Palgrave Global Media Policy and Business

The Palgrave Global Media Policy and Business Series has published to date (2017) 15 volumes since its launch in 2012. Concentrating on the social, cultural, political, political-economic, institutional, and technological changes arising from the globalisation of media and communications industries, the series considers the impact of these changes on matters of business practice, regulation and policy, and social outcomes. The policy side encompasses the challenge of conceiving policy-making as a reiterative process that recurrently addresses such key challenges as inclusiveness, participation, industrial-labour relations, universal access and freedom in an increasingly globalized and transnationalized world. The business side encompasses a political economy approach that looks at the power of transnational corporations in specific contexts - and the controversies associated with these global conglomerates. The business side considers as well the emergence of small and medium media enterprises.

Focusing on issues of media convergence, industry concentration, and new communications practices, the series analyses the tensions between systems based on national decision-making and publicly-oriented participatory structures and a more global perspective demarcated by commercialization, privatization and monopolization.

Based on a multi-disciplinary approach, the series tackles three key questions:

- To what extent do new media developments require changes in regulatory philosophy and objectives?
- To what extent do new technologies and changing media consumption require changes in business practices and models?
- And to what extent do privatisation, globalisation, and commercialisation alter the creative freedom, cultural and political diversity, and public accountability of media enterprises?

More information about this series at
http://www.palgrave.com/gp/series/14699

Robert G. Picard

Media and Communications Policy Making

Processes, Dynamics and International Variations

palgrave
macmillan

Robert G. Picard
Reuters Institute
University of Oxford
Oxford, UK

Palgrave Global Media Policy and Business
ISBN 978-3-030-35172-4 ISBN 978-3-030-35173-1 (eBook)
https://doi.org/10.1007/978-3-030-35173-1

Cover illustration: Federico Caputo / Alamy Stock Photo
Cover design: eStudioCalamar

This Palgrave Macmillan imprint is published by the registered company Springer Nature Switzerland AG.
The registered company address is: Gewerbestrasse 11, 6330 Cham, Switzerland

Preface

This book is the consequence of my four decades of scholarly examination of media and communications policies embracing the disciplines of communication, economics, law and policy, and political sociology. It led to faculty positions in departments and research centers in communications, economics and political science. That interdisciplinary background and knowledge led to invitations to participate in government inquires, parliamentary hearings and administrative policy processes in dozens of countries on five continents and in several intergovernmental organizations.

The intellectual and participatory journey accentuated the importance of the structures and processes in which policy is considered, the methods in which it is made and changed, the influences on its development and application, and the effectiveness of the policy choices. Although significant differences existed in governments and processes that I encountered, I discovered commonalities even when forms of governance, political philosophies and social contexts differed significantly. That perception was reinforced by influences from the emerging field of policy studies, which provided explanation and evidence about how policy initiatives develop and how policy is made.

Interest in media and communications policy has grown significantly, produced clusters of researchers in associations such as the International Communication Association and International Association for Media and Communication Research and is exemplified by the growth of the Telecommunications Policy Research Conference, which is nearing its 50th year. In addition, scholars in law, economics, political science and other disciplines have addressed policy issues. Today scholars contribute perspectives from multiple disciplines with which they are associated, but generally lack unifying approaches and theories for their work and most do not contextualize or analyze policy using policy studies methods. Consequently, the widely differing approaches make building broader understanding and theory of media and communications policy making difficult.

This book is based on those policy studies approaches for explaining why and how policy emerges, is implemented and is examined. An impetus for the volume was my growing awareness that much media and communications policy scholarship was narrow and drew little on the broader understanding of policy and policy making produced in other disciplines.

This book responds to the dearth of literature applying policy studies approaches and knowledge to media and communications. It is intended to help those concerned with media and communications policy to gain a better understanding of processes and influences in policy development, to reconsider the range of policy types used in media and communications governance and to consider that traditional policy practices may not be solving existing and emerging challenges. It should help build awareness that decisions in communications and media policy increasingly hinge on principles applied from other policy regimes and levels of governance. It is intended to develop better understanding about the overall impact of private, voluntary and community sectors on policy making and policy solutions and that merely focusing on the public sector limits perception and governance opportunities. It explores means for analyzing and evaluating policy and effectively engaging in policy advocacy.

Those learning and studying media and communications policy and law will benefit by better understanding of the contexts of policy making, influences upon it, its processes and the activities of policy actors. This book is intended to help provide those perspectives and to develop knowledge and skills in examining, comparing and advocating for media and communications policy. It will also provide those whose scholarship from a variety of disciplinary perspectives relates to media and communications policy with deeper understanding of policy structures, processes, influences and decision-making that will enrich and strengthen their work.

This book is intended for individuals knowledgeable about media and communications industries and systems, especially university postgraduate and doctoral students in those fields, media and communications activists and policy makers, individuals conducing policy analyses and scholars engaged in policy research focused on media and communications. It will also be useful to students and scholars in other disciplines, such as political science and political communication, who are wrestling with issues involving media and communications policy and understand their systems and operations. Because of their individual interests and objectives, it is expected that readers will use this book in differing ways.

Readers seeking to understand how policy is made and what influences its design and advancement will find knowledge about how policy making takes place, the factors that determine it forms, its developmental paths, that influence its elements and its outcomes. Readers who want to learn how to undertake effective policy research will find guidance on methods and approaches for researching and understanding policy making and considering the effects of different types of political and social systems on its processes. Those who want to participate in media and communications policy making will find the concepts and techniques explored in the book provide knowledge and methods for effectively engaging in policy-making processes.

The book is divided in three parts. Part I focuses on definitions, theories, approaches necessary to understand policy making and the practices of policy studies. Part II examines the differences and complexities of different levels of policy making and how varying policy-making structures and activities affect policy processes and influence outcomes. Part III focuses on techniques and methods of policy analysis, evaluation, and examination and on practical advocacy practices and issues and their influences on policy.

Readers will find boxed material throughout the book. These boxes serve several purposes. They highlight or expand upon concepts introduced in the chapters, provide illustrations of issues or ideas and present applications of analysis methods presented. The significance of each to different types of readers will vary.

Each chapter concludes with a summary and points for discussion designed to promote thought and debate about the nature of policy making and issues that its structures and processes raise. Suggested readings for each chapter explore the topics and issues introduced and citations throughout the chapters direct readers to related policies study literature and media and communications policy study examples that will be useful for further research.

Oxford, UK Robert G. Picard

Contents

List of Figures

PART I

Contexts and Means of Policy Making

CHAPTER 1

Introduction to Media and Communications Policy Studies

All around us, often invisibly, institutions and systems shape our lives, the ways we communicate, transact, entertain ourselves and learn about the world about us. Policy making is the way that society structures and instructs these institutions and systems. It involves organizing and influencing their elements and relationships to serve collective and individual needs and promoting well-being, safety, security, innovation and social progress. Deciding the best ways to achieve those outcomes is subject to considerable debate.

Without policy, much of what we take for granted in our daily lives would be impossible. Consider our mobile phones, for example. They would only be pieces of industrial design and useless technology unless policy decisions had spurred innovations in radio, telecommunications and electronics, allocated unique radio spectrum necessary for them to operate, formed standards for mobile interconnectivity to fixed, microwave and satellite telecommunications systems, produced a common address system to reach other phones and internet connections, provided authority for telecommunications companies to stretch wire and cable on governmental and private rights of way, and created and supported market structures and incentives for companies to build and operate the requisite infrastructures. These policy choices make possible the systems and markets necessary for us to call, text and share with friends, family and business partners around the world and to access all kinds of digital content wherever we happen to be. Similarly, when we switch on our television sets, few ever consider the policy behind their operations: technical standards for the sets are established to coincide with the technical standards for broadcast transmitters; licenses are given to firms to operate broadcast channels; operating standards are established; interconnectivity to cable, satellite and internet is standardized; content standards are promulgated; and broadcast carriage requirements for cable/satellite systems are all set by policy.

R. G. Picard, *Media and Communications Policy Making*, Palgrave Global Media Policy and Business,
https://doi.org/10.1007/978-3-030-35173-1_1

Hundreds of public policies at the national, regional and global levels influence the structures and operations of our media and communications systems. This book explores the policy processes and the environments in which these take place.

Why Study Policy and Policy Making?

The fundamental purposes of studying policy and policy making are to understand the policy-making environment, how policies are made and what influences their development, approval and implementation. Policy provides the bases for decision-making, providing principles, frameworks and approaches for dealing with issues that will become the bases of governmental action, laws and intervention.

Although related to political science, policy studies do not primarily focus on political philosophy, governmental structures and systems, parties, political behavior and political activity. Policy studies are more focused on how policy develops, how to critically analyze proposed and existing policy, how to develop better policy and how to advocate more effectively for policy. Policy making is nevertheless political by nature because it involves making decisions among preferences of varying actors and social interests and issues of power and influence arise in the decision-making processes. Policy studies is a branch of social science that draws from political science, political economy, economics, political sociology, management, communication studies and other established academic disciplines.

Policy studies use theory and evidence to develop and evaluate policies with the purpose of improving policy-making practices and their outcomes. In doing so, it is critical in evaluating institutional influences on policy making and decision-making and the effects of policies on people, enterprises and organizations.

Policy studies and its theories, models and approaches are thus central to investigation of policy making and outcomes regardless of what other disciplinary theories and methods are employed. Studying policy making is also crucial for those who may subsequently become participants in policy-making processes because it provides context and knowledge necessary to effectively engage in policy making.

Although the focus is on media and communications, this book is rooted in public policy and the activities that shape the types of communication in which we participate and consume. It is concerned with policy participants, processes, mechanisms and outcomes. It differs from much media and communications legal and policy research because of this approach. It is designed to help develop understanding of policy making in widely varying jurisdictions and contexts and to show how policy research facilitates comparative analysis. It is rooted in policy studies that are based on the idea that policy emerges from processes within a system involving institutions, and official and non-official actors (Birkland 2015).

At its most fundamental level, policy is the expression of what society wants—if the policy-making process is not skewed toward the interests of a few—and it guides the creation of mechanisms for pursuing those wants. Those interested in policy studies focus on policy institutions, systems and processes, rather than the outcomes in terms of laws, agencies, regulations and incentives that are primarily the purview of those in law and economics. The study of policy and policy making is thus concerned with why and how policy develops, what influences it and how it takes shape (Smith and Larimer 2013). Understanding these forces provides comprehension of how policy decisions are made, why certain policy emerges and how interested parties engage in policy processes and decision-making.

Policy does not develop in a vacuum. It is created as a response to issues, challenges, problems and the contexts in which they appear. It emanates from awareness that some condition or circumstance is creating undesirable conditions or impeding movement toward attractive possibilities. That awareness is rooted in recognition of the concepts that action produces consequence and change, that is, the ability to purposely and effectively alter factors that create the existing condition or circumstance or the ability to take steps to surmount factors that impede the achievement of the change. Good policy can improve lives; poor policy can worsen them. In its better forms, policy helps identify and shape conditions, organizes factors and relationships, ensures safety and security, enables progress and steers innovation to greater social needs. In its poorer forms, policy reduces competition, stifles innovation, limits the abilities of individuals to fulfill their needs and wants and constrains firms from providing desirable products or services.

Policy making thus involves empowerment, agency and effectuality within a system that can be influenced. This system becomes an institution of its own, in which purposive decisions are made and dynamics factors influence the policy system and processes (Easton 1965; Jenkins 1978). Policy responds to changes in the environment and seeks to create a difference. It is rare that new policy is pursued solely to maintain existing conditions and relationships, but the institutional nature of policy bodies, processes and stakeholders tend to preserve continuities and resist rapid changes in policy. There is thus a strong temporal element to policy making based on perceptions of what has been, what is and what can be.

The policy-making perspectives on why and how policy develops, what influences it, how it takes shape and their application to media and communications policy are the focus of this book. This policy-making approach focuses on why policy issues arise, the environments in which policy is pursued, how issues are identified and framed, the effects of policy-making institutions and processes on policy created and the tools available to pursue policy objectives at both the domestic and international levels. The book explores policy analysis methods, tools, their use and the insights they provide. It examines how existing policy is evaluated and how to identify means to improve it.

Before beginning that intellectual journey, common frames of reference need to be established. The remainder of this first chapter defines and explains fundamental terms, approaches and processes necessary for understanding policy making and its application to media and communications.

Delineating and Defining the Media and Communications Policy Field

The field of media and communications policy has historically been disorganized because of the disparate nature of individuals involved and the academic disciples in which those researchers developed. Consequently, media and communications scholars sometimes use basic terms differently depending upon their varying disciplinary backgrounds, national origins and linguistic traditions. A common understanding of terms related to and about the field is necessary if the policy discipline is to move forward (Picard 2016). An elementary step is to distinguish between the fundamental terms of policy, law, regulation and intervention. These are sometimes used synonymously, but they have precise meanings that should be recognized and employed.

Four Fundamental Terms

Clarity and precision in use of four fundamental terms are necessary for effectively understanding and studying policy and policy making.

Policy involves principles and objectives that steer public decision-making and intervention. Policy documents and frameworks typically establish the needs and rationales for policy, the intended results and the mechanisms for achieving the desired outcomes. These are designed to influence and steer policy-making activities. Policy is developed through political systems and processes (Kraft and Furlong 2017) that can be observed, defined, compared and evaluated.

Law denotes statutes, rules and practices established by legislative bodies, legal precedents, or fiat, compliance with which is enforced by government authority (Hart et al. 2012). Law is created as a social construct, influenced by dominant values and subject to constraints of legitimacy. Policy is typically implemented through the mechanism of authorizing laws enacted by relevant legislative bodies and/or by executive or administrative order depending upon the political system and agencies involved.

Regulation is a policy tool designed to achieve policy outcomes by prescribing desired conduct or proscribing undesirable conduct. It involves coercive power on actors who are the objects of policy (Baldwin et al. 2013). It can be established through law-making processes and promulgation of regulations by regulatory agencies under delegated authority. The term regulation is often erroneously used to indicate all mechanisms and tools of public governance activity, but those are better termed intervention.

Intervention denotes governmental activities that intrude on an industry and its activities. It involves the use of a variety of policy tools that influence industry structures through competition policy, licensing, fiscal and tax incentives, subsidies, prescriptive and prescriptive regulation and other measures designed to achieve policy objectives. These will be discussed in greater depth in Chap. 4. Regulation is a form of intervention, but it is important to understand that there are many tools other than regulation for achieving policy objectives.

The Emerging Concept of Governance

Governance is an emerging and disputed concept with multiple usages varying among disciplines and scholars (Puppis 2010). In political science and policy studies approaches, governance traditionally refers to state actions. Other expansive social science uses include institutions, processes, procedures and norms of decision-making and control that can be exercised by the state, systemic forces, the market, nongovernmental organizations or private activities (Terzis 2008). In this broader framework, governance is influenced by multiple social, institutional, economic and governmental factors (Ginosar 2013) and includes shared governmental and nongovernmental control exercised both domestically and internationally.

This book aligns with the policy studies' use of governance to indicate state policy making and the principles and frameworks designed to create policy effects. However, it recognizes that states and intergovernmental organizations are now partially relying on and legitimizing and sanctioning nongovernmental approaches within public regulatory frameworks for media and communications. Consequently, the volume includes the range of co-regulation and state accepted forms of self-regulation, policy networks and non-state policy decisions that create rules and policies that guide structures and behaviors domestically and internationally. This definition is thus more constrained than how it is employed by some media scholars (Karppinen and Moe 2013).

Delineating the Media and Communications Policy Field

A second definitional issue involves delineating the policy field in media and communications. Four terms regularly appear in the literature: media policy, communications policy,[1] information policy and telecommunications policy.

[1] The terms communication and communications are used inconsistently and erroneously as synonyms in media policy literature. Communication is the act of exchanging information and

Although each of these involves policy, they focus on distinct issues and are not synonymous. Each has roots in specific disciplinary fields and in the technologies with which they are associated when the terms emerged. Some now consider the latter term as overlapping or as a subset of the first three terms.

Media policy is concerned with industries and enterprises that produce and distribute content. It typically involves issues of structures and behavior, content issues and effects on citizens and society. Scholars involved in media policy tend to come from media studies, sociology, economics and business studies.

Communications policy focuses on systemic technologies, infrastructures, platforms and content distribution systems and networks. It considers their structures, operations, availability and accessibility to suppliers of content and consumers, and the behavior of firms involved. Scholars working on these issues tend to derive from communications studies, information technology, economics and business studies.

Information policy focuses on the flow and processing of information, with attention to issues involved in storage, access and distribution of information. It deals with issues such as information security, privacy and digital rights management and trading of rights. Scholars researching in this field tend to come from information technology, economics and legal disciplines.

Telecommunications policy typically refers to policies involving telephony and broadcasting. It emerged as a separate field from general media policy because of its focus on issues deriving from the unique properties and economic bases of those communications platforms. It is increasingly becoming a subdivision of communications policy because the technologies involved in telephony and broadcasting have been digitalized and are being integrated into common technologies and because systems and governments are often combining the agencies charged with overseeing telecommunications and communications policy. Scholars using this approach tend to have backgrounds involving broadcasting, engineering, economics and legal traditions.

The overlaps between these fields and the increasing movement of content and communication across platforms create challenges for delineating the fields and their issues (Braman 2004). Those engaged in media and communications policy research should pursue greater precision in terminology to ensure comprehensive and comparability of studies so that scholarship can be effectually used by policy researchers in other fields as well.

Existing media and communications scholarship has been primarily influenced by scholars embracing legal, political economics and political sociology approaches and to a lesser extent by those with political science, policy studies or governance studies backgrounds. Consequently, the bulk of scholarship has tended to take interpretivist approaches, to focus on specific policies or issues and to embrace strong normative traditions. Little media and communications

meaning, whereas communications involves the systems and technical means of communicating—the platforms subject to most policy activities. Consequently, this review will use the more definitive term *communications* policy.

scholarship concerned itself with the systems, processes and systemic influences on policy making. It has tended to be more concerned with outcomes than how these outcomes develop. This book will address that disconnect by showing the relevance of policy studies approaches, the concepts and methods they employ, the dynamic environment and the contested interests in policy making.

Understanding the Political Domain

Media and communications policy making cannot be conceived and addressed in isolation but must be undertaken through an interdisciplinary lens that includes political science, law, political sociology, political communication, organizational behavior and economics. Policy studies draw from those fields to focus on how policy is generated, what influences it, how policy decisions are made and what outcomes are produced. It seeks to understand and improve processes and outcomes. Policy making takes place in specific contexts that differ widely, are founded on differing political philosophies and have disparate governance structures and processes, but policy making can be studied in all of them. To do so effectively, however, requires understanding and employment of some fundamental political concepts.

Polity, Politics and the Public Sphere

Policy making can fundamentally be conceived as policy pursued in polities through politics in the public sphere. To understand and employ that conceptualization in research and practice requires clarity of those concepts.

Polity represents a form of organized community, bound together by a common identity and interests. The most recognizable polities are countries and provinces, but they can be other forms of organization such as political parties, associations and international organizations, because they are bound together with a common identity, have organizational structures and processes and make choices for the collective.

Politics denotes the processes and activities of decision-making within polities. It involves how power and authority are organized and distributed, how they are exercised and the ability of and means by which members of the polities influence decisions. The practice of politics raises issues of inclusion, participation, equality and equity.

The *public sphere* involves the space in which social developments, issues and matters of governance are discussed and determined. A public sphere exists in all polities, but the scope, scale and mechanisms vary widely depending upon the degree of inclusion, participation, equality and equity in politics. The sphere in authoritarian polities is narrower, existing primarily among and within the loci of power and involving the members of the public through participation in well-defined spaces with limits determined by those governing. In democracies, the sphere has more breadth, depth and mechanisms to permit public opinion to develop and be expressed independently from those governing.

These concepts will be used to inform analysis of policy making throughout this volume.

Competing Policy Domains

Media and communications policy alone does not influence communications in society. Several other policy regimes regularly influence media and communications companies, systems, structures and operations. These include those domains closely related to securities and finance, taxation, employment and labor, environment, trade secrets and privacy. Intersections and interactions with security policy, infrastructure policy, industrial policy, competition policy, intellectual property policy and cultural policy are also important in media and communications policy. These can also be used to influence media structures, behavior, content and effects, even though they may not be specifically media- or communications-centric policy domains.

Differing polities place divergent emphases on policy domains when making decisions. The European Union (EU) places significant emphasis on trade and competition policy domains, for example, whereas the United States places little emphasis on cultural policy. South Korea places great emphasis on security policy, whereas Chile does to a lesser extent. These differences come into play when issues in media and communications policies that overlap those domains are considered.

In many settings, these diverse policy arenas are often approached in isolation, without recognizing their influences on each other, with little concern for their effects on other policy objectives, or without policy makers clarifying and effectively managing priorities and trade-offs involved. This can create confusion in asserting and assessing policy needs.

To be most effective, media and communications policy needs to be coordinated with other domestic policies. Lack of harmonization among them is often a problem of larger nations and governments because coordination and regular contact among those responsible for the domains is limited. Authorizing and implementing legislation and rules for the different policy domains rarely promote interaction and coordination of effort because of their differences in purpose. This creates challenges, because communications policy does not exist in isolation and particularly needs to be coordinated with competition, industry/trade and cultural policy.

The movement of policy frameworks and approaches between policy domains and between countries or governance organizations is called *policy transfer*. These transfers include imitating or adapting policy and policy mechanisms from other uses, essentially borrowing from the knowledge and expertise of other policy makers who have experience dealing with the issues. Policy transfers involve many conceptual and policy challenges that need to be overcome to consider and transfer policy because of differences in the focuses and emphases in policy domains and individual national social, political and economic environments (Mossberger and Wolman 2003).

Rationales for Policy

Policy is made to alter conditions or change behavior for some purpose. It is founded in beliefs that state power can be exerted to influence and produce desired results. It is based on empiricist views that observation of contemporary social life can establish knowledge about how it operates. Policy attempts to rationally harness that knowledge to produce change and is thus based on empiricist concepts of reasoning, evidence and causation. Because policy and policy-making approaches almost universally embrace positivist approaches in the existing environment, this book emphasizes those approaches.

It is important to recognize, however, the contributions of postmodernist, Marxist and feminist critiques and explanations of policy and policy making (Barrow 1993; Cobb Jr 2002; Mazur 2002; Miller 2002). These offer critical insights on society and policy outcomes by focusing on systemic flaws and inequities that would require momentous political, economic and social transformation to fully address. Such critiques are beginning to appear in media and communications policy research, questioning issues such as the acceptance of ideas that social unity can be achieved, that political consensus can be reached, that existing politics can change society (Carpentier 2011) and that policy is gender neutral (Gallagher 2011; Mayer 2018). Such issues should be recognized as constraints and faults in policy making and not ignored in studying policy because they affect decisions and outcomes.

The dominant policy studies approach used in this book concentrates on existing policy structures, processes and actions (no matter how good or poor), how they affect policy outcomes and how they can be used to produce more immediate change.

Because policies are designed to produce outcomes, the reasons behind policy activities are important. Nearly all rationales for making policy can be attributed to five broad motivations:

1. to address existing challenges or problems
2. to avoid emerging challenges or problems
3. to pursue new opportunities and promote investment
4. to maintain social control and avoid civil disorder
5. to maintain existing power arrangements and legitimacy

The importance of each varies over time and among countries depending upon social, economic and technological conditions and public and private demands for state intervention. Specific policies will usually be described and framed differently in specific policy principles and rationales for action. However, it is infrequent that they do not fall into one of these broad rationales. In the domain of media and communications policy, some rationales influenced by normative perspectives on ideas of public goods, democratic needs, universal access, participation and representation in content are intended to address or avoid challenges and problems that are present.

Is Media/Communication Policy and Policy Making Unique?

Although some media and communications scholars have argued that making media and communications policy is different from that involving other industries and issues, that is not the case when it is approached from a policy studies perspective. It has been asserted there are fundamental differences between policy/regulation of communications and other industries because of political and social impact, economic and social welfare distinctions and the interaction of social and economic concerns in decisions (Napoli 1999). Such assertions of uniqueness are based on a very narrow view of social well-being. Many other policy fields face social welfare and economic choices and trade-offs that are equally socially significant, including health care, environment, housing, child services, education and transportation.

Media and communications policy and policy making is not unique but must address concerns about the roles of media and communications in content effects, information availability, political discourse and political participation in democratic politics that some of the other policy regimes do not. It must address broader factors than policy focused on dairy farming, aluminum manufacturing or mattress making. Those factors, however, do not make fundamental policy elements or policy-making processes and studies unique from the policy studies perspectives.

Content conveyed the media and communications serve important social functions and are beneficial to both individuals and society, but some content also creates risks and can produce harm. Media and communications activities play crucial roles linking the institutions and public in society. The arrangement of their roles varies depending upon nature of society and governance system, but the roles remain central to the operations of all society and maintenance of the social order. Consequently, media and communications policy making typically involves many more social, cultural and economic issues than policy for other industries (Napoli 2001, p. 20).

Conceptualizing Policy Making as Process and Stages

Policy scholars accept the view that policy making is a process that occurs in stages within policy-making mechanisms (Easton 1965; Jenkins 1978). This rationalist approach to policy making typically portrays these processes and stages as measured and orderly. Although there is a relationship between the concepts of process and stage, they should not be considered synonymous. The concept of *process* involves sequential action or movement through a series of actions or activities in which earlier activities influence subsequent actions to produce an outcome. A *stage* represents a type of activity that tends to be addressed individually or as independent from the others.

In policy studies, *policy stages* describe steps that lead to policy and its implementation (Althaus et al. 2013). Although scholars do not fully agree on the total number of stages or sub-stages, or their duration, or that all stages necessarily occur, nearly all recognize at least a half dozen stages. These include an *issue identification* stage in which awareness of an issue develops and the factors influencing the issue are exposed. Policy problems in this stage are often described and defined by media coverage, nongovernmental interest groups or political parties. The policy *agenda setting* stage involves getting the issue on the policy agenda of legislators or governmental agencies by raising policy makers' awareness of the issue and its import. This stage usually results from the activities of interest groups, think tanks, media and government personnel. The *policy formation* stage occurs when specific proposals to address issues are created and considered and a proposal is forwarded for consideration by a legislative body, executive authority or other official entity for consideration and action. Policy is then approved, revised and approved or rejected. Once this *approval* stage is completed, policy *implementation* takes place, during which budgeting is completed and the structures, mechanisms and regulations or rules necessary to turn policy into practice are put in place. After a period, the policy should undergo *evaluation* to determine its results and effectiveness and revisions may be sought to improve policy performance.

These stages are addressed within a policy process that is typically depicted as linear or cyclical and comprised of progressive steps, actions and choices. Linear models depict the process as consecutive stages in temporal order in which reasoned consideration and deliberation is given to a range of possibilities for addressing the issue, as portrayed in Fig. 1.1. Linear models portray finality in the outcome and its evaluation.

Other scholars prefer cyclical models that generally involve similar elements as their linear counterparts but portray the process as iterative, without an ultimate outcome. The two approaches equally portray careful thought and exercise of judgment throughout, but the cyclical models do not depict finality. Instead, they portray the process as ongoing with subsequent reconsideration of issues, potential solutions and actions (Howlett and Ramesh 2003), as shown in Fig. 1.2.

Policy process models are thus descriptive of typical activities in the policy process and represent a form of good practice. The rationalist nature of these models has been criticized, however, for being too idealized, orderly and deterministic because they do not convey that factors such as events, public

Fig. 1.1 Linear policy process model

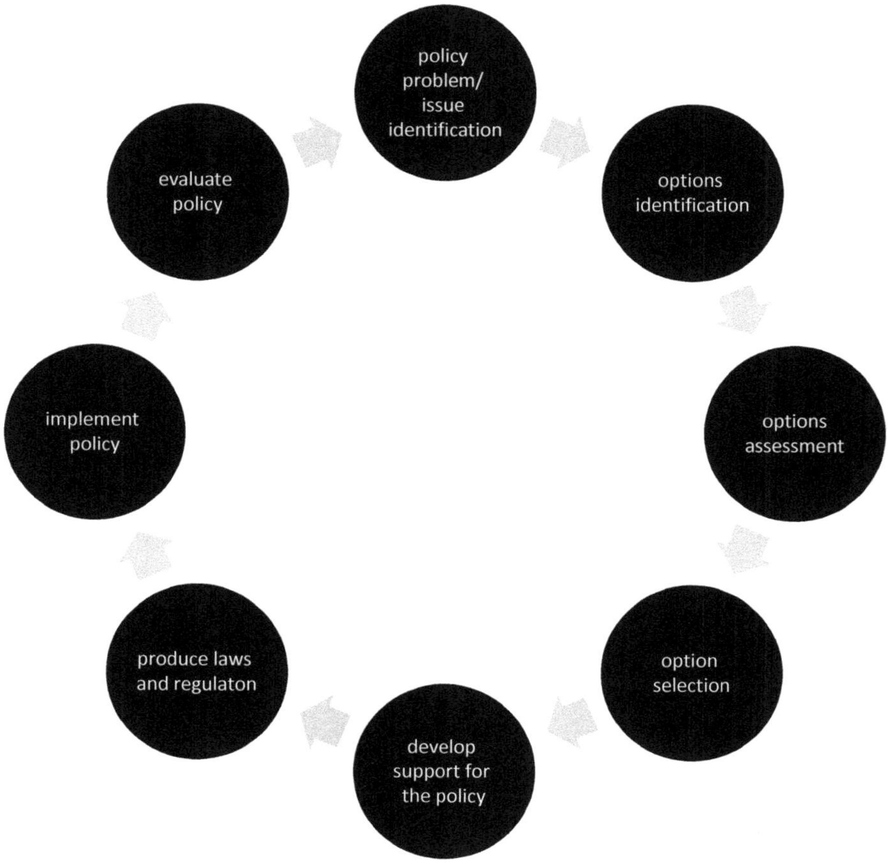

Fig. 1.2 Cyclical policy process

pressures, the nature of the political system, difficulties in gaining political consensus, institutional and elite influences, and bounded rationality that play important roles (Amy 1984; Fonnaini 1990; Jann and Wegrich 2006). The models also suggest that policy and its implementation are the ultimate outcomes, but in many cases, policy may be rejected, because deciding **not** to act is also a policy choice. Despite their limitations, policy stages and process models provide effective means for generally conceptualizing and locating the activities and actions that take place in policy making, but they should not be employed as deterministic because they are descriptive and not theoretical.

Those interested in policy making need to be aware that policy can emerge outside the orderliness of policy processes, that actual processes can be more dynamic—skipping steps or actions—and that policy making may not be as rational and deliberate as the idealized processes models indicate. This may occur because policy makers embrace a sudden reflexive reaction to a development, because public opinion is demanding a particular approach or policy or because of pledges made behind closed doors to some stakeholders.

Who Is Involved in Policy and Policy Making?
A wide variety of individuals and organizations engage in different stages of policy making, with larger numbers typically involved in open societies than in authoritarian societies. Among those who participate are:

Governmental
Heads of state
Offices of prime ministers and presidents
Legislative bodies
Courts
Government ministries and agencies

Commercial
Companies in the industry being addressed
Industry associations
Business organizations such as chambers of commerce
Topical lobbying groups/campaigns

Civic
Nongovernmental organizations
Citizens' groups
Scholars and experts

Policies Are Based on Values, Norms and Principles

Policy fundamentally involves decisions about what *ought* to be and thus involves values and norms that may be politically contested. These values and norms need to be transparent during policy making and in policy analyses so that the rationales and arguments of various parties can be clearly understood. This is crucial because debate is at the heart of effective policy making. Informed debate cannot take place unless disputing participants comprehend each other's positions and their bases.

Values are personal and social beliefs about what is important and their relative merit or importance. These influence priorities, choices and actions (Anderson 1979). Values include beliefs related to state of humankind, authority, relationships and social obligations. *Norms* are the common, usually informal, expectations of how individuals and institutions are expected to behave.

The values and norms embraced by stakeholders in policy debates become the bases for policy principles. These are coherent statements that help policy makers and organizations respond to issues and take part in legislative and administrative activities. Policy principles are more fundamental than policy objectives and specific policy tools because they are meant to inform the identification and development of those objectives and tools and to provide consistency in approaches to varying issues and actions. These principles are grounded in philosophical values and beliefs that can then be transferred into policy and practice by providing the fundamental criteria used in the decision-making processes. The principles thus inform political processes in which policy objectives and potential policy tools are considered (Picard and Pickard 2016).

In best practice, principles are articulated and then used to set policy objectives and determine the means to achieve them. Policy principles should be concerned about the effects of policy on all stakeholders, giving primacy to fundamental communications needs of society and seeking to balance social and economic benefits. This requires some prioritization of the principles. The significance of principles in communications and media policy making is beginning to be recognized. Studies have suggested principles for a variety of policy issues (Picard and Pickard 2016), government transparency policies (Dawes 2010) and media pluralism (Gibbons 2015), for example.

Individuals, private organizations and commercial enterprises, of course, place different emphasis on common shared values or may embrace some distinct separate values. When legislators and regulatory agencies consider principles, they should focus upon the deep-seated shared norms of society and embrace principles designed to reduce harm and strengthen beneficial activities for society as a whole.

Policy principles, objectives and mechanisms themselves are too distinct to national settings to be generalized across nations. They are influenced by numerous domestic philosophical, economic, industrial, political, social and cultural factors that make it difficult to directly transfer them among countries with similar effect. Principles, however, can be transferred among nations that share underlying values. Some fundamental values are embraced by all states, such as maintaining legitimacy, preserving order and promoting general welfare. Western and democratic nations share a variety of fundamental philosophical beliefs that can be the basis for developing domestic media and communications policy, as do postcolonial states, communist states and others with strongly held shared values.

Policy principles address a basic question of policy making: what is the public value being served? They set the bases for choices by specifying what is valued and why it is valuable to the public and society. Understanding the principles of differing stakeholders and the values and norms upon which they are based is fundamental to effective argumentation, debate and decision-making in democratic settings (Moore 1995; Benington and Moore 2011).

Principles underlying the processes, considerations and decisions in policy making should guide policy making. Because values and objectives in open societies emphasize different social and economic aspects, it is sometimes necessary to emphasize, balance or de-emphasize some principles in the process. The factors and rationales involved in these decisions should be clear, transparent and justified in the policy-making process.

Policy Making Involves Argumentation and Policy Narratives

Because policy making is a political act involving contestable norms and values, and multiple stakeholders with differing interests and perspectives, effective political communication and debate are necessary.

Good policy argumentation by all parties creates a policy narrative that explains developments and events within the framework set by the policy principles of those stakeholders. This narrative puts the complex factors involved together in a way that provides an easily communicable framework and explanation of what is being addressed. Policy narratives focus on salient elements and relationships to detail how they produced the issues being considered and then describe how altering those elements and relationships can produce different outcomes. It produces a way of thinking about challenges and what can be done about them.

Policy narratives are used to help develop an impetus for action, to gain consensus and to guide intervention toward achieving the desired outcomes. Different policy narratives exist simultaneously and produce conflicting demands on those who must determine the ultimate outcome of policy debates. These differing narratives result from varying values, ideologies or interests of stakeholders in the policy-making processes. Broad and conflicting policy narratives commonly appearing in media and communications policy making are (1) protection of free expression, (2) control of dangerous and damaging expression, (3) the necessity for public provision of services, (4) oversight and regulation of privately provided services and (5) the benefits of laissez-faire markets.

Policy debates are thus political contests in which narratives and the values, norms and policy principles upon which they are constructed are promoted and challenged. These take place in policy documents, media coverage, policy forums, hearings and the range of activities involved in policy making. These policy discussions are effective when multiple perspectives are equally expressed and considered.

The discourses used in argumentation and narratives in policy debates can be examined to understand the range of credible alternatives presented, the meaning behind the language used in proposals and discussions and how arguments influenced policy outcomes (Hajer 2002; Streeter 2013).

Final Words

Policy making is about making decisions. Policy studies focus on the factors involved in those decisions. The first question of all policy making is whether governmental intervention is necessary to achieve objectives. If policy makers determine that the answer to that question is yes, subsequent questions arise of how much intervention is required and what methods should be used. To begin answering these basic questions, and the more complex issues and questions that affect policy, policy makers should start with agreed-upon objectives, clear principles and established priorities.

Much media and communications policy research and discussion are Western centric and approach policy through the lens of one nation or group of nations with common policy and legal foundations. It tends to approach policy and policy making through a democratic political perspective and consider policy making in other political systems as inferior. In doing so it conveys and reinforces the view that only democratic societies can make good policy. Less democratic and authoritarian nations can and regularly make policy intent on improving social well-being and quality of life of their citizens, as well as making policy that reinforces their political and social systems. Oman, for example, has made health care a policy priority for several decades and the World Health Organization now ranks its overall health system performance as eighth in the world. By comparison, Sweden—a highly democratic society that places great policy emphasis on health care—is ranked at 23rd. Qatar has used media and communication policy to achieve mobile broadband penetration that is about 40 percent higher than that found in Italy.

A broader policy studies approach to media and communications policy thus focuses on the elements that affect the environment in which those questions and issues are addressed and the systemic practices that take place as decisions are made in whatever political system exists. It is designed to provide a richer understanding of the institutional arrangements, processes and influences on how decisions are made in individual nations and international organizations, to facilitate cross-national comparisons and to produce more effective evaluations of policies and policy systems and practices.

Chapter Summary

- Policy is the expression of what society wants and creates pubic mechanisms for pursuing those wants.
- Policy studies focus on why and how policy develops, what influences it and how it takes shape.
- Policy making takes place within an institutionalized system of decision-making.
- Four fundamental terms need to be distinguished in studying the field: policy, law, regulation and intervention.

- Media and communications policy involves overlapping fields variously called media policy, communications policy, information policy and telecommunications policy.
- Polity involves an organized community in which politics surrounding decision-making takes place; states have a public sphere in which citizens participate in the decision-making process.
- Policy making takes place in stages and moves through political processes.
- Policy is based on values and norms.
- Policy making is best guided by principles based on specified values and norms.
- Argumentation and effective narratives are used to pursue policy.

Discussion Points

1. How might the disciplinary backgrounds of policy scholars affect the salience of issues, policies, processes and outcomes?
2. How does politics aid and hinder the creation of good policy?
3. Why are policy process and stage models sometimes inadequate for explaining how policy is made?
4. Are there conditions and circumstances under which media and communications policy should take precedence over other policy regimes? Why?
5. What values and social norms do you believe are most important for media and communications policy making? Why?
6. To what extent do policy makers make independent decisions based on the rationales and narratives presented by stakeholders?

Bibliography

Althaus, Catherine, Peter Bridgman, and Glyn Davis. 2013. *The Australian Policy Handbook*. 5th ed. Crows Nest: Allen & Unwin.

Amy, Douglas J. 1984. Toward a Post-Positivist Policy Analysis. *Policy Studies Journal* 13 (1): 207–211.

Anderson, Charles W. 1979. The Place of Principles in Policy Analysis. *The American Political Science Review* 73 (3): 711–723.

Baldwin, Robert, Martin Cave, and Martin Lodge. 2013. *Understanding Regulation: Theory, Strategy, and Practice*. 2nd ed. Oxford: Oxford University Press.

Barrow, Clyde W. 1993. *Critical Theories of the State: Marxist, Neo-Marxist, and Post-Marxist*. Madison: University of Wisconsin Press.

Benington, John, and Mark Moore, eds. 2011. *Public Value: Theory and Practice*. Basingstoke: Palgrave Macmillan.

Birkland, Thomas A. 2015. *An Introduction to the Policy Process: Theories, Concepts, and Models of Public Policy Making*. 4th ed. Armonk: M.E. Sharpe.

Braman, Sandra. 2004. Where Has Media Policy Gone? Defining the Field in the Twenty-First Century. *Communication Law and Policy* 9 (2): 153–182.

Carpentier, Nico. 2011. Policy's Hubris: Power, Fantasy, and the Limits of (Global) Media Policy Interventions. In *The Handbook of Global Media and Communication Policy*, ed. Robin Mansell and Marc Raboy, 113–128. Oxford: Wiley-Blackwell.
Cobb, John B., Jr. 2002. *Postmodernism and Public Policy: Reframing Religion, Culture, Education, Sexuality, Class, Race, Politics, and the Economy*. Albany: State University of New York Press.
Dawes, Sharon S. 2010. Stewardship and Usefulness: Policy Principles for Information-Based Transparency. *Government Information Quarterly* 27 (4): 377–383.
Easton, David. 1965. *A Framework for Political Analysis*. New York: Prentice Hall.
Fonnaini, Robert. 1990. *The Myth of Scientific Public Policy*. New Brunswick: Transaction.
Gallagher, Margaret. 2011. Gender and Communication Policy: Struggling for Space. In *The Handbook of Global Media and Communication Policy*, ed. Robin Mansell and Marc Raboy, 451–466. Oxford: Wiley-Blackwell.
Gibbons, Thomas. 2015. Active Pluralism: Dialogue and Engagement as Basic Media Policy Principles. *International Journal of Communication* 9: 1382–1399.
Ginosar, Avshalom. 2013. Media Governance: A Conceptual Framework or Merely a Buzz Word? *Communication Theory* 23: 356–374.
Hajer, Maartin. 2002. Discourse Analysis and the Study of Policy Making. *European Political Science* 2 (1): 61–65.
Hart, H.L.A., Leslie Green, Joseph Raz, and Penelope Bulloch. 2012. *The Concept of Law*. 3rd ed. Oxford: Oxford University Press.
Howlett, Michael, and M. Ramesh. 2003. *Studying Public Policy: Policy Cycles and Policy Subsystems*. Oxford: Oxford University Press.
Jann, Werner, and Kai Wegrich. 2006. Theories of the Policy Cycle. In *Handbook of Public Policy Analysis: Theory, Politics, and Methods*, ed. Frank Fischer, Gerald J. Miller, and Mara S. Sydney, 43–62. New York: Routledge.
Jenkins, William I. 1978. *Policy Analysis: A Political and Organizational Perspective*. London: Martin Robertson & Co.
Karppinen, Kari, and Hallvard Moe. 2013. A Critique of 'Media Governance'. In *Communication and Media Policy in the Era of the Internet*, ed. Maria Löblich and Senta Pfaff-Rüdiger, 69–80. Baden-Baden: Nomos.
Kraft, Michael, and Scott Furlong. 2017. *Public Policy: Politics, Analysis, and Alternatives*. 6th ed. Washington, DC: CQ Press.
Mayer, Vicki. 2018. Media Policy and Governance. *Feminist Media Histories* 4 (2): 113–116.
Mazur, Amy G. 2002. *Theorizing Feminist Policy*. Oxford: Oxford University Press.
Miller, Hugh T. 2002. *Postmodern Public Policy*. Albany: State University of New York Press.
Moore, Mark. 1995. *Creating Public Value: Strategic Management in Government*. Cambridge, MA: Harvard University Press.
Mossberger, Karen, and Harold Wolman. 2003. Policy Transfer as a Form of Prospective Policy Evaluation: Challenges and Recommendations. *Public Administration Review* 63 (4): 428–440.
Napoli, Philip M. 1999. The Unique Nature of Communications Regulation: Evidence and Implications for Communications Policy Analysis. *Journal of Broadcasting & Electronic Media* 43 (3): 565–581.
———. 2001. *Foundations of Communication Policy: Principles and Process in the Regulation of Electronic Media*. New York: Hampton Press.

Picard, Robert G. 2016. Isolated and Particularised: The State of Contemporary Media and Communications Policy Research. *Javnost/The Public* 23 (2): 135–152.

Picard, Robert G., and Victor S. Pickard 2016. Essential Principles for Contemporary Media and Communications Policymaking. RISJ Report, April 2017. Oxford: Reuters Institute for the Study of Journalism, University of Oxford.

Puppis, Manuel. 2010. Media Governance: A New Concept for the Analysis of Media Policy and Regulation. *Communication, Culture & Critique* 3: 134–149.

Smith, Kevin B., and Christopher W. Larimer. 2013. *The Public Policy Theory Primer*. Boulder: Westview Press.

Streeter, Thomas. 2013. Policy, Politics, and Discourse. *Communication, Culture and Critique* 6 (4): 488–501.

Terzis, Georgios, ed. 2008. *European Media Governance. The Brussels Dimension*. Bristol: Intellect.

Suggested Readings

Anderson, Charles W. 1979. The Place of Principles in Policy Analysis. *The American Political Science Review* 73 (3): 711–723.

Braman, Sandra. 2004. Where has Media Policy Gone? Defining the Field in the Twenty-First Century. *Communication Law and Policy* 9 (2): 153–182.

Howlett, Michael, and M. Ramesh. 2003. *Studying Public Policy: Policy Cycles and Policy Subsystems*. Oxford: Oxford University Press.

Kraft, Michael, and Scott Furlong. 2012. *Public Policy: Politics Analysis, and Alternatives*. Washington, DC: CQ Press.

Picard, Robert G. 2016. Isolated and Particularised: The State of Contemporary Media and Communications Policy Research. *Javnost/The Public* 23 (2): 135–152.

Picard, Robert G., and Victor S. Pickard. 2017. Essential Principles for Contemporary Media and Communications Policymaking, RISJ Report, April 2017. Oxford, Reuters Institute for the Study of Journalism, University of Oxford.

Smith, Kevin B., and Christopher W. Larimer. 2013. *The Public Policy Theory Primer*. Denver: Westview Press.

CHAPTER 2

Policy-Making Environments and Locales

Comprehending the systems, processes and influences of policy making requires consideration of the environment, structures and locales in which they take place. This chapter introduces the levels at which media and communications policies are made, the governance structures involved, and the economic, social and cultural factors that influence those structures and processes. All of these must be considered when contemplating policy making in a specific milieu or comparing policy making across or between various locations.

Policy Making Occurs at Multiple Levels

Media and communications policy making takes place at more levels of governance than nearly all other activities subject to governance. Unlike foreign affairs, which takes place primarily at the national and multinational levels, or waste collection that is primarily the purview of local government, media and communications take place at the local, provincial/state, national, regional and global levels because the needs and requirements of communications and media necessitate coordination of activities across all those levels of governance. The arrangements and processes of policy making differ at various levels (Fig. 2.1).

The significance of these multiple layers of governance differs depending upon the issues being addressed. This is illustrated by the issues of broadband provision. Although the national government may develop broadband policies, implementation policies typically move downward to involve provincial/state government planning and control because of wide differences in geography and population distribution and to involve local governments who must decide whether and how cables will be strung on poles or laid under streets. Simultaneously policy moves upward to involve connectivity and other policy

R. G. Picard, *Media and Communications Policy Making*, Palgrave Global Media Policy and Business,
https://doi.org/10.1007/978-3-030-35173-1_2

Fig. 2.1 Locales of policy making and typical governance

involving neighboring states and global policy involving interconnectivity, transnational and multinational issues.

Policy making at the national and provincial/state levels is typically undertaken through legislative action in parliaments or other representative assemblies and through government agencies given authority to undertake policy making and oversight, such as the Australian Media and Communications Authority and the Moroccan National Telecommunications Regulatory Agency. Policy making at the regional and global levels is done through bilateral agreements negotiated between two countries or through multinational agreements between many countries negotiated through multinational organizations (Djelic and Sahlin-Andersson 2006; Hale and Held 2011; Karns et al. 2015; Ba et al. 2017; Hurd 2017), typically intergovernmental organizations under the United Nations (UN) such as the International Telecommunication Union or the World Intellectual Property Organization. Regional governance organizations such as the European Union or the Cooperation Council for the Arab States of the Gulf address issues across and within the nations participating (Acharya and Johnston 2007; Olsen and McCormick 2016; Leonard and Taylor 2016; Bandyopadhyay and Torre 2017). At the provincial/state level, governance is undertaken by entities such as the New York Public Service Commission in the United States that oversees cable television and internet in the State of New York or the Bavarian data protection regulator, Bayerisches Landesamt für Datenschutzaufsicht, in Germany. At the local level, policy making is undertaken by the county or city council, planning agencies and sometimes special media agencies or commissions (Bowman and Kearney 2016), such as the Vancouver Telecommunications Commission in Canada.

Depending upon the issues involved, policy may be made at one or more of the levels and those interested in policy need to understand all levels where action is required and whether one level is more powerful than another in addressing specific issues. It is important to understand which level deals with differing aspects of the issue and where decisions are made.

The significance of the different levels is illustrated by radio spectrum management. Electromagnetic spectrum is used for all technologies that transmit and/or receive radio wave transmissions. These include mobile telephones, satellite communication and television, microwave and radio, and other uses such as Bluetooth, ship and aircraft communication and even radio-controlled toys. Because spectrum is used in all nations, and usage must be coordinated or interference will render it unusable, transnational governance is necessary and conducted through the International Telecommunication Union, a specialized UN agency. Through its activities, spectrum frequencies are established for different uses and for use in different parts of the world. More decisions on allocation of spectrum use are shifted to regional and national governance and to local governance addressing issues such as placement of towers needed for radio spectrum use.

Unitary and Federalist States

An important distinction among countries is whether they are unitary or federalist states. This affects the locations of power, the institutions of governance, centralization and decentralization of governance and the ability to make policy and law (Elazar 1997).

In unitary states, the central national government is the source of all powers and attendant policies. It may choose to delegate authority to provinces, counties, cities and towns, but determines what powers they have and what issues they can address, and the central government can change that delegation or intervene. Unitary states are the most common form of state in the world.

Singapore is a unitary state with a parliamentary form of government and a government that derives its powers from the parliament. A small nation, it is essentially a city-state, and nearly all media and communication policies emanate from the parliament, cabinet, the Infocomm Media Development Authority and the Government Technology Agency.

Federalist states have a national government as well as provincial governments with significant power and autonomy (Watts 1998). The division of powers and degrees of coordination among levels of governance in federal states and federations differ significantly so it must be clearly understood when analyzing policy or undertaking comparative studies. National governments in federalist states tend to focus on international affairs, domestic issues common to the entire country and relations among provinces. Provinces focus on governance within their territories including delivery of social services such as transportation, education and health care.

Federalist states have national media and communications policies, but provincial and local governments have additional governance responsibilities as well, often for communications infrastructures and provincial media operations. The province of Quebec, Canada, for example, has a Ministry of Culture and Communications governing telecommunication services and rates, broadcasting services, internet, motion pictures and intellectual property, as well as linguistic promotion and protection, libraries, museums, arts and other cultural issues (Canada, Ministère de la Culture et des Communications 2018).

Institutional Influences on Policy Making

The most significant factors influencing policy making are governance, economic and social institutions (Fig. 2.2). Influences on the environment in which policy making takes place have significant impact on outcomes by affecting the philosophy of governance, establishing preferred policy approaches, shaping debate parameters and framing issues and questions.

Institutions are the established structures, processes, practices, norms and values that guide their actions. These vary considerably among countries, at different governance levels within countries and even for different forms of media and communications (Freedman 2006). It is thus important to understand them within the individual context(s) being considered when examining policy and policy making.

Governance Institutions' Influences on Policy Making

Various levels of government involved in policy making are all subject to political influence. Central political influences result from the type of political system in which the policy is made because authority and influences are systemically entrenched depending upon the structure of governance (Hague et al. 2016; Peters and Pierre 2016). This book concentrates on sovereign states—those

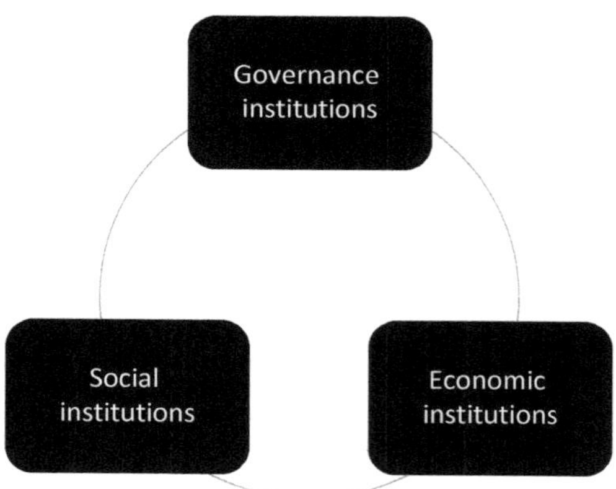

Fig. 2.2 Dominant institutions influencing policy making

with established governments, defined territories, permanent populations and the capacity to enter into relations with other sovereign states—but many of the analytical principles in this book can be applied to nations and chiefdoms that are subsumed within or transcend states and do not have the powers and recognition of sovereign states. Such stateless nations include the Zulu, who are dispersed in several countries of Southern Africa, and the Sami who are dispersed across northern Scandinavia and Russia.

Power and control are fundamental functions in all political systems (Smith 2009). Power is the capacity or ability to act to produce an effect through the exercise of authority or influence (Lukes 1986). Control is the actual exercise of that power to achieve a purpose. In many cases power need not actually be exercised to achieve an outcome because influence alone can do so. To understand policy making, one needs to be cognizant of the structural arrangements related to power and control, how they are divided or delegated and how they influence the policy process.

At a very basic level, governance institutions can be considered as either authoritarian or democratic. In the first, authority to govern resides with the leader based on heredity, as in the cases of monarchies, or by the seizure of power and the acquiescence of the public to that leadership (Linz 2000; Svolik 2012). In democratic systems, the authority to govern resides in citizens and the institutions and governance positions established for the exercise of power and control (Lijphart 2012). There is a great deal of variation in the ways governments operate within the two contrasting approaches.

In its extreme form, authoritarian governance prohibits all opposition and seeks to control private as well as public life, a form of governance called totalitarianism. The extreme form of democratic governance, direct democracy, is one in which the public decides all matters without limitations on their power. Few nations represent the polar positions today, and those that do tend to be toward the totalitarian end of the spectrum. Most democracies practice forms of representative governance in which representatives of citizens make decisions in governance bodies on their behalf. There is considerable variation in the practice of both authoritarian and democratic governance. Those differences must be carefully considered when comparing policy making between and among countries.

Two important political roles are resident in the leadership of both the basic systems, Head of State and Head of Government. The positions can be exercised by the same person or divided between persons. The head of state is the highest representative of the sovereign state and may have significant power or only ceremonial power depending on the form of government and the division of powers. Heads of state include kings and queens, emperors, presidents and sultans. When powers are divided or delegated, a head of government is typically responsible for operations of government and regular political activities. The amount of power in this position is also dependent upon the form of government and its division of power. Heads of government include individuals such as prime ministers, chancellors, presidents of councils of state and presidents of councils of ministers.

An important distinction among democratic political systems that influence policy making is that they are typically either parliamentary or presidential systems. Parliamentary systems typically have a head of government typically selected by the dominant party in the parliament. The head of government normally has significant executive power that is tempered by the influence and power of the head of state. In the case in the United Kingdom, for example, the government serves under royal prerogative and the prime minister is subservient to the monarch on certain nonpartisan issues. The monarch, for example, serves as commander-in-chief of the armed forces. In some cases, a head of state has no or very little executive power and is primarily symbolic or ceremonial. This is the case in Japan since 1947. The emperor is head of state, but nearly all executive power is held by the prime minister and cabinet, with the prime minister also serving as commander-in-chief of the military. In countries with presidential systems, the head of state and head of government are traditionally the same and possess all executive powers.

Policy making is directly affected by the amount of power held by and the control exercised by the head of state and head of government. Even when they have a great amount of power, heads of state and government rarely are closely involved in the day-to-day affairs of policy making, instead delegating the power downward through councils of ministers and administrative bodies.

Fig. 2.3 Common national government organization

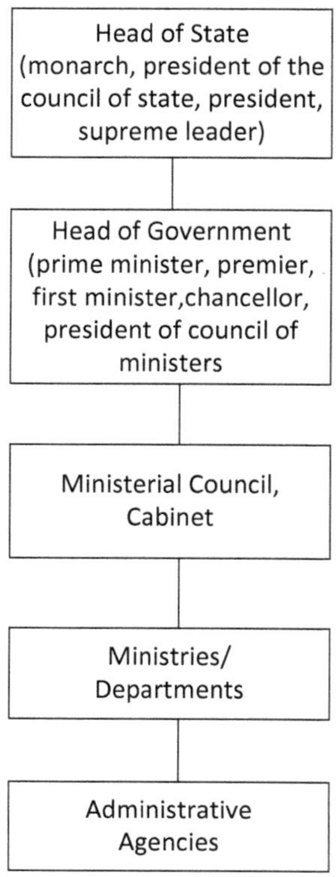

These may or may not be subject to the application of independent legislative and judicial power, depending upon the structure of government and division of powers. Administrative agencies are sometimes constituted independent of the executive and operate with varying degrees of autonomy. The Greek National Council for Radio and Television, for example, is structured and operates to make decisions independently of the government in power at a particular time.

Nearly every nation state has a cabinet or some form of the council of ministers that is headed by either the head of state or the head of government. These bodies are typically composed of top executives of each of the major state ministries or departments. Their purpose is to provide advice to the head, debate broad policy and coordinate action across the government. In some cases, these cabinets have separate decision-making powers on some matters (Fig. 2.3).

Policy making thus takes place in an environment in which the power relations and interactions among the executive and its administrative agencies, independent agencies, and legislative and judicial branches create political influences. Information, concerns, suggestions, proposals and decisions from each are subject to influence or authority from the others (Fig. 2.4).

In analyzing policy making in a country or comparing policy making among or between them, one must consider the form of government, the locations of policy generation and decision, the authority and power of legislative, administrative and judicial bodies, and the independence of those bodies in making policy. One must also be cognizant of issues of competency and authority that determine what issues the bodies may deal with, what approvals must be sought and what actions they may take on their own.

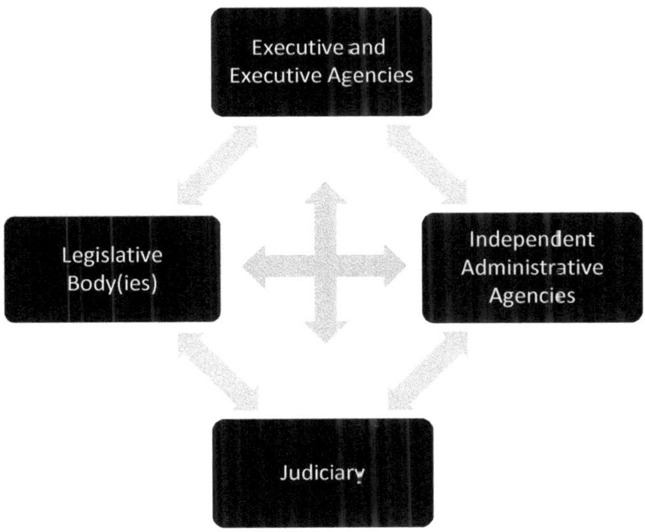

Fig. 2.4 Governance institutions exercising power in policy making

Media and Communications Administrative Agencies

Most media and communications activities are addressed through administrative agencies focused on their activities. As noted earlier, some activities related to broader issues such as competition policy, consumer protection and work safety may also be overseen by agencies dedicated to those issues. In most countries, the bulk of media and communications activities are overseen by telecommunications, communications or broadcasting agencies. These may be executive branch agencies operated within ministries or departments or agencies established with varying degrees of independence from the government. The number of agencies devoted to media and communications varies as well. In some countries, policy issues are divided between agencies focused on issues such as telecommunications or broadcasting, whereas they are combined in other countries.

Executive and Independent Agencies

An important distinction between administrative agencies is whether they are within executive branch control or are self-governing and separated from the executive branch. An agency that is more independent faces fewer immediate political pressures that influence its activities and decisions.

When structured within the executive branch, administrative agencies tend to follow the directions and pursue interests of the ruling government. In the Russian Federation, for example, Roskomnadzor (Federal Service for Supervision in the Sphere of Telecom, Information Technologies and Mass Communications) is a federal executive agency that controls and censors media and communications activities and content in ways that support the interests of the presidency. In Turkey, the Information and Communication Technologies Authority oversees a range of telecommunications and internet communications following policy established by the Ministry of Transportation, Maritime Affairs and Communications under which it is located so it is also influenced by the head of government.

When independence is desired, it is typically pursued through authorizing legislation that reduces political influence in the selection of agency leadership, creates financial independence and requires transparency and accountability for actions (Gilardi and Maggetti 2011; Schulz et al. 2013). Independence of media and communications agencies tends to be most often sought in democratic nations, but not all democratic nations do so. The Agência Nacional de Telecomunicações that oversees telephone and broadband in Brazil is an independent agency, for example, whereas the New Zealand Broadcasting Standards Authority operates under the Ministry for Culture and Heritage.

National contextual factors influence decisions to establish independent regulatory agencies. These include pressures for state reform, political leadership and the nature of existing institutions and structures, and differing national styles of regulation (Richardson 1982; Thatcher 2002). Independence moves regulation out of direct political control and promotes independent action, but some mechanisms for public oversight must be in place (Hanretty and Koop 2012, 2013).

Even when operating as independent agencies, the degree of independence varies creating a difference between *de jure* and de facto independence (Juwayeyi 2017). The Moroccan High Authority for Audiovisual Communication is an independent administrative agency, but its decisions tend to closely support interests of the king and his closest supporters. By contrast, the Austrian Regulatory Authority for Broadcasting and Telecommunications is also an independent agency but displays higher independence from governmental and direct political influence.

Although independent of direct government control and generally unelected, the leadership of independent administrative agencies generally employ a variety of political communication activities to establish their activities as being in the service of the public and to send signals to the industries they oversee when direct intervention is not desired (Puppis et al. 2014).

Research has shown that regulatory independence in developing nations tends to promote better network penetration by improving availability and access to services (Montoya and Trillas 2007). Independence does not completely free from influence, however. It has been shown that even partial state ownership of regulated firms, including telecommunications, can affect decisions of independent regulators (Edwards and Waverman 2006).

Factors Influencing Independence of Administrative Agencies

Many factors influence the degree of independence of administrative agencies from direct government and political pressure. Among the most significant factors are:

- Relationship of the agency to government and parliament
- The authority and latitude of actions the agency is authorized
- How agency board members are selected and the terms of appointment
- How the agency head is appointed and the term of appointment
- What is required for removal of the agency head or board members
- How the agency's financing is provided
- Who/what controls the agency's budget choices

Constructing agency structure, processes, leadership, staff and budget in ways that reduce external influences on those factors increases the possibility of independence, but there can never be absolute independence because the very existence of the agency is dependent upon establishment and legitimacy through political processes. That which can be established by the state can be altered or abolished if there is political will to do so.

Deeper understanding is needed of the influences on independent agencies in media and communications, the degrees of autonomy afforded various means of addressing the factors influencing their independence, their abilities to withstand external pressures and how long they can withstand prolonged political pressures. Media and communications policy research has not yet established that knowledge.

Specialized Versus Converged Administration

Because differing technologies of communications developed over time, countries traditionally tended to establish separate administrative agencies to address policy issues arising from their appearance. Countries established varying administrative oversight for communications activities provided through activities such as postal services, the press, telephony, radio, television, cable television, satellite television and the internet. The structures were influenced by who owned and operated the services.

Postal, telegraph and telephone services were owned and operated by governments in many countries well into the late twentieth century. Their administrative arrangements differed from countries in which telegraph and telephone services were provided by private companies regulated by government. In most countries, telephony issues were in the purview of a telecommunications administrative agency and broadcasting in a separate agency.

The development of technologies such as cable and satellite television, mobile phones and the internet in the latter part of the twentieth century created technological convergence and operational issues that did not fit easily or exclusively into the traditional telecommunications-broadcasting administrative separation and the remits of many administrative agencies. It raised questions such as whether the online operations of broadcasters should be under the authority of broadcasting regulatory agencies and the activities of internet search and aggregation firms were covered by the remits of communications regulators. This, combined with increasing privatization of communications services, began leading governments to adapt to this new environment by blending media and telecommunications policy (van Cuilenburg 2003), establishing new administrative structures and creating some converged media and communications policy to address emerging challenges (Collins 1995; Garcia-Murillo and MacInnes 2003). Despite convergence, there are still many differences in the administrative structures in which countries address issues of infrastructures, services, platforms and content.

Even with converged administrations, issues involving the appropriate structures, approaches and authorizations to oversee streaming video services such as Netflix and Hulu and data collection practices of online firms remain contentious. Other policy realms involving topics such as competition, industry and trade, and culture remain outside of this converged oversight in most countries and compete to oversee and influence many activities.

The Importance of Agency Competency

The abilities of agencies to address issues vary because of their competency to address policy matters. *Agency competency* involves the authority of an agency to make policy and to what and where it applies. Competency derives from the powers given it by executive and legislative action or in some case by judicial action.

The concept of competency refers to the ability, capability and aptitude to undertake an activity. One can say, for example, that an individual has the competency to operate a piece of equipment or carry out a task. In policy and legal use, however, the term specifically refers to the authority to act and exercise power. One can say, for example, that the Conseil Supérieur de l'Audiovisuel has the competency to regulate broadcasting enterprises in France.

Competency is important because it determines whether the state or agencies of the state may act, under what authority and under what circumstances. It involves the ability to intervene in activities or industries or to address certain types of issues. In practice, agencies involved in policy need both legal (sometimes called regulatory) competency and knowledge and skills-based competency to effectively operate. Competency differs from the concept of jurisdiction, which represents authority to administer law within a specific geographic area or level of government. In general, governments have jurisdiction within their countries, provinces and states within their territories, and counties and municipalities within their boundaries unless it has been specifically constrained. In some regional governance, such as the European Union, the issue of jurisdiction and competence has been addressed through country of origin provisions in regional policy (Smith 2015).

Three types of legal competencies are important in policy making: general, related and specific. *General legal competencies* of the state can be applied to media and communications but were not developed for media and communications intervention. General competencies involve those related to such issues as public order, state security, defamation and competition. These policy competencies are applicable to a variety of activities, including media and communications. *Related legal competencies* are not limited to media and communications but have direct relevance to its communication activates. Legal competency to protect public morals can be used to prosecute pornography appearing in media, and intellectual property protections may be enforced through prosecution and litigation of copyright infringement. *Specific legal competencies* are granted in media and communications for intervention involving specific communications technologies or activities of communications. This can lead to various media and activities being subject to different policy oversight.

Dispersal of competence creates conditions for regulatory competition and policy conflict. When competency is spread among agencies, tensions and rivalry arise about the degree of division of that competency. The relationship between different regulatory bodies that share decision-making competence can be viewed as *concurrent competence*, in which the competency of agencies complements each other, or *alternative competence*, in which one can substitute or another (Parisia et al. 2006).

Dispersal of competence can produce *policy competition* among ministries and agencies, leading to disputes about which may regulate what unless the distribution of competence is clearly delineated. In extreme cases, *policy collision* can occur if different ministries or agency establish conflicting policies or make conflicting rulings about the same issue.

Differences in approaches of when and how to intervene or disputes of where competency exists are evident in the United Kingdom over issues of media pluralism, for example. Competency is divided between Ofcom, which oversees the TV, radio and video-on-demand sectors, fixed-line telecoms, mobiles and postal services and the internet, and the U.K. Competition and Markets Authority, which ensures effective operations of economic markets. Ofcom tends to view pluralism in social and cultural terms, whereas the Competition and Markets Authority views it through competition and anticartel terms. The competition regulator may approve mergers and acquisitions among media firms that the communications regulator opposes. In such cases, the final decision is up to the cabinet and prime minister, and the decisions are often contentious.

Competency may also be absent because it has not been granted or has been deliberately constrained. This may have occurred because policy makers did not perceive an issue and did not assign competency, because of confusion or inaction on their part or because a deliberate choice was made not to provide authority to intervene.

Competency for Satellite Policy in the United States

The importance of legal or regulatory competency is illustrated by satellite policy in the United States. Because multiple issues and concerns are involved, competency is widely spread among administrative agencies and specifically divided to limit conflicts among the agencies.

The National Telecommunications and Information Administration (NTIA), an agency of the Department of Commerce, has competency for radio spectrum allocation and establishing spectrum of satellite and spacecraft control as well as the spectrum used for various types of communications using satellites.

The Federal Communications Commission, an independent agency, has competency involving concerns over satellite dishes, market issues and uses of satellites by broadcasters and cablecasters.

The Federal Aviation Administration (FAA) under the Department of Transportation has competency for nongovernment spaceports and the launch and reentry of private spacecraft that may be used to put satellites into orbit. The Department of Defense and National Aeronautics and Space Administration (an independent agency) oversee similar military and civilian governmental activities.

The National Oceanic and Atmospheric Administration, an agency of the Department of Commerce, has competency for spacecraft operations involving remote sensing and other activities.

Those conducting activities under oversight, advocating related policy or observing and studying policy must thus identify the agency or agencies with the appropriate competency(ies) to act on specific matters.

Procedural Aspects

To comprehend policy making in a country, one must consider the processes under which it is made.

An important issue involves the interests represented in the processes. Countries with procedures that include a wider number of participants are likely to produce policy that balances and services multiple interests; those with fewer participants represented are likely to serve a narrower range of interests. Knowing who is involved and represented in the processes is an important element in comprehending policy making and its outcome.

A second issue is the transparency of the processes and the extent to which they are clear and followed. Understanding whether the policy was made publicly or behind closed doors, whether documentation and rationales for decisions are available and clear and whether decision-making followed established protocols all provide insight into policy processes and results.

A range of procedural elements are used in varying countries. Knowledge of the traditional requirements and practices for a specific policy-making setting is fundamental.

Several elements are typically found in policy-making processes. *Consultations* are made with interested parties, seeking information and ideas to better understand the issues involved. These may be informal processes or involve formal processes in which written submissions are sought and may or may not be available to the public depending on the transparency involved.

Hearings are more formalized consideration of issues and proposals held by legislative and administrative agencies. These typically involve testimony and evidence from selected participants, who present the views of the organizations they represent and expert witnesses who provide analyses and recommendations. These are typically public but can be influenced by the choice of participants. It is typical for industry association leaders, company executives, consultants, industry analysts, scholars and civil society and advocacy groups to participate in consultations and hearings in open societies, but the participation is often narrower in less democratic nations.

Some governments, especially in Europe and those associated with the United Kingdom through the Commonwealth nations, issue *green papers* in which the ruling government reports its thinking and potential course of action on issues. These proposals are not binding and are a form of "trial balloons" in which governments issue a tentative policy proposal to judge reaction to it. At times governments will issue a *white paper*, a report that parses and discusses a policy issue and presents the government's philosophy, rationale and approach in addressing the issue. These are used to gain support for policy measures that will be pursued.

As policy moves toward implementation, legislative *bills* may be required to provide governance authorization and its legal and governmental bases. These are typically formal written documents that are used in debate and revision of the proposed laws.

Documents, reports, testimony and transcriptions resulting from all of these procedural elements are important objects used by those studying policy and policy making. Those who want to understand or participate in policy making seek to become involved in and influence the outcomes of the various elements.

Economic Systems and Institutional Influences on Policy

The economic system of a country and its economic institutions affect policy making, as do global and regional systems and institutions to which it has aligned itself. The types of policy made and the policy mechanism and tools selected are influenced by these economic factors.

The traditional economic system found throughout the world in centuries past was based on small-scale agriculture, hunting and individual labor with limited governance of those activities. It has been replaced by modern economic systems in developed and transitional countries, but it is still present in underdeveloped countries and underdeveloped provinces around the world. Modern economic systems are characterized by how they handle factors such as property rights, planning and competition (Gregory and Stuart 2004). Three fundamental types of modern economic systems exist and are categorized by the degree of governmental intervention and control of those factors (see Fig. 2.5).

Market economies are ones in which government does not intervene significantly in the market and planned economies are ones in which government plays a major role in the system. Mixed economies at the center balance aspects of both. Market and planned economies are ideal types. No market-based system exists without some government intervention and no planned economy system exists without some activities taking place outside the planned economy. In considering economic influences on policy, it is important to understand the degree to which intervention exists in an economic system, how it is evident and what institutional arrangements are involved in the intervention.

The economic system present in a country is highly influenced by a combination of culture, history, dominant political philosophy and governance

Fig. 2.5 Three types of modern economic systems

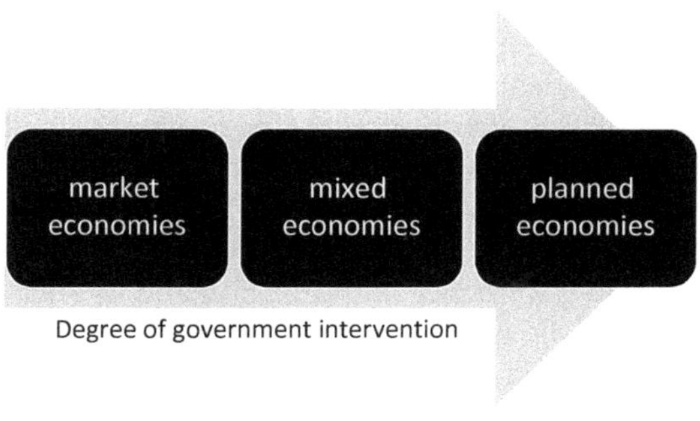

institutions. While it is tempting to simplistically label countries as capitalist or socialist, those distinctions are not very useful in understanding their economic systems. Vietnam, for example, is a socialist country politically and operates under a planned economic system. Those characterizations do not capture the fact that for more than 20 years the country has officially sanctioned private ownership and a market economy in some economic sectors. It has even moved some aspects of state-owned industries under market governance (Hayton 2011; Dinh 2013). Thus, some segments and activities of its economy are more explained by the mixed economic system model rather than the fully planned model.

Economic institutions included the economic system embraced, the dominant political economic philosophy, finance and banking, and important industries and major companies contributing to the national economy that are influential in all countries. Even when they are not officially part of governance, representatives of these serve on advisory boards or have access to leaders to advise and influence them privately.

Central banks influence national economies, banking system stability and commercial activity through their control over monetary policy and currency. Although government entities, they generally are independent from the ruling government to some degree. Decisions of central banks affect national economic conditions and their opinions on policy proposals, particularly those involving government budgets and taxation, are influential.

Dominant economic ideas have significant influence on policy making that affects not only the economy but all aspects of society. For the past century Keynesianism (Hall 1989), neoliberalism (Harvey 2007), various forms of Marxist economics (Freedman 1990; Fine et al. 2013) and hybrid approaches combining those economic philosophies have dominated worldwide, with Keynesianism and neoliberalism potent forces in democratic nations and Marxist economics in communist and socialist nations. Keynesianism emanated from the work of John Maynard Keyes and was especially influential between the 1930s and 1980s. It argued that government policies and spending can reduce economic downturns by stabilizing employment and economic output. Neoliberalism argues that deregulation, privatization of services, reduction in government spending and free trade improve overall economic conditions, a perspective that has been embraced by many countries in the past four decades. Marxist economic theory, rising from the works of Karl Marx, asserts that labor is a central factor in the economy and that without controlling capitalism, its benefits cannot be achieved.

At a broad general level, financial and business interests have been especially effective in influencing the environment during the past four decades through institutions such as the World Bank and the International Monetary Fund, through think tanks such as the Institute of Economic Affairs and the Council on Foreign Relations, through policy development organizations such as the World Economic Forum that have pushed a neoliberal approach to policy into prominence and through the use of experts and commentators in media (Beder

2001; Phalen 2014; Shoup 2015). The neoliberal approach was driven by stagnation of economies in Western nations and desires to benefit from the development of national economies in many nations elsewhere (Harvey 2003). Rejecting the idea that the state should be the preeminent force in governance, neoliberals asserted that the market is the most desirable source of governance and should be the primary influence on economic and social development. This has become the underpinning philosophy and policy justification for deregulation, privatization of public services and globalism in recent decades (Clarke and Pitelis 1995; Harvey 2007; Turner 2008; Roland and Stiglitz 2008; Eriksen 2014).

The influence of neoliberal philosophy on media and communications policy has been recognized by scholars of political economy of media and sociology (Freedman 2008; Pickard 2014). This has built upon earlier examinations of corporatization of media and trade dominance in media productions that grew throughout the last quarter of the twentieth century (Bagdikian 1983; Schiller 1989) and concerns about U.S. and Western dominance of global communications (Nordenstreng and Schiller 1993). Media and communications policies have been significantly altered by neoliberal policy approaches (McChesney 1999, 2004). The effects of neoliberalism have been especially evident in the privatization and deregulation of telephone and other telecommunications systems worldwide and deregulation of commercial broadcasting, cablecasting and internet provision in Western nations (Gershon 1993; Levy and Spiller 1996; Li and Xu 2004; Freedman 2008).

Socialist political and economic systems have also been influenced not only by neoliberalism at the global level but also by changing domestic developmental priorities and economic reforms that have introduced some market forces, private ownership and changes in banking and finance practices (Hayton 2011; Brundenius and Torres 2014; Kroeber 2016; Naughton 2018). This has required modernization of socialist economic theory and principles in ways that are not fully reconciled with socialist political theory.

It has been argued that the increased trade in media products and services and strengthening intellectual property rights have made media firms larger enterprises with more ability to influence national and global policy (May 2000). Media and communications have often been portrayed as being at the heart of globalization (Appadurai 1996; Castells 2000), but others have argued that this media-centric approach ignores the overall impact of neoliberal policy on other industries and that media are merely another beneficiary (Ampuja 2012).

Throughout the world, major industries upon which national economies are dependent—often oil and gas, minerals, steel and manufacturing industries—gain significant attention from policy makers and typically have noteworthy influence on national policies (McGillivray 2004; Felipe 2016). Large global corporations often wield significant transnational power for similar reasons (Mikler 2018). Similarly, media and communications firms in countries where they contribute meaningfully to gross domestic product and employment also tend to gain attention and influence (Flew 2011).

Decisions about media and communications policies and the effects of policy choices are highly influenced by economic concerns. These affect who makes choices, how choices are made, the economic and financial incentives and disincentives for varying choices, and the results they produce on individuals, companies and society (Picard 2011).

Understanding how economic influences on media and communications policy making in specific policy environments is vital for comprehending how and why various policies emerge.

Influences of Social Institutions on Policy

Social institutions represent influences deriving from both the organizational and non-organizational senses. They include religious organizations, associations and clubs, civil society groups, educational entities and libraries. But social institutions also involve the values and norms present in forms of government, business, families and a host of interactions in society.

Social influences result from values, beliefs and norms held across society and subgroups in society. These values, beliefs and norms are promoted in both private social interactions and public interactions and involve factors such as class, gender, race, equality, participation and the rights and privileges that influence social interaction. Governance and economic institutions are influenced by these social factors and they affect decisions in governance and policy.

Several types of social organizations are particularly active as social institutions in policy making: business groups, advocacy groups, cultural groups and religious organizations.

Business groups representing commercial interests are often active in policy making. These include chambers of commerce, small business associations and trade and industry groups representing banking, manufacturing, energy, pharmaceuticals and service industries. The Kenya National Chamber of Commerce and Industry is an example of such a group. All have some interests in media and communications policy, especially telecommunications—which is a central component of modern commerce. Companies in media and communications industries are represented by business and trade groups that vigorously support their interests worldwide. The Egyptian Publishers Association, for example, promotes the industry and its products but is also active in promoting copyright and postal policies beneficial to its members.

Civil society advocacy groups actively seek social and governance changes involving the issues upon which they focus. Some are short-term groups addressing an immediate policy question that disappear after a decision is made, whereas others involve long-standing organizations. Some groups deal with single issues, while others address multiple issues within their interest area. The Voice of the Listener and Viewer in the United Kingdom, for example, concentrates on issues involving public broadcasting, whereas Free Press in the United States addresses multiple policy issues involving print, broadcast and the internet. Some groups participate in governance processes, but others are marginalized by governance, economic or social institutions or by their own choice.

Cultural organizations and institutions focus on preserving and promoting cultural elements including history, language, values, art, literature, music, clothing and customs. These activities often center around museums, theaters, library, archives and cultural ministries, but private organizations also play roles in promoting culture and traditional values and may be active in policy making when issues involving culture appear. These types of institutions include, for example, the Jordan Academy of Arabic, which is the language academy devoted to preservation, study and development of proper use of the language, and the Daughters of the American Revolution in the United States that promotes elite heritage and historic preservation.

An important social influence in many countries results from religious institutions seeking to align policy with their beliefs, and these usually have significant ability to mobilize believers around issues related to their religious values and beliefs. Religion combines with political activity to support political preferences and can lead to political militancy (Bruce 2003), leading to varying models of church-state arrangements and influence emerging globally (Soper and Fetzer 2018). Religious influences can lead to church-state conflicts in open societies and societies in which religious influences are suppressed.

In a few countries, religious influence is so strong that religious leaders rule with their authority professedly originating from a deity they represent. In these theocracies, state structures, policies and activities enshrine the religious beliefs and practices (Ferrero and Wintrobe 2009). Contemporary theocracies include countries such as the Holy See (Vatican) and Iran.

In studying policy and policy making, understanding what social influences exist, at what governance levels that influence is exercised, by whom and on behalf of whom are crucial elements of analysis.

Media Capture, Policy Capture and State Capture

Policy and the absence of policy can be used by governments and stakeholders to pursue their self-interests, resulting in media capture, policy capture and state capture.

Media capture can occur when policy provides explicit control over content or creates and supports close relationships between government and media owners that influence content. The lack of adequate policy can also permit such conditions to arise (Besley and Prat 2006; Petrova 2008; Enikolopov and Petrova 2016).

Policy capture (sometimes called regulatory capture) and *state capture* describe conditions in which policy decisions are unduly influenced toward one outcome, usually by those of economic interests.

It has long been understood that administrative agencies can become so close to the firms they oversee that they focus on the industry's interests rather than public interests, undertake a soft approach to regulation and rarely engage in more than light-handed punishment for policy violations. Preventing such capture is critical for effective policy decisions (Carpenter and Moss 2013; OECD 2017). This is especially the case when industry development and promotion is also the remit of administrative agencies, as is the case of many media and communications administrative agencies.

State capture is an extreme form of capture that occurs when a firm, industry or a few economically powerful individuals unduly influence all mechanisms of governance in a country. Such conditions are usually established through high levels of corruption and reduced power in legislative and judicial institutions (Hellman et al. 2000; Leitner and Meissner 2016). In recent years such capture has been evident in transitional economies in Eastern Europe and South Africa. Media and communications firms are rarely involved in state capture themselves because most do not produce enough wealth necessary to undertake such capture. However, individuals and firms owning or controlling major sources of wealth such as oil and gas and minerals often acquire media and communications firms to help solidify their positions in society, gain available financial benefits and influence their portrayal and those of the political actors that they control.

Final Words

The environment and locales in which policies are central to understanding, participating in, and examining policy and policy making. These establish the settings in which governance, economic and social influences that affect policy principles, rationales, arguments and outcomes are exercised.

The influences are complex and can change, requiring continual reappraisal when viewing policy development and trajectories over time. Identifying factors that most steer policy at a point of time is crucial. Understanding the differences in settings is critical when comparing policy and policy making across countries and considering the viability of policy options.

Chapter Summary

- Public policy is made at a variety of levels under different conditions.
- The structures and powers of governance affect how policy is made in a country.
- Administrative agencies may be part of or independent of the ruling government.
- Administrative agencies in media and communications are increasingly merged because of technological changes.
- Dominant economic ideas influence policy choices.
- Major financial institutions and industries influence policy choices.
- Social institutions and their activities influence choices.
- Administrative agencies have only the competency or authority granted to them by government or legislative action.
- Administrative agencies can be captured by the industries and firms they oversee.

Discussion Points

1. Why is it more difficult to create global than national policy?
2. What governance levels are primarily involved in the regulation of internet services?
3. What are the advantages and disadvantages of independent administrative agencies?
4. How do economic influences affect policy making?
5. What evidence is there of policy capture in media and communications in your country?

Bibliography

Acharya, Amitav, and Alastair Iain Johnston, eds. 2007. *Crafting Cooperation: Regional International Institutions in Comparative Perspective*. Cambridge: Cambridge University Press.

Ampuja, Marko. 2012. Globalization Theory, Media-Centrism and Neoliberalism: A Critique of Recent Intellectual Trends. *Critical Sociology* 38 (2): 281–301.

Appadurai, Arjun. 1996. *Modernity at Large: Cultural Dimensions of Globalization*. Minneapolis: University of Minnesota Press.

Ba, Alice D., Cheng-Chwee Kuik, and Sueo Sudo, eds. 2017. *Institutionalizing East Asia: Mapping and Reconfiguring Regional Cooperation*. London: Routledge.

Bagdikian, Ben H. 1983. *The Media Monopoly*. Boston: Beacon Press.

Baker, C. Edwin. 2001. *Media, Markets and Democracy*. Cambridge: Cambridge University Press.

Bandyopadhyay, Sumana, and André Torre. 2017. *Regional Cooperation in South Asia: Socio-economic, Spatial, Ecological and Institutional Aspects*. Berlin: Springer.

Beder, S. 2001. Research Note – Neoliberal Think Tanks and Free Market Environmentalism, Environmental Politics. *Environmental Politics* 10 (2): 128–133.

Besley, Timothy, and Andrea Prat. 2006. Handcuffs for the Grabbing Hand? Media Capture and Government Accountability. *American Economic Review* 96 (3): 720–736.

Bowman, Ann, and Richard C. Kearney. 2016. *State and Local Government*. 10th ed. Boston: Cengage Learning.

Bruce, Steve. 2003. *Politics and Religion*. Cambridge: Polity Press.

Brundenius, Claes, and Ricardo Torres Pérez, eds. 2014. *No More Free Lunch: Reflections on the Cuban Economic Reform Process and Challenges for Transformation*. Berlin: Springer.

Canada, Ministère de la Culture et des Communications. 2018. Secteurs de Intervention. https://www.mcc.gouv.qc.ca/index.php?id=9. Accessed 21 Jan 2018.

Carpenter, Daniel, and David A. Moss, eds. 2013. *Preventing Regulatory Capture*. Cambridge: Cambridge University Press.

Castells, Manuel. 2000. *The Information Age: Economy Society and Culture, 3 Vols*. Oxford: Blackwell.

———. 2008. The New Public Sphere: Global Civil Society, Communication Networks, and Global Governance. *The Annals of the American Academy of Political and Social Science* 616 (1): 78–93.

Clarke, Thomas, and Christos Pitelis, eds. 1995. *The Political Economy of Privatization*. London: Routledge.
Collins, Richard. 1995. *Converging Media? Converging Regulation?* London: Institute of Public Policy Research.
Dinh, Hinh T. 2013. *Light Manufacturing in Vietnam: Creating Jobs and Prosperity in a Middle-Income Economy*. Washington, DC: International Bank for Reconstruction and Development/The World Bank.
Djelic, Marie-Laure, and Kerstin Sahlin-Andersson, eds. 2006. *Transnational Governance: Institutional Dynamics of Regulation*. Cambridge: Cambridge University Press.
Edwards, Geoff, and Leonard Waverman. 2006. The Effects of Public Ownership and Regulatory Independence on Regulatory Outcomes: A Study of Interconnect Rates in EU Telecommunications. *Journal of Regulatory Economics* 29 (1): 23–67.
Elazar, Daniel J. 1997. Contrasting Unitary and Federal Systems. *International Political Science Review* 18 (3): 37–251.
Enikolopov, Ruben, and Maria Petrova. 2016. Media Capture: Empirical Evidence. In *Handbook of Media Economics*, ed. Simon P. Anderson, Joel Waldfogel, and David Strömberg, 687–700. Amsterdam: North Holland.
Eriksen, Thomas H. 2014. *Globalization: The Key Concepts*. 2nd ed. New York: Bloomsbury Academic.
Felipe, Jesus. 2016. *Development and Modern Industrial Policy in Practice: Issues and Country Experiences*. Cheltenham: Edward Elgar Publishing.
Ferrero, Mario, and Ronald Wintrobe, eds. 2009. *The Political Economy of Theocracy*. New York: Palgrave Macmillan.
Fine, Ben, Alfredo Saad-Filho, and Marco Boffo. 2013. *The Elgar Companion to Marxist Economics*. Cheltenham: Edward Elgar Publishers.
Flew, Terry. 2011. *The Creative Industries: Culture and Policy*. London: Sage.
Freedman, Robert. 1990. *The Marxist System: Economic, Political, and Social Perspectives*. Washington, DC: CQ Press.
Freedman, Des. 2006. Dynamics of Power in Contemporary Media Policy-Making. *Media, Culture and Society* 28 (6): 907–923.
———. 2008. *The Politics of Media Policy*. Cambridge: Polity Press.
Garcia-Murillo, Martha, and Ian MacInnes. 2003. The Impact of Technological Convergence on the Regulation of ICT Industries. *International Journal on Media Management* 5 (1): 57–67.
Gershon, Richard A. 1993. International Deregulation and the Rise of Transnational Media Corporations. *Journal of Media Economics* 6 (2): 3–22.
Gilardi, Fabrizio, and Martino Maggetti. 2011. The Independence of Regulatory Authorities. In *Handbook on the Politics of Regulation*, ed. David Levi-Faur, 201–214. Cheltenham: Edward Elgar.
Gregory, Paul R., and Robert C. Stuart. 2004. *Comparing Economic Systems in the Twenty-First Century*. 7th ed. Mason: South-Western/Cengage Learning.
Hague, Rod, Martin Harrop, and John McCormick. 2016. *Comparative Government and Politics: An Introduction*. 10th ed. London: Palgrave Macmillan.
Hale, Thomas, and David Held, eds. 2011. *The Handbook of Transnational Governance: Institutions and Innovations*. Cambridge: Polity.

Hall, Peter A. 1989. *The Political Power of Economic Ideas: Keynesianism Across Nations.* Princeton: Princeton University Press.
Hanretty, Chris, and Christel Koop. 2012. Measuring the Formal Independence of Regulatory Agencies. *Journal of European Public Policy* 19 (2): 198–216.
———. 2013. Shall the Law Set Them Free? The Formal and Actual Independence of Regulatory Agencies. *Regulation & Governance* 7 (2): 195–214.
Harvey, David. 2003. *The New Imperialism.* Oxford: Oxford University Press.
———. 2007. *A Brief History of Neoliberalism.* Oxford: Oxford University Press.
Hayton, Bill. 2011. *Vietnam: Rising Dragon.* New Haven: Yale University Press.
Hellman, Joel S., Geraint Jones, Daniel Kaufmann, and Mark Schankerman. 2000. *Measuring Governance, Corruption, and State Capture: How Firms and Bureaucrats Shape the Business Environment in Transition Economies.* Washington, DC: The International Bank for Reconstruction and Development/World Bank.
Hurd, Ian. 2017. *International Organizations: Politics, Law, Practice.* 3rd ed. Cambridge: Cambridge University Press.
Juwayeyi, Murendehle M. 2017. The Malawi Communications Regulatory Authority: Issues of De Jure and De Facto Independence. *Communication Law and Policy* 22 (2): 213–253.
Karns, Margaret P., Karen A. Mingst, and Kendall W. Stiles. 2015. *International Organizations: The Politics and Processes of Global Governance.* 3rd ed. Boulder: Lynne Rienner Publishers.
Kroeber, Arthur R. 2016. *China's Economy: What Everyone Needs to Know.* Oxford: Oxford University Press.
Leitner, Johannes, and Hannes Meissner, eds. 2016. *State Capture, Political Risks and International Business: Cases from Black Sea Region Countries.* London: Routledge.
Leonard, Dick, and Robert Taylor. 2016. *The Routledge Guide to the European Union.* London: Routledge.
Levy, Brian, and Pablo T. Spiller, eds. 1996. *Regulations, Institutions, and Commitment: Comparative Studies of Telecommunications.* Cambridge: Cambridge University Press.
Li, Wei, and Lixin Colin Xu. 2004. The Impact of Privatization and Competition in the Telecommunications Sector Around the World. *The Journal of Law and Economics* 47 (2): 395–430.
Lijphart, Arend. 2012. *Patterns of Democracy: Government Forms and Performance in Thirty-Six Countries.* 2nd ed. New Haven: Yale University Press.
Linz, Juan J. 2000. *Totalitarian and Authoritarian Regimes.* Boulder: Lynne Rienner Publishers.
Lukes, Steven. 1986. *Power.* New York: New York University Press.
May, Christopher. 2000. *A Global Political Economy of Intellectual Property Rights.* London: Routledge.
McChesney, Robert W. 1999. *Rich Media, Poor Democracy: Communication Politics in Dubious Times.* Champaign: University of Illinois Press.
———. 2004. *The Problem of the Media: U.S. Communication Politics in the Twenty-First Century.* New York: Monthly Review Press.
McGillivray, Fiona. 2004. *Privileging Industry: The Comparative Politics of Trade and Industrial Policy.* Princeton: Princeton University Press.
Mikler, John. 2018. *The Political Power of Global Corporations.* Cambridge: Polity.
Montoya, Miguel Á., and Francesc Trillas. 2007. The Measurement of the Independence of Telecommunications Regulatory Agencies in Latin America and the Caribbean. *Utilities Policy* 15 (3): 182–190.

Naughton, Barry J. 2018. *The Chinese Economy: Adaptation and Growth*. 2nd ed. Cambridge, MA: MIT Press.
Nordenstreng, Kaarle, and Herbert I. Schiller. 1993. *Beyond National Sovereignty: International Communications in the 1990s*. Greenwood: Praeger.
OECD. 2017. *Preventing Policy Capture: Integrity in Public Decision Making*. Paris: Organization for Economic Co-operation and Development.
Olsen, Jonathan, and John McCormick. 2016. *The European Union: Politics and Policies*. 6th ed. Boulder: Westview Press.
Parisia, Francesco, Norbert Schulz, and Jonathan Klick. 2006. Two Dimensions of Regulatory Competition. *International Review of Law and Economics* 26 (1): 56–66.
Peters, B. Guy, and Jon Pierre. 2016. *Comparative Governance: Rediscovering the Functional Dimension of Governing*. Cambridge: Cambridge University Press.
Petrova, Maria. 2008. Inequality and Media Capture. *Journal of Public Economics* 92 (1–2): 183–212.
Phalen, Sean. 2014. *Neoliberalism, Media and the Political*. London: Palgrave Macmillan.
Picard, Robert G. 2011. Economic Approaches to Media Policy. In *The Handbook of Global Media and Communication Policy*, ed. Robin Mansell and Marc Raboy, 355–375. Oxford: Wiley-Blackwell.
Pickard, Victor. 2014. *America's Battle for Media Democracy: The Triumph of Corporate Libertarianism and the Future of Media Reform*. Cambridge: Cambridge University Press.
Puppis, Manuel, Martino Maggetti, Fabrizio Gilgard, Jan Biela, and Yannis Papadopoulos. 2014. The Political Communication of Independent Regulatory Agencies. *Swiss Political Science Review* 20 (3): 388–412.
Richardson, Jeremy, ed. 1982 and 2012. *Policy Styles in Western Europe*. London: Allan & Unwin/Taylor & Francis.
Roland, Gérard, and Joseph E. Stiglitz. 2008. *Privatization: Successes and Failures*. New York: Columbia University Press.
Schiller, Herbert I. 1989. *Culture, Inc.: The Corporate Takeover of Public Expression*. New York: Oxford University Press.
Schulz, Wolfgang, Peggy Valcke, and Kristina Irion, eds. 2013. *The Independence of the Media and Its Regulatory Agencies*. Bristol: Intellect Books.
Shoup, Laurence H. 2015. *Think Tank: The Council on Foreign Relations and the Empire of Neoliberal Geopolitics, 1976–2014*. New York: Monthly Review Press.
Smith, Martin J. 2009. *Power and the State*. London: Palgrave Macmillan.
Smith, Rachael Craufurd. 2015. Determining Regulatory Competence for Audiovisual Media Services in the European Union. *Journal of Media Law* 3 (2): 263–285.
Soper, J. Christopher, and Joel S. Fetzer. 2018. *Religion and Nationalism in Global Perspective*. Cambridge: Cambridge University Press.
Svolik, Milan W. 2012. *The Politics of Authoritarian Rule*. Cambridge: Cambridge University Press.
Thatcher, Mark. 2002. Delegation to Independent Regulatory Agencies: Pressures, Functions and Contextual Mediation. *West European Politics* 25 (1): 125–147.
Turner, Rachel S. 2008. *Neo-liberal Ideology: History, Concepts and Policies*. Edinburgh: Edinburgh University Press.
van Cuilenburg, Jan. 2003. Media Policy Paradigm Shifts: Toward New Communications Policy Paradigm. *European Journal of Communication* 18 (2): 181–207.
Watts, Ronald L. 1998. Federalism, Federal Political Systems, and Federations. *Annual Review of Political Science* 1 (1): 117–137.

Suggested Readings

Hague, Rod, Martin Harrop, and John McCormick. 2016. *Comparative Government and Politics: An Introduction*. 10th ed. London: Palgrave Macmillan.
Hale, Thomas, and David Held, eds. 2011. *The Handbook of Transnational Governance: Institutions and Innovations*. Cambridge: Polity.
Hanretty, Chris, and Christel Koop. 2012. Measuring the Formal Independence of Regulatory Agencies. *Journal of European Public Policy* 19: 2, 198–216.
Hurd, Ian. 2017. *International Organizations: Politics, Law, Practice*. 3rd ed. Cambridge University Press.
Schulz, Wolfgang, Peggy Valcke, and Kristina Irion, eds. 2013. *The Independence of the Media and its Regulatory Agencies*. Bristol: Intellect Books.
Smith, Rachael Craufurd. 2015. Determining Regulatory Competence for Audiovisual Media Services in the European Union. *Journal of Media Law* 3 (2): 263–285
van Cuilenburg, Jan. 2003. Media Policy Paradigm Shifts: Toward New Communications Policy Paradigm. *European Journal of Communications* 18 (2): 181–207.

CHAPTER 3

Politics in the Pursuit of Policy Outcomes

Policy is developed and exists with the deliberate purpose of producing an outcome. It is intentional and calculated, and a variety of elements bring the policy process into action and guide its course. It takes place through politically influenced processes. The robustness and effectiveness of a policy are dependent upon the policy process providing opportunities to extensively explore the nature of and factors contributing to the issues, to fully consider multiple means for addressing them, to facilitate effective decision-making and to properly implement the policy elements.

The policy process model introduced briefly in Chap. 1 depicts consecutive stages, building upon the activities of the previous stages, but its primary purposes are to clarify stages that occur in policy development and the order of best practice. In actual practice, the orderliness of the process, particularly in the early and middle phases, is sometimes muddled, and options consideration and assessment are narrowed by preconceived ideas or haste. Nevertheless, the model is useful in considering the phases and activities that typically place in policy making and its oversight, and it provides a means for organizing an understanding why and how policy issues gain attention and are addressed. This chapter considers the activities of participants in those phases and the issues that arise in the process (Fig. 3.1).

Policy processes are initiated when an issue or problem is identified and the need for policy action asserted. *Problem/issue recognition* may start in firms or industry, the public, advocacy groups, political parties, administrative agencies, the legislative branch of government, or at the top of the executive branch. Any of these actors may attempt to garner attention to the issues or developments and seek policy responses. Some issues will gain attention and action rapidly; others may be ignored and languish for extended periods of time.

Once an issue has gained recognition, the second step is *issue examination*, in which its characteristics, impact and causes reveal a clearer understanding of

R. G. Picard, *Media and Communication Policy Making*, Palgrave Global Media Policy and Business,
https://doi.org/10.1007/978-3-030-35173-1_3

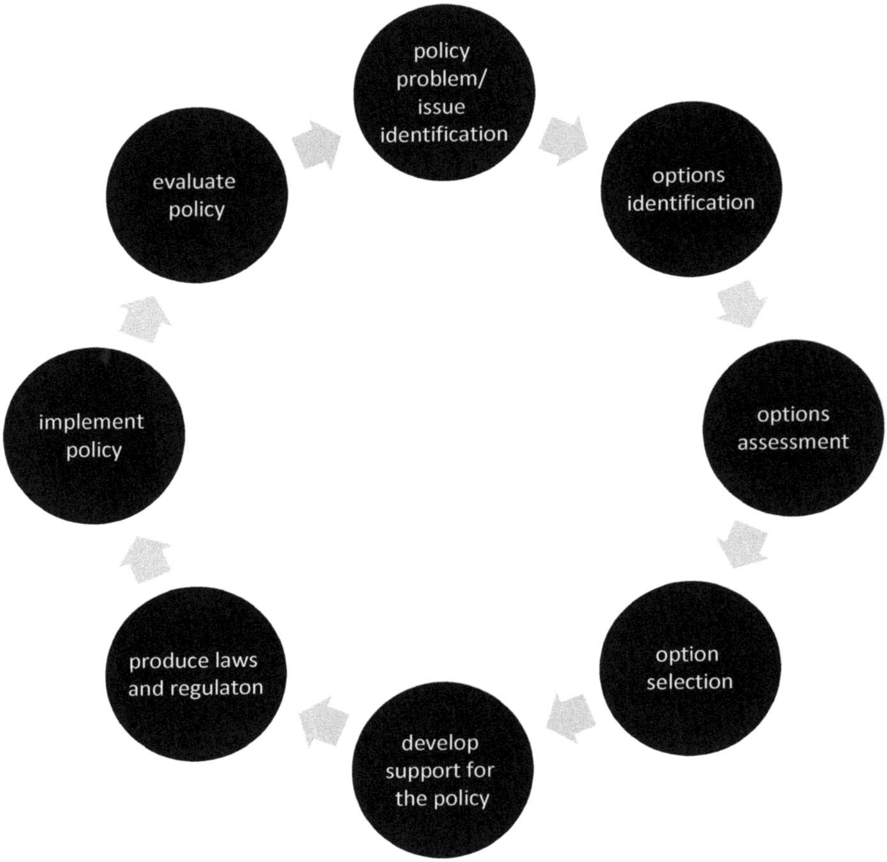

Fig. 3.1 Policy process model

its nature and the factors affecting it. The third stage in the process is *options identification*, in which the actions that public authorities can take in response to the issue using various policy approaches and mechanisms are determined. *Options assessment* involves considering what effects potential actions are likely to create and whether and the extent to which each option is likely to resolve the issue or problem receiving attention. The evaluation includes identifying the effort and costs involved in pursuing an option. Not making policy is also a policy option, because inaction can be strategic and deliberate, approving existing conditions and developments. The effects of policy inaction or avoidance have gained limited attention because it is difficult to document. It is argued that why and how policy makers and policy-making processes ignore or exclude viewpoints and public participation needs to be better explored (Freedman 2010), such as a study showing a "reoccurring pattern" of ignoring or avoiding discussion of market failure and its democratic effects in U.S. policy making

(Pickard 2014). Fuller considerations of methods used in examining issues, and identifying and considering options, will be explored more fully in Chap. 8 on policy analysis.

Once an issue has been explored and options established, those involved in the policy process select the policy preferences through *option selection* and pursue them through the governmental institutions that *produce laws and regulations* that design, formulate and enact the policy and provide the legal and budgetary bases for action. When policy is established, *implementation* occurs by relevant administrative agencies and ministries that establish the personnel, processes, regulations and enforcement necessary to pursue its implementation.

After a policy has been established and has operated for a sufficient period for its effects to be observed, often two to five years, it is best practice to revisit the policy through *evaluation* to determine its overall effectiveness, the extent to which it is producing the desired effects and whether unintended consequences are evident. Evaluation processes and methods will be explored more fully in Chap. 9.

Policy process explanations are based on a variety of approaches and theories that focus on institutions, diffusion of policy, narrative frameworks, uncertainties and irrationalities, and other factors influencing processes (Birkland 2015; Weible and Sabatier 2018). Ultimately, all these various policy process approaches recognize that processes involve a series of steps, although they may disagree about the tidiness of the processes and diverge about the significance of activities in the stages.

Gaining Attention Is Crucial in Starting the Process

Only when an issue is perceived as significant enough to warrant policy makers' time and efforts will the policy process begin, so gaining attention and having an issue recognized as needing action are crucial.

Whether the attention and recognition are raised from above or come from below in the political system affects the speed of policy-making activities (Fig. 3.2). Action initiated from leadership and policy makers tends to move more rapidly because of the advantages they have in raising awareness through public forums and initiating activity. Action initiated from below tends to take

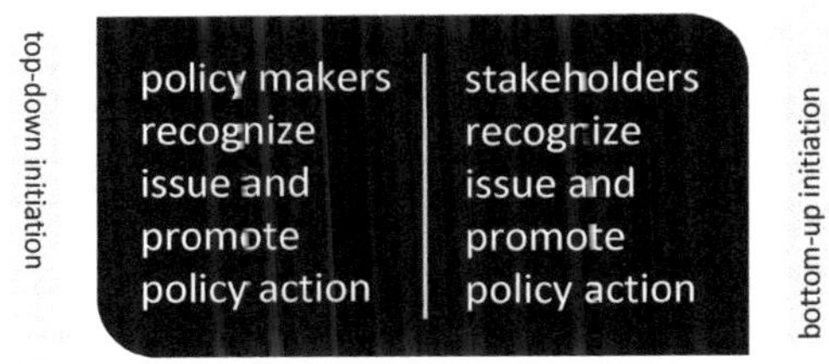

Fig. 3.2 Policy action can be initiated from above or below

longer because stakeholders doing so must gain the attention of policy makers and leaders and persuade them that some action is necessary or appropriate.

Bottom-up issue recognition is associated with ***agenda setting theory***, which posits that topics rise to public attention and are seen as requiring action through events and media coverage that elevate or relegate topics and issues though the amount of attention focused on and the relative importance attributed to them compared to that on other issues and topics (McCombs and Shaw 1972; Boydstun 2013). The approach is extensively used in political science, policy studies and media/communications studies to assert that media coverage, lack of coverage, and emphasis given to stories raise issues to, or keep them from, the ***public agenda***. Items on the public agenda are then often transferred to the ***policy agenda*** (McCombs and Shaw 1993; McCombs 2004; Weaver 2007). The approach recognizes that policy makers, interest groups, parties, heads of government and the public can become the impetus in raising issues and establishing agendas (Kingdon 2003; Birkland 2007; Zahariadis 2016), that using the networked public sphere enables rapid mobilization and public discourse in discussions of proposed new laws (Benkler et al. 2015) and that there are considerable variations among countries about how issues reach the agenda of legislatures, political parties and governments (Green-Pedersen and Walgrave 2014).

A challenge of top-down policy making at the national level is that nationwide concerns and media and communications tend to gain national policy makers' attention and take priority on their policy agendas. It has been shown, for example, that policy often does not recognize the significance of community television in local communities nor adequately distinguish it from nonprofessional content provision (Ali 2012).

Issues may gain attention when focusing events create awareness and induce the policy process to begin. Unexpected events and developments raise sudden awareness that some policy action is needed (Birkland 1998). These may result from accidents and disasters, civil disorder, large-scale violence, crises or other developments that gain significant attention.

After the Starwood Hotel chain owned by Marriott reported multiple types of data on 383 million guests had been breached, the State Attorney General and lawmakers in the state of California in the United States, for example, rapidly introduced a bill in 2019 to expand the state's data breach notification law to include mandatory notification of more of the types of data (Whittiker 2019). The rapid development and introduction of the legislation occurred because the Starwood breach of encrypted data focused attention on the fact that only certain types of information exposed were covered by the state's existing laws and led to rapid top-down policy action to include the omissions.

At other times attention develops more gradually, often in response to slowly appearing social issues, changes in public values and appearances of new technologies. Audio recordings began appearing in the late nineteenth century, for example, but they did not receive copyright protection against unauthorized copying under multinational treaties until 1961, protection that was strengthened in 1971 to halt importation and distribution of unauthorized recordings. A new treaty was established in 1996 to address illicit uses in the digital environment. To date, however, only about half the nations in the world have agreed to abide by the extended treaty (World Intellectual Property Organization 2019).

Multiple issues simultaneously contend for attention, including those involving the environment, immigration, criminal justice and social benefits and pensions. Creating a public focus on specific issues is highly influenced by the statements and actions of political leaders, but the approaches and methods for addressing them are often highly contested and gain substantial prominence in political debates, particularly in democratic nations. Media and communications policies only occasionally rise to the level that they are deeply contested in electoral politics or widespread national debate. Consequently, they often take a longer time to gain the attention of leading policy makers and tend to take place with less scrutiny than other issues. The challenges of internet hate speech, cyberbullying and stalking, and data privacy are now gaining significant attention among policy makers, but two decades have passed since the issues first appeared with the development of the internet.

Understanding how and why specific issues gain prominence and produce policies, the loci of their initiation and attention producing activities and what factors are involved in those activities provide an important understanding of the processes and outcomes of policy making.

How a Focusing Event Sets Media Policy Agenda

An Australian white supremacist attacked two mosques in Christchurch, New Zealand, in March 2019 with semiautomatic weapons, rifles and shotguns during prayer services, killing 51 people and injuring 49 others. The attacker livestreamed the assaults on Facebook Live and electronically distributed a manifesto just prior to the attack beginning.

The events horrified and galvanized the public and policy makers in New Zealand and worldwide to address issues of gun control (Westbrook and Greenfield 2019) and extremist and violent materials on digital media. This focusing event forcefully placed the need for action on both public and policy agendas by concentrating attention on extremists' online use and creating strong demands for policy action

Much of that response occurred because of the livestreaming of the attack and copies of that video were widely distributed on social media, including YouTube and Facebook (Timberg et al. 2019). The New Zealand Office of Film and Literature Classification rapidly banned the video, making distributing or exhibiting the video a crime and the Chief Censor of New Zealand banned distribution of the manifesto under the Films, Videos, and Publications Classification Act of 1993.

Larger digital companies took down and blocked uploads of the video, but numerous smaller social media and video sites operating outside New Zealand—especially in Australia—did not, leading to the introduction of legislation in Australia to fine or imprison managers of digital sites for carrying extremist and violent content.

The New Zealand government formed a royal commission of inquiry to investigate the attack and issues including the role of digital media in promoting extremism. The events set off a global discussion of the roles of digital platforms in strategies of extremist groups and individuals, with calls for policy action to address the risks of digital media in many nations.

A global summit in Paris hosted by French President Emmanuel Macron and New Zealand's premier Jacinda Ardern to combat violent and extremist content online brought world leaders and tech company executives together to discuss the issues. The Paris summit against online extremism produced pledges by governments and technology companies to increase efforts to counter the use of digital media by extremists (Curry and McMahon 2019). Pledges of support came from many firms including Facebook, Google, Microsoft, YouTube and Twitter and countries including Canada, Germany, India, Indonesia, Japan, Senegal and Spain.

Public Opinion, Narratives, Frames and Frameworks Influence the Process

Public opinion plays a role in all policy making because governments—regardless of forms—require support to be perceived as legitimate. These collective views about issues and how they should be addressed play roles in guiding priorities and actions. In democratic nations, however, public opinion plays a far greater role, with governments tending to be more responsive to citizens' opinions and policy preferences because of their electoral power, so public opinion plays significant role in creating the policy agenda. Public opinion and preferences have been shown to be a cause of policy rather than policy creating opinion (Page and Shapiro 1983). Even when elite influences are considered, public opinion has a substantial impact on policy and responsiveness to it (Burstein 2003).

Collective policy preferences tend to be rational and consistent over time. When preference changes occur, they are comprehensible and predictable rather than capricious (Page and Shapiro 1992). These factors tend to promote stability and continuity in policy rather than inducing chaotic rapid changes. However, when relevance of policy is perceived as declining because of changes in factors that initially led to the policy creation, when it is perceived to have diminished usefulness and effectiveness, or when dominant political philosophy is altered, public opinion can shift and lead to different preferences and demands.

Public opinion has an influence on all stages of the policy-making process but is especially salient in issue recognition, options assessment and options selection.

Rhetoric plays an important role in persuasive speech and raising issue awareness and creating demands for policy, and in the development and consideration of policy options. Language choices and styles are used to gain attention and persuade. Rhetoric often involves causal reasoning, moral evaluations and appeals to principle but can devolve into *moral panic* and *fear mongering*, in which unwarranted social concern is raised and strong instantaneous action is demanded.

Stakeholders and policy advocates often spend significant effort in trying to establish and control the *narratives* surrounding policy demands and development. The use of rhetoric and narratives defines issues and influences the ways they are conceived and are designed to create frames through which the public and policy makers will view, interpret and react to demands for action and policy proposals (Kelly 2012).

Policy narratives involve descriptions of issues or developments and why they are important. They typically use language that quickly categorizes the issues and those involved and conveys connotations about authority, righteousness, and good versus evil, and they can embrace or marginalize persons, groups or other states. These narratives create frames or mindsets for considering the issues addressed (Chong and Druckman 2007). The discourses of competing narratives and stakeholders can be examined to identify and investigate frames surrounding policy debates to better understand their motives and tactics (Chilton 2004; Fairclough and Fairclough 2012). Rhetoric and framing are not merely parts of debates over policy but can also be evident even in the naming of proposed policy and legislation. Effective policy narratives, especially conveyed in media reports, can strengthen and shift public opinion (Shanahan et al. 2011).

Framing is significant because it tends to activate unstated knowledge and opinions of those exposed to them. Language, semantics and the way the brain stores information create implicit memory that stimulates psychological responses predisposing individuals' perceptions of information or toward particular choices. Frames can thus be "prime" mental responses to issues and policy proposals (Scheufele and Tewksbury 2007). These can be especially strong if the frames and rhetoric set off a negative psychological reaction and if the policy issue has been negatively framed.

Framing is a more discursive and cognitive approach to understanding frames than that of *policy frameworks*, which has been used in policy studies and political science for several decades to identify general approaches to issues (van Hulst and Yanow 2016). The policy framework approach focuses on broader categorization of the policy within frameworks that involve complex, interwoven concepts, principles and objectives that can serve as foundations for policy debates, support policy formation and provide a touchstone to which proposed policy can be compared and assessed.

Monetary policy and fiscal policy frameworks are familiar examples of frameworks in economic policy that incorporate complex economics laws and theory, along with actions that can be taken by central banks, treasuries and other authorities to influence economic growth, exchange rates, borrowing, consumption or public spending.

In media and communications policy, two of the most germane and broad frameworks are the democratic needs framework and the economic framework. Policy developed within the *democratic needs framework* is focused on providing or protecting elements and functions necessary for citizens to knowledgeably and effectively participate in the democratic governance of society and its institutions. The *economic framework* is market centric and involves policies promoting achievement of market benefits, addressing market failures, and structural or financial constraints.

The democratic needs framework is based on the belief that a democratic deficit of inclusiveness and participation exists because of media and communications structures, elite control and commercialism (Baker 2006; Mueller et al. 2007; Picard 2007; Cammaerts and Carpentier 2007). The framework is based on a normative view of democracy and its communication needs (Baker 2006; Christians et al. 2009; Dahlgren 2009; Curran 2011). Unfortunately, much of the media and communications policy literature existing today that embraces the framework is based on idealized, underdeveloped or narrow conceptualizations of democracy and democratic theory and provides only limited agreed-upon criteria for policy development. Nevertheless, the framework is employed by many with little depth and critical thought.

The economic framework is based on concepts that support allowing the marketplace to determine outcomes and arguments that private interests will produce better results than intervention. This framework has been used to promote deregulation of telecommunications and broadcasting in hopes it would produce new technologies and services (Fowler and Brenner 1981; Holt 2011), to support privatization of provision (Eliassen et al. 1999; Greenstein 2015), to pursue "better" use of spectrum (Hazlett 1998; Cave and Webb 2016), and to argue for policy that protects competition and innovation (Bauer 2010). Critics regularly assert that the economic framework is gaining too much strength (Freedman 2006). Its supporters often employ it while ignoring market and competition prerequisites necessary for the economic framework to operate effectually and that market operations and failures can reduce its abilities to produce some media and communications products and services necessary in society.

More specific frameworks have been developed for addressing policy issues in internet and broadband development (Frieden 2003; Trkman et al. 2008) and for evaluating proposals governing internet access and service quality standards (van Schewick 2015). A layered model policy framework, spurred by the growth of data services and then the internet, has developed over the past four decades as technologists and policy makers have wrestled with how to adapt traditional siloed regulatory approaches to technological changes in telecommunications and broadcasting (Fransman 2002; Whitt 2004; Reed 2006; Sicker and Blumensaadt 2006). The layered framework approach asserts that traditional regulatory frameworks and policy designs setting separate policy approaches and objectives for voice services, data services and broadcasting (Fig. 3.3) should be shifted to an integrated and layered framework. This framework could better represent technical changes and create means by which

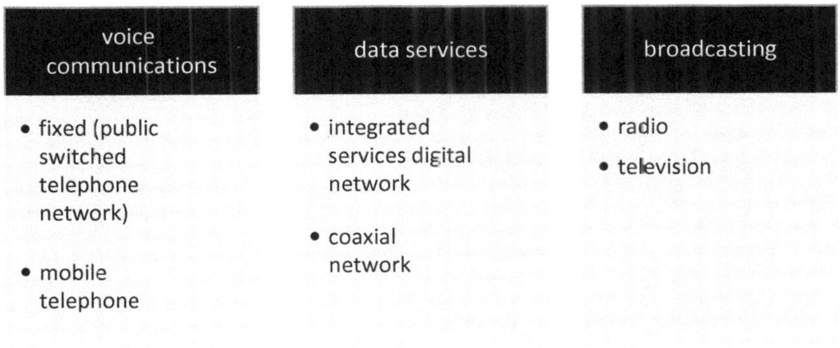

Fig. 3.3 Traditional regulatory framework in communications

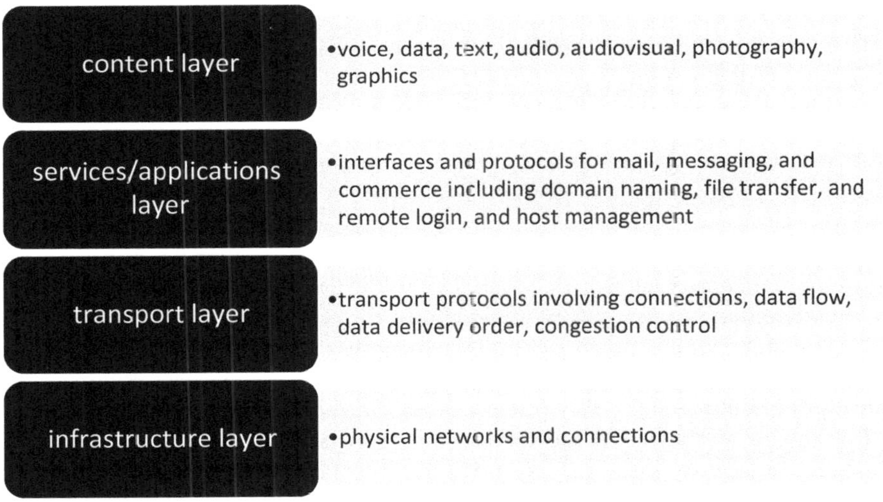

Fig. 3.4 Example of a layered regulatory framework

different objectives and strengths of policy could be pursued in varying levels. Thus, firms would deal with fewer regulatory issues and inconsistencies if they only operated in a single layer, such as those illustrated in Fig. 3.4. The framework has influenced policy approaches and convergence of regulatory authorities in many nations but has been criticized for being internet- and engineering-centric (Frieden 2003; Mindel and Sicker 2006) and because it tends to discount consumer or citizen interests.

Who Gets Involved in the Policy Processes?

A wide variety of individuals, firms and organizations can become involved in the process as *stakeholders*, meaning that they are affected by policy but have different interests and values that lead to divergent preferences. Stakeholders

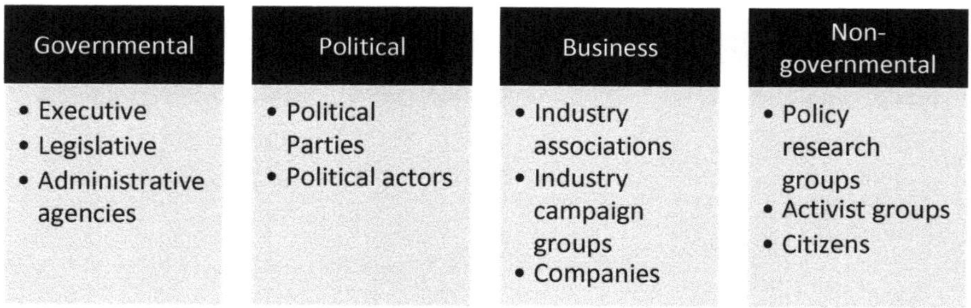

Fig. 3.5 Four main stakeholder groups

are not equal in policy processes because they have different amounts of power, influence and financial resources. This leads to varying access to leaders and policy makers, differential abilities to promote policy preferences publicly and privately, and disparities in capacity to take part in policy development and lobbying processes.

Commercial stakeholders may also seek governance at global, regional or national level to supersede other governance as a way of avoiding complying with differing regulations among nations or varying approaches in provincial governance. At times some commercial stakeholders will pursue highly self-serving policy that extracts unjust benefits used to protect revenue or markets against other competitors. This is usually through policy that creates beneficial conditions or regulation that provide advantages to the firm or disadvantages to others.

Stakeholders can roughly be divided into four categories (Fig. 3.5).

Some stakeholders may seek to align with other stakeholders and social institutions with similar interests or preferences to improve their abilities and strength in influencing policy outcomes (Hesmondhalgh 2005). This may take place through informal or formal discussions or negotiations, leading them to contribute different resources to the policy intervention or to divide the effort between or among themselves.

When governmental entities begin to address emergent issues but have not yet decided a preferred approach or crafted a preferred policy, they may initiate policy making by bringing stakeholders together in organized discussions or workshops conducted by regulatory agencies or trusted, neutral organizations or think tanks. This is designed to seek agreement of criteria for courses of action, to expand understanding of alternatives, to create buy-in that avoids win/lose situations and to build consensus for a policy.

Business Interests and Policy

Despite a widespread perception that companies and industries abhor governmental intervention in their concerns, business interests regularly seek policy, even regulation. This was starkly illustrated when Facebook CEO Mark Zuckerberg asked governments and administrative agencies to regulate the internet and some types of content (Zuckerberg 2019). This would help provide a more common regulatory regime globally and would focus attention on specific types of internet activities.

Business interests typically seek policies that help organize and stabilize their industries, reduce business risks and provide favorable treatments in tax law, environmental law, labor law, competition law and other areas that affect their operations and activities. The Cellular Operators Association of India that represents national and international mobile phone companies, for example, has sought lower spectrum use charges and improved treatment of business costs in application of the good and services tax.

Most communications and industries industry associations and many larger firms maintain governmental affairs offices and personnel who monitor and attempt to influence policies they find desirable and to vigorously oppose policies they deem disagreeable. The European Newspaper Publishers Association, for example, is based in Brussels representing its industry's views to the European Union institutions. In their activities governmental affairs personnel promote and advocate their points of view through production of policy reports, articles in trade publications, meetings with officials, testimony in hearings and other lobbying practices.

Companies and associations may also establish or support short-term advocacy groups focused on individual policy issues. These are sometimes named to give the impression that they are citizen groups rather than organizations tied to industries or specific companies.

A strategic approach to policy making links outcomes perceived as valuable with the requirements to achieve them. It involves developing policy advice based on conversations and input from a range of stakeholders both inside and outside of government to answer whether the purpose and objectives of the policy are publicly valuable (Benington and Moore 2011). Without the engagement of all stakeholders, including citizens, public value cannot be effectively pursued. Policy makers also need to consider whether the policy approach is politically and legally possible and whether administrative operational capability exists for policy implementation. These issues force policy makers and stakeholders to consider early on the value sought and range of issues that will be encountered in pursuing the policy, what kind of support and alliances may be needed, whether public or private intervention should be sought to pursue the objective and what kinds of resources will be required.

To pursue the objectives, three strategic areas of concern must be addressed (see Fig. 3.6).

The authorizing environment and resources must work together to create the possibility for value performance to be achieved. The authorizing environment will only be supportive if the performance objectives are acceptable and

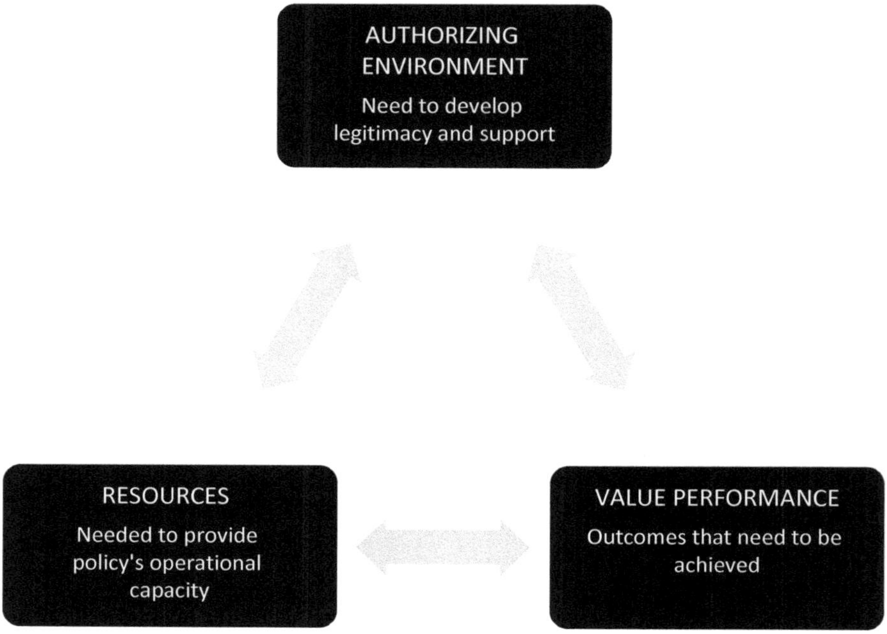

Fig. 3.6 The strategic triangle (Adapted from Moore 1995)

agreed upon and if the performance objectives cannot be achieved without that support.

Institutions of Policy

Policy institutions represent the spaces in which policy is developed and contested. These are guided by institutional norms and rules that direct or constrain their scope of activity and how policy activities take place. Because policy making takes place within institutions, those interested in policy and policy making must understand what institutions are involved, the order in which they become involved and the processes that take place within them. This requires identifying the institutions, how they are involved and their competencies to act. Those studying policy also need a clear understanding of the degrees of independence of the executive, legislative and judicial branches and administrative agencies and how they affect each other.

The fundamental design of institutions and administrative mechanisms is critical to their operations. Structures, authority and internal rules and procedures differ, as does the degree to which public and private interests are balanced. In Western nations, for example, those with Anglo-American traditions tend toward majoritarian policy making, in which political majorities wield great policy-making power, whereas other nations tend to employ more multi-stakeholder policy making.

A fundamental question in considering institutions is on whose behalf they operate—the governed or the governors. National assemblies, ministerial councils and administrative agencies involved in policy making may be more accountable to rulers than to the public, so the authorities and degrees of independence must be understood. Authority and oversight for media and communications may be delegated to independent administrative agencies that are not directly controlled by governments in power, but the degrees and scope of autonomy that they enjoy can vary widely.

There are a variety of policy spaces outside of legislative and administrative authorities in which various interests may be represented. These include policy conferences and forums and policy institutes. Although these do not have legislative and administrative authority, they often influence the thinking of policy makers.

Policy is never made with a clean slate. It is affected by previous policy and law. Existing policy, policy processes and policy trajectories are often overlaid on discussions and options for new issues and new technologies.

As policies are formulated into laws and regulations, policy contestation occurs as parties with different interests compete in the processes to obtain policy elements more beneficial for themselves. Effective policy processes seek optimal benefit for society and stakeholders; however, policy making involves the exercise of power and some parties often have more power and influence. Policy contestation is thus not merely about policy measures but about the values and norms that underlie and guide them and about the exercise of social power. It is important to identify and understand what and whose values and norms are being embraced, and how and why and what power is being exerted in the process to what effect.

Policy contestation also takes place among the institutions of government, but especially in more independent executive and legislative and executive bodies and agencies. Differing interests in policies produce competition among agencies over the approaches to policy, policy elements and application of policy. Consequently, differing policy regimes may address issues in different manners or conflict with one another. The development of digital terrestrial television just prior to the turn of the millennium, for example, led to conflicting approaches between the telecommunications and broadcasting regulators (Hills and Michalis 1997), and ultimately was a motivation for governments to converge regulation within new or reorganized regulatory bodies.

Differing concerns and conflicting approaches also lead to contestation among policy domains in governments. Industrial policy is intent on promoting industry development and economic growth; trade policy is devoted to supporting exchange of products and services with other countries, and competition policy is concerned with actions that create economic harm to competitors and consumers. Industrial policy and trade policy may work hand in hand, but competition policy may sometimes conflict with those policies, requiring governments to give preference to a policy regime. Differences in approaches and concerns exist even among policy regimes directly associated with media and communications. Most telecom and broadcast/cable/satellite policy have a technical emphasis intent on ensuring operability, interconnectivity and infrastructure development. These objectives tend to displace or downgrade other concerns within administrative institutions focused on them. Media policy tends to be more focused on addressing the effects of media structures, content provided, diversity and pluralism and other issues related to society and citizenship. Cultural policy tends to focus on issues related to national identity, values and norms, and domestic culture promotion and protection, and it may influence requirements in media policy regarding content production support and exhibition and broadcast quotas for motion pictures, broadcasts and streaming video.

It has been argued that cultural regulation approaches were progressively supplanted by industrial policies in the late twentieth century as state policies increasingly focused on economic growth and globalization and that citizen and consumer interests have been diminished (Abrahamson 2001; Lunt and Livingstone 2011). There are contested approaches even between media policy and cultural policy, despite many shared concerns, that make it difficult for those promoting each to see the value in the other and to link them together effectively (Napoli 2008).

Even when some agreement exists on the need for policy, the effectiveness of the application through various policy regimes can vary. Traditional policies and laws do not work well in addressing privacy on the internet because the issue involves multiple technologies and actors rather than single firms or governments that can be more easily observed and regulated (Zittrain 2008). Similarly, co-regulation of the press through self-regulatory mechanisms in the United Kingdom has been less effective and lagged behind the courts in addressing issues involving privacy protection for children using media (Morris and Davies 2018).

Convergence of communications technologies and operations has altered institutional arrangements for policy because the boundaries among industries and among administrative agencies overseeing their activities have been altered. The convergence of media technologies and the widening array of multifunctional infrastructures, platforms and networks that serve personal communications, commerce, banking, entertainment and information purposes have made traditional administration approaches less applicable and effective, leading to convergence of some media and communications administrative agencies in many countries, especially those dealing with telephony and internet infrastructures and services, broadcasting and digital media activities (Cowie and Marsden 1998; Garcia-Murillo and MacInnes 2003; Wu 2004). Mergers of these agencies were designed to improve coordination, to break down sector-based regulation and to produce converged policy and regulation that better addressed conditions and issues in the digital era (Iosifidis 2002). The effects of the mergers are not yet fully established.

Policy Capture and State Capture as Influences

A challenge of policy making is avoiding capture of administrative agencies or state apparatuses by private interests. As noted in the last chapter, policy capture is a form of policy failure that occurs when industries or individuals can highly influence the mechanisms that implement laws and regulations to achieve outcomes favorable to their interests rather than the public interest (Levine and Forrence 1990; Carpenter and Moss 2013).

Administrative agencies are highly significant because they make licensing decisions, promulgate behavioral regulations and can choose not to regulate some actions. Stakeholders with significant monetary interests in policy devote significant numbers of personnel and funds to influencing policy outcomes and regularly focus attention on regulatory agencies or their staff to encourage decisions and rules from which they benefit. This occurs through efforts influencing debate in policy forums, agenda setting, regulatory filings and meetings with regulators. It is also the result of revolving-door employment in which industry personnel become regulators and subsequently return to industry and vice versa. In its most corrupt forms, industry capture of regulatory agencies can also occur through bribery or threats.

Most capture is not highly evident, because a decision favoring commercial or private interests in itself is not evidence of capture. Determining when an agency is captured is observed over time through consistent rulings that diminish public interests in favor of private interests. It is evident when single stakeholder groups dominate the processes and information provision or when an agency's primary efforts are to develop and assist an industry and its major players rather than to monitor and regulate their behavior.

Capture becomes a graver concern when self-regulatory or co-regulatory bodies are involved (Puppis 2007), such as those involved in advertising content and practices, media behavior and consumer service. The government of Australia, for example, was instrumental in establishing the Communication Alliance in 2006, an industry-funded organization, to self-regulate technical, operational and consumer aspects of telephone, internet and equipment firms, including the consumer protection code (Australia n.d.; Communications Alliance n.d.). Within three years, a consumer group argued that its mechanism of consumer protection was unsustainable and that "many consumers experiencing detriment—financially, emotionally or socially" (Sengara et al. 2009, p. 12). The record since that time has not improved and the Alliance has been criticized as ineffective in terms of ensuring quality service provision (Gerrand 2011) and for lack of transparency and not publicly reporting customer service performance of telecom firms (Lee 2017).

An extreme form of regulatory capture, introduced in the last chapter, is state capture, in which private interests gain control of executive, legislative and regulatory institutions and processes through wholesale political corruption. Its focus on influencing the formation of laws and regulations is to their benefit. State capture most often appears in authoritarian states or weak and impoverished states where oligarchs and others seek to alter governmental intervention to their benefit (Hellman and Kaufmann 2001; Hellman et al. 2003). When state capture occurs, private actors control both the institutions and processes of policy to acquire wealth and additional power (Leitner and Meissner 2016).

Oligarchs in Southeast Europe and Central Asia have been particularly successful at state capture, intertwining business and political governance activities and owning or controlling media to their advantage (Gross 2008; Junisbai 2011).

Communications and Media Policy Often Responds to Economic Issues

Much media and communications policy regularly addresses economic issues involving markets, firms, consumers and social welfare. It includes structural and ownership choices, competition concerns, provision of state aid and measures to make investment and innovation attractive. It responds to issues of market failure and encompasses economic choices involving public and private goods, and natural monopolies. Policy allocates public resources and requires private action to achieve economic and social objectives, ideally pursuing optimal social welfare outcomes that balance multiple objectives and ensuring an equitable distribution of benefits and costs. It increases economic value and provides protection for content through copyright.

Public intervention can either slow or halt innovation and the development of new communications technologies and systems, or it can speed and promote its development. Policy makers regularly pursue national developmental and general economic benefits through media and communications and typically support activities that bring benefits to the state by contributions to the economy and state treasury and employment. These communications policies are thus linked to industrial policy, information society policies, national and local development policies and competition policies designed to help spur commerce and trade generally and lead to national economic growth.

Telecommunications, for example, involves fundamental economic questions involving whether there should be universal access, who should pay for infrastructure needed to achieve it, how should investments be protected and what returns should be allowed. Advanced telecommunications investments require significant investments and how to produce them requires significant thought and decision-making. Policy makers consider different ways to fund infrastructure construction and operation, with choices influenced by the size of the market, geographical challenges, population density, ability of customers to pay for services and capital availability from private and public sources. Governments are often limited in their abilities to fund such large-scale investments, a factor that led many to privatize telecommunications in the late twentieth century. Private firms also face constraints on the ability to generate capital to make large investments. Garnering the capital necessary to build and operate advanced telecom infrastructures induces some states to find ways to support private firms financing.

Typical mechanisms used are incentives for private investments in innovation, infrastructures and advance services by providing monopolies or limited competition and providing tax benefits that make the ventures more desirable and by providing subsidies and tax credits for serving rural and remote areas that otherwise could not be profitably served.

In broadcasting, fundamental questions have been who will pay for content creation and whose interests will be served by that content. States may choose public provision of broadcasting based on those questions or enact operating requirements and provide grants and tax benefits to commercial broadcasters for serving social purposes.

Economic issues and concerns are thus central in much policy making, as are debates about policy frameworks and approaches based on differing political economic philosophies. In the United States, for example, the Federal Communications Commission which has economic analyses in its policy processes and was criticized during the last part of the twentieth century and early millennium for emphasizing economic over social concerns (Freedman 2006), but the agency was recently controversially rebuked by some economists for relying more on political and populist sentiment than economic reasoning (Faulhaber et al. 2017; Winseck and Pooley 2017).

Economic analysis in media and communications policy making provides important understanding of issues and effects and potential effects of policy choices; however, over-reliance on economic reasoning can strip society of the ability to consider and discuss other aspects crucial for effective social decision-making.

Policy Processes Are Inherently Political

It is impossible to separate policy making from politics because the processes and institutions in which it is considered, developed and promulgated are political and decisions are influenced by power, ideology and the interests served. Policy studies approaches accept the roles of politics in the processes and offer means for organizing and understanding where, when and how those influences occur. The influences of these broader political issues can be both explicit and implicit in decisions throughout policy processes.

Politics has been central in choices that have shifted the balance of power of public and private interests in media and communications policy making since late twentieth century (Freedman 2006), have produced contemporary digital policies (Humphreys 2009) and resulted in contestation over policy frames and interests represented and have sometimes broken policy alliances between political actors (van den Bulck and Donders 2014).

The range of actors and politics involved in policy making varies depending upon issues being addressed and new actors and new governance locations shift some politics to new locations. These may shift the balance of public and private influence on policy and provide advantages to those with greater resources to use in influencing politics in multiple locales (Freedman 2006).

Policy making in media and communication can marginalize or exclude public participation and interests in policy processes (Freedman 2015) and the disregard interests through "policy silences" during explicit activities in the processes (Freedman 2010). Analyses of politics in policy thus need to pay attention to both explicit and implicit influences on the processes and outcomes.

Final Words

The processes of policy making guide choices among or seek to balance interests in formulating and establishing policy. During the processes the state, government, businesses and the public vie for policy outcomes in their interests. They compete for attention to policy issues, struggle to control narratives describing the issues, strive to affect the policy frameworks selected and contend over specific policy elements.

Despite the orderliness and linearity of processes conveyed by models, policy development can be irrational, hasty and responsive to events or perceptions and misperceptions. It can ignore broad interests in favor of narrow ones, can address indicators rather than causes of issues and can produce ineffective policy. In its best practice, however, it can be thoughtful and deliberate, incorporate profound understanding of the issues and seek optimal private and public outcomes.

The process elements employed, the participants, the ways issues and choices are portrayed and what options are considered all influence the outcomes that are produced as policy is created.

Chapter Summary

- Policies are made within general observable processes.
- Processes can be initiated by executive or legislative or actions and demands by stakeholders and interest groups.
- Language and contextualization of issues help establish narratives surrounding policy.
- Policy frameworks explain the general approaches, principles and concepts used in policies.
- The strategic policy approach formulates policy to fit the environment surrounding it, the resources needed and the outcomes desired.
- Policy making takes place within institutions and institutional processes in which power and influence are exercised and affect choices and outcomes.
- Policy making is political and involves contesting values, beliefs and philosophies.

Discussion Points

1. How and why does policy develop outside the orderliness depicted in traditional policy process models?
2. Why is it so difficult to gain policy action on some issues and developments?
3. Why is framing so persuasive in establishing the needs for and approaches to policy making?
4. Do policy frameworks help in the development of policy or merely in providing explanations for policy?
5. What are the best ways for policy making to address conflicts in policy regime approaches to media and communications policy issues?

Bibliography

Abrahamson, Bram Dov. 2001. Media Policy After Regulation. *International Journal of Cultural Studies* 4 (3): 301–326.

Ali, Christopher. 2012. Media at the Margins: Policy and Practice in American, Canadian, and British Community Television. *International Journal of Communication* 6: 1119–1138. Available at https://ijoc.org/index.php/ijoc/article/view/1316/750. Accessed 15 Oct 2019.

Australia, Department of Communications and the Arts. n.d. Telecommunications Self-Regulation. Available at https://www.communications.gov.au/policy/policy-listing/telecommunications-self-regulation. Accessed 1 Apr 2019.

Baker, C. Edwin. 2006. *Media Concentration and Democracy: Why Ownership Matters*. New York: Cambridge University Press.

Bauer, Johannes M. 2010. Regulation, Public Policy, and Investment in Communications Infrastructure. *Telecommunications Policy* 34 (1–2): 65–79.

Benington, John, and Mark Moore, eds. 2011. *Public Value: Theory and Practice*. Basingstoke: Palgrave Macmillan.

Benkler, Yochai, Hal Roberts, Robert Faris, Alicia Solow-Niederman, and Bruce Etling. 2015. Social Mobilization and the Networked Public Sphere: Mapping the SOPA-PIPA Debate. *Political Communication* 32 (4): 594–624.

Birkland, Thomas A. 1998. Focusing Events, Mobilization, and Agenda Setting. *Journal of Public Policy* 18 (1): 53–74.

———. 2007. Agenda Setting in Public Policy. In *Handbook of Public Policy Analysis*, ed. Frank Fischer, Gerald J. Miller, and Mara S. Sidney, 63–78. Boca Raton: CRC Press.

———. 2015. *An Introduction to the Policy Process: Theories, Concepts, and Models of Public Policy Making*. 4th ed. Armonk: M. E. Sharpe.

Boydstun, Amber E. 2013. *Making the News: Politics, the Media, and Agenda Setting*. Chicago/London: University of Chicago Press.

Burstein, Paul. 2003. The Impact of Public Opinion on Public Policy: A Review and an Agenda. *Political Research Quarterly* 56 (1): 29–40.

Cammaerts, Bart, and Nico Carpentier, eds. 2007. *Reclaiming the Media: Communication Rights and Democratic Media Roles*. Bristol: Intellect.

Carpenter, Daniel, and David A. Moss, eds. 2013. *Preventing Regulatory Capture*. Cambridge: Cambridge University Press.

Cave, Martin, and William Webb. 2016. *Spectrum Management: Using the Airwaves for Maximum Social and Economic Benefit*. Cambridge: Cambridge University Press.
Chilton, Paul. 2004. *Analysing Political Discourse: Theory and Practice*. London: Routledge.
Chong, Dennis, and James N. Druckman. 2007. Framing Theory. *Annual Review of Political Science* 10: 103–126.
Christians, Clifford G., Theodore L. Glasser, Denis McQuail, Kaarle Nordenstreng, and Robert A. White. 2009. *Normative Theories of the Media*. Urbana/Chicago: University of Illinois Press.
Communications Alliance. n.d. http://www.commsalliance.com.au/. Accessed 1 Apr 2019.
Cowie, Campbell, and Christopher T. Marsden. 1998. Convergence, Competition and Regulation. *International Journal of Communications Law and Policy* 1 (1): 1–32.
Curran, James. 2011. *Media and Democracy*. London: Taylor and Francis.
Curry, Bill, and Tamsin McMahon. 2019. Social-Media Giants Pledge Joint Action on Extremism at Summit with Trudeau, Other World Leaders. *The Globe and Mail*, May 15. Available at https://www.theglobeandmail.com/politics/article-social-media-giants-pledge-joint-action-on-online-hate-at-summit-with/. Accessed 23 June 2019.
Dahlgren, Peter. 2009. *Media and Political Engagement: Citizens, Communication, and Democracy*. Cambridge: Cambridge University Press.
Eliassen, Kjell A., Marit Sjovaag Nfa, and Marit Sjovaag, eds. 1999. *European Telecommunications Liberalisation*. London: Routledge.
Fairclough, Isabela, and Norman Fairclough. 2012. *Political Discourse Analysis: A Method for Advanced Students*. London: Routledge.
Faulhaber, Gerald R., Hal J. Singer, and Augustus H. Urschel. 2017. The Curious Absence of Economic Analysis at the Federal Communications Commission: An Agency in Search of a Mission. *International Journal of Communication* 11: 1214–1233.
Fowler, Mark S., and Daniel L. Brenner. 1981. Marketplace Approach to Broadcast Regulation. *Texas Law Review* 60: 207.
Fransman, Martin. 2002. Mapping the Evolving Telecoms Industry: The Uses and Shortcomings of the Layer Model. *Telecommunications Policy* 26 (9): 473–483.
Freedman, Des. 2006. Dynamics of Power in Contemporary Media Policy-Making. *Media, Culture & Society* 28 (6): 907–923.
———. 2010. Media Policy Silences: The Hidden Face of Communications Decision Making. *The International Journal of Press/Politics* 15 (3): 344–361.
———. 2015. Media Policy Fetishism. *Critical Studies in Media Communication* 32 (2): 96–111.
Frieden, Rob. 2003. Adjusting the Horizontal and Vertical in Telecommunications Regulation: A Comparison of the Traditional and a New Layered Approach. *The Federal Communications Law Review* 55 (2): 208–250.
Garcia-Murillo, Martha, and Ian MacInnes. 2003. The Impact of Technological Convergence on the Regulation of ICT Industries. *International Journal on Media Management* 5 (1): 57–67.
Gerrand, Peter. 2011. Unacceptable Quality of Service: Why Industry Self-Regulation Is Not Working. *Telecommunications Journal of Australia* 61 (4): 541–543.

Green-Pedersen, Christoffer, and Stefaan Walgrave, eds. 2014. *Agenda Setting, Policies, and Political Systems: A Comparative Approach*. Chicago/London: University of Chicago Press.

Greenstein, Shane. 2015. *How the Internet Became Commercial: Innovation, Privatization, and the Birth of a New Network*. Princeton: Princeton University Press.

Gross, Peter. 2008. Back to the (Uncertain) Future. Politics, Business and the Media in Romania. *Global Media Journal* 1 (4): 51–68.

Hazlett, Thomas W. 1998. Assigning Property Rights to Radio Spectrum Users: Why Did FCC License Auctions Take 67 Years? *Journal of Law and Economics* 41 (2): 529–576.

Hellman, Joel, and Daniel Kaufmann. 2001. Confronting the Problem of State Capture in Transition Economies. *IMF Finance and Development* 38 (3). Available at http://www.imf.org/external/pubs/ft/fandd/2001/09/hellman.htm. Accessed 2 July 2019.

Hellman, Joel S., Geraint Jones, and Daniel Kaufmann. 2003. Seize the State, Size the Day: State Capture and Influence in Transition Economies. *Journal of Comparative Economics* 31 (4): 751–773.

Hesmondhalgh, David. 2005. Media and Cultural Policy as Public Policy: The Case of the British Labour Government. *International Journal of Cultural Policy* 11 (1): 95–109.

Hills, Jill, and Maria Michalis. 1997. Technological Convergence: Regulatory Competition. The British Case of Digital Television. *Policy Studies* 18 (3–4): 219–237.

Holt, Jennifer. 2011. *Empires of Entertainment: Media Industries and the Politics of Deregulation, 1980–1996*. Rutgers: Rutgers University Press.

Humphreys, Peter. 2009. The Politics of Media Policy: How Political? *Cultural Trends* 18 (3): 263–272.

Iosifidis, Petros. 2002. Digital Convergence: Challenges for European Regulation. *Javnost/The Public* 9 (3): 27–47.

Junisbai, Barbara. 2011. Oligarchs and Ownership: The Role of Financial-Industrial Groups. Controlling Kazakhstan's 'Independent' Media. In *After the Czars and Commissars: The Press in Post-Soviet Authoritarian Central Asia*, ed. Eric Freedman and Richard Shafer, 35–58. East Lansing: Michigan State University Press.

Kelly, James T. 2012. *Framing Democracy: A Behavioral Approach to Democratic Theory*. Princeton: Princeton University Press.

Kingdon, John W. 2003. *Agendas, Alternatives, and Public Policies*. 2nd ed. New York: Longman.

Lee, Karen. 2017. ACMA Varies Compliance and Monitoring Arrangements for the Telecommunications Consumer Protections Code. *The Australian Journal of Competition and Consumer Law* 25 (1): 62–64.

Leitner, Johannes, and Hannes Meissner, eds. 2016. *State Capture, Political Risks and International Business: Cases from Black Sea Region Countries*. London: Routledge.

Levine, Michael E., and Jennifer L. Forrence. 1990. Regulatory Capture, Public Interest, and the Public Agenda: Toward a Synthesis. *The Journal of Law, Economics, & Organization* 6: 167–198.

Lunt, Peter, and Sonia Livingstone. 2011. *Media Regulation: Governance and the Interests of Citizens and Consumers*. London: Sage.

McCombs, Max. 2004. *Setting the Agenda: The Mass Media and Public Opinion*. Malden: Blackwell Publishing.

McCombs, Maxwell E., and Donald L. Shaw. 1972. The Agenda-Setting Function of Mass Media. *Public Opinion Quarterly* 36 (2): 176–187.

———. 1993. The Evolution of Agenda-Setting Research: Twenty-Five Years in the Marketplace of Ideas. *Journal of Communication* 43 (2): 58–67.

Mindel, Joshua L., and Douglas C. Sicker. 2006. Leveraging the EU Regulatory Framework to Improve a Layered Model for U.S. Telecommunications Markets. *Telecommunications Policy* 30 (2): 136–148.

Moore, Mark. 1995. *Creating Public Value: Strategic Management in Government*. Cambridge: Harvard University Press.

Morris, Brigit, and Máire Messenger Davies. 2018. Can Children's Privacy Rights Be Adequately Protected Through Press Regulation? What Press Regulation Can Learn from the Courts. *Journal of Media Law* 10 (1): 92–113.

Mueller, Milton L., Brenden N. Kuerbis, and Christiane Pagé. 2007. Democratizing Global Communication? Global Civil Society and the Campaign for Communication Rights in the Information Society. *International Journal of Communication* 1 (1): 267–296.

Napoli, Philip M. 2008. Bridging Cultural Policy and Media Policy. *The Journal of Arts Management, Law, and Society* 37 (4): 311–330.

Page, Benjamin I., and Robert Y. Shapiro. 1983. Effects of Public Opinion on Policy. *American Political Science Review* 77 (1): 175–190.

———. 1992. *The Rational Public: Fifty Years of Trends in Americans' Policy Preferences*. Chicago: University of Chicago Press.

Picard, Robert G. 2007. The Challenges of Public Functions and Commercialized Media. In *The Politics of News: The News of Politics*, ed. Doris Graber, Denis McQuail, and Pippa Norris, 2nd ed., 211–229. Washington, DC: Congressional Quarterly Press.

Pickard, Victor. 2014. The Great Evasion: Confronting Market Failure in American Media Policy. *Critical Studies in Media Communication* 31 (2): 153–159.

Puppis, Manuel. 2007. Media Governance as a Horizontal Extension of Media Regulation: The Importance of Self- and Co-regulation. *Communications* 32 (3): 330–336.

Reed, David P. 2006. Critiquing the Layered Regulatory Model. *Journal on Telecommunications and High Technology Law* 4 (2): 281–298.

Scheufele, Dietram A., and David Tewksbury. 2007. Framing, Agenda Setting, and Priming: The Evolution of Three News Media Effects Models. *Journal of Communication* 57 (1): 9–20.

Sengara, Ryan, Sal Humphreys, Jock Given, Marion McCutcheon, and Claire Milne. 2009. *Future Consumer: Emerging Consumer Issues in Telecommunications and Convergent Communications and Media*. Petersham: Australian Communications Consumer Action Network.

Shanahan, Elizabeth A., Mark K. McBeth, and Paul L. Hathaway. 2011. Narrative Policy Framework: The Influence of Media Policy Narratives on Public Opinion. *Politics and Policy* 39 (3): 373–400.

Sicker, Douglas C., and Lisa Blumensaadt. 2006. Misunderstanding the Layered Model(s). *Journal on Telecommunications and High Technology Law* 4 (2): 299–320.

Timberg, Craig, Drew Harwell, Hamza Shaban, Andrew Ba Tran, and Brian Fung. 2019. The New Zealand Shooting Shows How YouTube and Facebook Spread Hate and Violent Images—Yet Again. *New York Times*, March 15. Available at https://www.washingtonpost.com/technology/2019/03/15/facebook-youtube-twitter-amplified-video-christchurch-mosque-shooting/?utm_term=.99416f057b97. Accessed 29 Mar 2019.

Trkman, Peter, Borka Jerman Blazic, and Tomaz Turka. 2008. Factors of Broadband Development and the Design of a Strategic Policy Framework. *Telecommunications Policy* 32 (2): 101–115.

van den Bulck, Hilde, and Karen Donders. 2014. Of Discourses, Stakeholders and Advocacy Coalitions in Media Policy: Tracing Negotiations Towards the New Management Contract of Flemish Public Broadcaster VRT. *European Journal of Communication* 29 (1): 83–99.

van Hulst, Merlijn, and Dvora Yanow. 2016. From Policy 'Frames' to 'Framing': Theorizing a More Dynamic, Political Approach. *The American Review of Public Administration* 46 (1): 92–112.

van Schewick, Barbara. 2015. Network Neutrality and Quality of Service: What a Nondiscrimination Rule Should Look Like. *Stanford Law Review* 67: 1–166.

Weaver, David H. 2007. Thoughts on Agenda Setting, Framing, and Priming. *Journal of Communication* 57 (1): 142–147.

Weible, Christopher M., and Paul A. Sabatier, eds. 2018. *Theories of the Policy Process*. 4th ed. London: Routledge.

Westbrook, Tom, and Greenfield Charlotte. 2019. New Zealand Bans Military Type Semi-Automatic Weapons Used in Mosque Massacre. *Reuters*, March 21. Available at https://www.reuters.com/article/us-newzealand-shootout-ardern-guncontrol-idUSKCN1R205Z. Accessed 29 Mar 2019.

Whitt, Richard. 2004. A Horizontal Leap Forward: Formulating a New Communications Public Policy Framework Based on the Network Layers Model. *The Federal Communications Law Journal* 56 (3): 587–672.

Whittiker, Zach. 2019. California to Close Data Breach Notification Loopholes Under New Law. *Tech Crunch*, February 21. Available at https://techcrunch.com/2019/02/21/california-data-breach-laws/. Accessed 1 July 2019.

Winseck, Dwayne, and Jefferson D. Pooley. 2017. A Reply to Faulhaber, Singer, and Urschel's Curious Tale of Economics and Common Carriage (Net Neutrality) at the FCC. *International Journal of Communication*, 11(2017): 2702–2733. https://ijoc.org/index.php/ijoc/article/view/7543/2077. Accessed 18 Oct 2019.

World Intellectual Property Organization. 2019. WIPO Performances and Phonograms Treaty. Available at https://www.wipo.int/treaties/en/ip/wppt/. Accessed 29 Mar 2019.

Wu, Irene. 2004. Canada, South Korea, Netherlands and Sweden: Regulatory Implications of the Convergence of Telecommunications, Broadcasting and Internet Services. *Telecommunications Policy* 28 (1): 79–96.

Zahariadis, Nikolaos, ed. 2016. *Handbook of Public Policy Agenda Setting*. Cheltenham: Edward Elgar Publishing.

Zittrain, Jonathan. 2008. Privacy 2.0. *University of Chicago Legal Forum* 2008 (1): 65–119.

Zuckerberg, Mark. 2019. Mark Zuckerberg: The Internet Needs New Rules. Let's Start in These Four Areas. *Washington Post*, March 30. Available at https://www.washingtonpost.com/opinions/mark-zuckerberg-the-internet-needs-new-rules-lets-start-in-these-four-areas/2019/03/29/9e6f0504-521a-11e9-a3f7-78b7525a8d5f_story.html?noredirect=on&utm_term=.391b2de524e1. Accessed 23 June 2019.

Suggested Readings

Birkland, Thomas A. 2007. Agenda Setting in Public Policy. In *Handbook of Public Policy Analysis*, ed. Frank Fischer, Gerald J. Miller, and Mara S. Sidney, 63–78. Boca Raton: CRC Press.

———. 2015. *An Introduction to the Policy Process: Theories, Concepts, and Models of Public Policy Making*. 4th ed. Armonk: M.E. Sharpe.

Scheufele, Dietram A, and Tewksbury, David. 2007. Framing, Agenda Setting, and Priming: The Evolution of Three News Media Effects Models. *Journal of Communication* 57 (1): 9–20.

Shanahan, Elizabeth A., Mark K. McBeth, and Paul L. Hathaway. 2011. Narrative Policy Framework: The Influence of Media Policy Narratives on Public Opinion. *Politics and Policy* 39 (3): 373–400.

Weible, Christopher M., and Paul A. Sabatier, eds. 2018. *Theories of the Policy Process*. 4th ed. London: Routledge.

CHAPTER 4

Media and Communications Policy Mechanisms and Tools

Policy makers employ a wide variety of options to organize media and communications systems and markets, create operating requirements and influence behavior of firms in the pursuit of agreed-upon policy outcomes. The choice of options varies depending upon the media and communications system involved, legal bases for intervention and dominant domestic political philosophy. Policy mechanisms and tools are based on behavioral concepts of how firms and individuals are influenced and incorporate policy makers' perceptions of the assumptions of how companies and the public will respond to the tools selected (Schneider and Ingram 1990).

Not all options are selected in every country. This occurs because national history, political system, ideology and existing policies may limit the range of tools employed. The choices may be affected by policy trajectories created through previous choices of tools for the industry. The choice may also involve transfer of tools from another industry that experienced a similar issue or from another country or group of countries that are perceived to have dealt with the issue with effective policy (Dolowitz and Marsh 2000).

Countries may not have policies addressing some media and communications issues because they may not be domestically salient and germane or there may be little impetus or incentives to act. A country that does not create and launch its own communications satellites, for example, has little need to create policies related to satellite communications operations. At times, some states may not perceive domestic capability to address an issue effectively, so no policy option is selected. This absence of policy may create a policy void that permits undesirable actions by some stakeholders. A small East African nation, for example, may perceive it has little ability to effectively control U.S. and European internet firms and thus not create policy to do so.

R. G. Picard, *Media and Communications Policy Making*, Palgrave Global Media Policy and Business,
https://doi.org/10.1007/978-3-030-35173-1_4

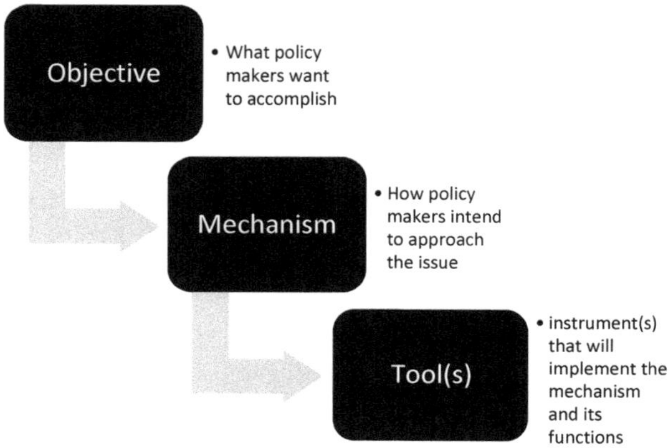

Fig. 4.1 Sequence of objective, mechanism and tools

Other countries may deliberately choose not to make policy, because the initial policy choice is whether or the state should intervene. Policy makers may thus intentionally choose to leave an issue alone, allowing stakeholders or the market to sort it out privately, as a means of avoiding over-regulation. This is often the case with new technological developments in which policy makers are wary of stifling innovation by domestic firms.

When deciding to intervene, policy makers link their objective with a mechanism to pursue it and tools that can support the mechanism (Fig. 4.1).

Policy Mechanisms and Policy Tools

Policy resulting from policy makers' decisions to intervene are based on choices of policy mechanisms and policy tools. *Policy mechanisms* are the approaches by which policy goals are pursued, the institutional means of pursuing a governance outcome. This ranges from facilitating a laissez-faire market mechanism to interventionist approach including market oversight, restricting firm behavior and public provision of services. *Policy tools* are the specific instruments used to execute mechanisms (Johns Hopkins Center for Civil Society Studies 2003). They are the concrete actions through which policy is interpreted and implemented (Bemelmans-Videc et al. 1998). Tools induce or influence functions or interactions within mechanisms as a means of producing a result. Many tools are available, including standard setting, licensing, tax credits, subsidies and public service broadcasting.

Policy makers tend to change the mechanisms and tools used for policy slowly, creating policy trajectories that are based upon previous uses. Trajectories can be based on the discourse surrounding policy, mechanisms employed or tools selected (Ball 1993). These trajectories create long-lasting policy principles and foundations and legal bases that provide systemic rationality that is only infrequently upended (Hayes 2001).

Policies and trajectories established in the United States to support development of roadways, waterways, railways and the telegraph, for example, significantly influenced the development of policy for radio and broadcasting (Picard 2015), and the trajectory of post-Cold War neoliberal policies significantly influenced approaches to global communication policy regarding the internet (Pickard 2007).

Example: Objective, Mechanism and Tools for Protecting Children

Policy makers might embrace a policy *objective* to protect children from exposure to sexual content. In pursuing that objective, they might employ the *mechanism* of reducing access to sexual content on television and related services and the internet by reducing its availability.

To make the mechanism function, policy makers will have choices among several available *tools*. For broadcasting, policy makers might prohibit programming with sexual content, limit its availability to times of day when children are less likely to be watching, require labeling or ratings of content for sexual content, require parental control technology on digital equipment or pressure broadcasters to self-regulate or voluntarily keep sexual content away from children. Policy makers could choose one or more tools to reduce access. Penalties such as loss of licenses could be levied or rewards such as tax credits could be available for voluntary compliance.

In seeking to control internet sexual content, policy makers might use tools requiring internet service providers (ISPs) to block it, requiring search engines to exclude it and browsers to provide parental controls, or requiring content labeling or ratings for sexual content. They could also put pressure on internet service providers, search engines and platforms to voluntarily keep sexual content away from children, highly tax revenue generated by carrying sexual content as a disincentive to provide it or offer incentives such as tax credits for reducing availability to children.

Policy Mechanisms

Policy mechanisms can be either informal or formal. Informal mechanisms include policy makers or regulators "having a word" with executives from industries or firms involved, a private conversation expressing concern or admonishment that may produce results without official action. Informal mechanisms can also be public statements conveying a similar message without directly indicating any parties involved or by making such a statement naming the parties to bring additional public pressure to bear. Most policy involves formal mechanisms of governance that oversee markets, service provision, growth, ownership, behavior, relationships and transactions.

Formal policy mechanisms are built upon perceptions of the underlying causes of issues or developments of concern, how various systemic or operational factors affect them and how policy action might affect related structures or behaviors. Useful mechanisms have some sort of validity based on theory and experience. The major mechanisms of policy in media and communications include public provision, promotion of competition and regulatory mandates. These and other media and communications policy mechanisms are often based on perceptions of issues involving universal service, natural monopolies and market failure.

Universal service involves providing service access to everyone, regardless of location and cost, and it may include provisions to overcome the inabilities to pay for services (Cremer et al. 2001). Universal service was perceived as providing public and network benefits and became a crucial factor in the mechanisms historically governing postal services, electrification, telephony and broadcasting in developed nations. National postal services, for example, were built on the concept of being able to deliver letters and parcels throughout entire countries, providing service even to rural and peripheral regions at a basic uniform price structure. This universal service concept has conflicted with efforts to liberalize postal service policy because much delivery work is uneconomical on its own (Crew and Kleindorfer 2000).

Natural monopolies exist in industries where huge startup costs and high fixed costs—usually due to infrastructure costs—make it impossible for effective competitors to arise because of economies of scale (Sharkey 1982). Policy makers who perceive the presence of natural monopolies in service tend to support mechanisms such as regulated monopolies or public provision of services. These factors were central to telegraph and telephone policies in the nineteenth and early twentieth centuries because of the costs of laying competing fixed telephony lines (Friedlander 1995).

Market failure occurs when economic and financial factors, resource requirements or other influences create an inefficient distribution of a good or service, either because of unwillingness or because of inability to provide service at a reasonable cost (Salanié 2000). These factors have created inefficiency and gaps in broadcasting (Ward 2006; Brown 2009) and broadband rollout (Ferguson 2004).

A fundamental choice of mechanism in media and communications involves the decision as to whether *public goods* should be pursued by public or private provision. Public goods are typically available for consumption by all members of society, rather than individual consumers, and are available to everyone on a non-rivalrous and usually non-excludable basis. Considerations of whether public intervention should occur usually involve determination that cost structures favor monopoly provision and that market failure is present, because private provision will not effectively provide universal service or meet the needs of some segments of society.

Consequently, roadways, utilities and parklands are public goods typically provided by public provision or controlled private provision. Many countries and municipalities consider basic utilities (water, electricity, sewage, etc.) to be public goods to be provided by public entities or through public regulation of private provision. Well into the twentieth century, large segments of media and communications were considered public goods, including postal services, telegraphy, telephone services and broadcasting. Policies in most states employed the mechanisms of public provision or highly regulated monopolistic private provision to provide these services. Policy makers began to reconsider the public provision and private monopoly approaches when new types of package and express mail services, telecommunications advances, and cable and satellite technologies appeared that facilitated rivalry and excludability. The decision over mechanism to employ need not be just whether to use the public or private mechanism but can include whether to create a system accommodating both.

Some argue that media content itself is a public good deserving public provision or public support for private providers. This is especially true of news and information necessary to support democratic participation (Curran 2011; McChesney and Pickard 2011; McChesney 2012) and cultural products such as film and television, especially genres that are not necessarily commercially viable (Lowe and Berg 2013; Raats et al. 2016).

Competition mechanisms can be used to promote effective competition among industry competitors, a requirement for operative markets to develop and survive. These mechanisms can include not only the use of tools such as competition/antitrust laws but also the employment of preferences for new or smaller competitors in awarding licenses, spectrum and operational approvals to reduce the effect of the largest companies on the market. The market-based mechanisms view policy as a means of ensuring that there is competition among firms and that a balance of power exists between firms and consumers.

Policy makers also have the choice of using the mechanisms of rewards and punishments to pursue objectives. These are typically mandates or incentives, or a combination of the two. Mandates direct or require that firms and individuals behave in a particular manner or provide specified services with penalties for noncompliance, whereas incentives provide benefits that reward them for doing so. Mandates tend to be more effective in situations where those regulated have no or little wish to carry out what is required; incentives tend to work best when actors are willing to carry out the requirements, but it is not cost-effective for them to do so. Policy makers might use these mechanisms to require broadcasters to produce domestic programming or to provide financial assistance or tax benefits for doing so voluntarily.

Categories and Administration of Policy Tools

Policy outcomes based on accepted mechanisms are typically pursued through four major types of policy tools: standards, regulation, incentives and disincentives. These may be employed individually or sometimes simultaneously. Policy tools thus make the mechanism function, just as provision of electricity makes an electric vehicle operable.

Standards are set by governmental and nongovernmental bodies—often backed or acceded to by governments—and are designed to spur industry growth by establishing agreed-upon technology that increases interconnectivity and reduces costs for producers of technology, commercial users of that technology and consumers. Standards are also promulgated to ensure that certain technologies, especially those that share resources such as spectrum or broadband lines, can effectively support all users.

Regulation is a form of intervention that requires or prohibits users from specified actions. Mandates that require action are called *prescriptive regulation.* Regulation that forbids action is called *proscriptive regulation.* In radio broadcasting, for example, broadcasters worldwide are required to operate on a specific frequency with specific levels of output power to avoid interference with others operating on the frequency in other locations. Most countries proscribe some type of content. Malaysia, for example, prohibits radio stations from carrying advertising for several goods and services, including tobacco products, fortune tellers or pork products (Baker and McKenzie 2012).

Incentives are policy tools that provide inducements for private behavior deemed to serve public interests. The Nigerian National Broadband Plan proposed a variety of tax and subsidy incentives to encourage commercial firms to increase the speed of broadband rollout, to share infrastructure, to serve economically inviable areas and to provide low-cost services (Nigeria, Federal Ministry of Communication Technology 2012).

Disincentives are tools that penalize private behavior that disregards or does not further public interests. These are non-criminal consequences, often levied through taxes or surcharges. Canadian tax policy, for example, does not allow advertising expenditures on U.S. stations that reach across the border to be deducted as business expenses, creating a disincentive to place advertising on U.S. rather than on Canadian stations (Canada, Canadian Revenue Agency 2018).

The degree of intervention with these methods is illustrated in Fig. 4.2, with the strength of intervention increasing as types toward the right are selected.

The administrative means used to intervene for these policy approaches can be either *direct* or *indirect*, that is, applied or provided directly to a firm or indirectly providing the firm benefit. Providing a telephone subsidy to provide low-cost service to individuals with lower incomes is thus a direct subsidy, whereas providing tax deductions for any mobile phone operators serving rural communities with low population density is an indirect benefit.

Decisions to intervene can be either *mandated* or *selective*, indicating whether the tool must be provided or applied to any entity that falls within its scope or meets stated qualifications or that agency administrators or designated persons have the opportunity to select which entities receive it. Providing a tax advantage to any firm that provides internet services to schools and hospitals, for example, would be a mandated intervention, but requiring the firm to apply to an agency to receive authorization for the tax advantage would be a selective intervention. Intervention may also provide general or specific aid, types of intervention primarily seen in subsidies. *General aid* permits firms to use the funds provided in any way by the private entity being supported, but *specific aid* must be used for a specified purpose by the firm (Picard 1983).

The degree of administrative choice tends to increase depending upon which of these forms is selected (see Fig. 4.3), with the strength of administrative decision increasing if types toward the right are selected.

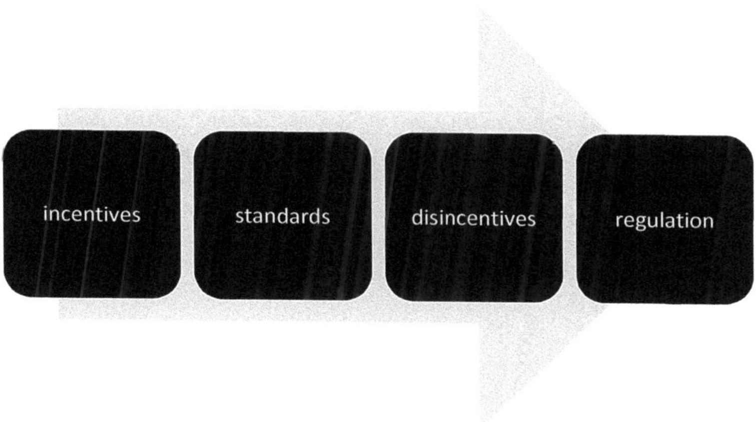

Fig. 4.2 Degree of intervention increases depending upon mechanism

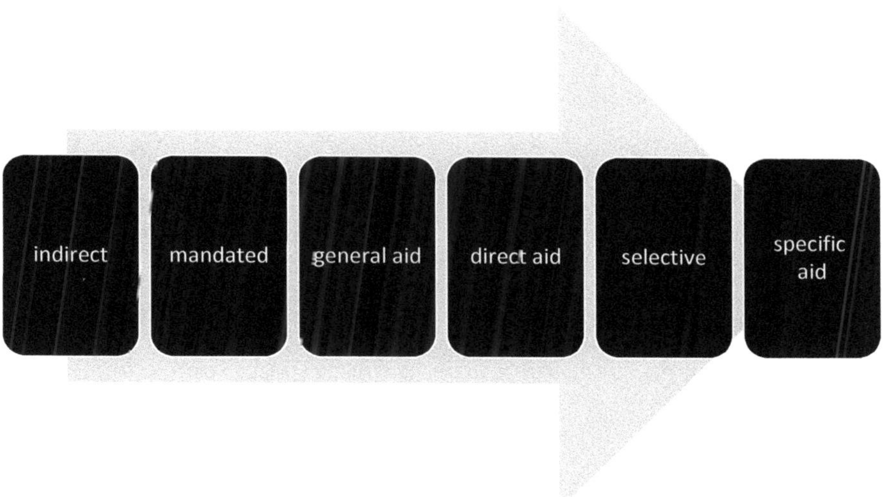

Fig. 4.3 Degree of administrative choice

A Diverse Selection of Policy Tools Is Available

Policy tools include both general tools used for a variety of policy purposes and specific tools fashioned to deal with unique issues, settings and purposes of specific industries or types of policy (Taylor Jr. 1977; Stevenson 2013). Tools are used in highly diverse policy areas, including international relations, economy, education, environment, public health, labor, agriculture, energy, business and industry, social benefits and transportation, as well as media and communications. Selection of tools is part of policy formulation in which the policy is designed and then constructed based on those tools (Sydney 2007). The range of tools available to governments for its operations and pursuit of policy have increased because of information technologies and communications improvements (Hood and Margetts 2007).

Even without creating separate policy for media and communications, policy makers can utilize tools from other policy areas in pursuit of objectives in the field. Tools provided in consumer law, privacy law, security law, competition laws and other fields are highly germane to contemporary issues and developments, even if they are not specifically constructed for media and communications activities.

In media and communications policy, the primary tools used by policy makers to intervene tend to be regulations, fiscal advantages and subsidies. *Regulations* involve decisions to proscribe or prescribe conduct, organize industries or control ownership. *Fiscal advantages* reduce costs for operations through preferential treatment or rates from government agencies or for government-provided or regulated services. *Subsidies* involve cash transfers to entities providing services or government payments of some costs. These include grants for audiovisual production, loan funds with government guarantees or low interest rates, and financial aid to maintain national news agencies. Governments are increasingly relying on public-private collaborations and supportive tools in the forms of fiscal advantages and operational interventions to achieve public purposes through private firms (Salamon 2002).

Purposes of Various Tools

Available tools serve a wide variety of purposes, ranging from industry facilitation to regulatory exemption and from structural intervention to public provision tools. It is important that the purposes of the tools are clear prior to determining which ones to employ and that the tools will actually carry out the desired effects in the mechanisms chosen (Fig. 4.4).

Industry Facilitation Tools

Industry facilitation tools are used by states to facilitate the development and operation of industries involved, creating conditions in which they can successfully operate and develop. In creating a regulatory environment, states seek to

Fig. 4.4 Primary purposes of policy tools

organize and stabilize industries, providing regulatory coordination among multiple providers of infrastructure, services and hardware and users. Companies and industries generally support policies that provide business stability, reduce business risks, promote desirable returns on investment and sometimes create protection from competition, particularly from new entrants or disruptive technologies.

Many states employ innovation policies, research funds, industry collaboration funds and education/training funds to help develop industries and provide the bases of knowledge and skilled workforces necessary for their existence. These tend to be used for emergent industries or industries that policy makers believe will create beneficial economic value (Vonortas et al. 2015), and media and communications industries are increasingly gaining attention in innovation policies (van Kranenburg 2017). Some states provide startup funds or loans to attract and support private investment in new industries and may use government investment funds such as sovereign wealth funds and pension funds to provide funding; others employ credit guarantees, subsidies and regional development funds to help address capital needs and constraints for infrastructure construction.

Some states choose to employ co-investment models of public-private partnerships that still incentivize innovation and efficiency or promote industry cooperation to improve service and upgrade capabilities. In the past, choices were traditionally public investment or private investment, but public-private partnerships and financing solutions are increasingly used for large infrastructure projects and for providing services to smaller underserved communities when other incentives are unable to produce commercially viable systems and services. The Canadian Infrastructure Bank, for example, co-invests with public entities and private firms in infrastructure projects, including broadband (Canadian Infrastructure Bank n.d.).

Many countries have used these tools in media and communications in recent years because of growth, employment and economic contributions. Broadband policies have been especially linked to innovation efforts, as have digital media (Choudrie and Middleton 2013; van Kranenburg 2017).

Policy-influenced standard setting is used in a wide variety of contexts including education, accounting, health care, safety and technology (Greenstein and Stango 2007). It is a crucial facilitation tool in media and communications that promotes coordination of technical and operating standards among equipment manufacturers and systems operators to ensure that technologies function together, connect effectively and are cost-efficient and safe. States may establish standards through policy, support private standard setting or accept standards created elsewhere.

When radio spectrum is required, states use the tool of spectrum allocation to facilitate industries needing spectrum and often give preferences to specific uses or users. The means by which spectrum is allocated is also a policy tool choice. Allocations can be made by spectrum agency administrators or through auctions in which private users bid to receive rights to use spectrum. This latter tool became especially popular for the allocation of radio spectrum to mobile telephony operators because it produced a large new source of revenue for state treasuries as multiple uses and reuses can be auctioned (Lin et al. 2014). Auctions have also been used in many countries to determine allotment of digital terrestrial television channels.

Structural Intervention Tools

Structural tools are used to form and govern media and communications industries and markets by determining or influencing what firms may participate, the number of participants and their impact on the industry or market or audience reach.

Fundamental structural intervention determines whether infrastructure and services will be provided by the state, private firms or both. Where infrastructure is viewed in strategic terms, nations are more likely to retain some ownership interests, although some maintain interests primarily for state revenue generation.

A primary structural intervention tool is *licensing*, in which firms are given permission to operate or use regulated resources such as radio spectrum or rights of way in ways that serve public or state interests. Television broadcasters must be approved to use spectrum, for example. Decisions on who can use a frequency are made by a state licensing authority based on criteria that often include financial ability, broadcast expertise and reputation. Other criteria may also apply. Nigerian law, for example, prohibits political or religious groups from obtaining a broadcast license (Nigeria n.d.). The use of the licensing tool is not restricted to broadcast media. Various states require various forms of licenses or registration for telephony, press, motion pictures, websites and other communication activities. Malaysia, for example, requires approval to own a printing press, and publishers of papers must obtain a publishing permit under the Printing Presses and Publications Act (Malaysia 2012).

A frequently used structural tool is ownership control that seeks to influence industry activity by controlling who can participate or how much of the industry a firm or individual can own. A common ownership tool in media and communications fully or partially restricts foreign ownership to ensure domestic control. For example, U.S. broadcasting stations are restricted to no more than 25 percent foreign ownership without special Federal Communications Commission approval (United States, Communications Act 1934), and foreign ownership of newspaper firms in India cannot exceed 26 percent, in great part due to post-colonial resistance to foreign ownership of all kinds (Sonwalkar 2001).

Ownership control is also used to limit the impact of a single owner in an individual medium or communications form or across media and communications. Restrictions can reside in tools specific to those industries and/or exist in competition law. Ownership intervention under competition law tends to focus on issues created by horizontal and vertical integration, whereas ownership intervention under the pluralism and diversity approach focuses on creating a variety of types of ownership and control. Pluralism is thus concerned with not only monopolization but ensuring owners represent different values and social and political perspectives, such as having including firms owned by minority groups or serving rural areas (Valcke et al. 2015). The rationales for this ownership approach are based on arguments involving democracy and participation (Baker 2006).

Historically, such restrictions were based on limited percentage of an individual medium output or cross-medium output owned or controlled by a single firm, but many nations have shifted to control based on the percentage of audience reached in the past quarter century (Doyle 2002). Competition law has not been particularly effective at promoting plurality and diversity, and the pluralism approach has failed to gain much support even where it has most received the greatest prominence (Picard 2017).

Fiscal Advantaging Tools

Advantages involve preferred or reduced fees or rates or preferred treatment for services or collections by government agencies or controlled entities that are provided to achieve a public purpose.

The most common advantages are tax reductions or credits that are provided to firms, lowering or removing corporate taxes, property taxes, sales taxes and other general business taxes. These are provided when policy makers believe that reducing such costs to firms will help develop an industry, attract businesses to a region, assist an existing industry experiencing financial difficulties or serve some other agreed public purpose (Klemm 2009; Hunter McMahon 2018). Tax breaks are sometimes criticized, however, for serving special interests rather than broader public needs and for difficulties in assessing their effectiveness (Jensen 2019).

U.S. federal and state authorities, for example, did not place sales taxes on internet commerce for many years as a means of promoting development of internet services and because of difficulties in collecting taxes on cross-border commerce (Hale and McNeal 2011). Many European nations provide value-added tax (VAT) exemptions for newspaper subscriptions and single-copy sales, but their equity and usefulness are increasingly being questioned (Nielsen and Linnebank 2011; Ots et al. 2016). The European Union ended differential application of VAT to printed books and newspapers and digital editions in 2016, extending the tax reduction to their digital products (Haines 2016).

Many nations provide postal, telecommunication and transportation rate reductions for newspapers and magazines to reduce the cost for distribution throughout their countries (Picard 1985; Murschetz 2013). Some countries provide low interest loans or loan guarantees for media and communications investments in facilities and infrastructures (Murschetz 1998). Arguments to provide tax breaks and charitable status to news organizations due to their declining financial positions are appearing and will require changes to policies and laws regarding those mechanisms and tools (Picard et al. 2016) and may conflict with competition law in some countries.

Operational Intervention Tools

These tools affect the ways companies operate and include apparatuses designed to regulate price setting or rates for media and communications goods and services to promote non-price competition or to ensure that use is not restricted by economic status.

Another form of operational intervention is requirements for universal service, requiring firms to serve territories or individuals that are not economically viable as well as profitable locations and populations. Other service requirements may include capacity or quality criteria.

Content requirements are frequently used by states in audio and audiovisual markets to promote domestic content and content industries for cultural and economic benefits. These often take the form of quotas, specifying a percentage of broadcast or exhibition that must be domestic. The European Union, for example, recently established a quota on audiovisual streaming services operating in Europe, including Amazon and Netflix, requiring that 30 percent of the content offered to be of European origin (Gershgorn 2018).

Other tools frequently found in telecommunications include required network access for competitors and those promoting shared infrastructure. In recent years, the operations of digital platforms and firms are increasingly being subjected to privacy regulation, data flow regulation, Data algorithmic regulation, and safety and ethical regulation because of issues arising from their operations.

Regulatory Exemption Tools

These tools release industries or firms from compliance with regulations for some public purpose. They almost always generate controversy and are often criticized as most serving private rather than public purposes.

U.S. policy makers have often used exemption tools. Policy makers, for example, provided an antitrust exemption for jointly operating newspapers under the argument that it would save editorial voices (Busterna and Picard 1993; Picard 2007), exempted newspapers from child labor laws so children could be used as independent newspaper delivery contractors (Linder 1990) and exempted platforms from regulations that would have legally considered publishers responsible for the content they carry (United States, Telecommunications Act 1996).

Public Provision Tools

States that determine that public provision of telecommunications and media services are desirable can do so through government agencies, state-owned firms, quasi-governmental organizations or other public institutions.

Many governments provide telephone services through tools including government agencies and state-owned or jointly owned firms. The United Arab Emirates, for example, provides phone services nationwide through the Emirates Telecommunications Corporation, a publicly traded firm in which the state owns controlling interest.

Public provision in broadcasting is most often pursued through state broadcasting, usually under the direction of the ministry overseeing communication. The Zimbabwe Broadcasting Corporation, for example, provides radio and television services under the direction of the Minister of Information with governing board members appointed by the national President (Zimbabwe Broadcasting Corporation 2018; World Intellectual Property Organization 2018). If more independence from the ruling government in power is sought, states sometimes create an independent agency or quasi-governmental corporation with a governance board that represents multiple political parties and interests selected in a process that reduces the direct influence of the ruling government. The United States, for example, uses this form of governance to oversee its international state broadcasting operations, including Voice of America, Radio Free Europe/Radio Liberty and broadcasting in the Middle East, Asia and elsewhere (United States, Agency for Global Media 2018).

Public provision in many democratic nations is pursued through the tool of public service broadcasting. These firms are funded by government or through government required reception licenses with the primary purpose of serving public needs. These are typically quasi-governmental corporations with governance structures designed to provide significant independence from the government of the day (Nissen 2006; Donders 2012). Changing broadcast technologies and public policies have reduced the role of public broadcasting in many nations, and some public broadcasters have had difficulties with maintaining independence in countries with autocratic rulers or ruling parties in recent decades (Tracey 1998; Polońska and Beckett 2019).

At times, states may pursue public provision through broadcasting services undertaken by educational institutions (Blakely 1979). This form was particularly evident in radio in the United States and some Latin American countries during the early to mid-twentieth century.

Subsidizing Tools

Subsidies are cash transfers to or expenditures on behalf of private entities made to pursue some public policy purposes (Picard 1983). In telecommunications and media, these include state payments to help build infrastructure in economically unfavorable regions and content production subsidies for film, television and radio broadcasters, and independent producers (Picard 2008). Some states provide organizational subsidies to ensure the economic survival of national news agencies.

Government advertising expenditures for public agencies and state firms are often seen as subsidies leading to questions about their potential influence on media firms' coverage and their transparency (Rockwell and Janus 2002; Besley and Prat 2006; Young 2007). Advertising that private firms or individuals are required to publish for regulatory or legal purposes can also be a form of subsidy if it is required to be placed in a specific medium, to the disadvantage of other media.

Significant subsidies exist for newspapers, particularly among Western nations (Murschetz 2013) but the extent to which they serve their purposes is increasingly questioned (Ots 2009), in part because their effects on firm economics and finances differ (Picard 1995). Domestic motion picture production is widely subsidized worldwide and exempted from World Trade Organization treaties as a cultural exception (Murschetz and Teichmann 2018).

Private Regulation Tools

Some policy makers have used tools forgoing public regulation in favor of private, usually industry-based, regulation (Haufler 2013). These have included a variety of self-regulatory tools including motion pictures, broadcast, cable and games rating systems, parental controls in digital technologies, content standards for advertising, broadcast and print media, and media councils that investigate and adjudicate complaints against media (Schulz and Held 2004; Shaver and An 2014), and a large amount of technical regulation in internet governance.

Private regulation lacks authority and power to enforce its decisions, unless governments endorse the private regulators and agree to use state authority and power to enforce their decisions.

Consumer Tools

Consumer tools provide information that help the public understand what they are consuming and give them the ability to make informed choices. Most general consumer policies and regulations apply to media and communications firms. When specifically employed in media and communications policy, such tools tend to focus on transparency of factors that might influence those choices.

Tools include requirements for information clarity. In telecommunications, some countries are requiring clear and comparable price and service information that allows the public to consider various call, text and data use plans and their pricing to make informed choices about which mobile phone plans and firms to select. Similarly, some policy makers are attempting to establish clear language requirements to ensure that platform and software use agreements make clear how the firms will use consumers' personal information and data.

A policy tool requiring transparency of ownership of media and communication firms is gaining favor as a means of establishing who controls media firms because there is often a lack of information or ownership is deliberately obscured using secretive offshore firms or shares held in the name of investment firms. Austria, for example, requires media companies to publicly disclose ownership information annually, providing details about their owners, shareholders, beneficial owners and anyone with indirect interest and influence on the firm (Austria 2011).

Content quality labeling policies are gaining interest as a means of combating misinformation and disinformation, particularly as content is disaggregated in social media. Suggestions that a trademarked certificate that stories originated with new organizations adhering to good journalism practice have arisen but not yet gained traction (Amos 2009; McCallum 2019).

Tool Selection Influences Success of the Policy

Policy making is most successful when the proper tool(s) are selected to influence the mechanisms of the policy. Tools must be fit for purpose, effective, efficient and meet legal requirements.

South Korea, for example, has long had policies of heavy research investment and support for telecommunications infrastructures for national security reasons, but also for industrial policy purposes to help develop technologies that can be manufactured and sold in international markets (Larson 1995; Kim and Kelly 2010). Although initially employing highly state-centered policies, it has moved over the years toward policies encouraging private investment and joint public-private projects (Jin 2011, 2017).

Choices of policies are influenced by national policy style—the dominant ways of public problem solving, tool preferences and perceptions of whether they will be effective, efficient and accepted as legitimate (Bemelmans-Videc et al. 1998). Some mechanisms and tools are more contentious than others. Shifting costs to suppliers usually gains more opposition than shifting costs to consumers or taxpayers. Removing sources of revenue and profits, or inhibiting opportunities to pursue them, often produces contention and opposition of commercial firms.

In considering policy tools, it is important to reflect on assumptions underlying choices. Many policy advocates and policy makers are very willing to spend other peoples' money or make them spend more to serve desired purposes. There are also tendencies in some to expect that private investment and activity will solve nearly public problems. In some there is a propensity toward believing public funding and operation will ensure quality public provision of services. All of these will affect the outcomes of policy—especially if they are inappropriate for dealing with the problem or issue being addressed.

Mechanisms and tools are effective if they accomplish the policy intent by producing the desired results and affecting behavior as anticipated. If the intent of a policy is to reduce violent content in music broadcast on radio and television, for example, it can only be deemed effective if that content disappears or is substantially reduced.

Motion picture production and distribution is a policy concern in many nations, but they address it with varying policies depending upon the underlying reason for the policy. New Zealand, for example, focuses on economic impact of production on the national economy and pursues policies designed to attract foreign production to make films and videos in that country. U.S. policy is focused on distribution and trade policy concerns, so it focuses on protection against piracy and free trade policies in intergovernmental organizations. Ireland is primarily concerned with improving domestic cultural promotion so it uses a variety of motion picture subsidy and support policies.

Policies need to be efficient making good use of time, effort and resources. This means that the administration and application of the policy must be systematic and well run, that the costs are appropriate for the issue or problem being addressed and that the policy does not overburden administrator or firms the policy is affecting.

To be successful, policies also need to be in accord with legal requirements created by constitutional or basic governance laws and legislation. If not, they are likely to be halted by judicial or executive decision as unlawful or overreach by the policy makers involved.

Changes in technology and industry structure often require policy reconsideration and changes in choices of mechanisms and tools selection; thus significant reconsideration has been given to policy mechanisms and tools in media and communications in recent decades. These produced changes in domestic and international telecommunication through the introduced competition (Crandall and Flamm 1989), forced consideration of how converged media altered efficacy of existing policy (Collins 1995), induced the impetus for greater internet intervention (Brousseau et al. 2012; Glenn 2017) and induced reconsideration of the use of domestic content policies (Picard et al. 2016).

Chapter Summary

- There are many policy options available to organize industries, fashion operating requirements and influence behavior of media and communications firms.
- Options used in a country are influenced by political philosophies, previous policy choices and executive, legislative and legal factors.
- Policy mechanisms reveal how factors related to the issue or challenge being addressed may be influenced.
- Tools serve various purposes and need to be selected based on the policy intent and mechanism employed.
- Properly selected tools increase the likelihood of policy success.

Discussion Points

1. What influences decisions about what types of policy mechanisms to employ?
2. Can a policy mechanism pursued be fallacious?
3. Why does the selection of policy tools influence the success of the policy?
4. What keeps some countries from using certain types of policy tools?
5. Why are some countries less willing to use direct subsidies than others?

Bibliography

Amos, Owen. 2009. 'Kitemark' Could Distinguish Journalism from 'Web Noise.' *Press Gazette*, January 1. Available at https://pressgazette.co.uk/kitemark-could-distinguish-journalism-from-web-noise/. Accessed 19 June 2019.

Austria. 2011. Media Transparency Act, Official Gazette 125/2011.

Baker, C. Edwin. 2006. *Media Concentration and Democracy: Why Ownership Matters*. New York: Cambridge University Press.

Baker & McKenzie. 2012. *Guide to Media and Content Regulation in Asia Pacific*. Sydney: Baker & McKenzie.

Ball, Stephen J. 1993. What Is Policy? Texts, Trajectories and Toolboxes. *Discourse: Studies in the Cultural Politics of Education* 13 (2): 10–17.

Bemelmans-Videc, Marie-Louise, Ray C. Rist, and Evert Vedung, eds. 1998. *Carrots, Sticks & Sermons: Policy Instruments and Their Evaluation*. New Brunswick: Transaction Publishers.

Besley, Timothy, and Andrea Prat. 2006. Handcuffs for the Grabbing Hand? Media Capture and Government Accountability. *American Economic Review* 96 (3): 720–736.

Blakely, Robert J. 1979. *To Serve the Public Interest: Educational Broadcasting in the United States*. Syracuse: Syracuse University Press.

Brousseau, Eric, Meryem Marzouki, and Cécile Méadel, eds. 2012. *Governance, Regulation and Powers on the Internet*. Cambridge: Cambridge University Press.

Brown, Allan. 2009. Economics, Public Service Broadcasting, and Social Values. *Journal of Media Economics* 9 (1): 3–15.

Busterna, John C., and Robert G. Picard. 1993. *Joint Operating Agreements: The Newspaper Preservation Act and Its Application*. Norwood: Ablex Publishing.

Canada, Canadian Revenue Agency. 2018. Advertising. https://www.canada.ca/en/revenue-agency/services/tax/businesses/topics/sole-proprietorships-partnerships/report-business-income-expenses/completing-form-t2125/line-8521-advertising.html. Accessed 26 Dec 2018.

Canadian Infrastructure Bank.. n.d. Available at https://cib-bic.ca/en/lobby. Accessed 6 May 2019.

Choudrie, Jyoti, and Catherine Middleton. 2013. *Management of Broadband Technology and Innovation: Policy, Deployment and Use*. London: Routledge.

Collins, Richard, ed. 1995. *Converging Media? Converging Regulation?* London: Institute of Public Policy Research.

Crandall, Robert W., and Kenneth Flamm. 1989. *Changing the Rules: Technological Change, Competition, and Regulation in Communications*. Washington, DC: Brookings Institution Press.

Cremer, Helmuth, Farid Gasmi, Andre Grimaud, and Jean Jacques Laffont. 2001. Universal Service: An Economic Perspective. *Annals of Public and Cooperative Economics* 72 (1): 5–43.

Crew, Michael A., and Paul R. Kleindorfer. 2000. Liberalization and the Universal Service Obligation in Postal Service. In *Current Directions in Postal Reform*, ed. Michael A. Crew and Paul R. Kleindorfer, 3–28. Boston: Springer.

Curran, James. 2011. *Media and Democracy*. London: Taylor and Francis.

Dolowitz, David P., and David Marsh. 2000. Learning from Abroad: The Role of Policy Transfer in Contemporary Policy-Making. *Governance* 13 (1): 5–53.

Donders, Karen. 2012. *Public Service Media and Policy in Europe*. London: Palgrave Macmillan.

Doyle, Gillian. 2002. *Media Ownership: The Economics and Politics of Convergence and Concentration in the UK and European Media*. London: Sage.

Ferguson, Charles H. 2004. *The Broadband Problem: Anatomy of a Market Failure and Policy Dilemma*. Washington, DC: Brookings Institution Press.

Friedlander, Amy. 1995. *Natural Monopoly and Universal Service: Telephones and Telegraphs in the U.S. Communications Infrastructure, 1837–1940*. Reston: Corporation for National Research Initiatives.

Gershgorn, Dave. 2018. The EU Is Giving Netflix and Amazon Two Years to Make 30% of Their Catalogs European. *Quartz*. https://qz.com/1508022/netflix-and-amazon-have-two-years-to-make-30-of-their-catalogs-european/. Accessed 19 Dec 2018.

Glenn, Carol M. 2017. *Controlling Cyberspace: The Politics of Internet Governance and Regulation*. Santa Barbara: Praeger.

Greenstein, Shane, and Victor Stango, eds. 2007. *Standards and Public Policy*. Cambridge: Cambridge University Press.

Haines, Anjana. 2016. European Commission Unveils VAT Rules for E-commerce Businesses. *International Tax Review*. http://www.internationaltaxreview.com/Article/3647310/European-Commission-unveils-VAT-rules-for-e-commerce-businesses.html. Accessed 31 Dec 2018.

Hale, Kathleen, and Ramona McNeal. 2011. Technology, Politics, and E-Commerce: Internet Sales Tax and Interstate Cooperation. *Government Information Quarterly* 28 (2): 262–270.

Haufler, Virginia. 2013. *A Public Role for the Private Sector: Industry Self-Regulation in a Global Economy*. New York: Carnegie Endowment for World Peace.

Hayes, Michael T. 2001. *The Limits of Policy Change: Incrementalism, Worldview, and the Rule of Law*. Washington, DC: Georgetown University Press.

Hood, Christopher C., and Helen Z. Margetts. 2007. *The Tools of Government in the Digital Age*. 2nd ed. Basingstoke: Palgrave Macmillan.

Hunter McMahon, Stephanie. 2018. *Principles of Tax Policy*. St. Paul: West Academic Publishing.

Jensen, Nathan. 2019. *Incentives to Pander: How Politicians Use Corporate Welfare for Political Gain*. Cambridge: Cambridge University Press.

Jin, Dal Young. 2011. *Hands On Hands Off: The Korean State and the Market Liberalization of the Communication Industry*. Cresskill: Hampton Press.

Jin, Dal Yong. 2017. *Smartland Korea: Mobile Communication, Culture, and Society*. Ann Arbor: University of Michigan Press.

Johns Hopkins Center for Civil Society Studies. 2003. *Policy Tools and Government Performance: Report on a Conference Co-Sponsored by the U.S. General Accounting Office, the U.S. Office of Management and Budget, and The Johns Hopkins University*. Baltimore: The Johns Hopkins Center for Civil Society Studies.

Kim, Yongsoo, and Tim Kelly. 2010. *Building Broadband: Strategies and Policies for the Developing World*. Washington, DC: The International Bank for Reconstruction and Development/World Bank.

Klemm, Alexander. 2009. Causes, Benefits, and Risks of Business Tax Incentives. Working Paper WP/09/21. Washington, DC: International Monetary Fund.

Larson, James F. 1995. *The Telecommunications Revolution in Korea*. Oxford: Oxford University Press.

Lin, Peng, Xiaojun Feng, and Qian Zhang. 2014. *Auction Design for the Wireless Spectrum Market*. Berlin: Springer.

Linder, Marc. 1990. From Street Urchins to Little Merchants: The Juridical Transvaluation of Child Newspaper Carriers. *Temple Law Review* 63: 829–864.

Lowe, Gregory F., and Christian E. Berg. 2013. The Funding of Public Service Media: A Matter of Value and Values. *International Journal on Media Management* 15 (2): 77–97.

McCallum, Zoe. 2019. Journalism Vs Churnalism: The Push for "Quality Marks" in Online News. *Inforrm's Blog*, February 26. Available at https://inforrm.org/2019/02/26/journalism-vs-churnalism-the-push-for-quality-marks-in-online-news-zoe-mccallum/. Accessed 19 June 2019.

McChesney, Robert W. 2012. Farewell to Journalism: Time for a Rethinking. *Journalism Practice* 6 (5–6): 614–626.

McChesney, Robert W., and Victor Pickard. 2011. *Will the Last Reporters Please Turn Out the Lights: The Collapse of Journalism and What Can Be Done About It*. New York: The New Press.

Murschetz, Paul. 1998. State Support for the Daily Press in Europe: A Critical Appraisal: Austria, France, Norway and Sweden Compared. *European Journal of Communication* 13 (3): 291–313.

———, ed. 2013. *State Aid for Newspapers: Theories, Cases, Actions.* Berlin: Springer.

Murschetz, Paul Clemens, and Roland Teichmann. 2018. *Handbook of State Aid for Film: Finance, Industries and Regulation.* Berlin: Springer.

Nielsen, Rasmus Kleis with Geert Linnebank. 2011. Public Support for Media: A Six-Country Overview of Direct and Indirect Subsidies. RISJ Report. Oxford: Reuters Institute for the Study of Journalism, University of Oxford.

Nigeria, Federal Ministry of Communication Technology. 2012. *Nigeria's National Broadband Plan 2013–2018.* https://www.researchictafrica.net/countries/nigeria/Nigeria_National_Broadband_Plan_2013-2018.pdf. Accessed 24 Dec 2018.

Nigeria, National Broadcasting Commission. n.d. Procedure of Obtaining a Broadcast License. Available at http://www.nbc.gov.ng/pages/licensing. Accessed 30 Dec 2018.

Nissen, Christian S., ed. 2006. *Making a Difference: Public Service Broadcasting in the European Media Landscape.* Eastleigh: John Libbey Publishing.

Ots, Mart. 2009. Efficient Servants of Pluralism or Marginalized Media Policy Tools? *Journal of Communication Inquiry* 33 (4): 376–392.

Ots, Mart, Arne H. Krumsvik, Marko Ala-Fossi, and Pernilla Rendahl. 2016. The Shifting Role of Value-Added Tax (VAT) as a Media Policy Tool: A Three-Country Comparison of Political Justifications. *Javnost/The Public* 23 (2): 170–187.

Picard, Robert G. 1983. State Intervention in U.S. Press Economics. *Gazette* 30: 3–11.

———. 1985. Patterns of State Intervention in Western Press Economics. *Journalism Quarterly* 62 (1): 3–9.

———. 1995. Free Press and Government: The Ignored Relationships of U.S. Newspapers. In *Media Structure and the State: Concepts, Issues, Measures*, ed. Karl Erik Gustafsson, 133–148. Göteborg: Göteborg University, School of Economics and Commercial Law.

———. 2007. Natural Death, Euthanasia, and Suicide: The Demise of Joint Operating Agreements. *Journal of Media Business Studies* 4 (2): 41–54.

———. 2008. Subsidies for the Media. In *The International Encyclopedia of Communication*, ed. Wolfgang Donsbach, vol. 11, 4891–4895. Oxford: Wiley-Blackwell.

———. 2015. Business and Market Challenges and Their Effects on the Foundations and Trajectory of U.S. Broadcast Policy. *Journal of Media Business Studies* 8 (2): 45–62.

———. 2017. The Sisyphean Pursuit of Media Pluralism: European Efforts to Establish Policy and Measurable Evidence. *Communication Law and Policy* 22 (3): 255–273.

Picard, Robert G., Valerie Belair-Gagnon and Sofia Ranchordás, ed. 2016. The Impact of Charity and Tax Law and Regulation on Not-for-Profit News Organizations. Reuters Institute, University of Oxford, and Information Society Project, Yale Law School, Yale University.

Pickard, Victor. 2007. Neoliberal Visions and Revisions in Global Communications Policy from NWICO to WSIS. *Journal of Communication Inquiry* 31 (2): 118–139.

Polońska, Eva, and Charlie Beckett, eds. 2019. *Public Service Broadcasting and Media Systems in Troubled European Democracies.* London: Palgrave Macmillan.

Raats, Tim, Tom Evens, and Sanne Ruelens. 2016. Challenges for Sustaining Local Audio-Visual Ecosystems: Analysis of Financing and Production of Domestic TV Fiction in Small Media Markets. *Journal of Popular Television* 4 (1): 129–147.

Rockwell, R., and N. Janus. 2002. The Politics of Coercion: Advertising, Media and State Power in Central America. *Journalism* 3 (3): 331–353.
Salamon, Lester M. 2002. *The Tools of Government: A Guide to the New Governance.* Oxford: Oxford University Press.
Salanié, Bernard. 2000. *Microeconomics of Market Failure.* Cambridge, MA: MIT Press.
Schneider, Anne, and Helen Ingram. 1990. Behavioral Assumptions of Policy Tools. *The Journal of Politics* 52 (2): 510–529.
Schulz, Wolfgang, and Thorsten Held. 2004. *Regulated Self-Regulation as a Form of Modern Government: A Comparative Analysis with Case Studies from Media and Telecommunications Law.* Bloomington: Indiana University Press.
Sharkey, William W. 1982. *The Theory of Natural Monopoly.* Cambridge: Cambridge University Press.
Shaver, Mary Alice, and Soontae An, eds. 2014. *The Global Advertising Regulation Handbook.* London: Routledge.
Sonwalkar, P. 2001. Opposition to the Entry of Foreign Press in India, 1991–1995: The Hidden Agenda. *Modern Asian Studies* 35 (3): 743–763.
Stevenson, Charles A. 2013. *America's Foreign Policy Toolkit: Key Institutions and Processes.* Los Angeles: CQ Press.
Sydney, Mara S. 2007. Policy Formulation: Design and Tools. In *Handbook of Public Policy Analysis*, ed. Frank Fischer, Gerald J. Miller, and Mara S. Sidney, 79–88. Boca Raton: CRC Press.
Taylor, William B., Jr. 1977. *A Survey of Policy Tools Available to Local Governments to Influence Industrial Development.* Cambridge, MA: John F. Kennedy School of Government, Harvard University.
Tracey, Michael. 1998. *Decline and Fall of Public Service Broadcasting.* New York: Oxford University Press.
United States, Communications Act of 1934. Available at https://transition.fcc.gov/Reports/1934new.pdf. Accessed 30 Dec 2018.
United States, Telecommunications Act of 1996, Sec. 5. Available at https://transition.fcc.gov/Reports/tcom1996.txt. Accessed 31 Dec 2018.
United States, Agency for Global Media. 2018. https://www.bbg.gov/. Accessed 31 Dec 2018.
Valcke, Peggy, Miklos Sukosd, and Robert G. Picard, eds. 2015. *Media Pluralism and Diversity: Concepts, Risks and Global Trends.* London: Palgrave Macmillan.
van Kranenburg, Hans, ed. 2017. *Innovation Policies in the European News Media Industry: A Comparative Study.* Berlin: Springer.
Vonortas, Nicholas S., Phoebe C. Rouge, and Anwar Aridi, eds. 2015. *Innovation Policy: A Practical Introduction.* Berlin: Springer.
Ward, David. 2006. Can the Market Provide: Public Service Media, Market Failure and Public Goods. In *Making a Difference: Public Service Broadcasting in the European Media Landscape*, ed. Christian S. Nissen, 51–64. Eastleigh: John Libbey Publishing.
World Intellectual Property Organization. 2018. Zimbabwe Broadcasting Services Act 3/2001, 22/2001, 26/200, 6/2003. Available at https://www.wipo.int/edocs/lexdocs/laws/en/zw/zw036en.pdf. Accessed 31 Dec 2018.
Young, Sally. 2007. Following the Money Trail: Government Advertising, the Missing Millions and the Unknown Effects. *Public Policy* 2 (2): 104–118.
Zimbabwe Broadcasting Corporation. 2018. Available at http://www.zbccorporate.co.zw/. Accessed 31 Dec 2018.

Suggested Readings

Hood, Christopher C, and Helen Z. Margetts. 2007. *The Tools of Government in the Digital Age*. 2nd ed. Houndmills/Basingstoke/Hampshire: Palgrave Macmillan.

Murschetz, Paul, ed. 2013. *State Aid for Newspapers: Theories, Cases, Actions*. Berlin: Springer.

Murschetz, Paul Clemens, and Roland Teichmann. 2018. *Handbook of State Aid for Film: Finance, Industries and Regulation*. Berlin: Springer.

Salamon, Lester M. 2002. *The Tools of Government: A Guide to the New Governance*. Oxford: Oxford University Press.

PART II

Three Levels of Policy Making

CHAPTER 5

Global Policy Making

Global policy making emerged as technologies permitted media and communication flow among many countries worldwide and issues arose concerning governing the technologies and processes employed, as well as issues resulting from that communication. These developments required transnational policy rather than merely individual domestic or regional policy.

Global policy making in communication has existed for about 150 years, spurred by increasing connectivity and movement of telegraph messages and postal items worldwide. The International Telegraph Union (now the International Telecommunication Union or ITU) and the Universal Postal Union (UPU) were established in 1865 and 1874 respectively to coordinate national services and facilitate standards of interconnectivity and operations in their fields. As newer communications technologies successively emerged—wireless, radio and television, microwave, satellite, internet—needs to coordinate and regulate their operations at the international level emerged and led to additional global policy. Much of that policy is based on earlier international approaches to communication policy guided by international law (Mansell and Raboy 2014), but newer forms of governance are appearing.

Contemporary developments in communication technology, globalization of media and communication firms and the changing economics of their operations have made national policy less effective in addressing issues, leading some to suggest that broader global approaches are particularly required in the contemporary environment (Iosifidis 2011).

Global policy making is structured by the principles and practices of international law and primarily takes place through intergovernmental organizations (IGOs) established to facilitate relations among states and collective public decision-making. Other policy, however, is made through nongovernmental international organizations that provide private governance of some issues,

R. G. Picard, *Media and Communications Policy Making*, Palgrave Global Media Policy and Business,
https://doi.org/10.1007/978-3-030-35173-1_5

especially standards and practices that facilitate operations of technologies and interconnectivity. This form of global governance of communication networks can be characterized as creating a form of global civil society, according to Manuel Castells (2008). Critics of that view argue that the extent of participation and representation in the sphere is highly constrained (Weber 2009; McLaughlin and Pickard 2005). Private governance mechanisms are not unique to media and communications. They are found in many fields including business, finance and labor, and raise issues of governance accountability and transparency in those cases as well (Graz and Nölke 2008).

Sovereignty as a Fundamental Principle of Global Policy

The concept of national sovereignty is central to all discussions of global policy making. Sovereignty involves the power of states to self-govern and create policies and laws on internal affairs without interference from other states (Hofbauer 2016). Governments are thus sovereign over their territories, the people within them and domestic activities (Biersteker and Weber 1996). Although there are differences in concepts of how states gain sovereignty, once the sovereignty of a state is recognized by other states, its ability to exercise independence is established. The rise of global economic and transborder technological activity has altered international economics, politics and relations in recent decades (Holsti 2004), but international intervention abridging sovereignty remains limited under international law, primarily to preserve peace or serve humanitarian purposes (Lyons and Mastanduno 1995).

The principle of sovereignty is part of international law that governs relations among states with generally accepted rules and practices. This body of law is applied almost exclusively to the behavior of countries, rather than individuals, and involves principles related to statehood, territoriality, maritime law, international organizations, responsibilities of states, human rights, diplomatic relations and treaties (Crawford 2012; Shaw 2017). Because of the principle of sovereignty, the rules and practices embodied under international law are applicable to states that have agreed to be governed by them, usually through approval of multinational treaties.

Global policy making of all kinds is influenced by this fundamental concept, and it is generally recognized that states cannot be obligated to comply with international policy and law without their express agreement. Nevertheless, international governance is increasingly addressing global issues by creating mechanisms to facilitate and incentivize that agreement by states (Kreijen 2002).

Treaties Are the Bases of Policy in Intergovernmental Organizations

Treaties are the primary political mechanism of global governance, agreements made between sovereign states that accept obligations governed by international law. By accepting those obligations, states voluntarily give up some degree of sovereignty on specific issues to the intergovernmental organization involved (Sarooshi 2005). Most global governance involves multinational treaties facilitated through intergovernmental organizations. The primary organizations involved in creating and overseeing the treaties in media and communications are the International Telecommunication Union, Universal Postal Union and World Intellectual Property Organization. Although not specific to media and communications, the World Trade Organization (WTO) also plays a significant role in policy making because its treaties govern trade in products and services, including media products, data services and intellectual property.

Treaties are essentially contracts that states sign with other states to create policy and international legal requirements relating to various issues (Hollis 2014). These treaties bind countries to adhere to certain policy principles in their domestic policy and law and behave in prescribed ways in the international sphere (Aust 2014). Treaties between two countries are called bilateral treaties and those involving more countries are called multilateral (sometimes multinational) treaties. Bilateral treaties address issues that primarily concern two countries, whereas multilateral treaties address issues with broader significance involving multiple states.

When the United Kingdom and Ireland began moving toward switchover to digital terrestrial television broadcasting, for example, they entered a bilateral agreement to coordinate and govern the transition of stations to new spectrum in both countries. The agreement was undertaken because the United Kingdom governs broadcasting in Northern Ireland and the technical coordination was needed to ensure that both Ireland and the United Kingdom were making decisions that did not hinder the switchover in either Northern Ireland or Ireland (Commission for Communications Regulation and Ofcom 2012). This agreement thus dealt with an issue specific to the two states, rather than an issue involving multiple states that might require a multilateral agreement.

Multilateral treaty making is exemplified by the International Telecommunication Union updating the International Telecommunication Regulations to bring internet operations under its remit. The treaty, which came into effect in 2015, contains provisions permitting states to block some internet content and authorizing intergovernmental action involving security and internet crime (Hill 2014). The World Conference on International Telecommunications convened in 2012 to amend the International Telecommunication Regulations and 89 nations agreed to the provisions, but European and North American nations, as well as India and Japan, did not agree. Continuing efforts by the ITU to deal with internet issues remain highly contested (Glenn 2017). This situation is not uncommon. Although many multinational treaties exist, their acceptance by states varies widely. In some cases, a minority of states are parties to the treaties and in others nearly all states are parties.

How Treaties Are Made in Intergovernmental Organizations

Intergovernmental organizations exist to permit states to jointly address issues of common significance. IGOs are part of the broader group of international organizations influencing and governing global governance that include many nongovernmental organizations (Frederking and Diehl 2015). The most accepted intergovernmental organizations range from the Food and Agriculture Organization to the World Meteorological Organization and these are specialized agencies of the United Nations (UN). These IGOs operate under a charter, a form of treaty, that defines its scope and functions and is created by representatives of states for which the organization is germane. States become members of the IGO once the founding treaty is ratified by the government of their home states. Ratification may be made by legislative action, executive action or royal decree depending upon the form of government and procedures established in various states.

Once an intergovernmental organization has been established it goes about its work considering issues within its scope (Karns et al. 2015). Most IGOs are administered by a secretariat that includes administrative and technical experts led by personnel appointed through processes governed by the member states. Major decisions regarding operations and the establishment of policy and regulations are typically overseen by assemblies of the membership. Proposed policies and treaties develop through committee meetings and then drafts are put forward to the members for deliberation and then debate in conferences or assemblies. Even though a new treaty is adopted by the IGO, it is not binding on members unless their governments specifically ratify the treaty and notify the organization that they are committing themselves to adherence to its provisions.

Global policy making is slower compared to domestic and regional policy making because it involves many states with widely differing interests. Greater time is required because not only must the IGO go through its processes but each of the states must go through their individual executive and legislative processes to ratify a treaty. In Japan, for example, both the House of Representations and the House of Councillors of its parliament must ratify treaties and may not take up the issue concurrently.

The process of creating a treaty in the organization may take years itself and some states may take many years before ratifying it. Sometimes a treaty or even membership in the IGO might not have been highly relevant to a state so it may have not agreed to or ratified the treaty when it was originally put forward but may decide to do so some years later. The International Telecommunication Union's Radiotelegraph Convention was signed in 1906 to govern wireless communication with ships at sea by 27 countries. Its annexes became the bases of the Radio Regulations that have been expanded and revised more than a dozen times in the past century to account for changes in technology and radio spectrum use. In 1950, the ITU had 56 member states. Today that number has increased to 193.

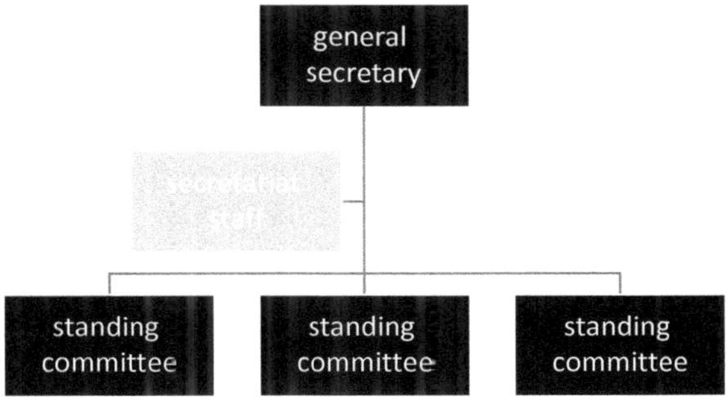

Fig. 5.1 Typical administrative structure of intergovernmental organizations

A state joining a treaty is not obligated to adhere to the agreement in perpetuity. Changes in government or policy may lead countries to alter commitments to respect the agreement so treaty provisions generally establish means by which countries can withdraw from treaties and the obligations they impose. There are also some provisions in international law that permit denunciation or withdrawal from treaties if those provisions are not specifically included in a treaty. In most cases, withdrawal requires that notice be given and specifies an advance time period before actual withdrawal takes place.

Treaties often authorize governance processes and rulemaking activities within the general scope of the treaty. These are typically carried out by some form of standing committees or administrative panels or commissions authorized to deal with specific issues, under the oversight of the secretariat of the intergovernmental organization (Fig. 5.1). These groups may also raise new issues and typically can make recommendations for treaty amendments or new treaties when needed. It is increasingly common for nongovernmental organizations and experts to participate in some form at the standing committee levels. The general secretary and standing committee members are typically elected by member states and the secretariat staff are employees. The specific structures and administrative processes for each intergovernmental organization are outlined in its establishing treaty and any constitution or bylaws that may exist.

Member States in Intergovernmental Organizations

Member state is the traditional term used to indicate a country that has joined an intergovernmental organization or similar confederation of states (Harrington 2018), although a few international organizations—such as the World Trade Organization—merely call them a member. No state can be compelled to join an intergovernmental organization or to adhere to its governance. The number of potential member states for intergovernmental organizations is dependent upon the number of countries recognized as sovereign states.

The actual number of countries in the world is disputed depending on whether some territories or autonomous regions are included, and that decision is highly politicized and determined by recognition extended by each sovereign state. Overall the number of countries recognized internationally has more than doubled since 1900, rising from 77 sovereign countries in 1900 to 106 in 1950 and to at least 193 today. The United Nations recognizes 195 countries, 193 member states and 2 non-member states with observer status (i.e., The Holy See and the State of Palestine). When it was founded in 1945, the UN had 51 member states, reaching 99 in 1960, 144 in 1975 and 189 in 2000.

The rise in the number of sovereign states worldwide and member states in international organizations resulted from decolonization and independence movements worldwide that asserted sovereignty that was recognized by the international community. This increase has significantly affected global policy making.

Most multinational treaties made before the Second World War and intergovernmental organizations established thereafter involved relatively few signatories by today's standard. The International Telegraph Convention of 1865, for example, was signed by 20 countries, primarily European and adjacent states. That number grew as telegraph cables were laid globally. When the World Intellectual Property Organization (WIPO) was founded in 1967, 51 states signed the agreement.

Intergovernmental organizations governing media and communications are made up of member states and sometimes other territories, autonomous regions, industry organizations and firms that have observer or some form of associate membership status with limited participation rights. Member states take part in actual treaty construction and approval but may consider concerns and advice from non-member states and organizations.

The number of member states of the major intergovernmental organizations contributing to global governance of media and communications now includes most states. The International Telecommunication Union now has 193 member states; the World International Property Organization now has 191 member states; the Universal Postal Union has 192, and the World Trade Organization has 164 member states.

The rise in membership in these organizations has had a significant influence on their operations and governance activities. In earlier years, Western nations tended to play decisive roles in directing the organizations and their global governance activities because they were the primary signatories. Although there is still significant influence from Western nations, their influence has been reduced by the larger number of member states, many of whom consult each other and coordinate their efforts to pursue mutual interests and can now outvote Western and other major economic powers in the organizations.

The broader membership has pushed intergovernmental organizations to pursue issues of greater interest to countries outside the West. These have included development agendas, crafting exceptions to treaties that benefit poorer nations and recognizing concerns of states with non-Western values and political approaches. The larger number of states, differing political philosophies and varying interests requires increased negotiation among member states in creating new policy and regulation.

Factors Influencing State Positions on Global Policy

National interests play fundamental roles in the policy positions states take in international governance. Varying national philosophies, interests and priorities affect international policy making. Because the policy is negotiated among states, each state engages in the policy debate within a framework of their own perspectives, approaches to policy and national interests that they want to advance or protect.

In preparing for international policy discussions, national agencies overseeing media and communication, trade and culture generally prepare policy documents outlining their interests and concerns. Consultations are held with their agency leaders and other executive personnel to decide on how the government will instruct its representatives and diplomatic personnel taking part in discussions and negotiations at the global level.

A wide variety of factors influence the positions taken on global policy by governments in this decision-making process, shown in Fig. 5.2.

In considering potential policy, the initial concerns of states tend to focus on the amount of sovereignty that must be ceded to the intergovernmental organization regarding the policy, whether the policy presents any national security

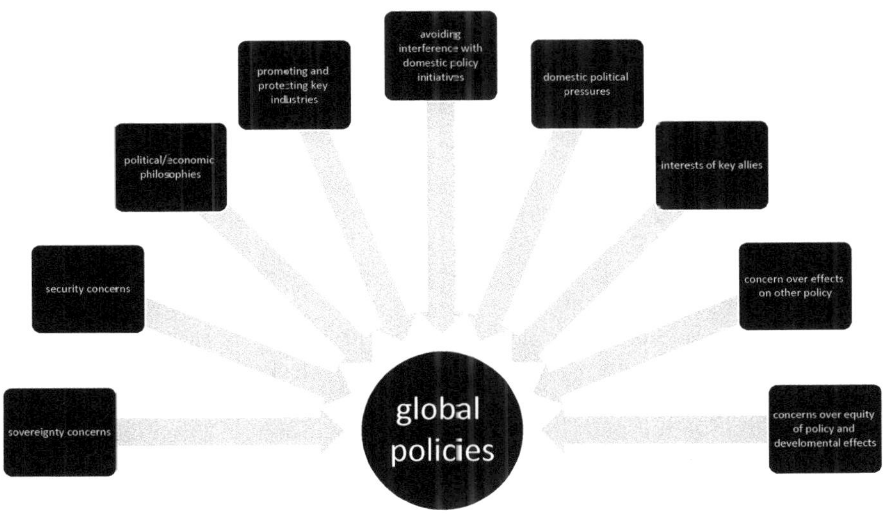

Fig. 5.2 Influences on global policies

issues, and the extent to which proposed policy is aligned with dominant political and economic philosophies of the state.

Significant attention is given to the effect of proposed policies on key industries in states. Thus, states whose media and communications industries produce large amounts of intellectual property tend to ensure that the rights to that property are protected globally. States with large electronics manufacturing industries desire policies that standardize technical requirements, so their products are usable globally or can be easily adapted to differing regional standards. Similarly, concerns about how proposed policy might affect domestic policy initiatives, such as state subsidies for broadband development or the state's international broadcasting activities, are considered.

Domestic political pressures from political parties, industry associations and citizens groups are weighed in decisions, as well as pressure from key state allies promoting their interests. States generally tend to harmonize their policy approaches with their positions on other policy issues taken in international governance so that reasonable consistency is maintained. Finally, they may consider the equity of the position on other nations or effects on developments in other nations if they have a commitment to global economic and social progress.

When analyzing policy and policy making, it is important to identify and understand the importance of the different factors on a country's positions and how those factors compare to those of other countries in the process.

The Four Primary Intergovernmental Organizations Involved in Media/Communications Policy Making

International Telecommunication Union

The ITU is the oldest of communications governance organizations, established in 1865 to coordinate telegraph traffic and standardize practices among nations (Lyall 2016). It became a specialized UN agency in 1947. As telephone and radio technologies emerged, it began carrying out similar functions needed for them to operate and it now carries out a wide variety of activities involving fixed telephones, wireless communication, broadcasting and satellite communications (Codding Jr. and Rutkowski 1982; Allison 2014).

Its most significant tasks today are the governance of radio spectrum that is used for broadcasting, mobile phones, navigation at sea, in the air and on the ground, and even radio-controlled models and toys. It sets technical and operational standards that are used worldwide in all telecommunications fields to ensure compatibility and interoperability.

The organization is made up of member states. Hundreds of members from the private sector involved in telecommunications also take part in various sector activities, particularly in standards creation, but do not take part in the diplomatic decision-making.

The Necessity of Global Radio Spectrum Management

All types of communications today rely on the use of the electromagnetic spectrum that involves energy radiation in the form of electromagnetic waves. Although the production, distribution and detection of radio, microwaves, ultraviolet, infrared, visible light and x-ray waves differ, they all are dependent upon use of portions of the electromagnetic spectrum. Because the spectrum used for these and other activities is a natural phenomenon not constrained by national boundaries or unique to earth itself, the need to coordinate use among states became rapidly evident (Cave and Webb 2016).

Use of radio spectrum became fundamental to contemporary communication in the late nineteenth century with the creation of wireless telegraphy. Since that time uses of radio spectrum have expanded momentously to include such diverse uses as two-way radio, radio and television broadcasting, satellite communications, mobile telephones and Wi-Fi.

Fundamental challenges in use of frequency ranges in the radio spectrum are that some frequencies are better for some uses than others and that if two operators in proximity to each other use the same frequency, it creates interference that makes it unusable for both. These issues led to global radio spectrum governance more than a century ago, with the recognition that sovereign states control use of spectrum within their boundaries.

The International Telecommunication Union was tasked with overseeing spectrum and allocating frequencies to states for choices of how to use them. Assignments are made by the ITU Radiocommunication Bureau. The ITU Plenipotentiary Conference every four years sets general policy carried out by the secretariat and its administrative sectors, considers treaty revisions and oversees allocation decisions by the Radiocommunication Bureau. When frequency allocations are made to states, it is up to the communication agency(ies) of the state to determine how it is used, who will use it and the processes employed in making those decisions (Mazar 2016).

The ITU works with regional groups because of the proximity of states and common interests in effective regional frequency management. In Europe, creating and improving regional spectrum management has existed since the creation of the European Community in the 1950s, but actual use decisions remain in the hands of national authorities. European coordination of policy is undertaken by the Conférence Européenne des Postes et Télécommunications through the European Radiocommunications Office, working together with the European Union and national governments (Ryan 2005).

Most countries' frequencies for military use are managed separately from frequencies for civilian use, which can create policy conflicts. The development and rollout of Bluetooth technology in Europe, for example, was slowed by French government opposition to the spectrum frequency sought, because it was already in use for other purposes by the French military.

Universal Postal Union

The Universal Postal Union was created in 1874 by the multinational Treaty of Berne to establish a global postal system based on the domestic postal services of member states. The UPU established common policy for sending and receiving mail, replacing individual bilateral agreements that were previously the norm.

The need for global postal governance was spurred by the rise of literacy and postal use in Europe and North America, the need for communications with colonies and trade centers worldwide, and global immigration (Codding Jr 1964; Walsh 2000). Nations with significant needs and interests in international services, such as the United States, engage in significant efforts to influence the course of the international postal policies (John 2015).

UPU policy establishes standards for mail size and weight, establishes common rates for international postage, ensures that foreign and domestic mail are handled similarly and creates payment formulas among nations based on the total weight of mail exchanged. The Union became a specialized agency of the United Nations in 1948. It currently has 190 member states (Lyall 2016). The UPU oversees the international movement of letters, express mail and parcels and is working to establish a global electronic postal system.

Members meet at the Universal Postal Congress every four years to consider changes to the UPU's operations, policies and regulations.

World Intellectual Property Organization

Copyright and related rights cover such materials as press and literature, motion pictures and video, radio and television content, photography, visual and graphic arts, music and theatrical productions, and software and databases. The existence of rights allows their owners to sell or license the use of the copyrighted materials. The rights cover reproduction, translation, adaptation, arrangement, alteration, public performance, broadcast, communication to the public, distribution and rental of the copyrighted material.

WIPO was created in 1967 and is charged with overseeing multiple forms of intellectual property, including copyrights and patents. WIPO replaced the United International Bureaux for the Protection of Intellectual Property that had been created to administer the Berne Convention. WIPO administers existing copyright and related rights treaties and is the coordinating organization when new forms of rights are established and put forward in treaties (May 2006). The organization has 191 member states but is increasingly integrating a wider variety of private stakeholders into its activities (Kwakwa 2006).

Internationalizing Copyright and Related Rights

Copyright and related rights are property rights defined, given and enforced by states that protect economic value for the owner with the purpose of spurring greater production. Copyrights are granted by national laws that apply only within their sovereign territory. This limitation thus does not provide protection outside the country granting the property right. As trade increased in the nineteenth century, efforts to provide protection internationally emerged and became the impetus for the Berne Convention for the Protection of Literary and Artistic Works in 1886. This treaty obligated states that signed the convention to recognize and protect copyrights granted by other states who were also signatories. Ten countries initially ratified the treaty and that number has grown to 175. The convention became the basis of global policy making involving copyright and related rights as newer communications technologies emerged.

Global policy making involving copyright is primarily under the governance of the World Intellectual Property Organization, a specialized intergovernmental organization of the United Nations. The general processes for policy making through the creation of a new treaty is seen in Fig. 5.3 and generally similar elements and processes are used by other intergovernmental organizations.

In this process, the Standing Committee on Copyright and Related Rights considers emerging copyright issues and means for coordination of laws internationally. As part of its work, it can forward recommendations to the WIPO General Assembly for a diplomatic conference to address a specific issue through a proposed treaty. The General Assembly determines whether there is enough interest among member states to call a diplomatic conference, which finalizes negotiations on a treaty and obtains approval of diplomats representing their member states.

The initial acceptance by country representatives approving the treaty at diplomatic conferences must then return to their member states for ratification and implementation in national law.

Fig. 5.3 Governance processes of WIPO

World Trade Organization

The World Trade Organization is not a communication policy-setting body per se but establishes policy governing international trade and has been used to create specific policy related to media and communications products and services.

The intergovernmental organization grew out of the General Agreement on Tariffs and Trade signed in 1948 to begin standardizing taxation and trading practices to improve international trade. The agreement has been revised several times and became a treaty overseen by the World Trade Organization when it was established under an agreement of 124 countries in 1994 (van den Bossche and Zdouc 2013). WTO governs trade in goods, services and intellectual property rights and provides mechanisms for dispute resolution among signatory states (Matthews 2003; Hoekman and Mavroidis 2015).

The General Agreement on Trade in Services lays out principles governing audiovisual services such as motion pictures, television programming and radio and television broadcasts and other distribution services (Geradín and Luff 2004). Trade policy involving audiovisual products and services has been highly contentious because many nations do not agree to provisions requiring their entry because of cultural and political policy reasons.

Governance particularly significant to media and communications appeared in the Trade-Related Aspects of Intellectual Property Rights Agreement governance, which specifically addressed intellectual property rights including copyright and digital rights management, providing multinational media and communications companies greater protections for the rights they owned and traded (Matthews 2003; May 2009). In addition to general trading governance, the provisions strengthened antipiracy measures but weakened cultural protections for film and audiovisual content (Pauwels and Loisen 2003).

Many scholars of the political economy of communications have criticized WTO governance as favoring large nations and multinational firms, making it difficult for developing nations to develop internal media and communications systems and content, and reducing democratic debate on policy measures (Winseck 2002; May 2009; Iosifidis 2011). Policy makers in the nations agreeing to place their nations under the provisions of WTO treaties did so prioritizing perceived trade benefits higher than domestic media and communications benefits of not ratifying the treaties. The extent to which the public worldwide understood and could influence that prioritization varied.

Nongovernmental Organizations in Global Communications Governance

In addition to intergovernmental organizations, nongovernmental international organizations play important roles in governance, setting policies to structure and guide media and communications activities. The role of all private governance has grown significantly in recent decade and is increasingly seen as a legitimate exercise of authority (Hall and Biersteker 2002). This private governance is voluntary and typically involves issues of technology standards, accepted practices and other forms of self-regulation. This private policy making affects the structures and operating principles of much modern communications technology.

The European Telecommunications Standards Institute, for example, is an independent, not-for-profit organization of telecommunications and broadcast equipment makers, network operators, service providers, broadcasters and others that establishes technical standards for fixed and mobile telephony, broadcasting and internet technologies so that interoperability and connectively is promoted. Its digital television standard is the most used throughout the world.

The Internet Corporation for Assigned Names and Numbers (ICANN) is a not-for-profit international organization that creates policies that underlie the operations of the internet worldwide. It coordinates the assignment of identification addresses necessary for routing messages through the internet (Kleinwächter 2000). ICANN was established as part of privatization of technical functions previously undertaken by the U.S. government, and it maintains address and internet protocol systems, provides name dispute resolution and carries other related functions that are crucial for internet operability. The technical functions and processes of ICANN allow it to act as a private internet governance mechanism (Klein 2002; Musiani et al. 2015). Because it is central to the internet system, ICANN has faced criticism from many observers and governments. It has been suggested that ICANN become an intergovernmental organization under the United Nations, but it remains a multi-stakeholder private organization (Braman 2006).

Another important international organization, the International Electrotechnical Commission, provides basic electrical standards and disclosure information for electrical and electronic devices, including consumer devices in telecommunications, computing and other personal electric devices. It works closely with national electrical standards organizations and manufacturers to carry out its purposes of coordinating and overseeing practices in the production of electrical equipment.

Small States and Global Governance

The ability of countries to engage internationally and to influence international policies varies significantly, with larger nations often using their economic weight, technological expertise and geopolitical influences to promote advantageous international law and treaties.

The inferior ability of smaller countries to influence world affairs has led smaller countries to put greater emphasis on international organizations and alliances in their relations with powerful states and economic interests (Panke 2012). Because it is difficult for them to achieve parity in negotiations of bilateral treaties with larger countries, they tend to favor participation in multinational organizations such as the specialized agencies, for example, International

Telecommunication Union, World Intellectual Property Organization and World Trade Organization, in dealings with communications issues and in the multinational treaties established by those entities. These preferences have been explored by political science and policy studies as small state theory that explores how they navigate between forces and interests of larger states and their own (Vital 1967; Rothstein 1968; Keohane 1969; Elman 1995; Panke 2012).

In policy making smaller countries face policy challenges different from larger states because they have differing public resources and capabilities for communications infrastructures and operations and smaller regulatory agencies with lessor expertise. Such factors make fashioning communications systems, as well as domestic policies to support identity, cultural and domestic political needs, challenging (Puppis 2009). Consequently, when faced with complex issues policy makers and regulators in many smaller states tend to mimic policies developed in larger countries or follow the recommendations of multinational organizations.

Even those with stronger national policy making sometimes have difficulty resisting the momentum of international policy making.

Challenges in Global Governance

Global governance differs from the state-based modes of regulation because collective policy making tends to be horizontal rather than top-down; it moves policy away from the participation of those affected by the outcomes, and it tends to promote newer forms of policy making and governance such as co-regulation and self-regulation (Raboy and Padovani 2010). Because it is distant and less directly accountable to the public, its legitimacy is dependent upon the transparency, impartiality and responsiveness of its institutional structures and processes and the policy it creates (Ó Siochrú et al. 2002).

Some fundamental factors challenge global governance activities and affect the abilities of states and media and communications firms to influence decision-making.

The development and spread of satellite and internet communications have created conditions in which transborder communications is the norm. This has reduced the impact of national media and communications policies on the domestic environment and diminished national sovereignty (Price 2002; Picard et al. 2016).

A major challenge is the degree of democratic governance of global institutions, particularly in private nongovernmental international organizations. Even in intergovernmental organizations there are concerns about the extent to which member states represent the interests of citizens and democratic communications practices, because the types of governments involved vary widely, including many authoritarian states and states in which policy capture has taken place. Issues of who decides what, for what purposes and objectives, and with what effects are central to debates and concerns about the degree of democratic participation and representation in the processes (Braman 2006; Mueller et al. 2007).

Another challenge involves pressures for and against policy making by global media and communications firms and the states in which they were originated. These actors often seek policy that supports their development and strategies and work to stop policy that might conflict with their interests. States from which companies originate typically have significant economic and incentives to ensure their success globally (Mikler 2018). Other interests that might play more significant roles in domestic policy making, such as equity issues and effects on citizens and democracy, tend to be given less import in their decisions of policy to pursue at the global level.

Inequities in global policy making based on national size and economic advantage are also a challenge. Countries with larger economies tend to utilize more types of media and communications systems and radio spectrum, for example. In global policy making they tend to have more capacity and experience in dealing with the requirements of these technologies and have previously made policy at the domestic and regional levels that may influence the policy trajectory at the global level. In addition, they tend to exercise their influence and power over other states with which they have had historical ties or that are economically dependent upon them. They also tend to use their influence in multiple intergovernmental and private international organizations to pursue preferential policies and then to seek coordination across organizations that are beneficial (Karns et al. 2015).

History, Politics, Economics and Culture Affect Perceptions of Global Policy Making

Global media and communications policy making are affected by underlying concerns in countries based on their histories, political systems, level of development, culture and perceived power. These factors influence perceptions of policies proposed by other states and the kinds of policies that are deemed desirable.

Policy makers in post-colonial countries are concerned about influences of their former colonial masters. When global policy proposals are put forward, they often consider them through this lens to determine whether the policy is a means of economic or political subjugation. In terms of media and communications, they are concerned whether it will give advantages to firms from their former rulers against their own companies and thus undermine their independence and sovereignty.

Countries south of the equator, even those without colonial histories, tend to worry about the influences of countries with strong economies north of the equator and how they might affect their economies and development. Eastern countries worry about policy influences from Western countries for political, economic and development reasons, but also for significant cultural reasons when media and communications are involved. The BRICS nations tend to question global media and communications policy for all the above reasons, but especially for any potentially negative effects on their increasing development and economic growth.

Western nations tend to perceive global policy making in terms of how it will affect trade, domestic economics and firms from their countries. They also consider policy proposed by others in terms of any effects it may have on freedom of expression, democracy and other values in Western political philosophy.

Small states are particularly concerned about large neighbors for political and economic reasons. In media and communications, they are concerned about global policies that may affect their culture and identity by providing overwhelming access to media and communications companies from the larger countries, as well as to economic losses that their economies may experience from the use of those products.

As the number of member states involved in global policy making in media and communications increases, the ability of global media and communications companies and the states from which they originated to exploit global opportunities is reduced because other countries often jointly pursue their interests and force greater negotiation with advantaged parties. Sometimes they can pursue policies unnecessary or undesirable to more powerful countries. In such cases, powerful parties may ignore them, actively oppose them or refuse to accept them. This issue has led to an increased focus on private or nongovernmental policy.

Inequities based on size or inequities based on technological advantages are also a challenge. Nations with highly developed technologies and technological production can produce media and communications systems and operations that can spread globally well ahead of global policy development. These nations tend to seek policies early to support technological innovation. The full implications may not be seen by other nations or set policy trajectories that are difficult to alter later. Because of their technical expertise and experience, advanced nations often make significant use of intergovernmental and nongovernmental international organizations to influence acceptance of standards and practices before additional treaty developments may be required (Klein 2002; Hall and Biersteker 2002; Haufler 2013).

Although global policies or their absence have drawn significant attention as globalization of media and communications has increased in the past five decades, global policy making remains relatively limited to facilitating communications, encouraging the flow of content products and protecting the value of content products. Both proponents of policies supporting globalization and their critics have brought great attention to global governance, often at the cost of diminishing attention to domestic policy. This has often conveyed the erroneous perception that domestic policy and regional policy has lost importance, primarily because of the dominance of global policy discourse and a lag in domestic policy makers responding to global developments (Flew et al. 2016).

Chapter Summary

- Policy making at the global level addresses media and communications issues that need to be addressed with cross-national policy and law.
- Only countries that agree to comply with global policies are subject to them under international law.
- Global policy making is based on multinational treaties.
- Global governance of communications and media activities has existed for about 150 years.
- Intergovernmental organizations are governance groups that have states as decision-making members.
- Global media and communications activities are affected by both specialized and more general policy-making bodies.
- Nongovernmental international organizations affect some aspects of media and communications, including standards and accepted practices.
- Inequities exist in global policy making that tends to advantage large, economically powerful and technologically advanced countries.

Discussion Points

1. Why is it possible for countries with widely varying political philosophies and systems to come to an agreement on some policies?
2. If a state isn't a party to a multinational treaty, can its media and communications system still be influenced by it?
3. What happens when a state has agreed to a treaty that is subsequently amended, and the state does not agree with the amendments?
4. Why do some observers and states believe that private international governance is less democratic than that in intergovernmental organizations?
5. What advantages do technologically advantaged states have in governance activities?

Bibliography

Allison, Audrey L. 2014. *The ITU and Managing Satellite Orbital and Spectrum Resources in the 21st Century*. Berlin: Springer.

Aust, Anthony. 2014. *Modern Treaty Law and Practice*. 3rd ed. Cambridge: Cambridge University Press.

Biersteker, Thomas J., and Cynthia Weber, eds. 1996. *State Sovereignty as a Social Construct*. Cambridge: Cambridge University Press.

Braman, Sandra, ed. 2006. *The Emergent Global Information Policy Regime*. London: Palgrave Macmillan.
Castells, Manuel. 2008. The New Public Sphere: Global Civil Society, Communication Networks, and Global Governance. *The Annals of the American Academy of Political and Social Science* 616 (1): 78–93.
Cave, Martin, and William Webb. 2016. *Spectrum Management: Using the Airwaves for Maximum Social and Economic Benefit*. Cambridge: Cambridge University Press.
Codding, George A., Jr. 1964. *The Universal Postal Union: Coordinator of the International Mails*. New York: New York University Press.
Codding, George A., Jr., and Anthony M. Rutkowski. 1982. *The International Telecommunication Union in a Changing World*. Boston: Artech House.
Commission for Communications Regulation and Ofcom, Band IV/V Bilateral Co-ordination Agreement Between the Administrations of Ireland and the United Kingdom of Great Britain and Northern Ireland, June 2012. http://static.ofcom.org.uk/static/broadcasting/Web_Ireland_United%20Kingdom%20800MHz%20DTT%20Clearance%20Agreement_06July12.pdf. Accessed 11 Nov 2018.
Crawford, James. 2012. *Brownlie's Principles of Public International Law*. 8th ed. Oxford: Oxford University Press.
Elman, Miriam Fendius. 1995. The Foreign Policies of Small States: Challenging Neorealism in Its Own Backyard. *British Journal of Political Science* 25 (2): 171–217.
Flew, Terry, Petros Iosifidis, and Jeanette Steemers, eds. 2016. *Global Media and National Policies: The Return of the State*. London: Palgrave Macmillan.
Frederking, Brian, and Paul F. Diehl, eds. 2015. *The Politics of Global Governance: International Organizations in an Interdependent World*. 5th ed. Boulder: Lynne Rienner Publishers.
Geradín, Damien, and David Luff, eds. 2004. *The WTO and Global Convergence in Telecommunications and Audio-Visual Services*. Cambridge: Cambridge University Press.
Glenn, Carol M. 2017. *Controlling Cyberspace: The Politics of Internet Governance and Regulation*. Santa Barbara: Praeger.
Graz, Jean-Christophe, and Andreas Nölke, eds. 2008. *Transnational Private Governance and Its Limits*. London: Routledge.
Hall, Rodney B., and Thomas J. Biersteker, eds. 2002. *The Emergence of Private Authority in Global Governance*. Cambridge: Cambridge University Press.
Harrington, Alexandria. 2018. *International Organizations and the Law*. London: Routledge.
Haufler, Virginia. 2013. *A Public Role for the Private Sector: Industry Self-Regulation in a Global Economy*. New York: Carnegie Endowment for World Peace.
Hill, Richard. 2014. *The New International Telecommunication Regulations and the Internet: A Commentary and Legislative History*. Berlin: Springer.
Hoekman, Bernard M., and Petros C. Mavroidis. 2015. *World Trade Organization (WTO): Law, Economics, and Politics*. 2nd ed. London: Routledge.
Hofbauer, Jane A. 2016. *Sovereignty in the Exercise of the Right to Self-Determination*. Leiden: Martinus Nijhoff.
Hollis, Duncan B. 2014. *The Oxford Guide to Treaties*. Oxford: Oxford University Press.
Holsti, K.J. 2004. *Taming the Sovereigns: Institutional Change in International Politics*. Cambridge: Cambridge University Press.
Iosifidis, Petros. 2011. *Global Media and Communication Policy: An International Perspective*. London: Palgrave Macmillan.

John, Richard R. 2015. Projecting Power Oversees: U.S. Postal Policy and International Standards Setting at the 1863 Paris Postal Conference. *Journal of Policy History* 27 (3): 416–438.

Karns, Margaret P., Karen A. Mingst, and Kendall W. Stiles. 2015. *International Organizations: The Politics and Processes of Global Governance*. 3rd ed. Boulder: Lynne Rienner Publishers.

Keohane, Robert O. 1969. Lilliputians' Dilemmas: Small States in International Politics. *International Organization* 23 (2): 291–310.

Klein, Hans. 2002. ICANN and Internet Governance: Leveraging Technical Coordination to Realize Global Public Policy. *The Information Society: An International Journal* 18 (3): 193–207.

Kleinwächter, Wolfgang. 2000. ICANN Between Technical Mandate and Political Challenges. *Telecommunications Policy* 24 (6–7): 553–563.

Kreijen, Gerald, ed. 2002. *State, Sovereignty, and International Governance*. Oxford: Oxford University Press.

Kwakwa, Edward. 2006. Institutional and Procedural Reform at the World Intellectual Property Organization. *International Organizations Law Review* 3 (1): 143–152.

Lyall, Francis. 2016. *International Communications: The International Telecommunication Union and the Universal Postal Union*. London: Routledge.

Lyons, Gene M., and Michael Mastanduno, eds. 1995. *Beyond Westphalia?: National Sovereignty and International Intervention*. Baltimore: Johns Hopkins University Press.

Mansell, Robin, and Marc Raboy, eds. 2014. *The Handbook of Global Media and Communication Policy*. Oxford: Wiley-Blackwell.

Matthews, Duncan. 2003. *Globalizing Intellectual Property Rights: The TRIPS Agreement*. London: Taylor & Francis.

May, Christopher. 2006. *World Intellectual Property Organization (WIPO): Resurgence and Development Agenda*. London: Routledge.

———. 2009. *The Global Political Economy of Intellectual Property Rights: The New Enclosures*. 2nd ed. London: Taylor & Francis.

Mazar (Madjar), Haim. 2016. Radio Spectrum Management: Policies. In *Regulations and Techniques*. Chichester: Wiley.

McLaughlin, Lisa, and Victor Pickard. 2005. What Is Bottom-Up About Internet Governance? *Global Media and Communication* 1 (3): 357–373.

Mikler, John. 2018. *The Political Power of Global Corporations*. Cambridge: Polity.

Mueller, Milton L., Brenden N. Kuerbis, and Christiane Pagé. 2007. Democratizing Global Communication? Global Civil Society and the Campaign for Communication Rights in the Information Society. *International Journal of Communication* 1 (1): 267–296.

Musiani, Francesca, Derrick L. Cogburn, Laura DeNardis, and Nanette S. Levinson, eds. 2015. *The Turn to Infrastructure in Internet Governance*. London: Palgrave Macmillan.

Ó Siochrú, Sean, Bruce Girard, and Amy Mahan. 2002. *Global Media Governance: A Beginner's Guide*. Lanham: Rowman and Littlefield.

Panke, Diana. 2012. Small States in Multilateral Negotiations. What Have We Learned? *Cambridge Review of International Affairs* 25 (3): 387–398.

Pauwels, Caroline, and Jan Loisen. 2003. The WTO and the Audiovisual Sector: Economic Free Trade or Cultural Horse Trading. *European Journal of Communication* 18 (3): 291–313.

Picard, Robert G., Charles Davis, Franco Papandrea, and Sora Park. 2016. Platform Proliferation and Its Implications for Domestic Content Policies. *Telematics and Informatics* 33: 683–692.
Price, Monroe. 2002. *Media and Sovereignty: The Global Information Revolution and Its Challenge to State Power*. Boston: MIT Press.
Raboy, Marc, and Claudia Padovani. 2010. Mapping Global Media Policy: Concepts, Frameworks, Methods. *Communication, Culture & Critique* 3 (2): 150–169.
Rothstein, Robert L. 1968. *Alliances and Small Powers*. New York: Columbia University Press.
Ryan, Patrick S. 2005. European Spectrum Management Principles. *Journal of Computer and Information Law* 23: 277–324.
Sarooshi, Dan. 2005. *International Organizations and Their Exercise of Sovereign Powers*. Oxford: Oxford University Press.
Shaw, Malcolm M. 2017. *International Law*. 8th ed. Cambridge: Cambridge University Press.
van den Bossche, Peter, and Werner Zdouc. 2013. *The Law and Policy of the World Trade Organization*. 3rd ed. Cambridge: Cambridge University Press.
Vital, David. 1967. *The Inequality of States: A Study of Small Power in International Relations*. Oxford: Oxford University Press.
Walsh, Tim. 2000. Globalization, Posts, and the Universal Postal Union: A Functional Critique. In *Current Directions in Postal Reform*, ed. Michael A. Crew and Paul R. Kleindorfer, 483–506. Boston: Springer.
Weber, Rolf H. 2009. *Shaping Internet Governance: Regulatory Challenges*. Berlin: Springer.
Winseck, Dwayne. 2002. The WTO, Emerging Policy Regimes and the Political Economy of Transnational Communications. In *Global Media Policy in the New Millennium*, ed. Marc Raboy, 19–38. Luton: University of Luton Press.

Suggested Readings

Hoekman, Bernard M., and Petros C. Mavroidis. 2015. *World Trade Organization (WTO): Law, Economics, and Politics*. London: Routledge.
Iosifidis, Petros. 2011. *Global Media and Communication Policy: An International Perspective*. London: Palgrave Macmillan.
Ó Siochrú, Sean, Bruce Girard, and Amy Mahan. 2002. *Global Media Governance: A Beginner's Guide*. Lanham: Rowman and Littlefield.
Raboy, Marc, and Claudia Padovani. 2010. Mapping Global Media Policy: Concepts, Frameworks, Methods. *Communication, Culture & Critique* 3 (2): 150–169.
Puppis, Manuel. 2009. Media Regulation in Small States. *International Communication Gazette* 71 (1–2): 7–17.

CHAPTER 6

Regional Policy Making

Regional policy making occurs when states in regions of the world undertake forms of intergovernmental cooperation and governance. It results from common interests, from experiencing similar challenges and from shared cultural traits or political philosophies, in response to the disinterest of global policy makers in the issues, from perceptions that global processes will not be effective or efficient, and sometimes as a prelude to global policy making.

Regional governance can also go beyond global governance to take additional steps, to adapt global policy to the specifics of the region and to work cooperatively to implement both global and regional policy measures.

In most parts of the world, regional common interests and concerns have led to the development of cooperation through regional intergovernmental organizations that have grown significantly in recent decades (Hawdon 1996). These typically take the forms of regional councils, associations and cooperative networks and most typically developed from earlier bilateral and larger multinational intergovernmental meetings.

Regional cooperation initially emerged to deal with security cooperation, economic stability and trade issues, and these issues tended to generate significant support among nations for regional intergovernmental organizations (Volgy et al. 2009). Over time, these governance organizations have expanded their scopes, or additional ones have been created, to address issues such as the environment, health, education, migration, humanitarian assistance, energy and communications. Some competition among the intergovernmental organizations for membership exists so support for organizations varies in regions throughout the world. There are also differences in the organizational structures, operations and membership (Acharya and Johnston 2007; Reinalda 2013). At times, some nations join intergovernmental organizations in order to participate, even if they are not fully supportive of the values and activities of the organizations, because they can engage in internal resistance to governance.

R. G. Picard, *Media and Communications Policy Making*, Palgrave Global Media Policy and Business,
https://doi.org/10.1007/978-3-030-35173-1_6

Other members may find it difficult to incentivize or coerce them into more cooperative activities (Fawn 2013).

The regional governance classification is often fluid, tending to be one of convenience. In some cases, it is used to include all countries on continents and subcontinents or smaller groupings of nations under those categories. In many cases, the regional category is linked to existence of the cooperative institutions that have been established and the states affiliating with them. Contemporary regionalism is an extension of the internationalism formed in the second half of the twentieth century at the global level and the interest blocs that emerged among contiguous and proximate states. In many cases, regionalism began with bilateral relationships that expanded into multinational relations among several and many nearby nations. It has the advantage of bringing policy making closer to the locations affected.

As with global governance, participation in regional cooperation and governance is voluntary and involves much diplomacy because of sovereignty issues and differing national interests involved. Most regional organizations are structured and operate in accordance with the general principles and practices of intergovernmental organizations at the global level. More nongovernmental organizations tend to become more involved in regional governance activities than global activities.

Regional intergovernmental organizations include larger organizations such as the African Union, Arab Union, Association of Southeast Asian Nations, Council of Europe, European Union (EU) and Organization of American States. Many smaller sub-regional organizations such as the Caribbean Community, Economic Community of West African States and Nordic Council serve smaller regions. The EU is the most expansive and integrated of the regional governance organizations (Ginsberg 2010; Leonard and Taylor 2016), and cooperation and governance in Asia are also well developed through multiple organizations (Cheema et al. 2011; Rothman et al. 2017). The frequency with which regional governance organizations deal with media and communication issues, the types of issues in which they engage and the extent to which member starts are bound to follow their actions vary.

Regional policy making does not take the place of global or domestic policy making but allows countries to jointly address common issues with nearby states. Regional policy making can take place through bilateral agreements or multinational agreements, which tend to be completed more quickly at the regional level than at the global level because fewer national interests are involved. Policy making is not required to choose between multinational or bilateral objectives but can employ both to achieve objectives, as has been the case in trade in media products and services (Calabrese and Briziarelli 2011). Direct cooperation among regional policy makers is increasing outside the global governance mechanisms (Canedo and Crusafon 2014).

The creation of communications infrastructures and their improvement are important objectives globally because they are perceived as backbones to regional development, facilitate business and trade, and contribute to the growth of national and regional economies (Saunders 1983; Qiang and Pitt 2003; Torero and von Braun 2006; Stephenson 2008).

The economics of telecommunications make regional cooperation desirable (Cecot and Wallsten 2009). A significant impetus for regional policy making in telecommunications has also been resistance to transferring policy and regulation from advanced nations, particularly in the Northern Hemisphere. That influence was possible because global intergovernmental organizations have a strong influence through networks and interactions worldwide (Kim and Barnett 2000). The growth of regional policy making is still influenced by those organizations but has facilitated the abilities of member nations to have more influence in the development and enactment of policy than previously possible at the global level (Wavre 2018).

Influences on the Strength of Regional Governance

A variety of factors influence the capabilities and strength of regional governance organizations (Fig. 6.1). These affect the ability of intergovernmental organizations to establish and implement policies.

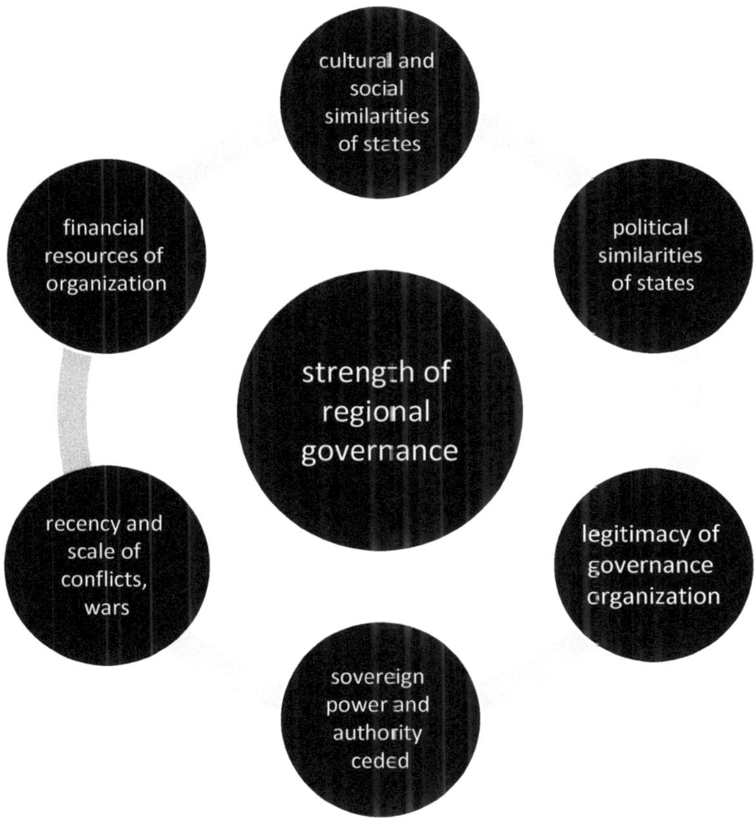

Fig. 6.1 Factors influencing the strength of regional governance

The degree of cultural and social similarities of states in the organization affects how nations perceive and trust each other and understand their similar interests. Political similarities of states also affect how they relate to each other. A regional governance organization made up solely of democracies is likely to have more strength than one including democracies, monarchies and authoritarian states because states share more common political philosophies and systems.

The legitimacy of the governance organization, that is, the extent to which it is perceived as having rightful authority and influence, will affect its strength. That legitimacy is directly affected by the amount of sovereign power and authority ceded by member states.

The financial resources at the regional governance organization's disposal significantly affect its strength. Many regional intergovernmental organizations have limited financial resources to allocate to activities promoted in policy, such as construction of communications infrastructures. Consequently, they can only urge members to assist, facilitate the investments or leave financing to global or regional development banks. When member states provide significant financial resources, the organization can directly support activities promoted in policy.

Influences on Policy Activities and Choices

The range of policy activities and policy decisions made in regional intergovernmental organizations varies significantly, as do the implementation of policy and the abilities of the organizations to require actions by member states. This occurs because of multiple influences on the activities and choices (Fig. 6.2).

Policies made in global governance have an influence on regional governance if member states are bound by the global policy making. World Trade Organization (WTO) policies and treaties have been particularly significant and have influenced regional trade agreements regarding media, communications and cultural products and intellectual property rights. International Telecommunication Union (ITU) policies and procedures are passed down and often work through regional governance organizations.

The dominant ideologies of states in regions affect policy approaches and frameworks utilized in regional governance, as do regional interests and needs that may differ from those in other regions or globally. Dominant members of regional intergovernmental organizations influence policy making by exercising power and influence over processes and other states. Countries such as Brazil, Germany, the United States, Russia, China, India, South Africa, the United Arab Emirates, Iran and Saudi Arabia exercise significant influence in their regions because of both physical and economic size.

The interests of stakeholders in policy affect the policies of regions. In media and communications issues, for example, the trade and financing interests of major manufacturers of related hardware in China, South Korea, Taiwan and

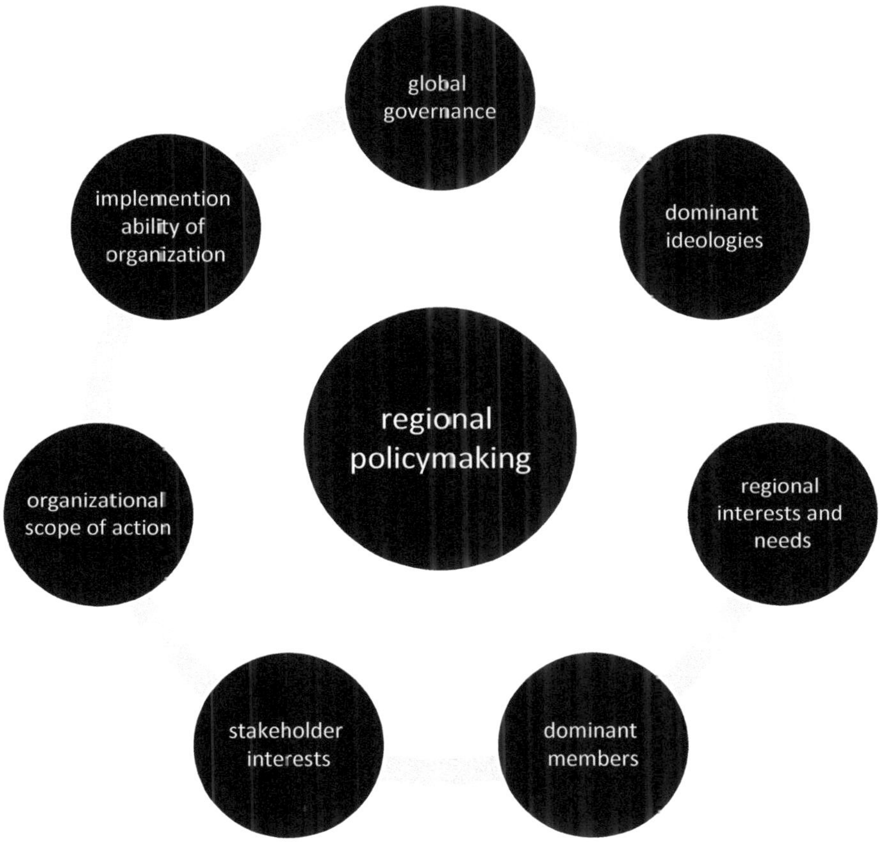

Fig. 6.2 Influences on regional policy activities and choices

Japan work to ensure supportive regional policy or to block detrimental policy, usually with the willing concurrence of their national governments.

The organizational scope of action for regional intergovernmental organizations affects the types of issues addressed and types of actions that they can take. Thus, the organizational treaties for the organizations set out the topics that they will address and their authority to administratively make policy. These vary widely among organizations and are one reason why many new governance organizations focused on specific topics have emerged. The ability of organizations to implement policy is also an important aspect in understanding regional policy making. Organizations with limited administrative staff and structures can rarely undertake policy implementation effectively on their own and thus tend to leave implementation to member states. The oversight of national implementation is also dependent upon the size and effectiveness of the regional organization and the authorities delegated to it to enforce implementation.

The structures and processes of regional governance generally mirror those of global governance, requiring domestic agreement with and commitment to action because of national sovereignty. Consequently, they are created by treaty and their basic structures and process tend to mirror those of global governance, but often in a more streamlined form because of the smaller number of countries involved.

Regional Cooperation and Governance in Media and Communications

In media and communications, regional cooperation and governance is more evident in communications policy than in media policy—except for within the European Union. Most cooperation has pursued common interests in telecommunications infrastructure development, including fixed, mobile, undersea cables, satellite systems and radio spectrum allocation, and in dealing with issues such as cybercrime.

Regional organizations related to the International Telecommunication Union promote technical, interconnectivity and developmental objectives at the regional level. These include the Asia-Pacific Telecommunity, African Telecommunications Union, European Conference of Postal and Telecommunications Administrations, Inter-American Telecommunication Commission, Arab Spectrum Management Group and Regional Commonwealth in the Field of Communications (former Soviet Republics). For spectrum issues, the ITU divides the world into three regions, roughly the Americas, Asia, and Europe, the Middle East, and Russia and former Soviet states, in which the states participate in spectrum management and allocation decisions.

Which Regional Governance Group Should a Country Join?

Governments face an increasing array of regional intergovernmental organizations with which to align. Large nations with significant financial resources and larger numbers of governmental personnel might consider joining many, but the expenses of joining, annual contributions, maintaining representatives, attending meetings and participating in joint projects encourage many countries to choose among the organizations or to participate in more limited ways.

Asian countries, for example, can pick from several dozen organizations ranging from the Asia-Pacific Economic Cooperation to the Centre on Integrated Rural Development for Asia and the Pacific and from the International Network for Bamboo and Rattan to the Asian Productivity Organization.

In addition to the practical decisions of resources, the importance of the intergovernmental organization activities to the nation's needs and priorities play roles in the decision. New Zealand, for example, would have little to gain by participation in the Mekong River Commission and Japan would have little direct interest in the work of the Bay of Bengal Initiative for Multi-Sectoral Technical and Economic Cooperation. More nations might find participation in the Asia-Pacific Economic Cooperation, Association of Southeast Asian Nations, Asia Cooperation Dialogue and Asian Development Bank useful.

Technical cooperation and assistance have been important aspects of regional governance within both the ITU and other organizations closer to the nations involved. Technical cooperation involves a range of activities through which assistance is provided to help assess, plan and implement projects, often involving systems, networks and advanced technologies, when local knowledge and skills are absent or insufficient. It has often been part of foreign aid and development activities of developed nations or voluntarily provided by leading firms. Significant technical assistance was coordinated in telecommunications development through the International Telecommunication Union and its regional branches to help develop strategies, integrate technological advances and upgrade connectivity (Hudson 1991). Technical cooperation in the second half of the twentieth century between major powers and developing nations was often criticized for its lack of focus on building effective local capacity (Berg 1993) and for providing significant benefits and power to Western telecommunications firms (Hills 1994).

Regionally operated cooperation programs organized by bilateral actions and multinational regional organizations have been preferable by countries in many parts of the world, making it possible to share experience and knowledge, within a context less influenced by former colonial states or other major powers. This has led many intergovernmental organizations to develop policies and programs for regional technical cooperation and assistance, particularly in telecommunications.

Historically, one area of significant regional cooperation was in satellite system development, especially during the latter half of the twentieth century. Satellites played and continue to play important roles in telephone calls, broadcasting and internet connections, and are used to exchange news, television programming and television channels among regional states. They have been used strategically to improve basic telephone systems as part of development initiatives (Hudson 2006; Nair 2008; Cochetti 2015) and as direct broadcast satellites in ways that alter domestic broadcasting markets and challenge the abilities of national governments to effectively govern audiovisual content (Negrine 2013).

Many regional satellite systems were developed in and operated through intergovernmental cooperation organizations such as Intelsat, PanAmSat and Intersputnik, with smaller and sub-regional satellite proposals and operations such as ArabSat being developed through regional efforts to meet more localized needs (Berger 2001; Cochetti 2015). Cooperation is undertaken not only to spread costs effectively, but because satellite footprints by technical necessity may serve needs in more than one country.

Many intergovernmental satellite operations have been restructured or privatized in recent years, but some regional operations remain intergovernmental because governments see them as important to continuing regional development efforts (McCormick and Mechanick 2013). Today, however, most satellite communications worldwide remain state or commercially provided. Some regional systems are now private, but states still maintain some financial interests in them.

Policies to promote other telecommunications development through state firms and intergovernmental organizations have been progressively pushed aside by privatization and WTO commitments to liberalizing telecommunications (Mathew and Cottier 2003). This has produced rapid but uneven development of infrastructure by private firms, most with monopolies, and limited public oversight over telephone prices and customer service.

Regional media and communications policy making outside of the European Union has received only limited attention and scholarly research.

Overview of Regional Policy Making in Media and Communications

The purpose of this section is not to address all intergovernmental activities and organizations in the regions affecting media and communications, but to provide a broad understanding of what types of organizations are active in the regions, the types of issues being addressed by regional policy making and trends in policy making.

Africa

With 54 countries, the African continent is one of the most diverse regions of the world. There are different Africas that are often categorized as Saharan, sub-Saharan, central, southern, eastern or western. These have different histories, cultures and varying levels of economic and social development, and they engage differently in African-wide and sub-regional governance.

Major intergovernmental organizations include the African Union, Economic Community of West African States, East African Community, Southern African Development Community, Community of Sahel-Saharan States and Arab Maghreb Union. Most regional policy activities have related primarily to telecommunications rather than media and involved intergovernmental organizations such as the Conference of African Ministers of Transport, Communications and Planning and the African Telecommunications Union.

Much of the interest in communications in Africa was the result of member states gaining independence in the mid-to-late twentieth century and attempting to adapt inherited systems and develop communications systems designed to serve domestic needs. These systems were almost universally state enterprises with aging technologies, insufficient national availability and limited use. The African Telecommunications Union, a specialized agency of the African Union, has been influential in promoting telecommunications planning, cooperation and reform, but its processes and activities have been critiqued for lacking clear strategy and performance standards (McCormick 2005).

African regions and national governments began relying upon assistance provided through the ITU to help evaluate and improve telecommunications and to begin exploring restructuring opportunities (Hudson 1991). Countries in Africa felt increased pressure toward privatization because of the lack of government funds needed for large-scale investments in infrastructures and neoliberal policies promoted by World Bank, International Monetary Fund, and World Trade Organization, but there was reluctance by many governments to give up ownership and control over telecommunications (Noam 1999).

Desires to improve infrastructure and dependence on transnational satellite operations led African states to explore how to establish their own systems. Regional policy making to support developments included the Conference of African Ministers of Transport, Communications and Planning facilitating development of regional satellite communication. The Pan African Telecommunications Network was part of the African Union during its existence and worked to overcome deficiencies created by existing communications networks, creating policy and developing cooperation to create joint satellite communications (Mukasa 1992).

Regional policy and cooperation through the Southern African Development and Coordination Conference has been perceived as particularly useful in promoting telecommunications planning and advancement in southern Africa in the post-colonial era, as have similar activities in East Africa through the East African Community (Dymond 1987; Mukasa 1992; Mureithi 2002).

Ultimately, many nations privatize their public telecommunications operations because of financial limitations and commitments involving telecommunications as part of World Trade Organization accession. These changes of course led to rapid expansion of communications systems but did not result in development of domestic knowledge and skills, increased reliance on international firms and exacerbated rural and urban disparities and did not provide much policy for consumer protection (Mureithi 2002).

Asia and Pacific

Regional governance takes place through the Asia-Pacific Economic Cooperation group, the Association of Southeast Asian Nations, the South Asian Association for Regional Cooperation and other intergovernmental organizations. South Asian governance is increasingly focusing on cooperation in improving telecommunications, the internet, energy and transport infrastructures and applications of competition policy.

Despite significant regional support and development of regional policy frameworks for improving telecommunications, especially broadband infrastructure, little regional action has occurred, and it has been primarily left up to nations, development banks and private firms to finance telecommunications investments, doing little to improve the situations in poorer nations (Cecot and Wallsten 2009). Reasons for regional ineffectiveness in producing outcomes are economic conditions in the region, internal disputes and concerns about the roles of larger countries in the region (Shaheen 2013).

Few regional efforts have involved development of broadcast satellites because of the existence of highly commercialized digital satellite and cable operations created by elites, often with the support of states (Atkins 2002).

Europe

Regional policy making in Europe takes place through intergovernmental organizations such as the European Union, Council of Europe, Central European Initiative, European Free Trade Association, Council of the Baltic Sea States, Nordic Council and European Conference of Post and Telecommunications.

The Council of Europe has addressed issues such as transborder television broadcasting (Council of Europe 1989) and cybercrime (Webster 2003). The European Conference of Post and Telecommunications has played a major role in the creation, integration and restructuring of European telephone and broadband systems (Natalicchi 2001). The Nordic Council has for decades funded much research, including NORDICOM, which documents and distributes media and communications research. The European Union is extensively involved in media and communications policy making, setting principles and standards that are subsequently implemented in national policies, as well as overseeing an array of other policy regimes—competition policy, cultural policy and so on—that affect media and communications structures and operations.

The European Union

The EU is the most extensive and sophisticated regional policy-making organization in the world, starting first as a trade and economic organization in the middle of the twentieth century, but with aspirations that led to its expansion into a governance organization attempting to unite Europe and create common social and cultural bases as well (Leonard and Taylor 2016; Olsen and McCormick 2016). It is particularly strong in comparison to other regional governance because of its long history and development and because member states explicitly give up significant amounts of sovereign powers and authority in accession.

The EU has a particularly strong influence in policy diffusion among member states because it sets broad principles of policy to be implemented at the national level and it influences domestic policy makers' perceptions of benefits of particular policy options (Braun and Gilardi 2006). The European Union has struggled to reduce elite rule and integrate public participation in governance (Magnette 2003; Ward 2004; Steffak et al. 2007), a factor made more complex by significant lobbying (Bouwen 2002; Klüver 2013). It has been criticized for lack of transparency and accountability (Harlow 2002; Arnull and Wincott 2003), for being highly separated from the public political processes in its democratic member states and for remaining subject to intense lobbying by elite interest groups (Klüver 2013; Greenwood 2017).

Initial EU media and communications policies focused on promoting European audiovisual content production, distribution and consumption and on improving and liberalizing domestic and EU telecommunication infrastructures and services (Cave and Crowther 1996; Schneider 2001; Bartle 2005). As time passed, EU policies set the stage for rapid deployment of new media and communications technologies that significantly altered the broadcast landscape and created an economically powerful audiovisual industry (Crusafon 2015).

The growth of the commercial broadcasting sector, and competition policy conflicts involving state aid, led the EU to consider and regenerate the role of public service broadcasting (Iosifidis 2010; Donders 2012). The increasing range of media-related issues created by contemporary technological developments has led it to significantly widen the scope of its policy making (Humphreys 1996; Donders et al. 2014; Simpson et al. 2016).

Media and communications policies and related cultural policies are applied within the framework of EU competition and trade policies, so policies must be coordinated, or specific exceptions put in place. The EU was established as an economic union and then expanded into a political and social union, so competition and trade policies and their implementing laws and regulations have existed since its inception and are applicable to all other policy developments.

Competition and trade policy are fundamentally opposed to private or state action that inhibits competition, alters markets in favor of some competitors or restricts trade with other nations. Its primary application is to ensure effective markets in and among its member states of the EU and to ensure its firms have access to markets outside the EU (Nazzini 2012). Media and communications policy and cultural policy involving media often promote or require state action such as subsidies, advantages or regulations to support domestic media cultural objectives and communications infrastructure objectives. These by nature may sometimes conflict with the objectives of competition and trade policy and any disputes must be addressed by the European Commission, Directorate-General for Competition, or adjudicated by the Court of Justice.

The Middle East and North Africa

Regional cooperation and governance organizations include the League of Arab States, Cooperation Council for the Arab States of the Gulf and the Organisation of Islamic Cooperation. There are fewer intergovernmental organizations in the Middle East and North Africa than in most other regions of the world.

The countries in the Middle East and North Africa have not developed strong cooperation in development, security and trade because of lack of common interests, continuing conflicts and foreign interference, despite a significant degree of cultural and religious similarities (Harders and Lengrenzi 2016). These factors have produced waves of cooperation and disunity for decades, with efforts to promote regional interests being more fruitful at times through the Organisation of Islamic Cooperation, League of Arab States and Greater Arab Free Trade Area. Some sub-regional bilateral cooperation is gaining support in the absence of broader regional collaboration and integration.

The European Union and its member states have had significant influence on telecommunications in the Middle East and North Africa, but regional policy makers have also adopted telecommunications policy ideas from other developing countries. Most communications development efforts have been pursued at the national level.

Some cooperation in the region has improved satellite television broadcasting, which in recent years has moved to serve broader external audiences created by migration of Arab populations globally (Kraidy 2002).

Central and South America and the Caribbean

Regional policy making in Central America and South America and the Caribbean takes place through intergovernmental organizations such as the Organization of American States, Caribbean Community, Mercosur, Community of Latin American and Caribbean States, and the Association of State Telecommunication Undertakings of the Andean Community.

Mercosur—the South America trade block—has created a framework for trade in cultural industry products and services that is directly aligned with neither the North American economic framework nor the European economic and cultural framework approach (Galperin 1999), but extensive cooperation between Mercosur and the EU on audiovisual content has grown and produced some concurrence in policy approaches (Canedo and Crusafon 2014; Sarikakis and Ganter 2014).

The digital policy frameworks in Latin America have been strongly influenced by the economic approaches of both the United States and the European Union, moving away from cultural and audiovisual policy approaches that were more influential in the past. EU and American interests have been particularly successful in using Mercosur to promote the policy transfer (Sarikakis and Ganter 2014).

Caribbean initiatives have sought to improve communications infrastructures and developed system resilience following hurricanes and other natural disasters.

Challenges in Regional Governance

Perhaps the greatest challenge in regional governance is creating trust and cohesiveness among states for effective cooperation and governance. There tends to be more trust when countries have greater cultural and social similarities because those factors tend to create more understanding among nations. Creating trust and cohesiveness is not easy because neighboring states often have more disputes than states that are widely separated. In some cases, states must overcome histories of conflicts. These may exist if one of the states was created as a result of civil war or was a breakaway territory. Regional disputes involving water and fishing rights and access to oil and gas deposits and other natural resources may have led to border disputes and even armed conflict. Such disputes need to be overcome before effective regional governance can occur.

Identifying common interests and needs that draw member states together is crucial, because addressing issues with more common interests is likely to gain support from multiple countries. Even when adjacent states share a common need, however, they may have low priority on the policy agendas of some countries and higher priority on the agendas of others.

Even when general policy approaches have consensus, reaching agreement on how to proceed and who should undertake the activities required is sometimes a challenge, because states must balance global policy commitments and domestic pressures. Regional governance is sometimes better at pooling knowledge held in multiple smaller countries to develop comprehensive strategies and policy approaches than implementing them.

Helping member states improve their conditions is often a stated goal of regional intergovernmental organizations, but is often difficult in practice because increasing the economic competitiveness of an adjacent state may be undesirable for neighboring states benefiting from competitive superiority. There is also often a need to overcome resistance to sharing wealth from wealthier states to poorer states. This issue exists even for transfers among provinces in domestic policy making but is often exacerbated when transfers among states are involved.

Chapter Summary

- Regional policy making addresses issues and concerns that may be more localized or disregarded in global policy making, or collectively implement global policy frameworks.
- The institutional structures and practices of regional policy making are similar to those of global policy making.
- Regional policy-making organizations have grown significantly in the past four decades.
- The concerns and effectiveness of regional policy vary widely.
- The strength of regional governance is influenced by member cohesiveness and its legitimacy, authority and financial resources.
- National, regional and international influences, as well as structural capabilities, affect regional policy approaches and outcomes.
- Improving communications capabilities has been a major focus of regional governance.

- Most regional policy bodies focus on communications and information technologies; media policies receive most consideration among European intergovernmental organizations.

Discussion Points

1. What benefits are obtained by creating regional and sub-regional governance organizations?
2. Why do so many regional intergovernmental organizations form and break apart after a few years?
3. Why do so many regional governance organizations follow the approaches and frameworks of global governance?
4. Is it feasible for regional governance to establish and implement policy at odds with global governance?
5. Why do regional intergovernmental organizations cooperate with similar organizations from other regions?

Bibliography

Acharya, Amitav, and Alastair Iain Johnston, eds. 2007. *Crafting Cooperation: Regional International Institutions in Comparative Perspective*. Cambridge: Cambridge University Press.

Arnull, Anthony, and D. Wincott. 2003. *Accountability and Legitimacy in the European Union*. Oxford: Oxford University Press.

Atkins, William. 2002. *The Politics of Southeast Asia's New Media*. London: Routledge.

Bartle, Ian. 2005. *Globalisation and EU Policy-Making: The Neo-Liberal Transformation of Telecommunications and Electricity*. Manchester: Manchester University Press.

Berg, Elliot J. 1993. *Rethinking Technical Cooperation: Reforms for Capacity Building in Africa*. New York: United Nations Development Program.

Berger, Lee. 2001. Proposed Legal Structure for the Silksat Satellite Consortium: A Regional Intergovernmental Organization to Improve Telecommunications Infrastructure in Central Asia and the Trans-Caucasus Region. *Law and Policy in International Business* 3: 99–143.

Bouwen, Pieter. 2002. Corporate Lobbying in the European Union: The Logic of Access. *Journal of European Public Policy* 9 (3): 365–390.

Braun, Dietmar, and Fabrizio Gilardi. 2006. Taking 'Galton's Problem' Seriously: Towards a Theory of Policy Diffusion. *Journal of Theoretical Politics* 18 (3): 298–322.

Calabrese, Andrew, and Marco Briziarelli. 2011. Media Imperialism: Bilateral Trade Agreements as Instruments of Media Governance. In *Handbook of Global Media and Communication Policy*, ed. Robin Mansell and Marc Raboy, 383–394. Oxford: Wiley-Blackwell.

Canedo, Daniele, and Carmina Crusafon. 2014. The European Audiovisual Policy Goes Abroad: The Case of Inter-Regional Cooperation with Mercosur. In *The Palgrave Handbook of European Media Policy*, ed. Karen Donders, Caroline Pauwels, and Jan Loisen, 526–541. London: Palgrave Macmillan.

Cave, Martin, and Peter Crowther. 1996. Determining the Level of Regulation in EU Telecommunications. A Preliminary Assessment. *Telecommunications Policy* 20 (10): 725–738.

Cecot, Caroline, and Scott Wallsten. 2009. South Asia Telecommunications Development and the Role of Regional Cooperation. In *The Service Revolution in South Asia*, ed. Ejaz Ghani, 296–306. Washington, DC: The International Bank for Reconstruction and Development/World Bank.

Cheema, G. Shabbir, Christopher A. McNall, and Vesselin Popovski, eds. 2011. *Cross-Border Governance in Asia: Regional Issues and Mechanisms*. Tokyo: United Nations University.

Cochetti, Roger. 2015. *Mobile Satellite Communications Handbook*. 2nd ed. Hoboken: Wiley.

Council of Europe. 1989. European Convention on Transfrontier Television. Available at https://heinonline.org/HOL/LandingPage?handle=hein.journals/intlm28&div=113&id=&page=. Accessed 13 Apr 2019.

Crusafon, Carmina. 2015. The European Audiovisual Space: How European Media Policy Has Set the Pace of Its Development. In *European Cinema and Television*, ed. Ib Bondebjerg, Eva Norrup Redvall, and Andres Higson, 81–101. London: Palgrave Macmillan.

Donders, Karen. 2012. *Public Service Media and Policy in Europe*. London: Palgrave Macmillan.

Donders, Karen, Caroline Pauwels, and Jan Loisen. 2014. *The Palgrave Handbook of European Media Policy*. London: Palgrave Macmillan.

Doyle, Gillian. 2002. *Media Ownership: The Economics and Politics of Convergence and Concentration in the UK and European Media*. London: Sage.

Dymond, Andrew. 1987. Reducing the Number of Missing Links: Regional Cooperation and Telecommunications Development in Southern Africa. *Telecommunications Policy* 11 (2): 121–134.

Fawn, Rick. 2013. *International Organizations and Internal Conditionality: Making Norms Matter*. London: Palgrave Macmillan.

Galperin, Hernan. 1999. Cultural Industries Policy in Regional Trade Agreements: The Cases of NAFTA, the European Union and MERCOSUR. *Media, Culture and Society* 21 (5): 627–648.

Ginsberg, Roy. 2010. *Demystifying the European Union: The Enduring Logic of Regional Integration*. Plymouth: Rowman & Littlefield.

Greenwood, Justin. 2017. *Interest Representation in the European Union*. 4th ed. London: Palgrave.

Harders, Cilja, and Matteo Lengrenzi, eds. 2016. *Beyond Regionalism? Regional Cooperation, Regionalism and Regionalization in the Middle East*. London: Routledge.

Harlow, Carol. 2002. *Accountability in the European Union*. Oxford: Oxford University Press.

Hawdon, James. 1996. *Emerging Organizational Forms: The Proliferation of Regional Intergovernmental Organizations in the Modern World-System*. New York: Praeger.

Hills, Jill. 1994. Dependency Theory and Its Relevance Today: International Institutions in Telecommunications and Structural Power. *Review of International Studies* 20 (2): 169–186.

Hudson, Heather E. 1991. Telecommunications in Africa: The Role of the ITU. *Telecommunications Policy* 15 (4): 343–350.

———. 2006. *From Rural Village to Global Village: Telecommunications for Development in the Information Age*. New York: Routledge.
Humphreys, Peter. 1996. *Mass Media and Media Policy in Western Europe*. Manchester: Manchester University Press.
Iosifidis, Petros, ed. 2010. *Reinventing Public Service Communication: European Broadcasters and Beyond*. London: Palgrave Macmillan.
Kim, Kyungmo, and George A. Barnett. 2000. The Structure of the International Telecommunications Regime in Transition: A Network Analysis of International Organizations. *International Interactions* 26 (1): 91–127.
Klüver, Heike. 2013. *Lobbying in the European Union: Interest Groups, Lobbying Coalitions, and Policy Change*. Oxford: Oxford University Press.
Kraidy, Marwan M. 2002. Arab Satellite Television Between Regionalization and Globalization. *Global Media Journal* 1 (1). Available at http://repository.upenn.edu/asc_papers/186. Accessed 13 Apr 2019.
Leonard, Dick, and Robert Taylor. 2016. *The Routledge Guide to the European Union*. London: Routledge.
Magnette, Paul. 2003. European Governance and Civic Participation: Beyond Elitist Citizenship? *Political Studies* 51 (1): 144–160.
Mathew, Bobjoseph, and Thomas Cottier, eds. 2003. *Telecom Regulatory Framework and Effect on Competition: The WTO Agreements on Telecommunications*. New York: Peter Lang.
McCormick, Patricia K. 2005. The African Telecommunications Union: A Pan-African Approach to Telecommunications Reform. *Telecommunications Policy* 29 (7): 529–548.
McCormick, Patricia K., and Maury J. Mechanick. 2013. *The Transformation of Intergovernmental Satellite Organisations: Policy and Legal Perspectives*. Leiden: Martinus Nijhoff Publishers.
Mukasa, Stanford G. 1992. Toward Pan-African Cooperation in Satellite Communication: An Analysis of the RASCOM Project. *Africa Media Review* 6 (2): 13–30.
Mureithi, Muriuki. 2002. Evolution of Telecommunications Policy Reforms in East Africa: Setting New Policy Strategies to Anchor Benefits of Policy Reforms. *The African Journal of Information and Communication* 3: 58–54.
Nair, G. Madhavan. 2008. Role of Communications Satellites in National Development. *IETE Technical Review* 25 (1): 3–8.
Natalicchi, Giorgio. 2001. Wiring Europe. In *Reshaping the European Telecommunication Regime*. London: Rowman and Littlefield.
Nazzini, Renato. 2012. *The Foundations of European Union Competition Law: The Objectives and Principles of Article 102*. Oxford: Oxford University Press.
Negrine, Ralph, ed. 2013. *Satellite Broadcasting: The Politics and Implications of the New Media*. Reprint ed. London: Routledge.
Noam, Eli, ed. 1999. *Telecommunications in Africa*. New York: Oxford University Press.
Olsen, Jonathan, and John McCormick. 2016. *The European Union: Politics and Policies*. 6th ed. Boulder: Westview Press.
Qiang, Christine Zhen-Wei, and Alexander Pitt. 2003. *Contribution of Information and Communication Technologies to Growth*. Washington, DC: The International Bank for Reconstruction and Development/World Bank.
Reinalda, Bob, ed. 2013. *Routledge Handbook of International Organization*. London: Routledge.

Rothman, Steven B., Utpal Vyas, and Yoichiro Sato, eds. 2017. *Regional Institutions, Geopolitics and Economics in the Asia-Pacific: Evolving Interests and Strategies*. London: Routledge.
Sarikakis, Katharine, and Sarah Ganter. 2014. Priorities in Global Media Policy Transfer: Audiovisual and Digital Policy Mutations in the EU, MERCOSUR and US Triangle. *European Journal of Communication* 29 (1): 17–33.
Saunders, Robert J. 1983. *Telecommunications and Economic Development*. Baltimore: World Bank/Johns Hopkins University Press.
Schneider, Volker. 2001. Institutional Reform in Telecommunications: The European Union in Transnational Policy Diffusion. In *Europeanization and Domestic Change*, ed. Maria Green Cowles, James Caporaso, and Thomas Rissee, 60–78. Ithaca: Cornell University Press.
Shaheen, Irum. 2013. South Asian Association for Regional Cooperation (SAARC): Its Role, Hurdles and Prospects. *IOSR Journal of Humanities and Social Science* 15 (6): 1–9.
Simpson, Seamus, Manuel Puppis, and Hilde Van den Bulck, eds. 2016. *European Media Policy for the Twenty-First Century: Assessing the Past, Setting Agendas for the Future*. London: Routledge.
Steffak, Jens, Claudia Kissling, and Patricia Nanz, eds. 2007. *Emergent Patterns of Civil Society Participation in Global and European Governance*. Basingstoke: Palgrave Macmillan.
Stephenson, Philip. 2008. *Telecommunications and Growth*. Saarbrücken: VDM Verlag.
Torero, Maximo, and Joachim von Braun, eds. 2006. *Information and Communication Technologies for Development and Poverty Reduction: The Potential of Telecommunications*. Baltimore: Johns Hopkins University Press.
Volgy, Thomas J., Zlatko Šabič, Petra Roter, and Andrea K. Gerlak. 2009. *Mapping the New World Order*. Chichester: Wiley-Blackwell.
Ward, David. 2004. *The European Union Democratic Deficit and the Public Sphere: An Evaluation of EU Media Policy*. Amsterdam: IOS Press.
Wavre, Veronique. 2018. *Policy Diffusion and Telecommunications Regulations*. London: Palgrave Macmillan.
Webster, Amalie M. 2003. The Council of Europe's Convention on Cybercrime. *Berkeley Technology Law Journal* 18 (1): 425–446.

Suggested Reading

Acharya, Amitav, and Alastair Iain Johnston, eds. 2007. *Crafting Cooperation: Regional International Institutions in Comparative Perspective*. Cambridge: Cambridge University Press.
Doyle, Gillian. 2002. *Media Ownership: The Economics and Politic of Convergence and Concentration in the UK and European Media*. London: Sage.
Galperin, Herman. 1999. Cultural Industries Policy in Regional Trade Agreements: The Cases of NAFTA, the European Union and MERCOSUR. *Media, Culture & Society* 21 (5): 627–648.
Ginsberg, Roy. 2010. *Demystifying the European Union: The Enduring Logic of Regional Integration*. Plymouth: Rowman & Littlefield.
Ward, David. 2004. *The European Union Democratic Deficit and the Public Sphere: An Evaluation of EU Media Policy*. Amsterdam: IOS Press.

CHAPTER 7

Domestic Policy Making

Policy making in media and communications is primarily domestic, with policies heavily influenced by domestic social and political norms and practices embodied in domestic governance structures and institutions. Policy was historically made in a nationally bounded system characterized by scarcity, time and distance constraints and unidirectional communication. Today, the nationally bounded system has broken down, although preferences for national policy and domestic media content remain. The system is now characterized by abundance, immediacy and multidirectional communication often provided by firms external to countries, requiring some new domestic policy approaches.

Global and regional policy making, especially agreements states have made with the World Trade Organization, constrains the ability of national governments in some telecommunications, media and cultural policy making (Puppis 2008; Picard et al. 2016). Although globalization and regionalization have moved some media and communications policy making away from states, individual states still play important roles in facilitating and governing media and communications and maintaining regulatory functions. Policymakers are more effectively responding to technology and issues poised by globalism at the domestic level (Flew et al. 2016).

Policy making differs in all nations. Even when there are similarities in political philosophy, structures and general processes, individual differences influence the rationales, objectives, development of policy, mechanisms pursued, implementation and practices surrounding policy. Examining domestic policy making thus requires attention to the variations and subtleties of the domestic policy system and practices. Domestic policy takes place within the governmental, social and political environments discussed in Chap. 2, guided by the strength of states and polities, forms and institutions of governance in place and their institutional designs, norms, capabilities and processes. These central factors influence policy making and its outcomes.

R. G. Picard, *Media and Communications Policy Making*, Palgrave Global Media Policy and Business,
https://doi.org/10.1007/978-3-030-35173-1_7

Accounting for these factors is important in probing domestic policy, most especially in examinations of comparative policy making and outcomes among countries. The differences require accounting for the effects of varying institutional influences and their strengths (Scharpf 2000), and care is needed because there can be large differences even among functionally similar systems (Turnpenny et al. 2008).

Influences on Domestic Policy Outcomes

Domestic policy worldwide is influenced by the form and institutions of government, the rationales for policy, the nature of policy consultation and systemic outcome-skewing factors (Fig. 7.1). These factors are central to understanding why and how domestic policy is created and who or what influences that process. When examining policy making or a specific policy in a country, how these individually and collectively affect the process and the outcome needs to be considered.

The model of the influences on domestic media and communications policy can be applied to both democratic and autocratic countries and to

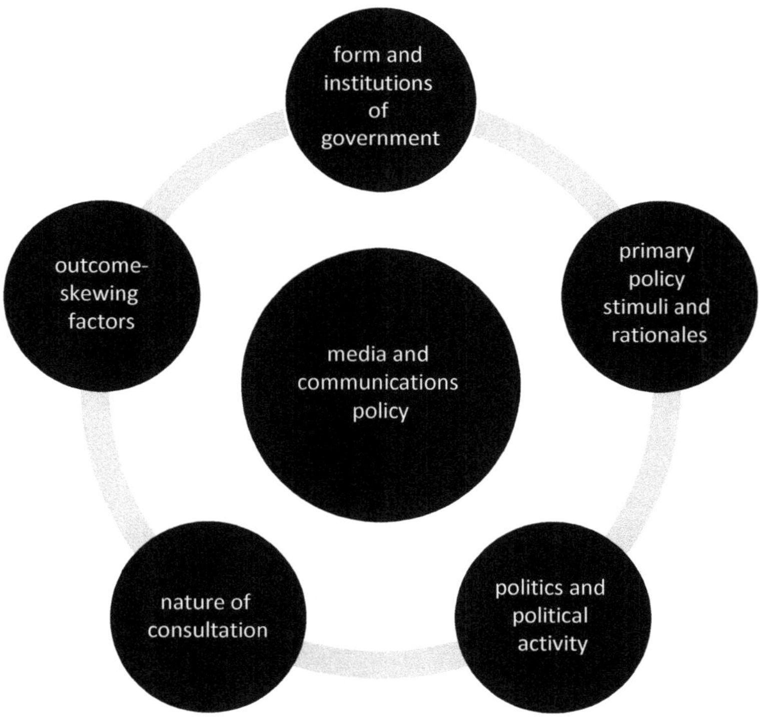

Fig. 7.1 Influences on domestic media and communications policy

situations where special interests—including business and state interests—exercise unusual influence.

When studying policy, identifying the extent and significance of the influences on processes and outcomes is crucial. Influences may be stronger than others in some countries, so it is crucial to assess their impact when comparing processes and outcomes in different states.

Form and Institutions of Government

As discussed in Chap. 2, the form of government, the government institutions involved and whether processes or decisions take place in democratic or autocratic milieux have a significant influence on how policy is made. The roles of heads of states and governments, ministers and leaders of governmental institutions must be considered. Identifying the standard processes and roles of individuals and institutions is vital, as is understanding factors that influence how and why deviations occur.

Policy Making in a Restrictive State: The Case of Saudi Arabia

Saudi Arabia is an absolute monarchy and home of the most holy site in the Islamic world. Both factors have significant influence on media and communications policy, which is one of the more restrictive in the world (Duffy 2013). The country is ruled by a monarch, Salman bin Abdulaziz Al Saud, who serves both as head of state and prime minister, and head of the Council of Ministers. Media and communications policy is made by royal decree, decisions of the Council of Ministers, ministries, and by regulatory agencies (United States CIA and Department of State 2012). All must ultimately have the assent of the monarch.

The country has a Consultative Assembly with the authority to propose laws and regulations to the Council of Ministers and the king but cannot enact or enforce them on its own. The Transportation, Communications, Information Technology Committee addresses media and communications policy issues, particularly those related to infrastructure planning.

The ministries and agencies most involved in media and communications policy include:

- The Ministry of Culture and Communication, which operates state broadcasting and the state news agency and oversees private media (Saudi Arabia Ministry of Culture and Communication 2016)
- The Ministry of Communication and Information Technology, which oversees telecommunications, including telephone and internet systems, and government digital initiatives (Saudi Arabia Ministry of Communication and Information Technology 2016)

(*continued*)

(continued)

- The Communication and Information Technology Commission, which is charged with establishing telecommunications policy and ICT regulation (Saudi Arabia Communication and Information Technology Commission 2016)
- The King Abdulaziz City for Science and Technology, a specialized development cluster, is specifically charged with formulating policies and national plans for science, technology and innovation, and deals with issues related to digital media and internet oversight (Saudi Arabia King Abdulaziz City for Science and Technology 2016).

Islam is recognized as the state religion in the basic law of governance, and the king is the official custodian of the mosques in Mecca and Medina (where Mohammed lived and died). Islam is integrated into government through its legal system based in Sharia law, the religious police and direct influence over policy involving mosques, culture and education through the Ministry of Islamic Affairs, Endowments, and Guidance and a Council of Senior Scholars that directly advises the king on Islamic issues.

In practice, infrastructural and technical policy issues tend to arise first in the Ministry of Communication and Information Technology, the Communication and Information Technology Commission, and King Abdulaziz City for Science and Technology, and then move to the Council of Ministers. Other forms of media and communication policy may also emanate from those agencies, but also from the Ministry of Culture and Communication, the Ministry of Justice and the Ministry of Commerce and Industry. Because of their varying focuses, differences between the ministries and agencies emerge, and these are debated and decided within the Council of Ministers.

Once a policy is put in place by the Council of Ministers or by a royal decree, the relevant ministries and agencies construct and administer rules and regulations for implementing the policy.

Domestic media and communications infrastructures and operating firms are state firms, private firms with the state holding a controlling interest, or private firms related to the royal family or government officials that act as regime agents.

The combination of a monarchical form of government, strong state influence in media operations, primary policy rationales that media and communications should support the monarchy, the state, national development and Islam, and limited public consultation produce strongly centralized and coordinated policy affecting all media and communication systems operating in the country. Media and communication policy making is thus primarily driven by centralized executive planning and decision-making, in coordination with technical and subject experts.

The form and institutions of government affect how the policy process begins and takes place. Pronouncement of preferred policy approaches or policy elements by the head of state or government may start a top-down process to establish policy, or public desires for action may be taken up by political parties and initiate a bottom-up process based in legislative and administrative institutions. Industry actors are often able to initiate policy processes through legislative or administrative overtures that may later enter political processes and become politicized.

Where the executive is the source of law as well as its administration, the processes will differ significantly from states in which those roles are well divided between the executive and legislature. Similarly, the amount of autonomous authority granted to administrative agencies and ministries will affect processes and implementation requirements, as well whether the legal system is based in statutory or common law.

Primary Policy Stimuli and Rationales

The developments or issues that induce policy making and its rationales have a fundamental role in influencing its establishment and elements. Being aware of why the need or desire for policy has arisen is an important part of understanding domestic policy making and its processes.

Policies whose rationales involve social control, maintenance of political power, democratic facilitation, cultural promotion, servicing public needs, or economic growth and development will heavily affect the types of policies created. It is possible for various actors in the process to have differing rationales when addressing an issue; thus, identifying those differences and how they affect the process and policy are necessary.

Most countries perceive improving domestic communications infrastructures and media offerings as policy priorities, because of the importance to governance, commerce and social development. They thus produce a range of policies to support communications improvements, expanded operations and availability.

Although there is a general policy impetus to improve communications abilities in nations around the world, the desire to provide all types of communication available and unfettered access and use is not universal. In countries in which media and communications are wielded as instruments of power, incentives to permit and create systems and platforms that enhance communications abilities of subjects or citizen are diminished. In some cases, policies develop and offer advanced communications capabilities only to regime supporters, or to people in the regions and cities where the greatest support exists, or they create mechanisms to limit the sources and range of communication.

Technological change is often an impetus for policy development or change, because it may not be covered by existing policy, may create opportunities for new approaches, or may allow secondary rationales to rise in importance or even new rationales to emerge. Rationales to maintain influence over critical infrastructure often lead to policies of heavy regulation or state investment. In 2018, for example, the Italian government purchased an influential share of Telecom Italia during a struggle between major foreign investors, to increase its ability to direct decisions about infrastructure investments (Bernabei 2018).

External Forces Drive Digital Television Policy in Mongolia

Mongolia is nestled between Russia and China and has a population of 3 million people, with the vast majority speaking Mongolian and related dialects. Despites its small population, it has a television market served by about 140 channels and transitioned to digital terrestrial television as its primary broadcast technology in 2014.

The policy to switch technologies has been primarily driven by the rationales of technological modernism and the desire to match technological developments in more developed nations in Asia and the West. In planning and implementing the changes, the agencies responsible for the shift—the Information Technology, Post, and Telecommunications Authority and the Communications Regulatory Commission—received assistance from the International Telecommunication Union. All three have been primarily concerned with technical aspects of the change. Under their guidance, the government has made significant expenditures to replace the existing analog network.

The digital terrestrial television policy initiative has taken place primarily as a technological regulatory issue within a general legislative and regulatory framework in which policy considerations such as universal service, program diversity and quality and the effects of change on disadvantaged groups and small broadcasters have not gained significant consideration.

One observer has noted that the government's "piecemeal approach to media legislation creates uncertainties for commercial televisions, public broadcasters and digital media service providers in terms of market structure, programmes, services and regulation" (Baasanjav 2016, p. 8).

Politics and Political Activity

All governance involves politics, but the forms and extent of the politics and associated political activity vary and influence policy differently. Politics involves the relations of those involved in decision-making, the exercise of influence and power in the institutions and processes of governance. Politics and related activity involved in policy making must be considered in an extant case because of the wide differences in which they are practiced in domestic settings. Politics is dependent upon the form of government, relations between the executive and the legislative branches and their degrees of autonomy and power.

Important factors that influence the range of political activity permitted and how policy making takes place include whether the governance is democratic or autocratic, whether party governance exists and whether a single or multi-party system is in place. All countries have some sort of national assemblies representing public interests, but their composition, authorities, scope, structures and operations vary widely. These assemblies may be unicameral or bicameral, in which a second chamber represents interests different from the first. Power and influence are exercised in all governance forms, but the processes that take place, who exerts power and influence and how it is wielded will vary.

Politics and political activity play important roles in creating domestic policy and tend to be more contested in complex democratic states. Whereas policy making tends to respond primarily to the priorities and wishes of leaders and dominant parties in more autocratic states, policy-making institutions of democratic governance tend to diffuse power and authority and typically respond to a broader range of interests. This tends to create a more politically complex environment in which political activity in shaping and determining policy occurs.

Policy making at the domestic level tends to occur more rapidly than at the global or regional levels, because the latter have fewer avenues in which policy demands can arise and more competing interests that must be accommodated. Pressures from the public to provide services and respond to media and communications problems tend to gain attention and influence the priorities of domestic parties and national leaders more swiftly.

Stakeholders make significant efforts to influence policy development and choice through political activities (Klüver 2013). Business interests use access to legislators, legislative staff and administrative agency staff to lobby for their preferred policy outcomes (Bouwen 2002). Nongovernmental civil society organizations also advocate for their positions, but generally do not have as ready access as lobbyists for large economic interests. Research has shown that lobbying activities are the preferred means of influencing political activities in richer countries, and that corrupt practices are more often utilized in poorer countries (Campos and Giovannoni 2007).

Nature of Consultation

The nature of consultation that takes place in policy processes to determine the need for, and preferential elements of, policy, and the reactions to draft policy, are also vital for understanding influence in policy making. Who is consulted, at what policy stage the consultation takes place, whether the consultation is legitimate or merely procedural and the extent to which consultation informs policy development and outcome are all important elements that require consideration.

At its fundamental level, consultation is designed to create political legitimacy, that is, acceptance of the results in society. Consultations are designed to gain participation of interested parties and to produce knowledge and advice relevant to the issue being considered. Depending upon the state and issue involved, consultation may be expert-based, include only stakeholders directly involved, or be open to the wider public and civil society organizations. Digital technologies are providing methods to obtain, organize and meaningfully comprehend large numbers of contributions to consultations from the general public (Coleman and Shane 2012), but they need to ensure that it is the public responding to the consultation. This challenge was starkly illustrated in the United States by the manipulation of the Federal Communications Commission's public consultation on net neutrality, to which more than 21.7 million members of the public made submissions. Subsequent investigation revealed that more than half of the comments were from duplicate email addresses, fraudulently used names and dead persons, and that hundreds of thousands of comments supporting the repeal of net neutrality—a position favored by large internet service providers—were posted by web robots multiple times (Pew Research Center 2017).

The nature and timing of consultation is significant. It may take place before policy development to help policy makers gain a better understanding of the issues and interests involved. It may take place after the policy has been developed to obtain reaction to it. The nature and time of consultation are important, because they determine whether those taking part can influence perspectives about its context and its actual development or can merely express opinions and positions about what has been developed and provide policy makers a means to gauge how action to implement will be received.

Spain, for example, uses public consultations to gather views of citizens, organizations and associations about how emerging issues should be addressed, what concerns are central and what factors need to be addressed before policy is developed. It also conducts consultations regarding specific policy or project proposals. The government initiated a consultation on a draft proposal for a digital service tax that would place a levy on service provision, advertising and e-commerce in 2018, which became an official proposal submitted to the parliament in 2019 (Sweet 2019).

At times, consultations executive and legislative institutions may not be used to actually develop policy, but as a form of political posturing in which policy makers demonstrate they are addressing an issue through the consultation, even if they do not intend to act or wish to delay taking action.

Outcome-Skewing Factors

Identifying and comprehending outcome-skewing factors and their degree of influence on policy is crucial. These include factors such as the strength of state and governmental influence, the extent to which stakeholder groups (companies, financiers, political actors, citizens, etc.) shape the outcome and systemic factors based in economics, social standing, gender and minorities that marginalize interests in policy making. Outcome-skewing factors can affect decision-making processes in political activities, but they may also determine whether decisions can be made and what options may be considered.

Security Interests

National security interests commonly play significant roles in domestic media and communications policy making, typically creating policies that serve security needs and providing preferences for the ability of governments to carry out their activities and communicate to their subjects or citizens.

Central aspects of policy typically involve ensuring crucial communication capabilities, weaponizing communications technologies against adversaries and protecting domestic communications infrastructures and technologies (Khetri 2005; Lewis 2006). Concerns about the adequacy infrastructures in times of conflict and crisis, redundancy of infrastructure in case of damage or failure and ensuring domestic control and that foreign interests and owners are unable to negatively interfere with system decisions and operations are all common elements of security interests that skew policy.

Issues of use of technologies for telecommunication and internet surveillance have grown significantly in recent years (Slobogin 2007; Lemieux 2018). Such surveillance is associated with both democratic and autocratic states, with technological capabilities and sizes of governments influencing the extent to which they are involved.

U.S. policy has supported military interests in and uses of communications technologies throughout U.S. history, for example, and this has influenced infrastructures and their operations and promoted strategic communication of U.S. national interests and security (Schiller 2008). The pursuit of domestic security objectives induced Taiwan to create and implement information security policy to help protect businesses upon whose economy the country is dependent and critical infrastructures against interference by foreign powers and criminal actors (Ku et al. 2009).

Economic Interests

Domestic economic interests are often an outcome-skewing factor, with governments often favoring policies inducing investment, producing beneficial domestic economic impact and supporting activities of domestic firms against foreign competitors. Robust industrial policies supporting technological development have been credited with the success of Japanese and Chinese information and communication technological developments and their national economic benefits (Fan and Watanabe 2006). These industrial policy approaches promote national industry developments and competition (Iosifidis 1997) but can sometimes underpin or weaken competition and media policy approaches (Bauer 2010) and are central to contemporary debates regarding creative industries and copyright (Freedman 2008).

In some states, economic interests are so strong that they can skew or determine policies. In countries where media and communications activities make larger contributions to gross domestic product and employment or foreign trade, policy makers tend to give the industries greater attention and work to help develop, support and protect them. Media and communications policies tend to become more linked to and influenced by national innovation, commerce and trade rationales and by national strategies and policy mechanisms addressing them. This requires those taking part in or observing policy making to pay attention to and understand added policy complexity and intervention and how it will influence media and communications policy outcomes. In many cases, policy and legislative actions ostensibly addressing other issues than media or communications policy may have provisions that significantly affect those industries and functions.

Skewing of outcomes because of economic concerns is more likely to occur in the executive branch when administrative agencies are specifically tasked with industry development objectives as well as protection of public interest objectives, and in autocratic states in which media and communications industry regime agents and allies are present. The influence of policy capture (regulatory capture) and state capture by economic interests needs to be considered in states in which they are present. Policy that is weak, poorly enforced, or produces insignificant penalties for violations of regulations can be indicative of policy capture (Latzer 2007). Although some policy capture involving media and communications firms is not uncommon (especially that initially produced with the appearance of new technologies), it is rare for these firms to be involved in state capture because they do not have the economic strength and resources needed unless they are subsidiaries of large industrial and financial conglomerates creating the capture.

In many countries, often those with authoritarian tendencies, policy decisions tend to skew in favor of firms and owners that act on behalf of the government or are allied with the government, thus providing them economic benefits and incentives. This creates and sustains a configuration of interests between media and communications firms and government or rule, in which the behavior of firms supports the government or ruler. Such arrangements and firms require limited direction and oversight, because the benefits they provide the owners, such as income and position, are dependent upon the government or ruler. The benefits of these arrangements to state, government or ruler are that they do not need to own the firms to obtain their support, do not need to threaten or punish owners to obtain compliance and are able to use the private firms as evidence of liberal governance.

In the strongest form of alignment, these arrangements make the firms *regime agents* that act on behalf of the state or government, providing legitimacy and fully supporting its activities. Under such conditions, it is nearly impossible to separate the regime agent from the regime, often because owners are related to the ruler, hold positions in the regime, or are so fully dependent upon and entwined with the regime that they cannot act otherwise. Al-Jazeera (sometimes transliterated to Al Jazeera), the broadcast and satellite channel operator based in Qatar, for example, is a private firm but was established with government loans and sustained by government grants, and both private investors and the state own shares in the firm (Miles 2005; El-Nawawy and Iskandar 2008). *Regime allies* are found in less intertwined forms of alignment that are characterized by media and communications firms supporting the state, government or ruler to obtain benefit based on licenses, franchises and revenue dependent upon the patron regime. In these cases, they voluntarily align and behave in supportive manners to maintain the benefits of the patronage.

Domestic Cultural Influences

Strong national cultural factors can also skew policy. Dominant beliefs, values and customs can heavily influence and skew policy decisions, indirectly through social norms or directly through intervention in policy making. These are more often manifest in media rather than in communications policy.

The promotion and protection of domestic culture and cultural expression plays important policy roles in many nations, especially those with smaller populations or dependent upon external sources of content. Cultural promotion and protection is also strong in some countries, such as France, where distinct cultural elements such as language, arts, cuisine and heritage are deemed critical to identity and national cohesiveness (Ahearne 2002). These concerns are typically manifest in efforts to provide state support for domestic content production, creation of domestic content quotas and ownership restrictions (Sarikakis 2007; O'Regan and Goldsmith 2006; Picard et al. 2016).

Religion has a particularly strong influence in many states, particularly when policy involves media content and behavior. Media governance in Iran, for example, is deeply affected by the Shia branch of Islam, and its impact on policy cannot be disregarded. How proposed policies relate to Islamic principles are openly debated, and policy decisions and their implementation involving audiovisual media, the internet, cinema and other content media often involve contested interpretations and applications of that religious belief (Menashri 2001; Semati 2008). Religion can also play a role in media structure, as in the case of the Netherlands, where public service broadcasting is built upon social groups including religious associations (Daalmeijer 2004), or in Latin America, where Catholic institutions were often the first to be granted non-state broadcasting licenses (Lugo-Ocando 2008).

Size of State Influences Domestic Policy and Policy Making

The size of a country measured in physical, population and economic terms influences the size of government, its institutions, the policy issues it faces and the amount of policy and law it produces. This occurs because the geography involved may require greater administration; a larger population has greater needs for social service, and domestic and international business and national interests require more attention. Size creates governance complexity, so the processes and institutions involved in policy tend to grow and proliferate. Understanding how size affects policy making and policy is particularly important when comparative analysis of domestic policy is involved.

Size of country creates legislative differences, for example. As size grows, the number of representatives in legislative bodies typically increases, and larger numbers of committees and working groups are created that add layers into policy processes and bring increasing number of legislative staff into the process. Smaller countries tend to have fewer representatives and committees, many have legislatures that meet only part time and legislators and committees have fewer staff and produce lower legislative output.

Small states also typically have a relatively small number of administrative personnel in ministries and agencies. Consequently, they may oversee multiple issues and carry out a wide variety of duties. Personnel tend to be less specialized than those in larger states and governments. There tends to be a lower number of ministries and agencies in smaller states, and policy making tends to involve more consultation and cooperation among them than in larger states. This reduces the complexity of the policy-making process. By contrast, larger states more often have multiple ministries and agencies with narrower objectives and higher degrees of independence that require policy makers to navigate the interests and processes of multiple governance structures.

Country size also affects media and communications systems and the number and capabilities of domestic firms. Small countries face economic hurdles in relying on the market to produce media and communications systems and providers, and struggle with external ownership and content issues exacerbated by modern technologies and globalization (Trappel 1991; Lowe and Nissen 2011). They are usually more interventionist in media and communications policy and must balance domestic needs with risks of becoming overly protectionist and isolationist in content (Puppis 2009). Larger countries face some unique economic issues as well, particularly because costs of some communications systems infrastructure rise in urban areas with large populations, and costs of serving sparsely populated rural and wilderness regions are high (Picard and Wildman 2015).

Size affects the needs and capabilities of communications systems and their complexity, the number of media outlets and necessity for some types of formal policy and legislation. In smaller countries, relations between the state and providers may be more informal and decisions made more collectively, reducing the need for some formal policy making and legislation. In larger states, the sheer number and geographic distribution of providers may force more formality into the process.

Policy making is also affected by the number and size of provincial and local governments in a country and the degrees to which governance power has delegated to them. Although broader policy is typically made at the national level, a good deal of implementing policy regarding media and communications systems tends to take place at the provincial and local levels. In recent years, several nations, including Canada and the United Kingdom, have devolved significant policy-making power to the provincial and subnational levels.

Structures and Relations Among Policy Institutions Affect Processes

The way in which policy-making institutions are structured and the relations among them determine how policy is initiated, developed, considered and implemented. The institutional design of governance, the capabilities and constraints on the institutions and the authority and responsibilities distributed among institutions affect the paths that policy making follows among states.

The processes primarily involve executive administrative agency and legislative institutions. The judiciary is not directly part of primary policy-making process but may become involved to rule on processes and outcome. In some cases, its previous rulings may influence choices made during subsequent policy-making processes by constraining the range of options available. When courts and their rulings involve policy, they are primarily concerned with issues of policy concurrence with fundamental governance law, such as constitutions, determining whether policy was produced following legally established practices, interpreting disputed provisions and resolving conflicts among laws and regulations.

Policy processes typically follow one of three major paths: one initiated by the head of government, one initiated by the legislature, or one initiated by an administrative agency. In most countries, all three forms are possible, but some are most frequently present. It is possible for policy demands from the public or civic society organizations to stimulate a policy process, but their efforts are typically focused on urging one of the governance institutions to consider the issue and initiate one of the policy-making processes.

Head of Government-Initiated Process

In this form, the impetus comes from a head of government indicating that a policy should be developed and providing some direction of the preferred approach. This occurs in both democratic and autocratic political systems.

Heads of government are rarely directly involved in developing the specifics of policy, but typically direct their ministerial council or cabinet to discuss and add detail. The relevant ministry or administrative agency becomes involved to assist development by adding technical details and establishing administrative mechanisms and processes (Fig. 7.2). Once the policy proposal is accepted by the head of state and ministerial council, it can be implemented by the administrative agency/ministry, or, if new or additional legislation is needed to authorize implementation of the policy, it can be sent to the legislature to do so. During that process, the legislature will work with the relevant ministry or agency and ultimately send completed legislation back to the executive for approval.

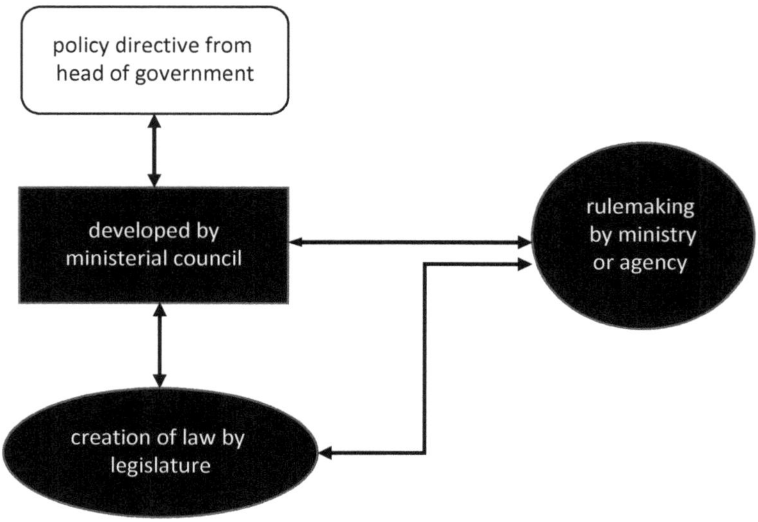

Fig. 7.2 Basic structures and relations in policy initiated by the head of government

Legislature-Initiated Process

When the policy process begins in the legislature, it begins with a policy proposal that is debated and developed within committees, ultimately being crafted as law to implement the policy and its measures. In this process, the legislature normally consults with the relevant administrative agency or ministry on technical and administrative details.

Once legislation has been approved, it is forwarded to the executive branch for acceptance or rejection. The decision of the executive is often discussed between the head of state and ministerial council or cabinet, and sometimes with the ministry or agency involved (Fig. 7.3).

Agency- or Ministry-Initiated Process

Administrative agencies and ministries can initiate and implement policy themselves, within the authority delegated to them and their regulatory processes. If the policy does not represent a major change or have any political implications for the government, the ministerial council and head of state may choose to allow it to proceed without their intervention.

When significant new policy is necessary or is outside the delegated authority of the agency and ministry, they will typically forward it for discussion and development by the head of state and ministerial council, revising the policy according to their advice before implementing it or sending it to the legislature for further development and approval and creation of law that may be required for its implementation (Fig. 7.4).

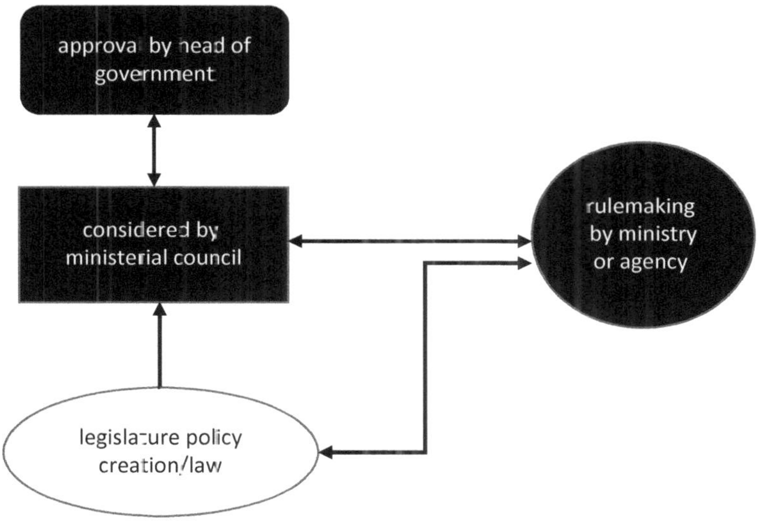

Fig. 7.3 Basic structures and relations in policy initiated by the legislature

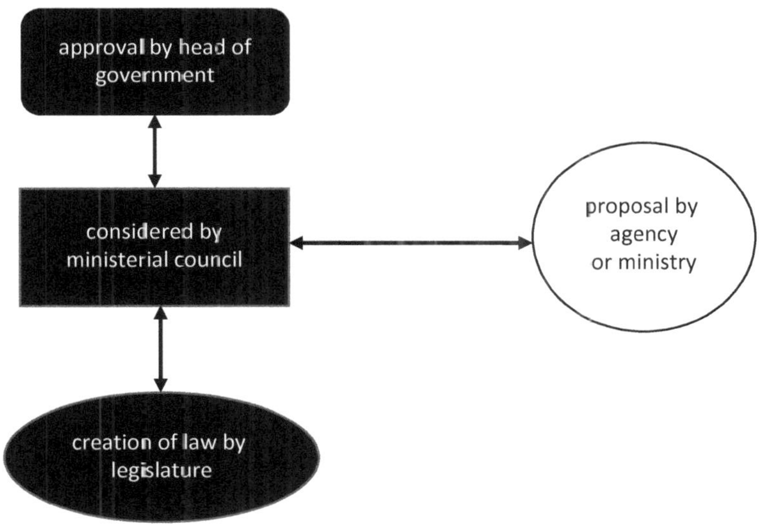

Fig. 7.4 Basic structures and relations in policy initiated by an administrative agency/ministry

Institutional Norms Affect Processes and Policy Outcomes

The specific domestic policy settings, processes and typical intervention forms employed as a result of the initiation of policy processes by institutional actions differ among states. It is therefore important to understand what the norms are for a country being considered. Through knowledge of these factors, one can better assess the stimuli for policy, whether normal policy development and implementation channels and practices are being followed, their influences on policies, why particular mechanisms and tools were selected and the effectiveness of the decision-making process.

Social and Political Systems Norms

Policy making and policy in all societies is influenced by prevailing social and political system norms involving power, authority, hierarchy and processes that are based in dominant social values and practices. Significant influences are norms related to preserving the state, protecting existing power relations, maintaining social order and control and adhering to dominant political philosophy. Consequently, policies tend to promote media and communications systems and activities that support and operate within those norms and to constrain those that challenge or threaten those norms.

Use of communication as an instrument of state power internally and externally is a fundamental function of government, and policies typically include measures to support it. Sometimes, particularly in more autocratic states, policies to protect and preserve current leadership are enacted. This is illustrated by Russian policy makers enacting legislation in 2019 to jail individuals for online "disrespect" of government officials. The bill was passed with the support of Vladimir Putin and he signed it into law (Bennetts 2019; Tamkin 2019).

Legislative Norms

The power and sizes of legislative bodies affect their roles and participation in policy making. In some states, their role may be primarily to affirm decisions of the executive, in others to establish law implementing policy determined in the executive branch, and in others they may involve actual policy-setting as well. Legislative processes are influenced by whether the legislature is uni- or bicameral. In cases where there is an upper and lower chamber, the lower most often has greater legislative power, and the upper house is typically designed to identify and explore issues needing legislative or executive action, examine and agree with or reject lower chamber actions and safeguard broad social, political and cultural standards.

How issues and proposals arise for legislative consideration needs to be understood. In some cases, the executive and its ministers submit them to the legislature for concurrence or implementing legislation; in other countries, the legislature can act on its own, creating legislation that is sent to the executive for approval. In more democratic states, there are some mechanisms to override the decisions made by the head of government to approve or disapprove legislation.

The processes by which policy consideration takes place in individual legislative settings differ, with decisions being made about what issues and proposals to consider and the means for addressing them. Legislative bodies operate with sets of rules that govern whether these decisions may be made by legislative leadership, committees, or by member debate. The legislative forums in which the issues will be debated, legislation developed and decisions taken on its provisions are subject to rules as well. Where multiparty legislative settings exist, more deliberation and negotiation take place to consider various positions. The amount of support needed to approve proposed measures varies, as does the extent to which members of parties in legislative bodies are subject to party discipline or are more independent during voting. These factors can move proposals toward acceptance or rejection or toward seeking changes, delaying, or halting consideration of proposals.

In considering the role of legislative bodies in the policy-making process and how policy and legislation are developed within it, one needs to identify the influences of leaders, the committees that are most important to the process for a given issue and the norms and procedures by which issues are introduced, proposals reviewed and options deliberated.

Intervention Norms

Policy mechanisms and tools used domestically are heavily influenced by dominant domestic political philosophies and policy traditions. These influence the types and degrees of intervention. Despite its unique issues, media intervention tends to follow the domestic norms and patterns of intervention involving other industries (Picard 1985).

It is especially notable in policy terms when efforts are made to deviate from those norms. In the United States, which has long eschewed direct subsidies, many journalists are now supporting efforts to create direct intervention to support news organizations as a result of the changing economic bases of journalism, actions they would have heavily criticized in the past.

Final Words

Because of variations in domestic policy making, it is important for those considering their processes and outcomes to identify the specificities and nuances present in a given country. This chapter has provided means for recognizing and classifying the domestic influences on policy making and policy and show where and how they affect the processes.

When analyzing policy making in an individual country, a researcher must pay attention to the influences present, and where and how they occur and affect policy. When comparing policy between or among countries, the domestic influences in all countries involved must be taken into account to determine why variations in policy occur.

Chapter Summary

- The specifics of policy making differ in all states
- Policy-making institutions, processes and practices influence the policy produced
- Why policy is being considered influences the policy developed
- The extent to which those affected by policy decisions participate in the process varies
- National security, economic interests and cultural demands have strong influences on media and communication policy
- Domestic norms affect policy processes and choices

Discussion Points

1. Why might one want to compare policy-making processes among different countries?
2. Why does the appearance of new technologies so often require the development of new policy?
3. Why do public consultations sometimes produce few new ideas or involve a small range of elites? How can those limitations be overcome?
4. Is it undesirable for security, economic, or cultural factors to affect policies? Why or why not?
5. Do simpler policy-making arrangements in smaller states necessarily produce poorer policy?

Bibliography

Ahearne, Jeremy, ed. 2002. *French Cultural Policy Debates: A Reader*. London: Routledge.

Baasanjav, Undrah. 2016. The Public Interest and Mongolian Digital Television Transition. *International Journal of Digital Television* 7 (1): 7–22.

Bauer, Johannes M. 2010. Regulation, Public Policy, and Investment in Communications Infrastructure. *Telecommunications Policy* 34 (1–2): 65–79.

Bennetts, Marc. 2019. Russia Passes Law to Jail People for 15 Days for 'Disrespecting' Government. *The Guardian*, March 6. Available at https://www.theguardian.com/world/2019/mar/06/russian-parliament-outlaws-online-disrespect. Accessed 8 Mar 2019.

Bernabei, Stefano. 2018. Italy Buys into Telecom Italia to Shield Strategic Interests. *Reuters*. Available at https://www.reuters.com/article/us-telecom-italia-vivendi-cdp/italy-buys-into-telecom-italia-to-shield-strategic-interests-idUSKCN1HC0GJ. Accessed 12 Jan 2019.

Bouwen, Pieter. 2002. Corporate Lobbying in the European Union: The Logic of Access. *Journal of European Public Policy* 9 (3): 365–390.

Campos, Nauro F., and Francesco Giovannoni. 2007. Lobbying, Corruption and Political Influence. *Public Choice* 131 (1–2): 1–21.

Coleman, Stephen, and Peter M. Shane, eds. 2012. *Connecting Democracy: Online Consultation and the Flow of Political Communication.* Cambridge, MA: MIT Press.

Daalmeijer, Joop. 2004. Public Service Broadcasting in The Netherlands. *Trends in Communication* 12 (1): 33–45.

Duffy, Matt. 2013. *Media Laws and Regulation of the GCC Countries.* Doha: Doha Center for Media Freedom.

El-Nawawy, Mohammed, and Adel Iskandar. 2008. *Al-Jazeera: The Story of the Network That Is Rattling Governments.* New York: Basic Books.

Fan, Peilei, and Chihiro Watanabe. 2006. Promoting Industrial Development Through Technology Policy: Lessons from Japan and China. *Technology in Society* 28 (3): 303–320.

Flew, Terry, Petros Iosifidis, and Jeanette Steemers, eds. 2016. *Global Media and National Policies: The Return of the State.* London: Palgrave Macmillan.

Freedman, Des. 2008. *The Politics of Media Policy.* Cambridge: Polity Press.

Iosifidis, Petros. 1997. Pluralism and Media Concentration Policy in the European Union. *Javnost/The Public* 4 (1): 85–104.

Khetri, Nir. 2005. Information and Communication Technologies, Strategic Asymmetry and National Security. *Journal of International Management* 11(4): 5M3–580.

Klüver, Heike. 2013. *Lobbying in the European Union: Interest Groups, Lobbying Coalitions, and Policy Change.* Oxford: Oxford University Press.

Ku, Cheng-Yuan, Yi-Wen Chang, and David C. Yen. 2009. National Information Security Policy and Its Implementation: A Case Study in Taiwan. *Telecommunications Policy* 33 (7): 371–384.

Latzer, Michael. 2007. Regulatory Choice in Communications Governance. *European Journal of Communication* 22 (3): 399–405.

Lemieux, Frederic. 2018. *Intelligence and State Surveillance in Modern Societies: An International Perspective.* Bingley: Emerald Publishing.

Lewis, Ted G. 2006. *Critical Infrastructure Protection in Homeland Security: Defending a Networked Nation.* New York: Wiley.

Lowe, Gregory F., and Christian Nissen. 2011. *Small Among Giants: Television Broadcasting in Smaller Countries.* Göteborg: NORDICOM.

Lugo-Ocando, Jairo. 2008. *The Media in Latin America.* Maidenhead: Open University Press/McGraw-Hill.

Menashri, David. 2001. *Post-Revolutionary Politics in Iran: Religion, Society and Power.* London: Routledge.

Miles, Hugh. 2005. *Al Jazeera: The Inside Story of the Arab News Channel That Is Challenging the West.* New York: Grove Press.

O'Regan, Tom, and Ben Goldsmith. 2006. Making Cultural Policy: Meeting Cultural Objectives in a Digital Environment. *Television and New Media* 7 (1): 68–91.

Pew Research Center. 2017. Public Comments to the Federal Communications Commission About Net Neutrality Contain Many Inaccuracies and Duplicates. November 29. Available at http://www.pewinternet.org/2017/11/29/public-comments-to-the-federal-communications-commission-about-net-neutrality-contain-many-inaccuracies-and-duplicates/. Accessed 6 Mar 2019.

Picard, Robert G. 1985. Patterns of State Intervention in Western Press Economics. *Journalism Quarterly* 62 (1): 3–9.

Picard, Robert G., and Steven S. Wildman, eds. 2015. *Handbook of the Economics of the Media.* Cheltenham: Edward Elgar Publishing.

Picard, Robert G., Valerie Belair-Gagnon, and Sofia Ranchordás, eds. 2016. The Impact of Charity and Tax Law and Regulation on Not-for-Profit News Organizations. Reuters Institute, University of Oxford, and Information Society Project, Yale Law School, Yale University.

Puppis, Manuel. 2008. National Media Regulation in the Era of Free Trade: The Role of Global Media Governance. *European Journal of Communication* 23 (4): 405–424.

———. 2009. Media Regulation in Small States. *International Communication Gazette* 71 (1–2): 7–17.

Sarikakis, Katharine, ed. 2007. *Media and Cultural Policy in the European Union*. Amsterdam: Editions Rodopi.

Sarikakis, Katharine, and Sarah Ganter. 2014. Priorities in Global Media Policy Transfer: Audiovisual and Digital Policy Mutations in the EU, MERCOSUR and US Triangle. *European Journal of Communication* 29 (1): 17–33.

Saudi Arabia, Communication and Information Technology Commission. 2016. http://www.citc.gov.sa/English/Pages/default.aspx. Accessed 7 May 2016.

Saudi Arabia, King Abdulaziz City for Science and Technology. 2016. http://www.kacst.edu.sa/eng/Pages/default.aspx. Accessed 7 May 2016

Saudi Arabia, Ministry of Communication and Information Technology. 2016. http://www.mcit.gov.sa/En/Pages/default.aspx. Accessed 7 May 2016

Saudi Arabia, Ministry of Culture and Communication. 2016. http://www.saudinf.com/main/c6e.htm. Accessed 7 May 2016.

Scharpf, Fritz W. 2000. Institutions in Comparative Policy Research. *Comparative Policy Studies* 33 (6–7): 762–790.

Schiller, Dan. 2008. The Militarization of U.S. Communications. *Communication, Culture & Critique* 1 (1): 126–138.

Semati, Mehdi, ed. 2008. *Media, Culture and Society in Iran: Living with Globalization and the Islamic State*. London: Routledge.

Slobogin, Christopher. 2007. *Privacy at Risk: The New Government Surveillance and the Fourth Amendment*. Chicago: University of Chicago Press.

Sweet, Pat. 2019. Spain to Introduce Digital Services Tax. *Accountancy Daily*, January 22. Available at https://www.accountancydaily.co/spain-introduce-digital-services-tax. Accessed 4 Mar 2019.

Tamkin, Emily. 2019. With Putin's Signature, 'Fake News' Bill Becomes Law. *Washington Post*, March 18. Available at https://www.washingtonpost.com/world/2019/03/18/with-putins-signature-fake-news-bill-becomes-law/?utm_term=.3f5767d87d39. Accessed 28 Mar 2019.

Trappel, Josef. 1991. Born Losers or Flexible Adjustment? The Media Policy Dilemma of Small States. *European Journal of Communication* 6 (3): 355–371.

Turnpenny, John, Måns Nilsson, Duncan Russel, Andrew Jordan, Julia Hertin, and Björn Nykvist. 2008. Why Is Integrating Policy Assessment So Hard? A Comparative Analysis of the Institutional Capacities and Constraints. *Journal of Environmental Planning and Management* 51 (6): 759–775.

United States US Central Intelligence Agency and US Department of State. 2012. *Saudi Arabia: A Brief Comprehensive Study of Saudi Arabia, Country Studies*. Washington, DC: Zay's Place.

Suggested Readings

Bauer, Johannes M. 2010. Regulation, Public Policy, and Investment in Communications Infrastructure. *Telecommunications Policy* 34 (1–2): 65–79.
Flew, Terry, Petros Iosifidis, and Jeanette Steemers, eds. 2016. *Global Media and National Policies: The Return of the State*. London: Palgrave Macmillan.
Latzer, Michael. 2007. Regulatory Choice in Communications Governance. *European Journal of Communication 22* (3): 399–405.
Puppis, Manuel. 2009. Media Regulation in Small States. *International Communication Gazette* 71 (1–2): 7–17.

PART III

Policy Reviews, Advocacy and Future Research

CHAPTER 8

Policy Analyses

An important aspect of policy making is policy analysis, in which interested parties examine the need for policy, clarify issues of concern, explore alternatives and assert a preferential course of action. Understanding the purposes and creation of policy analyses is important if one is to effectively produce them or consider analyses produced by other parties.

Policy analysis is a form of research that assesses potential policies with the purpose of helping policy makers and advocates make decisions about what courses of action to pursue. It is designed to clearly identify what issues or problems are being addressed, the underlying factors that create or influence them, the potential actions to address them, the extent to which the various policy options can be expected to alter underlying factors or conditions that create the issues or problems and how the options align with the philosophy and policy principles of the policy makers or advocacy organization.

Policy analysis provides explanation based on information, developments and evidence that is understandable to those who need to make decisions. Effective and valuable policy analysis requires that the examination be made with the sincere purpose of improving understanding of the challenges and issues involved, accurate and honest portrayals of options and their potential outcomes, genuine consideration of the range of options and authentic reflection upon the possibilities.

Policy analysis involves ex ante research and examination to inform policy decisions. It takes place in the initial stages of the policy process model. Policy evaluation is a term principally used to indicate ex post research and examination after policy implementation. Evaluation will be explored in the next chapter.

R. G. Picard, *Media and Communications Policy Making*, Palgrave Global Media Policy and Business,
https://doi.org/10.1007/978-3-030-35173-1_8

The Importance of Evidence in Analyses

Evidence-based policy is a contemporary public administration and regulatory approach based on the use of relevant scientific, economic, financial and performance documentation. It is an important part of policy analyses and is now being widely used in many political and social policy and administrative environments (Cartwright and Hardie 2012; Stoker 2016). It is designed to provide fundamental data and information that are used concurrently with regulatory values, preferences and expertise to promote best practices and consistency in regulation.

Evidence-based policy making is a rationalist approach to policy making and policy analysis that relies on systematic reviews of knowledge and experience, as well as original research (Bogenschneider and Corbett 2010). Its uses are sometimes criticized for the ways evidence questions are constructed, evidence relied upon and the belief that evidence will overcome political judgment and contested values (Marston and Watts 2003; Pawson 2006). Nevertheless, well-used evidence provides significant understanding of issues and conditions, what approaches have worked in other contexts and what may be useful concepts and ideas to adopt in policy making.

The evidence-based approach asserts that policy should be based on evidence of actual conditions, not merely perceptions or anecdotal indicators. Evidence-based policy making involves systematic reviews, quantitative and qualitative analysis, modeling, forecasting, research on relevant markets, identification of market successes and failures, identification of potential regulatory measures, cost-benefit analysis of proposed policies and impact assessment of existing policies (Majchrzak and Markus 2013).

Good evidence-based analysts are wary of unconcernedly adopting policies from other settings because they cannot be expected to produce similar outcomes if there are differences in conditions. Consequently, evidence needs to be sought to ensure that policy adoption does not ignore important factors that might make policy effective.

The evidence-based policy-making approach is increasingly being applied in media communications policy debates and has been used to assess such diverse policy issues as the role of privatization in telecommunications development (Parker and Kirkpatrick 2005), effects of media coverage of suicide (Hawton and Williams 2005) and programs to reduce bullying on the internet (Farrington and Ttofi 2009).

Although evidence is useful, it must be used and relied upon critically. Statistical data can be skewed because of the purpose for which it was collected, whether the data are a direct measure or proxy measure of the phenomenon and what data were not collected, available, or relied upon. Limitations on data about media and cultural industries in national industrial statistics have been widely noted ((European Commission 2001; Eurostat 2001; Cardona 2002; Picard and Toivonen 2004). Although many national statistics offices have made efforts to improve data available for evidence purposes, many gaps and omissions remain because much relevant data are proprietary or uncollected by any organization.

Elements of Policy Analyses

Good analyses take place in steps as part of an assessment process that involves identifying and explaining issues and challenges; considering available knowledge and evidence; detailing, evaluating and comparing options; and recommending courses of action (Fig. 8.1). The elements create a logical progression for developing understanding that leads to decision-making.

Policy Problem and Objective Identification

This initial task of a policy analysis defines and delineates the policy problem, that is, the issues and what policy makers are trying to accomplish. Effective analyses start by clarifying the issues, distinguishing symptoms of problems from the issues themselves and clearly stating the rationale(s) for acting and the primary objectives of policy intervention. Plainly identifying the issues involved in the policy problem and the policy objectives is crucial for good policy analysis because they influence the analytical strategy and subsequent steps in the analysis process and policies recommended. Poorly constructed policies often focus on indicators of issues, rather than on the fundamental issues themselves, and the objectives of policies are sometimes vague and unclear, so this first step is crucial for valuable analyses.

Issue identification often begins by addressing what has precipitated interest in the topic, such as a focusing event or larger trends that have revealed the issue. It delineates and clarifies the issue and the relationships between events and developments and the central issue itself. Stakeholders often have varying perceptions of the policy problem or issue. Good analysis helps capture these differences and provides a broader context (Hansberger 2001).

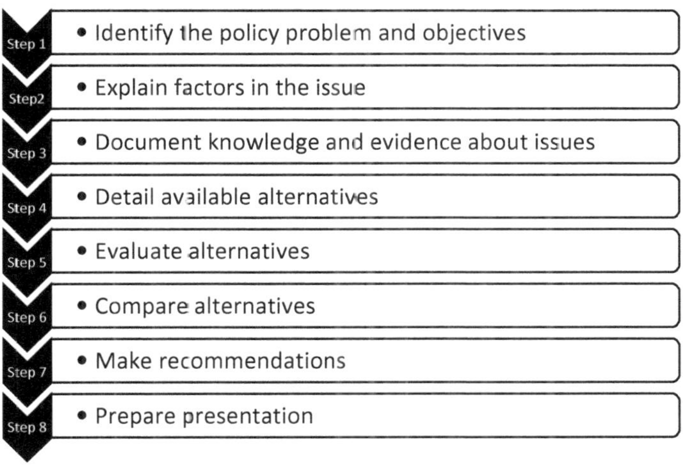

Fig. 8.1 Steps in the policy analysis process

The analysis then specifies the objective(s) of policy action, stipulating what the intervention is intended to accomplish. This process is crucial if one is to establish the fundamental nature of the issue and effective approaches addressing it. Issue and objective identification require clear-headedness and precision to separate indicators of the issue, perceive the larger picture and parse the fundamental nature of the issue. Poorly or narrowly defined issues can constrain thinking and lead to courses of action that may not provide beneficial solutions to the fundamental challenges being addressed.

During and following the economic crisis of 2008–2011, for example, rapidly declining advertising income led news organizations in North America and Europe to rapidly reduce journalistic employment and reduce news coverage. Those who depicted this issue as a revenue challenge in commercial media firms and the objective as preserving established news providers narrowed the issue and consequently focused on policy options and tools such as subsidization, tax breaks and exceptions to competition and media cross-ownership laws. Observers who described the issue as resulting from a fundamental change in news production, distribution and consumption and the objective of creating mechanisms and tools to support quality journalism took a more holistic approach to options that included for-profit and not-for-profit media, encouraging startup digital news providers, helping established firms adjust to the new environment and news production funds.

Issue and objective identification should also provide the rationale for addressing the issue. It should describe how it is associated with related issues, its relative importance and the policy principles that support acting upon the issue. This provides motive and justification for giving the issue attention and action.

Explain Factors in the Issue

This analysis step describes the various factors that influence the issue being addressed and how they are interrelated. This is an informational task designed to provide understanding to subject area experts and to provide fundamental understanding to those who are not specialists in the issue but will nevertheless have to make decisions. A legislator who operates an insurance agency or metal fabricating company, for example, may need such information to understand factors influencing cable/satellite television markets or internet telephone services. A regulatory specialist in competition law at a ministry of communications may find the discussion helpful in comprehending the issues of program genre diversity on broadcast television.

An explanation of factors involved in a policy proposal to extend the duration of copyright, for example, would outline what is concerning those who are promoting the extension; explain the purposes and history of copyright; describe how the copyright system works; indicate what goods and services are covered by copyright; define important concepts and terms; reveal how it relates to the economy, employment and culture as a whole; specify its bases in both national law and international treaties; indicate who the stakeholders are; and describe how and why they would be expected to react to a proposed change in copyright duration.

This step thus provides the bases upon which policy makers can consider the significance of the issue, evidence about the issue and potential courses of actions.

Document Knowledge and Evidence

This step lays out what is known and unknown about the issue, its scale and scope, existing evidence about the issue and factors influencing it.

This is not an academic literature review designed for purposes of scientific research, but a cohesive comprehensible summary of existing knowledge and evidence. It usually relies on academic research, research by government agencies and reports by think tanks, trade associations and nongovernmental organizations. It addresses differences among approaches to the issue and the findings and the bases of divergent viewpoints of subject area experts.

The review should be sufficiently broad to convey understanding of issues addressed and raised in existing research and the state of existing knowledge. It should assess the quality, quantity and consistency of existing studies and evidence and include contradictory and negative viewpoints. It is important that this review does not "cherry pick" evidence promoting a particular point of view, but it can provide evidence and rationales for giving specific approaches or research greater credence.

Whenever possible, the review should include statistical information related to the topic that helps to explain the scale and scope of the issue. The evidentiary strength of that data should be critically evaluated, providing readers a level of confidence in the evidence available and the conclusions or recommendations that might be based upon it. Some types of research, for example, economic modeling, provide evidence of potential outcomes of choices. Models are useful, but do not fully reflect reality. These should be assessed to understand what assumptions are employed, what factors are included or excluded and how those affect the results and the overall quality of the evidence. In addition, important evidence and relevant perspectives produced by other quantitative and qualitative methods should be included.

Good analysis maintains analytical integrity and does not use misleading data and evidence or ignore contradictory evidence. It makes values and beliefs transparent, so users can understand how the evidence is being interpreted. In making the appraisal of existing research, it is important to identify necessary and sufficient conditions, remember that correlation is not "cause and effect" and keep in mind that "proof" is elusive.

A comprehensive knowledge review includes exploration of how other states/provinces, countries, regional governments and intergovernmental organizations and agencies address the issue and the outcomes of their choices.

Care must be taken in comparing and potentially transferring policy from another location or governance location because many factors can make them ineffective when applied elsewhere (Bauer 2010).

Detail Available Alternatives

This step moves beyond understanding the issue, its context and related evidence to answer the question, "What can be done about it?" This undertaking is designed to clarify what could be done, how it would be done and the effort required.

A policy analysis lays out and discusses alternative policy approaches and/or specific policies that are or can be considered. The initial option for any issue is to do nothing and to wait for further developments or evidence. Other options are then presented, based on the various approaches identified in the knowledge review and any proposals already made by various stakeholders.

This section of the analysis should be direct and clear about each option. It should lay out what would be necessary to be done to pursue the options—such as pursuing legislation in a parliament or congress or seeking rulemaking in a regulatory agency; whether and how the option requires altering current policy, law or regulation; and the extent to which the option involves coordination of policies and activities of multiple agencies. It should reasonably estimate cost, feasibility, acceptability, challenges expected in implementation and impediments to the policy. The analysis should also clarify what the alternative will and won't do, an estimate of its effectiveness of each alternative in addressing the policy problem, potential unintended consequences and the extent to which it promotes equity.

Evaluate Alternatives

Thoughtful consideration of the alternatives is important for decision-making because it provides those reading the analysis an understanding of their differences, implementation requirements and likely outcomes. Each alternative is considered separately and systematically using an established set of criteria. The criteria are specified and applied consistently throughout the process.

There are multiple ways to consider options (Nagel 2002; Wollmann 2006). Criteria often include factors such as equity, efficiency, administrative ease, cost and concurrence with other policies, laws and regulations. Political feasibility and alignment with the values and principles of the organization for which the analysis is made are also common elements. The risks of regulating, not regulating, over-regulating and under-regulating should be considered.

In addressing the likely outcomes of the options, estimation is made about the extent to which they address the fundamental issue and objectives and the underlying factors involved.

Compare Alternatives

This step is designed to compare the alternatives individually considered in the previous step. It highlights the positive and negative aspects of each, the costs and benefits of implementation, the capability of the administrative agency to oversee the approaches and potential unintended consequences.

The analysis discusses the comparison and often provides a quick reference chart or graphic summary of the assessment.

Make Recommendations

The final step in the analysis is to recommend a course of action. The recommendations may suggest one or more alternatives, or even none of the alternatives, as desirable and preferred. Recommendations should explain the reasoning for the choices, grounded in the information and evidence provided and the comparison of alternatives. This step is essentially making the argumentative case for the options favored.

In making recommendations, it is important to add the extent to which the proposed policy intervention is proportionate to the issue and conditions being addressed, and to clarify how it will be effective in addressing them. Uncertainties and limitations in pursuing the suggested actions should be clarified.

Finally, the recommendations should indicate what steps are needed to pursue the preferred alternative. These should describe what actions are needed and by whom, or which governance bodies to pursue and implement the policy.

Prepare Presentation

Completing the process is not the ultimate objective of policy analysis. The objective is to provide guidance on how an agency, organization, or client should think about the issues, options and potential courses of action. It is to be an aid to considered decision-making. To accomplish that task, the analysis needs to be prepared and presented to an audience to consider and act upon. This is typically done as a written document or report, a policy brief and/or a slide deck for presentation in a meeting.

The material needs to be prepared keeping in mind the audience who will read or view it and crisply and concisely convey its message (Swain and Swain 2015). The presentation needs to clearly introduce and contextualizes the issue and answer the question of why policy to address it is needed now. It should progress logically and provide robust evidence, possible solutions and recommendations.

As with all professional presentations, the written reports, brief and/or slide decks should be a visually attractive, professional presentation that conveys the import of and proficiency with which the analysis was undertaken. Well-designed report and presentation templates and presentation folders can enhance how they are received by their audience.

Analyses from Others Need to Be Used Carefully

When considering policy analysis that others have produced in decision-making and research, it is important to consider whether the source is reliable and its reputation for producing dependable analysis based on verifiable information and supportable argumentation. Many political organizations, advocacy groups and nongovernmental organizations produce quality analyses and argumentation despite taking sides in a policy debate.

Policy analyses need not be devoid of values, beliefs, or preferences, but should be truthful and sincere. Unfortunately, some less reputable providers of analyses sometimes base their work on misleading or false information, hyperbole and hysteria, and provide little good analysis. They often present perspectives promoting or protecting the interests they represent, and ignore or denigrate other perspectives.

It is good practice to ensure that analyses and information relied upon were produced by reputable organizations, to carefully review their findings and citations and to examine their arguments to ensure that they are grounded in the data and information presented and based on rational contemplation.

Common Approaches and Methods Used in Analysis

A wide variety of examination and research methods are commonly found in policy analyses, and it is important to be familiar with them and what they reveal. This section introduces the approaches and methods, but those involved in producing analyses need to develop deeper understanding of the approaches and methods that they choose to employ. This provides an overview of different methods that are often employed or encountered to familiarize readers with their uses. More extensive discussions of policy research methods can be found in volumes specifically devoted to methodology (Bardach 2005; Holland 2007; Cartwright and Hardie 2012; Majchrzak and Markus 2013; van den Bulck et al. 2019).

The choice of method is dependent upon the purpose of the research and must be able to answer the questions posed. Both quantitative and qualitative approaches are appropriate and useful, providing different types of evidence, insight and understanding. Most research in policy analysis still relies on quantitative research, in part because it is given strong emphasis in policy studies education (Morçöl and Ivanova 2010), but the use of qualitative methods is growing rapidly—especially in media and communications policy studies in which researchers come from a wider variety of disciplines more supportive of qualitative studies.

Purposes Served By Various Analysis Methods

A wide variety of analysis methods support various aspects of policy analyses, but the choice of which to employ should be based on the purposes and needs of the analysis. Some of the common uses of methods to pursue analysis purposes are:

Understanding the current policy environment
PEST analysis (Political, Economic, Social, and Technical analysis)
SWOT analysis (Strengths, Weaknesses, Opportunities, and Threats analysis)
Stakeholder Analysis

Focusing attention
Risk analysis
Delphi Technique
Legal research

Exploring a policy approach
SWOT analysis (Strengths, Weaknesses, Opportunities, and Threats analysis)
Cost-Benefit Analysis
Economic analysis
Modeling

Decision-making
Decision Tree Analysis
Cost-Benefit Analyses

Strategic Approaches in Analysis

Many analyses include strategic tools for considering options, their desirability and their efficacy. Common types of strategic analysis include PEST analysis, SWAT analysis and risk analysis that are now used in a wide variety of public administration and policy analysis. These provide means to help improve policy choices by understanding how those policy proposals fit within the current policy environment, problematic parts of the policy approach that will need to be addressed and how policy addresses public needs. These approaches help policy makers think strategically about issues and conditions, those who will be involved in the policy-making processes and to plan strategy for pursuing policy.

PEST Analysis

PEST analysis is a strategic technique used to clarify the milieu and its implications for issues and policy approaches being considered that may affect the feasibility of proposed approaches or policy. It is based on identifying relevant political, economic, social and technological (PEST) influences that are germane to the issues or policy choices being considered. It contextualizes the issue or potential choices within broader relevant contexts, identifies significant factors underlying the issue or that may affect how it is addressed and provides insight into the viability and effectiveness of choice options.

Political influences include the amount of current governmental involvement relevant to the issue, existing policies and legal/regulatory frameworks, political philosophies and makeup of the executive and legislature and domestic and international political pressures to make or alter policy. *Economic influences* involve the state of the economy evidenced in factors such as gross domestic product, inflation, interest rates, employment, personal income, living standards and other indicators that may influence decisions and the success of the policy approach. *Social influences* include demographic factors such as gender, age, ethnicity and disability, public attitudes and cultural values that are relevant to the decisions being made. *Technical influences* involve availability and capacity of technologies, innovation, research and development of technologies, rates of technological change and issues of technology cost and quality. An extended analysis called PESTLE is sometimes used to focus on legal and environmental influences if they are especially relevant.

PEST analysis produces a narrative that is typically abridged in summary graphics identifying the most important factors inducing action and influencing policy choices. A PEST analysis for an emerging nation considering the introduction of digital terrestrial television, for example, might produce a summary such as the one shown in Fig. 8.2. This would be accompanied by a narrative report exploring each of the points raised and their relationship to and influence on the decision to move from analog to digital broadcasting.

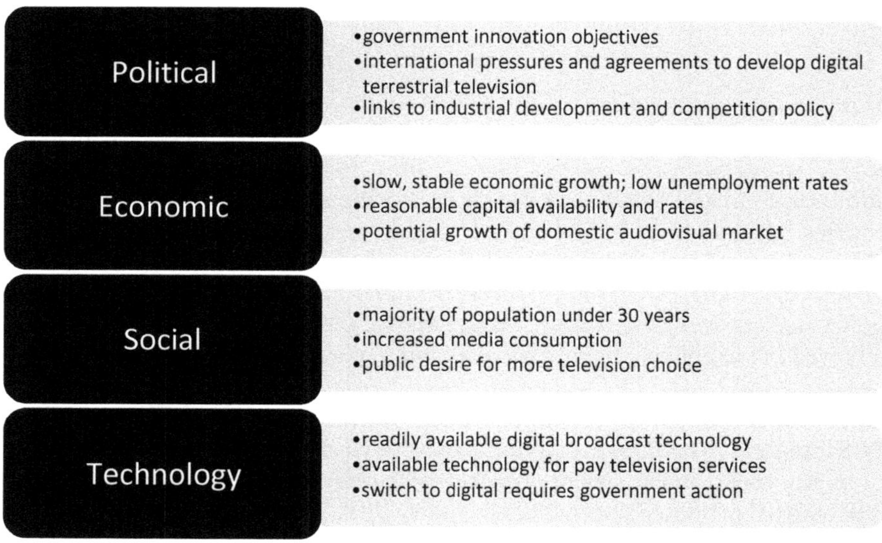

Fig. 8.2 Sample PEST analysis for digital terrestrial television in a country

SWOT Analysis

SWOT analysis identifies the strengths, weakness, opportunities and threats (SWOT) poised by potential policy approaches and choices to help policy makers capitalize on strengths and opportunities and ameliorate or minimize their weaknesses and threats. It is a method used in issue and solution exploration in public policy (Veselý 2007). Like all strategic tools, it is better applied in some types of policy analyses than others and tends to work better for analysis of specific discrete approaches and policies rather than analyzing broader complex policy regimes.

Strengths are those conditions that provide advantages such as strong government-industry relations, technological competence, or existing technological regulatory framework. *Weaknesses* are factors that disadvantage policy making such as lack of legal authority or technological competence, small administrative staff, or lack of strategic direction. *Opportunities* are environmental conditions or factors supporting the policy change such as market conditions, growth potential for industry, or broad support for altering existing policy. *Threats* are conditions or factors that create concerns if existing policy is maintained or new policy established.

Like PEST analyses, SWOT results are typically a written narrative and a condensed graphic display of the most important factors, as illustrated in a sample SWOT for a publicly owned telecommunications firms considering a switch to 5G mobile technology (see Fig. 8.3).

Once the analysis is competed, specific items to which policy should respond can be identified and mechanisms can be selected to address.

Stakeholder Analysis

Stakeholder analysis is a form of environmental research that identifies the different interests, perspectives and influence of various stakeholder groups that will take part in the policy process and debates. The analysis can lead to pursuing policy initiatives that balance interests or create opportunities for coopera-

Strengths • Would modernize system to newest standard • supports policies for education and health care delivery in rural areas	**Weaknesses** • high investment cost required • public operator lacks technical expertise • consumers require new phones
Opportunities • skipping 4G technology rollout • employment of domestic construction and telecom workers	**Threats** • lack of domestic capital • reliance on foreign capital and technology firms

Fig. 8.3 Sample SWOT results considering rollout of 5G technology

tion with some stakeholders in pursuing policy. The analysis helps identify key stakeholders, their varying needs and the issues on which to engage them.

Analysis tends to focus on their power, influence, needs and perspectives on the policy issue under consideration.

Delphi Technique

The Delphi method is a technique used to gather and assess the views of experts about current conditions, what is expected to happen in the future, its likelihood and what should be done about it with the purpose of eliciting the consensus of the experts (Linstone and Turoff 1975). The technique essentially uses an expert focus group for environmental scanning and forecasting.

The method can be employed with experts present together or individually reporting their views. The technique relies on structured questions that the experts answer and justify and takes place in two or more rounds of activity. In the first, each is asked to provide their views and assessment. The results are then collated and presented back as the consensus answer to which the experts are invited to suggest and justify revisions.

Risk Analysis

Risk analysis seeks to identify the probability of negative outcomes if no policy action is taken or potential policy options are pursued. This type of analysis considers systemic risks and the factors that are most likely to create poor consequences. Analysis involves risk identification, determining the probability and impact of their effects and any potential mitigation that may be possible.

Risk analysis is used to identify factors most needing to be addressed by policy, as well as the risks of not acting or of policy failing.

The European Commission uses a risk-based approach to monitor developments affecting media pluralism (Valcke et al. 2010; Centre for Media Pluralism and Media Freedom 2016).

Modeling and Forecasting Approaches in Analysis

These approaches use statistical and methods to describe conditions, markets and market behavior to forecast their future development, and to reveal how policy interventions might alter them.

Modeling

Modeling is often used in policy analysis to understand the environment, make predictions about how changes may affect it and seek evidence on cause and effects. It uses a variety of formal modeling techniques including computational and econometric models.

The validity and reliability of models are dependent upon how well the conditions and intervening factors are modeled, the levels of abstraction and assumptions employed. Some policy analysis uses advanced modeling techniques as a means of developing theory (Moss 2002).

Predictive models use statistics and other data to model conditions and predict how changes created by policy will create different outcomes. A wide variety of approaches and techniques are available, and the choice of which to employ needs to be appropriate for the use and for available data (Kuhn and Johnson 2013). Because of uncertainties involved, the best practice is to provide probabilities of different outcomes modeled. This type of predictive modeling is found in the Barwise and Picard study (2014) of the effects of potential reduction of financial support for the BBC on the public service broadcaster, commercial broadcasters, independent television programming sector and viewers.

Causal modeling reveals causal relationships among variables and is typically displayed in causal diagrams that indicate the causal relationship among variables (Mulaik 2009). Models are built using causal assumptions and then tested against data with statistical analysis to determine the extent to which and how well they explain what can be observed in the data. Causal modeling seeks to establish more than association or correlation, by identifying necessary and sufficient conditions producing effects. Structural equation modeling using factor analysis, path modeling and other techniques is used to establish the causality (Hoyle 2014)

Econometric Analysis

A variety of methods is used in economic analysis, including describing market and industry conditions and projecting and forecasting future developments with and without proposed policy interventions. Econometric models are used to evaluate the effects of policy alternatives and to perform cost-benefit analyses. The potential effects of policies on the economy are often examined using general equilibrium, rational expectations and optimal growth models.

Economic approaches consider the choices and uses of resources at the individual, firm, industry and societal levels and how the benefits of these choices can be maximized. Economic analysis provides means to examine the inner workings of industries and firms, policy initiatives and public agencies, but also methods for analyzing how choices and uses of resources affect consumer and social welfare. Much of this analysis is based on modeling techniques.

The importance of economic analysis in all types of public policy decisions involving markets and social welfare has grown over the past century. Analysis has been applied in the examination of the effects of policies involving health, transportation, the environment and a variety of other social issues. The increasing use of economic evidence in media and communications policy is part of a broader shift in policy making toward an evidence-based approach, when considering proposed policies and evaluating their outcomes. These approaches should not take the place of non-economic analysis, but they can provide quantifiable analytical criteria to be used alongside other methods.

Policy makers are placing greater emphasis on private investment and consumer choice because public funding for additional communication and media services is limited and competing demands for other financing of social services such as education, health and social welfare are high. As a result, the roles of regulation and economic incentives in achieving desired policy outcomes are growing in importance, and economic analysis is helping to inform debates about the viability of alternative policy options.

Achieving optimal balance in policy ultimately requires economic trade-offs. For instance, pursuing universal access to broadcasting and a variety of providers may involve providing access to public service or state broadcasting services and allowing commercial providers to serve only those areas that are commercially viable. Promoting the development of strong commercial players may be traded off against anti-siphoning rules with respect to sports and other major national events to ensure their availability on free-to-air television. And promoting consumer welfare may involve controlling and regulating the prices of cable television services as well as the mix of services offered.

Cost-Benefit Analysis

Cost-benefit analysis is used to identify, estimate and evaluate the costs of different potential policies and the benefits that they might produce. It involves techniques for examining those costs and benefits, including changes in individual, company and social behavior, and the cost-effectiveness of the proposed measures. This type of measurement does not merely consider financial outcomes, but social ones as well (Campbell and Brown 2015).

The method establishes the costs to implement, administer and support results from a policy or project (Boardman et al. 2017). These include expenditures required for facilities and equipment, personnel time and effort and management and oversight required.

Cost-benefit analysis developed as a business investment tool, but is now widely embraced for social cost-benefit analyses by governments and policy makers to estimate the impact of decisions to initiate a policy or even do nothing. Identifying and estimating costs and benefits involving policy require great attention and care because policies often affect varying social groups and enterprises in different ways, in different time frames, and there is often a good deal of uncertainty about effects that will be produced.

Although application of cost-benefit analysis to media and communications policy is appropriate and useful, it alone is insufficient for evaluating many policy options and decisions because their rationales are often intended to address issues that markets and economic efficiency measures alone will leave unanswered. These include questions such as whether it is better to service rural areas with wired or wireless communications and how does one serve community members that are unable to afford access to communications.

Decision Trees as a Decision-Making Tool

To help policy makers clarify and envision the decisions they are making, policy analyses often include decision tree analysis in their discussion of alternatives and recommendations.

Decision trees graphically display and highlight potential decisions, possible consequences, probabilities of outcome and requirements (Magee 1964).

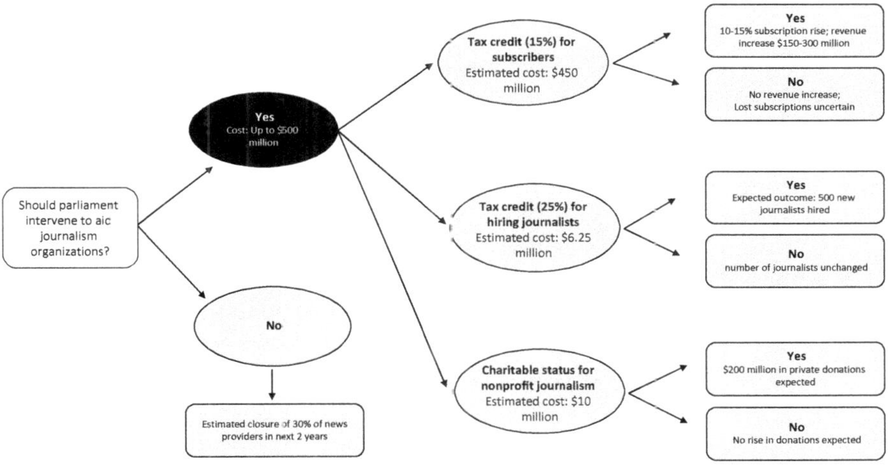

Fig. 8.4 Decision tree illustrating options for supporting journalism

Adapted from operations research and decision research, trees now are also used in policy making to map potential decisions. Effective decision trees account for uncertainties and risks, costs and other important factors.

Decision trees can be effectively used in policy analysis when considering alternative approaches or policy options. They are indicate the directions that potential decisions take policy makers and can help classify and predict outcomes.

A decision tree considering options for public intervention to support journalism activities is illustrated in the following graph (Fig. 8.4).

Final Words

Robust analyses are vital to making a case for policy or for altering policy. These planned and orderly examinations of issues that assert policy proposals need to be complete, realistic and credible to serve the purposes for their preparation. The methods used in analysis and the evidence provided should be appropriate for their uses and the conclusions being drawn.

Analyses should carefully consider and assess alternatives, their likely outcomes and should provide reasoned recommendations based on the analysis. They should make clear what is known and not known, what risks are involved in choices and what factors may intervene in achieving expected results.

Analyses can be used in a number of ways: to engage supporters and guide the activities of organizations that commission or produce them, to inform other organizations that may be willing to collaborate in promoting action in areas of agreement and to provide policy makers understanding of the background to an issue, various ways in which it can be addressed and why a course or course of action are preferable to others.

Chapter Summary

- Policy analyses explore why policy is needed, the conditions and issues of concern and options for addressing them.
- Policy analyses are either action-oriented or extended analysis that provide deeper understanding and critical review.
- The process of analysis involves identifying issues, explaining relevant factors, documenting knowledge and evidence and explaining, evaluating and comparing policy option.
- Robust evidence based on systematic reviews, statistics, and quantitative and qualitative research is an important part of policy making.
- Many methods with different uses and varying degrees of sophistication are used in policy analyses.

Discussion Points

1. Who is the audience when you produce a policy analysis?
2. How much evidence is necessary in a policy analysis?
3. How do you decide what analysis approaches and methods to use in a policy analysis?
4. Where can you get assistance when more robust and sophisticated analysis methods are required?
5. Why is it important for analyses to be thorough and use information and data carefully?

Bibliography

Bardach, Eugene. 2005. *A Practical Guide for Policy Analysis*. 2nd ed. Washington, DC: Congressional Quarterly Press.

Barwise, Patrick, and Robert G. Picard. 2014. *What If There Were No BBC Television? The Net Impact on UK Viewers*. RISJ Report. Oxford: Reuters Institute, University of Oxford.

Bauer, Johannes M. 2010. Learning from Each Other: Promises and Pitfalls of Benchmarking in Communications Policy. *Info* 12 (6): 8–20.

Boardman, Anthony E., David H. Greenberg, Aidan R. Vining, and David L. Weimer. 2017. *Cost-Benefit Analysis: Concepts and Practice*. 4th ed. Cambridge: Cambridge University Press.

Bogenschneider, Karen, and Thomas J. Corbett. 2010. *Evidence-Based Policy Making: Insights from Policy-Minded Researchers and Research-Minded Policy Makers*. London: Routledge.

Campbell, Harry F., and Richard P.C. Brown. 2015. *Cost-Benefit Analysis*. 2nd ed. London: Routledge.

Cardona, Jeannie. 2002. Cultural Statistics in Europe: Updates and Trends. UNESCO International Symposium on Cultural Statistics, Montréal, Canada, 21–23 October.

Cartwright, Nancy, and Jeremy Hardie. 2012. *Evidence-Based Policy: A Practical Guide to Doing It Better*. Oxford: Oxford University Press.

Centre for Media Pluralism and Media Freedom. 2016. *Assessing the Risk for Media Pluralism in EU and Beyond: Application of the Media Pluralism Monitor Tool (MPM 2016) in 30 European Countries*. Florence: European University Centre. http://cmpf.eui.eu/News/All/1601MPM2016Grant.aspx. Accessed 09 Dec 2018.

European Commission. 2001. Executive Summary: Identification and Evaluation of Financial Flows within the European Cinema Industry by Comparison with the American Model. Study for the European Commission, Directorate General for Education and Culture, Unit C1. Brussels: European Commission.

Eurostat. 2001. *Special Feature on Publishing and Printing*. Brussels: Eurostat Structural Business Statistics Unit.

Farrington, David P., and Maria M. Ttofi. 2009. Reducing School Bullying: Evidence-Based Implications for Policy. *Crime and Justice* 38 (1): 281–345.

Hansberger, Anders. 2001. What Is the Policy Problem? Methodological Challenges in Policy Evaluation. *Evaluation* 7 (1): 45–62.

Hawton, Keith, and Kathryn Williams. 2005. Media Influences on Suicidal Behaviour: Evidence and Prevention. In *Prevention and Treatment of Suicidal Behaviour: From Science to Practice*, ed. Keith Hawton. Oxford: Oxford University Press.

Holland, Jeremy. 2007. *Tools for Institutional, Political, and Social Analysis of Policy Reform: A Sourcebook for Development Practitioners* Washington, DC: The International Bank for Reconstruction and Development/The World Bank.

Hoyle, Rick H., ed. 2014. *Handbook of Structural Equation Modeling*. New York: Guilford Press.

Kuhn, Max, and Kjell Johnson. 2013. *Applied Predictive Modeling*. Berlin: Springer.

Linstone, Harold A., and Murray Turoff, eds. 1975. *Delphi Method: Techniques and Applications*. Boston: Addison-Wesley Educational Publishers.

Magee, John F. 1964. Decision Trees for Decision Making. *Harvard Business Review* 42 (4): 126–138.

Majchrzak, Ann, and M. Lynne Markus. 2013. *Methods for Policy Research: Taking Socially Responsible Action*. 2nd ed, 2013. London: Sage.

Marston, Greg, and Rob Watts. 2003 Tampering with the Evidence: A Critical Appraisal of Evidence-Based Policy Making. *The Drawing Board: An Australian Review of Public Affairs* 3 (3): 143–163.

Morçöl, Göktuğ, and Nadezda P. Ivanova. 2010. Methods Taught in Public Policy Programs: Are Quantitative Methods Still Prevalent? *Journal of Public Affairs Education* 16 (2): 255–277.

Moss, Scott. 2002. Policy Analysis from First Principles. *Proceedings of the National Academy of Sciences of the United States of America*, Vol. 99, No. 10, Supplement 3: Arthur M. Sackler Colloquium of the National Academy of Sciences. Sackler Colloquium on Adaptive Agents, Intelligence, and Emergent Human Organization: Capturing Complexity Though Agent-Based Modeling (May 14, 2002), 7267–7274.

Mulaik, Stanley A. 2009. *Linear Causal Modeling with Structural Equations*. Boca Raton: CRC Press.

Nagel, Stuart S. 2002. *Handbook of Public Policy Evaluation*. Thousand Oaks: Sage.

Parker, David, and Colin Kirkpatrick. 2005. Privatisation in Developing Countries: A Review of the Evidence and the Policy Lessons. *Journal of Development Studies* 41 (4): 513–541.

Pawson, Ray. 2006. *Evidence Based Policy: A Realistic Approach*. London: Sage.

Picard, Robert G., and Timo E. Toivonen. 2004. Issues in Assessment of the Economic Impact of Copyright. *Review of Economic Research on Copyright Issues* 1 (1): 20–29.

Stoker, Gerry, ed. 2016. *Evidence-Based Policy Making in the Social Sciences*. Cambridge: Polity Press.

Swain, John W., and Kathleen Dolan Swain. 2015. *Effective Writing in the Public Sector*. London: Routledge.

Valcke, Peggy, Robert Picard, Miklos Sükösd, Beata Klimkiewicz, Brankica Petkovic, and Cinzia dal Zotto. 2010. The European Media Pluralism Monitor: Bridging Law, Economics, and Media Studies as a First Step towards Risk-Based Regulation in Media Markets. *Journal of Media Law* 2 (1): 85–113.

van den Bulck, Hilde, Manuel Puppis, Karen Donders, and Leo van Audenhove, eds. 2019. *The Palgrave Handbook of Methods for Media Policy Research*. London: Palgrave Macmillan.

Veselý, Arnošt. 2007. Problem Delimitation in Public Policy Analysis. *Central European Journal of Public Policy* 1 (1): 80–100.

Wollmann, Helmut. 2006. Policy Evaluation and Evaluation Research. In *Handbook of Public Policy Analysis: Theory, Politics, and Methods*, ed. Frank Fischer and Gerald J. Miller, 393–404. Boca Raton: CRC Press/Taylor & Francis.

Suggested Readings

Campbell, Harry F, and Richard P.C. Brown. 2015. *Cost-Benefit Analysis*. 2nd ed. London: Routledge.

Cartwright, Nancy, and Jeremy Hardie. 2012. *Evidence-Based Policy: A Practical Guide to Doing It Better*. Oxford: Oxford University Press.

Majchrzak, Ann, and M. Lynne Markus. 2013. *Methods for Policy Research: Taking Socially Responsible Action*, 2nd ed. London: Sage 2013.

Swain, John W., and Kathleen Dolan Swain. 2015. *Effective Writing in the Public Sector*. London: Routledge.

van den Bulck, Hilde, Manuel Puppis, Karen Donders, and Leo van Audenhove, eds. 2019. *The Palgrave Handbook of Methods for Media Policy Research*. London: Palgrave Macmillan.

CHAPTER 9

Policy Evaluation and Policy Examination

Policy evaluation is the final stage in the policy process mode introduced in Chap. 1, in which the implementation and effects of a policy are reviewed, the need for the policy reconsidered and continuation, revision or ending the policy is proposed. Related to evaluations are policy examinations, extensive and authoritative reviews of the entire policy problem, intervention rationales, policy frameworks, mechanisms and tools and results through in-depth, rigorous methods, usually undertaken by scholars in universities and researchers at policy institutes.

Policy Evaluation

Policy evaluation takes place after policy has been implemented through laws and regulations and has been in place for enough time for its existence and administration to produce results. Evaluation is a way of holding those responsible for making and implementing policy accountable, to assess the effectiveness and efficiency of their efforts, to improve the policy and its implementation and to learn from the experience to improve future policy making.

Evaluations are crucial when policy mechanisms and tools use or reduce public funds, or provide regulatory benefits that are enjoyed only by particular firms or industries, because there is a need to ensure the policy scheme is producing public benefits.

Findings of evaluations should help inform changes in decisions, become the bases of new policy analyses and be integrated into the evaluation phase of policy cycle (Wollmann 2006). Evaluation is especially important when policy evolves over time because it instigates policy reconsideration and can produce change in policy agendas (Weiss 1999).

Effectiveness evaluation considers the degree to which the policies, processes and programs are accomplishing what was intended. Efficiency evaluation

R. G. Picard, *Media and Communications Policy Making*, Palgrave Global Media Policy and Business,
https://doi.org/10.1007/978-3-030-35173-1_9

reflects on whether they are making good use of resources to efficiently produce the outcomes. Evaluation considers the performance of the policies and their implementation by developing and using evidence.

In carrying out evaluation, policy researchers need to examine whether policy is effective in maximizing desired outcomes, the mechanism(s) behind the approach to ensure the choice is based on sound understanding of the problem and its causes and that the appropriate policy tools are being used to address the problem (Johns Hopkins Center for Civil Society Studies 2003). Evaluation considers how the policy, mechanisms and tools were implemented, the effectiveness of the implementation and administrative activities and the extent of support that exists for retaining the policy.

The primary purpose of evaluations is to assess the value of the policy and its impacts and to provide accountability for public intervention and resources expended. Evaluation can be used systematically to monitor and grade policies and their outcomes (Vedung 2000), and high-quality evaluations are especially important for those advocating for policy change (Gardner and Brindis 2017). Evaluations can be carried out by researchers commissioned by policy makers, by administrative agencies, or by stakeholders. Sometimes they are carried out by legislative committees or by independent commissions.

Three basic approaches are used in evaluations: (1) outcome evaluation that focuses on whether the policy produced intended consequences, (2) impact evaluation that looks at its overall effects and (3) program evaluation that considers individual programs or projects established as part of the policy.

Outcome evaluation seeks to determine the effectiveness and efficiency of the policy and its administration, whether modification should be made to the existing policy and its operation, whether it should be ended, or whether new policy is necessary. Evaluation can consider policies, processes, programs and initiatives associated with it, thus considering how well they are implemented and their outcomes (Weiss 1997).

Although many developmental policies and programs have, for decades, endeavored to improve media as a means of improving underdeveloped regions, systematic significant evaluation has long been absent, leading to misunderstanding of the usefulness of the efforts and the effectiveness of Western developmental theories (Manyozo 2012; Picard 2017). Contemporary reconsideration has concluded that media development efforts are often too narrowly focused on press freedom and the interests of their international supporters and do not address significant issues such as public participation and government accountability well (Noske-Turner 2017).

Impact evaluation goes beyond the question of whether results are being produced to examine economic and social impact. Impact evaluations have been used to address a range of policies and programs including teaching teachers about media literacy (Scull and Kupersmidt 2011), assessing how media literacy affects children's perceptions of media content involving violence and unhealthy practices (Bickham and Slaby 2012) and the impact of handset subsidies in Korea (Kim et al. 2004). Impact evaluations tend to consider systemic or community-level impacts, consider impacts on more stakeholders and rely on greater data collection and analysis. Social impact assessment focuses on impact on people's lives (Becker 2001; Vanclay et al. 2015) and has been used in many forms of policy evaluation.

Many evaluations focus on broader issues of policy, but *program evaluations* consider individual programs or projects carried out by different parties as a result of policy implementation (Vedung 2000). Programs are specific activities established under a policy that are intended to meet stated objectives and achieve specified goals in the short- to mid-term. An example would be a program to promote media literacy among high school students to help them identify misinformation and disinformation in social media. *Program evaluations* focus on program- or project-level evaluations, program administration aspects such as expenses and oversight of projects and administrative measures of results produced (Weiss 1997).

Program evaluation thus would identify the original objectives and goals, and seek evidence against which to compare implementation, administration and outcomes. These evaluations enquire as to whether the program or project is being properly operated and how useful it is. Evidence is developed through discussions or surveys with stakeholders, administrative staff and those receiving program services. The evaluation would include developing knowledge about awareness of the program, its reputation, consistency in application of principles and processes, what worked well and what did not, what factors inhibited better implementation, who was served by the program and who was not and what could be done to improve it.

Evaluations are sometimes carried out by policy actors including political parties and activist groups. In order to serve their fundamental purposes, evaluations must have credibility, be accurate, be undertaken in a transparent manner and be available for others to review. In considering completed policy evaluations, it is important to understand who produced them, the source of their funding, their scope and the criteria used for evaluation (Wollmann 2006).

Criteria for Evaluation

Those conducting evaluations need to select criteria being used before carrying out evaluation, providing a justification for what elements are included or excluded and a rationale for which elements will carry more weight in the evaluation and why. This is important as a guide for the evaluators, but also so that subsequent users of the evaluation can understand its bases.

Evaluations typically include assessments of the effectiveness and efficiency of the policy and its administration, its consequences and whether the policy remains viable or needs revision or replacement. They regularly include evaluation of economic, administrative and social impacts. Economic evaluations assess the impact on industry and the public. When considering impact of policy on an industry and its firms, evaluations tend to focus on issues such as whether the policy created risks for providers, increased or reduced revenue and profits, affected innovation, the costs required for compliance, employment effects and effects on valuations of firms. When considering economic impact on the public, evaluations tend to focus on changes in demand and consumption produced, what costs consumers bear because of the policy and benefits received. Social considerations evaluated involve the equity of the policy and its impacts, and effects on well-being, democratic participation and quality of life.

When an evaluation is being made, it is important to specify and clarify the criteria being used for the assessment. In an evaluation of the democratic impact of EU media policy, for example, the researcher asserted criteria of democratic needs and norms against which to assess whether policies supported the democratic roles of communications and citizen access to information and ability to participate in debates (Ward 2004).

A policy evaluation of the welfare effects of public television in the Netherlands established program-level and aggregate-level criteria to explore issues of quality and consumption following a change in policy for distributing funds to public television (Poort and Baarsma 2016).

Evaluations also focus on the coherency with other policy initiatives within the policy domain and between domains (May 2006; Rodrigo et al. 2009) and the degree to which a policy is transparent and promotes accountability (Finkelstein 2000; Fox 2007).

The Evaluation Process

Thoughtful evaluations take place through a disciplined and orderly process. They are systematic and guided by procedures that set out a series of questions for considering policy performance. They provide the bases for evaluations to move through stages that focus on different issues and aspects of a policy and its implementation (Fig. 9.1).

Effectiveness Is a Central Evaluation Criterion

The first part of the evaluation process concerns effectiveness, that is, what has changed because of implementation of the policy and the use of its tools. This requires examining what the conditions and factors were that created the issue or problem being addressed and what they are at this point, adjusting for any other intervening factors. This is typically done using statistical analysis, case studies, interviews and other social science methods.

When past and current conditions have been established, evaluators need to return to the purposes of the policy that were identified in original policy analyses, statements from the policy makers and implementing legislation and rules. Once evaluators clarify and understand the original objectives, they can then assess the extent to which the changes accomplish those objectives, identify items that have not been achieved and determine why they are not being realized.

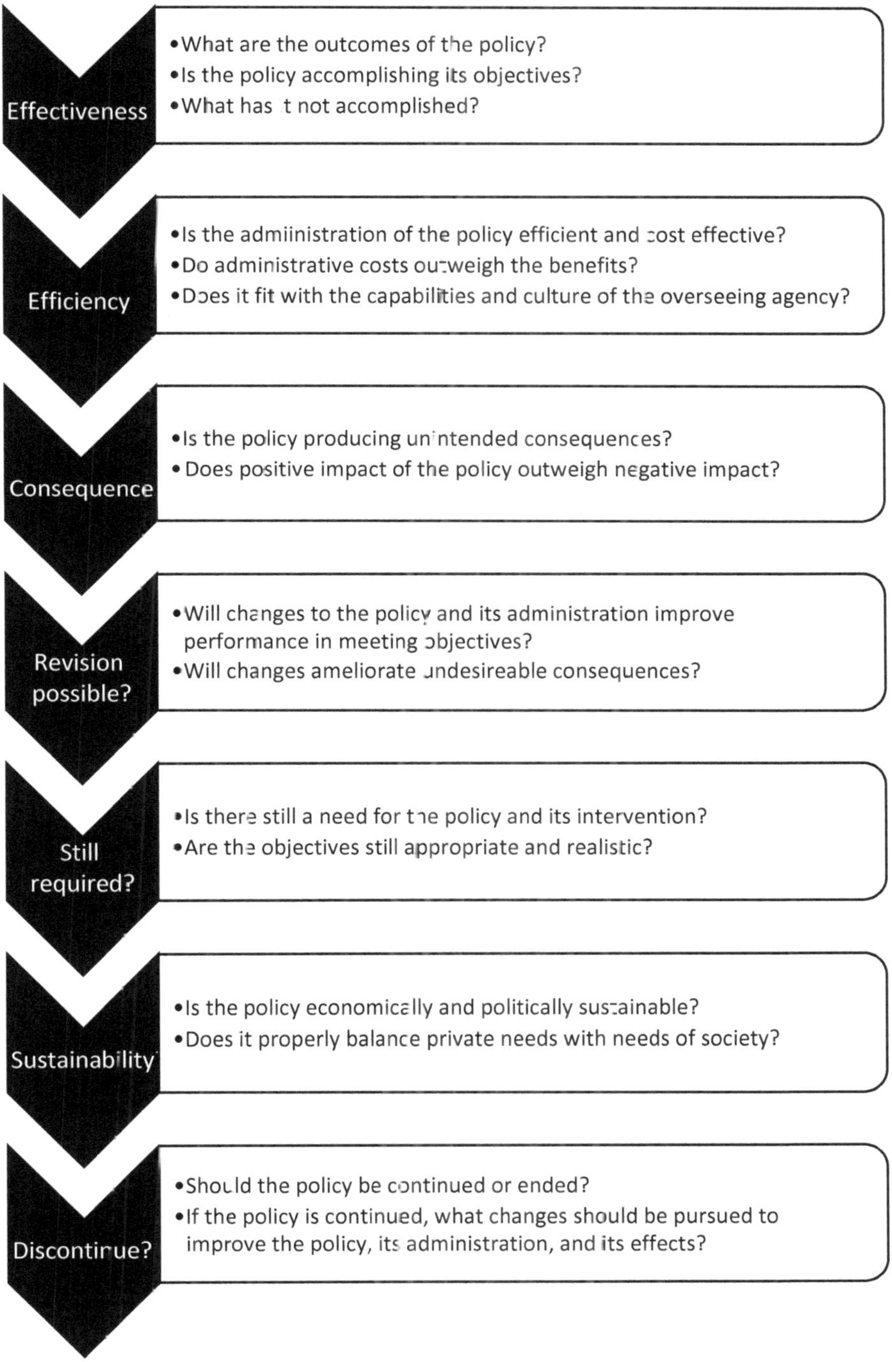

Fig. 9.1 The evaluation process

Policy evaluations, for example, have revealed that the Telecommunications Act of 1996 failed to deliver inter-sector and cross-platform competition, in part because it promoted too many self-interests of stakeholders in separate and uncoordinated sections of the legislation, and because it equated consumer choice with public interest (Aufderheide 2006). An evaluation of European policy makers' failure to establish effective media pluralism policy found they were unsuccessful in creating objectives, embracing mechanisms and tools needed, and that policy makers often sacrificed pluralism in pursuit of industrial policy and other media policy goals (Picard 2017).

Efficiency Concerns Focus on Policy Administration

Evaluation of the efficiency of a policy focuses on the time, effort and expense required to implement and administer the policy. It focuses on the organization and operations required by the policy and the extent to which they are practical, functional, make appropriate use of personnel and expenditures and provide adequate value for the expense involved.

Part of this type of evaluation considers what is happening to the administration and the administrative costs associated with the policy. These often start with an evaluation of whether the policy implementation fits with the capabilities and culture of the overseeing agency and if deficiencies in that area are so great that a different administrative setup might be preferable. The evaluation than considers whether administration of the policy is efficient and cost-effective and if administrative costs outweigh the benefits produced by the policy.

Consequences: Is the Policy Producing Intended and Unintended Consequences?

Policies can produce both intended and unintended results. Policy evaluation considers whether the existing policy is producing the intended results and how well it is doing so. If the assessment determines that it is not producing the intended result, it considers whether changing the mechanisms and tools of the policy is likely to achieve the results or whether the policy needs to be scrapped and a new approach pursued.

As noted earlier, unintended consequences may be either harmful or beneficial. A review of indigenous broadcast policies in Australia, for example, found that the government failed to use satellite policies in the 1980s and 2010 to support community and indigenous broadcasters, creating disadvantages for them. The decisions, however, led to the indigenous people creating a commercial television licensee and using the state digital television switchover to their advantage, and transparency requirements in the 2010 policy producing clarity and more equality in satellite policy (Rennie 2013).

Is Policy Revision Possible?

If policy is not producing expected results or producing negative unintended consequences, evaluations consider whether and how it might be altered to improve performance or reduce negative outcomes. This part of the evaluation process considers what laws, regulations, or processes may need adjustment, the feasibility of doing so, how those changes will affect stakeholders and their potential for creating negative consequences.

If policy revision is unlikely to produce better performance or reduce negative consequences, consideration may need to be given to ending the policy or completely reconsidering it (May 1992).

Is the Policy Still Required?

Consideration needs to be given to whether the conditions addressed persist and outcomes sought remain valid. Time, policy effects, social change, economic developments, technology and other factors may have altered the need for the policy by ending the conditions generating the initial issue(s) that produced the policy.

Consideration should be made as to whether the policy thus continues to produce results and whether removing the policy will lead to reappearance of the issues instigating the policy. Thus, issues of the objectives and the extent to which they remain appropriate need to be contemplated. A 25-year-old policy requiring telecom operators to provide rural school libraries with internet connectivity may be outdated if broadband connectivity has subsequently been extended to all schoolrooms.

Is the Policy Sustainable?

Sustainability involves the ability of current approaches to be continued and whether it is negatively affecting current and future social and industry needs and other policy options. The concept of sustainability originally developed out of policy concerns involving the environmental and human development (Dixon and Fallon 1989; Dovers 1996), but has since been extended to many other policy topics including state budgets, energy, education, trade and to evaluating the efficacy of current policies (See, e.g., Talvi and Végh 1998; Chalk and Hemming 2000; Cox and Béland 2013).

In considering whether the current policy approach is sustainable, one of the basic questions is whether it is producing diminishing results, whether trends and developments in society and technology are bypassing or reducing the effectiveness of the policy and whether it is worth continuing the existing policy given its reduced ability to produce objectives. Tax breaks and production financing assistance for domestic motion picture production, for example, may not be sustainable in their current form if the average annual number of beneficiaries has declined from 44 to 7 over the past 25 years; significant questions about the reasons for the decline need to be raised and whether the existing policy addresses them.

The economic sustainability of the policy also needs to be considered. This involves addressing questions of whether the costs of administering the policy are increasing at a rate that can be absorbed and whether the agency or ministry doing so is able to continue providing the personnel, time and effort required to continue pursuing the policy. It also involves assessing how the policy transfers costs to industries and firms, and whether that remains viable in light of technical developments, industry trends and consumer choices. A policy of taxing television broadcast advertising to create funds to support production of quality children's programming, for example, may have been viable when established, but its sustainability might be in question today because audiences are increasingly viewing content from cable/satellite channels and digital streaming services, and broadcast television advertising expenditures are being reduced.

Political sustainability also needs to be considered. This includes assessing whether changes in the political environment or government have altered support for the policy, or whether austerity measures or demands for different types of policy may affect its continuation. Many governments in recent years have been reducing funding for social welfare programs, including pensions, healthcare and unemployment benefits, for example. These state cuts to these vital and popular services make it politically difficult to argue for and expect expansion of funding for public provision of broadcasting or significant subsidies for media.

Policies that do not equitably balance private and public needs are not likely to be sustainable in the long term because the benefits they provide are one-sided. Over time, the inequitable nature of such policies and the harm they produce become increasingly visible, raise ethical issues and lead to backlash and demands for change.

Discontinue: Should the Policy Be Continued or Ended?

If a policy or its administration is not performing well, producing significant negative consequences, or is unsustainable, an evaluation needs to consider whether it should be ended. If reasonable revisions cannot be made, an evaluation normally will recommend termination. If revisions can be made to the policy or adjustments made to its administration to make it more effective and efficient or to address other deficiencies, continuance with modifications will normally be recommended.

Evaluations Should Consider if Policy Drift or Bureaucratic Drift Is Evident

Evaluations should consider whether policy drift or bureaucratic drift is evident. *Policy drift* describes policy that was implemented to serve specific purposes, but over time has produced different effects because needs for the policy and the conditions for which it was established have evolved and changed. The institutionalized policy thus "drifts" away from the issues and conditions it was originally intended to address because policy makers have not revised or reformed the policy for contemporary conditions (Hacker 2004). A policy choice to have multiple public service broadcast channels to provide more choice for viewers, for example, may or may not be have remained germane and effective in the era of digital terrestrial television, satellite television and digital streaming.

A second type of drift, *bureaucratic drift*, occurs when policies are implemented, but how they are applied are shifted in the direction desired by the administrative bureaucracy rather than by the original policy makers. Preferences of agency administrations and organizational culture can direct policy interpretation and its application, so it drifts away from its original intent (McCubbins et al. 1987). A policy to provide support for independent radio producers, for example, may be expanded by agency bureaucrats to include centralized radio broadcast production for numerous stations owned by the same firm, arguing it is within the meaning of a policy supporting an independent producer eligible for aid.

Policies that have been enacted thus need regular review and oversight from policy makers to ensure that policies remain appropriate and viable, and are applied as intended.

Policy Drift in Media Subsidies

The second half of the century produced multiple subsidies for media, many designed to serve specific public purposes of promoting pluralism and diversity in Western nations. Since their establishment, however, enormous changes in technologies and media systems have occurred and significantly altered the media environments in which these subsidies are provided.

Despite those changes, little revision or reform of the policies and those subsidy tools has occurred, allowing their funding to decline in real terms, diminishing their effectiveness in promoting pluralism and diversity, by not altering approaches and mechanisms or adjusting the tools to account for contemporary conditions (Picard 1986; Picard and Grönlund 2003; Ots 2009). The policies have drifted from their original purposes and objectives.

The lack of reform has been attributed to limited political attention, incumbent industries and firms protecting their interests in the subsidies and a perception that there are a few desirable, cost-effective and governable alternatives to the existing policies. Despite significant media transformation, subsidies "largely remained frozen in their late-20th century form" and had lost effectiveness due to policy drift, according to one observer (Nielsen 2014).

Controlling policy drift requires placing time limits on policy and its implementing laws, regular evaluation of existing policy and reconsideration of the rationales, assumptions, policy approaches and mechanisms and tools employed to address issues. Although methods for addressing policy drift exist and can be easily pursued, recognizing that drift is occurring, there is a need to reduce drift, and developing the political will to do so are complicated because inertia, well-established policy trajectories and resistance from within entrenched policy structures and stakeholders can hinder action (Hacker et al. 2015).

Responding to Policy Failure

The evaluation should consider whether and the extent to which policy failure has occurred. *Policy failure* transpires when it does not achieve its stated objectives. Failure can result from the policy itself being unsuitable, poorly implemented, ineffectively administrated, or affected by environmental changes. Evaluators need to consider all four to determine why a policy has been unsuccessful. They need to reflect on whether it relies on the wrong mechanism(s) and policy tool(s), to determine whether it was a failure because implementation did not provide appropriate authority or resources (Birkland 2015) and to establish whether administrators negatively affected how it was carried out because of lack of knowledge, capacity, or other factors (Taylor and Thorold 2017).

Policy is rarely a clear failure or success after implementation, but usually falls on a spectrum between the two outcomes (McConnell 2010), so evaluators need to consider whether it can be improved or whether different policy is needed. It is important to adapt when failure or weakness is identified in a policy evaluation. Policy makers should consider what different approaches, frameworks, mechanisms and tools exist and their potential for replacing existing policy.

Policy Learning Should Be Emphasized

Evaluations should seek to establish what lessons can be learned from the policy experience that can inform future policy choices and their use. This should include both instrumental learning about what mechanisms and tools work and don't work and why, as well as social learning about setting the context and goals for policy making (May 1992).

Policy learning is also evident when policies are transferred from other policy regimes, administrative arrangements, or institutions, but can create varying degrees of effectiveness in new settings (Stone 1999). Although learning from others can be useful at times (Dolowitz and Marsh 2000; Bulmer and Padgett 2004), much learning appears to be political rather than instrumental, and emulation with little adaptation is evident (Radaelli 2009).

Challenges of Evaluations

Gaining agreement for officially sanctioned evaluations to take place is sometimes problematic, and there may be debate about the scope and focus of the assessments. Evaluations may be unwelcomed by some stakeholders because current policy is beneficial for them and simultaneously welcomed by others because of perceptions that the policy is not appropriately balancing interests of stakeholders.

Organizational resistance to evaluation may arise within the bureaucracies administering the policy and its application because of inertia or opposition to how it may affect existing processes, organizational structures, agency budgets, job roles and employment. Such resistance affected the privatization processes and degree of independence granted in telecommunications governance reform in Brazil, for example (Prado 2013).

Evaluations also sometimes face difficulties when the policy frameworks and theories underlying policy were never specified or are not clear. This requires evaluators to reconstruct the original bases and intent for policy making (Leeuw 2003).

Seeking policy learning from evaluations requires clarity on what learning is sought, particularly in policy experiments and pilots, and often requires use of multiple methods in undertaking evaluations (Sanderson 2002).

Policy Examinations

Policy examinations are deep assessments and substantial explorations of existing policy typically undertaken by subject area experts and typically published as reports, journal articles, or books. They often become part of evidence in subsequent policy analyses or evaluations.

These studies are comprehensive and authoritative reviews and assessments that typically are produced in universities, policy institutes, international organizations and reputable think tanks. Such studies follow many of the steps in practice-oriented analysis but differ in terms of depth, strength of use of existing knowledge, links to theory, concerns with validity and reliability, reliance on reputable sources of information and evidence, contribution of original research, use of reliable data and information and efforts to compare and generalize findings.

Policy examinations develop deep understanding of a policy problem, provide extensive original analysis of information and data and develop theory or approaches that have greater generalizability. They often examine the history and development of policy and links them to factors that led to the previous decisions. It goes beyond mere policy description or simple criticism to examine evidence, explain causes of conditions and identify how they may be more effectively addressed.

This is a type of policy study rooted in the belief that policy should be constructed on a knowledgeable foundation of information developed through thorough and effective policy research, not merely perceptions and opinion (Majchrzak and Markus 2013). It includes original research, rather than merely relying on knowledge produced by others, as is normally the case in most policy analysis. It typically involves statistical and economic study using a range of social science research methods, historical research and legal research, as well as political economy and other critical research approaches.

This broader approach is intellectually honest and keeps critical distance between evidence and its interpretation and the subjective biases of the authors or the sponsoring institutions. It makes the political philosophies and policy preferences of the authors transparent when assessments, arguments, or recommendations are made.

An examination of policy related to children and their interest, for example, found that the technology is amplifying harm to children and that there are growing policy demands and actions to protect children. However, it found that the efforts involve numerous discrete and uncoordinated policy approaches using both public and self-governance mechanisms and lacked a unifying approach to the issues (Livingstone 2011). Scholarly policy examination is also illustrated by a review of policies on access to telecommunications for individuals with disabilities that revealed widely differing national approaches and significant social exclusion because of the lack of enabling policies (Jaeger 2006).

The Contemporary State of Policy Literature and Evaluations

The nature and approaches taken in policy literature and evaluations vary widely because of the varied interests of scholars and researchers in policy. Media and communications policy literature produced by scholars with legal backgrounds rarely recognize contributions made by scholars using economics approaches. Economic scholars seldom acknowledge the literature produced by political sociologists, who infrequently cite scholars taking historical approaches, who—in turn—never seem to appreciate the work of political economists. Few political sociologists and political economists acknowledge that institutions, power arrangements and processes are material to understanding policy making.

The body of media and communications policy literature is disconnected and atheoretical, and conveys different and inconsistent understandings of policy that often ignore institutional influences on policy making. It tends to portray policy debate and decision-making in win-lose terms, takes highly normative stances and regularly champions preferred policies with inadequate evidence or recognition that the rationales for and effectiveness of the policy may have changed over time.

The bulk of that policy literature describes individual policies in a specific governance setting, includes few robust comparative policy studies and contains insufficient meaningful policy evaluations and examinations. Much of the literature is unconcerned with policy institutions, processes and influences, and rarely addresses the intricacies and subtleties of policy making. It often conveys the idea that policy making can only be studied in democratic nations. Adding policy studies concepts and approaches introduced in this book will help improve knowledge produced in the future.

Most media and communications policy literature is found in journals and tends to be narrowly focused on a particular policy issue or trend in a given setting, such as an exploration of Australian regulatory monitoring of telecommunications consumer protection (Lee 2017) or implementation of the addressable digital system in West Bengal, India (Pandit 2019).

Most book-length literature of media and communications policy involves national or regional policy studies or reviews, such as the implications of European telecommunications liberalization (Eliassen et al. 1999), media and cultural policy and its application in Western Europe (Humphreys 1996; Sarikakis 2007; Simpson et al. 2016), the influence of the European Union on media policy (Terzis 2008) and policy and policy making in U.S. broadcasting (Napoli 2001). Alternatively, the book literature addresses specific issues and makes arguments for new policy approaches, such as the globalization challenges to national governance and the increasing significance of global governance (Price 2002; Iosifidis 2011), which need to focus on citizen and consumer concerns (Ward 2004; Feintuck and Varney 2006; Freedman 2008; Lunt and Livingstone 2011), how innovation policy is being applied to media (van Kranenburg 2017), how the WTO agreements have affected telecommunication competition and governance (Mathew and Cottier 2003) and issues in the independence of media regulatory agencies (Schulz et al. 2013).

Many edited compilations often contain compartmentalized chapters of whatever topics interested the contributing authors. Natascha Just and Manuel Puppis' *Trends in Communication Policy Research* (2012) includes a range of topics including accountability, content control in digital settings and gender issues and methods such as network analysis and document analysis, but only one chapter addresses policy process aspects. In recent years, appearance of handbooks featuring reviews of various research topics has followed similar patterns (Mansell and Raboy 2014; Donders et al. 2014), but some are beginning to take a more focused approach on issues such as state aid for motion pictures (Murschetz and Teichmann 2018) or research methods (van den Bulck et al. 2019).

Although this expansive body of literature on telecommunications and media policy issues and trends provides helpful understanding to specific issues and the application of policy to them, there is limited literature addressing the specifics of policy making in the field. The most significant is perhaps a chapter arguing for using policy process models (van den Bulck 2012).

Like media and communications policy literature, telecommunications policy literature tends to focus on the law or narrow policy topics. A good deal of book-length literature describes existing law and regulation of telecommunications (Benjamin and Speta 2015; Walden 2018) and effects of technological changes on existing legal and regulatory mechanisms (Nuechterlein and Weiser 2013) rather than on policy making. Some literature focus on specific issues such as regulatory failure in addressing localism in media (Ali 2017) and the development and effects of commercialism in broadcasting (Streeter 1996).

Edited volumes have tended to present diverse and unconnected papers presented at conferences and generally describe or critique specific policies rather than addressing the institutions, processes and various influences on that policy. This issue is exemplified by Gillet and Vogelsang's *Competition, Regulation and Convergence: Current Research Trends* (1999) that presents papers addressing such disparate topics as product bundling practices, telephone number portability and funding universal access.

Journal literature on telecommunications policy tends to be narrow and nation-specific, such as a study of telecommunications reform in South Africa (Gillwald 2005), or it compares policies and policy making in a limited number of nations, such as a comparison of policy-making changes in China and India (Liu and Jayakar 2012). A few have addressed policy making from a policy studies perspective, such as a review of institutions in U.S. telecommunications policy making in the inaugural issue of *Telecommunications Policy* that found multiple institutions involved and little coordination in policy decisions (Polishuk 1976). A recent examination of telecommunications policy literature (Kim and Oh 2018) found that less than 5 percent directly involved governance issues, confirmed the diverse disciplines involved in policy research and identified changes and gaps in topics studied.

Literature on telecommunications policy research methods is sparse. This is partly a result of its diverse disciplinary homes producing inconsistent and non-combinable approaches (Rowland 1986). A contemporary review of the use of case studies in telecommunications policy studies found these differences make theory building difficult because theory is used to explain the cases rather than to extend or test the theories (Sutherland 2016).

It should be noted that there is a significant amount of literature on media and communications industries, structures and operations that touch up policy, but are not policy examinations or policy studies per se. Many of these recognize existing policy, but do not approach their description or critiques using methods and approaches of policy studies or directly address the issues about which they are concerned within the policy structures and processes, deeply discuss how they were developed, or examine the influences on decisions that occurred in them. Studies of motion pictures, social media, telephony, broadcasting and journalism often address existing law or policy or make appeal for policy, but without robust understanding of policy making, policy mechanisms and tools, the effectiveness of policy choices, or examining them using policy studies approaches and methods.

Common Methods in Evaluations and Policy Examinations

Policy evaluation employs some of the methods used in pre-implementation policy analysis (discussed in Chap. 8), but evaluations usually measure actual performance of the policies and compare those against previously relied upon assumptions, beliefs and projections to determine how accurate and reliable they were and how well the choices of policy mechanisms and tools, and their implementation, have performed.

In evaluation, because the policy has already been in place, the predictive approaches and modeling used in policy analysis before implementation are replaced by multivariate and other analysis based on actual data and performance. Evaluation tends to rely on analysis of impact on stakeholders, legal research involving implementing laws and regulation and any significant court decisions and cost-benefit analyses using actual costs and benefit data rather than projections.

Policy examinations use a variety of methods and disciplinary approaches that provide useful means for pursuing policy studies when combined with thorough grasp of policy-making structures, processes and issues and policy research approaches. The choice of approaches and methods used is very much dependent upon the intent of the examinations and issues being examined.

Elite Interviewing

Discussion with those who fashioned a policy, sought or seek alternative policy and stakeholders affected are also frequently used in evaluations to gain their perspectives about its effects and efficacy. This is a form of elite interviewing, an ethnographic method that requires cognizance of the researcher's preferential positions and involvement in the research (Herzog and Ali 2015).

Interviewing policy makers and stakeholders about their roles in and perspectives of policy is useful because it provides primary sources for understanding rationales, purposes and choices made in policy making. Using such interviews presents selection, access, recollection and other issues, so methods need to be carefully planned and transparent (Herzog and Ali 2015).

Policy Tracing

This type of analysis involves investigating the origins of a policy, its development and its trajectory. It is designed to explain conditions and forces producing the policy and engagement in policy making and the roles of stakeholders and advocacy activities in creating the final policy. Tracing can employ a variety of methods common in historiography, archaeology and genealogy to establish the heritage of a policy and map its development (Ball 1993; Gale 2001).

Tracing is useful in examining policy trajectories and policy transfers. A policy tracing study, for example, might focus on the origins of provisions requiring consumer-controlled content blocking capabilities, where they developed, for what technology and how and why the policy provisions were transferred to internet browsers and services.

Cost-Benefit Analysis

This type of analysis was introduced in the previous chapter on analysis using estimated costs and benefits of policy alternatives. In evaluation and policy studies, however, actual costs can be reviewed, and the actual benefits produced considered. This helps inform decisions about whether the policy is cost-effective or should be revised or dropped.

Cost-benefit analysis have explored such diverse topics as telecommunications policies in economic development (Leff 1984), assessing the efficacy of distance education evaluation (Cukier 1997), and costs and benefits fixed rural broadband policy in Europe (Schneir and Xiong 2016).

Policy Experimentation

Policy experimentation provides opportunities to explore effects of potential policies when dealing with new issues and technologies and when evidence of the best option is not clear. This experimentation provides opportunities to employ limited-scale testing to obtain additional evidence. Experimentation can involve laboratory experiments, surveys, trials, or field experiments testing alternates in different locales that were conducted during the life of the policy. To be effective, the objectives of the experimentation must be clear, and robust assessment methods must be employed.

Policy experimentation has been influenced by the development of experimental political science (Morton and Williams 2010) and economics (Levitt and List 2009). Experimental political science developed into a recognized field of study in the past four decades, with distinct approaches to developing evidence on political issues (Druckman et al. 2011).

Public agencies sometimes participate in the experimentation process, trying out different policies, regulations and rules in different locales or on different groups of people or technologies to determine which produce better outcomes.

In policy applications, experimentation tends to involve trials and testing of policy, with the robustness and usefulness of the experiments influenced by the purposes of the trials and methods employed (Martin and Sanderson 1999; Ettelt et al. 2015). Effective experiments seek causality and generalization and are transparent about methods employed (Danielson 2007).

Herzog and Beck (2016) have asserted the need for more systematic experimentation in media policy development. Experiments have been used to gain insight in a few countries in recent years.

Legal Research

Legal research involving policy issues is designed to help decision-making by developing understanding of the legal bases and issues being considered and potential courses of action. The research goes beyond establishing relevant legal principles and laws and how they are applied, as is typically done in legal practice research. Legal research is an in-depth, extended research that deeply explores the issues and the ability of existing law and legal approaches to address them. Extended legal research provides analysis and commentary about public and social policy, often critiques existing law and advocates for alternative interpretations or changes in law.

This type of research typically starts with a description of an emergent issue or set of circumstances to which law should be applied and establishes the principles of law, statutes and precedents from past application. It then asserts a clear thesis or argument, identifies the legal issues or disputes about their application and applies the argument to the conditions, asserting how and why law should be applied for better outcomes. The research often considers how it might apply in different legal systems or jurisdictions and evaluates the feasibility of actions needed to implement the argument when policy or legislative changes are required.

Legal research has addressed issues such as how European law is addressing must-carry policies in digital television and efforts to extend policy to other digital distribution systems (Valcke 2006), the evolution and use of competition law to achieve policy goals (Larouche 2000) and legal protection of minors as motion picture actors (Krieg 2004).

Political Sociological Approaches

These approaches focus on the settings, behavior and relationships between policy actors and activities that are used to investigate issues involving institutions and processes, how policy makers go about their work and how people take part in the processes. Interpretive approaches based on institutional ethnography, participant observation, case studies, interviews and secondary data analysis are common in this type of research.

This type of research has explored the role of policy actors in global communication policy (Padovani and Pavan 2011), actor networks in harmonizing European telecommunications policy (Schneider et al. 1994) and the European Union's use of isomorphic processes to induce national policy action (Radaelli 2000).

Discourse Analysis

Discourse analysis is used in policy studies to examine the language used, arguments made and scope of discussion in policy making to identify how they influence policy development (Hajer 2002; Streeter 2013). This form of analysis focuses on establishing meaning in dialogue and texts (Wetherell et al. 2001). Critical analyses using the method explore how the interests of elites and those with power are represented, how perspectives of others are downplayed and the consequences of those actions (van Dijk 1993; Wodak and Meyer 2009).

This approach has been used to explore how discourse about the emergence of cable television affected perceptions of the technology and policy established to regulate its operations (Streeter 2009) and the implications of changing the language of policy discussions from "cultural industries" to "creative industries" (Garnham 2005).

Feminist Approaches

Feminist approaches challenge the notion that policy and policy making are gender neutral (McPhail 2003). The question of what makes a policy feminist remains debated (Mazur 2002), however, especially outside of social policy fields. What is agreed is that feminist approaches apply critical methods to understanding how policy concerns relating to women and families are determined and the roles and limitations on participation of women in that policy making (Hawksworth 1994). Common themes in this form of analysis in media and communications focus on the roles of women in policy making and media governance and limitations on participation (Mayer 2018). Feminist approaches tend to use qualitative research methods such as ethnography, content analysis and discourse analysis, but the range of methods is expanding (Fonow and Cook 2005).

Political Economic Approaches

Political economic analyses focus on systems and processes in which large-scale decision-making involving both politics and economics takes place and how those two fundamental factors influence the systems and processes. These approaches emphasize how individuals relate to society, the roles of powerful institutions such as the market and the state, how relationships are governed and how public and private interests are represented.

These approaches often use interpretive frameworks to explore meaning in secondary data and relevant social science research studies.

The methods of political economic research place significant attention on systems, infrastructures and processes, and are highly useful in identifying their effects. Most studies of the political economy of media and communications, however, take a broader perspective and can be improved by more specifically examining where in the policy-making systems, structures and processes, and at what decision points, the influences they focus upon were or are exercised.

Political economic approaches have explored topics including systemic influences on film production (Wasko 1999, 2005), the development and expansion of intellectual property rights (May 2000) and the role of the World Trade Organization in transnational communications policy (Winseck 2002).

Historical Research

Historical policy studies look to the past to explain the origins of policy or how policy makers dealt with issues at a juncture or in a specific period. These studies are intent on explaining the factors influencing decisions made and/or how those influence contemporary choices. These seek explanations of why and how events and developments occurred and societies changed, relying heavily on documents, artifacts, letters and interviews with participants and witnesses, and interpreting them through various explanatory frameworks.

Examples of historical research include a comparison of U.K. and U.S. policy approaches to radio in 1920s that suggested the U.S. might learn from the U.K. experience (Jome 1925) and studies on how commercialism and corporate libertarianism influenced telecommunications and media policies in the twentieth and early twenty-first centuries (McChesney 1993; Pickard 2014), and how engineers, investors and businesses influenced policy makers to create the telecommunications industry in the United States (John 2010). Excellent work on policy in the development of postal standards and services has been contributed by Kielbowicz (1989, 1990, 2005) and John (2015) on governmental use of national power and policy to support internet development, governance and growth (Goldsmith and Wu 2008), and there is notable historical research on media and communications policy reforms and their effects (Horwitz 1991, 2001).

Final Words

Policy evaluations and examinations are only as rigorous and useful as the processes in which they are conducted and the methods selected to investigate the policy. This chapter, and the previous one on policy analysis, have presented steps in conducting such research and issues that should concern researchers when carrying out these forms of policy research.

Selecting the proper research methods is crucial, and decisions of what methods to use in policy evaluations and examinations need to informed by the purposes of the research and the performance criteria established. Some purposes may require empirical data, which require use of quantitative approaches; some purposes may require highly nuanced understanding of relationships, perceptions and actions, which require use of qualitative approaches; others may require use of multiple methods. It is rare for good policy evaluations and examinations to rely upon single methods.

Whatever methods are selected, researchers should be cognizant of the benefits and limitations, be transparent upon how and why they were selected and ensure that conclusions drawn are consistent with the method and its evidence.

Chapter Summary

- Good evaluations and policy studies focus on answering questions about what to do with the policy.
- Evaluation is made to determine whether existing policy is effective and efficient, and if it needs to be revised or dismantled.
- Evaluations can focus on outcomes, impact or program performance.
- Explicit evaluation criteria must be established before carrying out the research.
- The potential for policy drift and bureaucratic drift should be considered.
- Identifying policy failure and policy learning are important aspects of evaluations.

Discussion Points

1. What are the primary differences between policy analysis and policy evaluation?
2. What should evaluators do when they find information that is not supportive of the policy?
3. What might be appropriate ways to establish the criteria to be used in an evaluation?
4. How might one overcome resistance to evaluations being undertaken?
5. What factors might make one consider that a policy is unsustainable or a failure?

Bibliography

Ali, C. 2012. Media at the Margins: Policy and Practice in American, Canadian, and British Community Television. *International Journal of Communication* 6: 1119–1138. Available at https://ijoc.org/index.php/ijoc/article/view/1316/750. Accessed 15 Oct 2019.

Ali, Christopher. 2017. *Media Localism: The Policies of Place*. Urbana: University of Illinois Press.

Aufderheide, Pat. 2006. The 1996 Telecommunications Act: Ten Years Later. *The Federal Communications Law Journal* 58 (3): 407–413.

Ball, Stephen J. 1993. What Is Policy? Texts, Trajectories and Toolboxes. *Discourse: Studies in the Cultural Politics of Education* 13 (2): 10–17.

Becker, Henk A. 2001. Social Impact Assessment. *European Journal of Operational Research* 128 (2): 311–321.

Benjamin, Stuart M., and James B. Speta. 2015. *Telecommunications Law and Policy*. 4th ed. Durham: Carolina Academic Press.

Bickham, David S., and Ronald G. Slaby. 2012. Effects of a Media Literacy Program in the US on Children's Critical Evaluation of Unhealthy Media Messages About Violence, Smoking, and Food. *Journal of Children and Media* 6 (2): 255–271.

Birkland, Thomas A. 2015. *An Introduction to the Policy Process: Theories, Concepts, and Models of Public Policy Making*. 4th ed. Armonk: M. E. Sharpe.

Bulmer, Simon, and Stephen Padgett. 2004. Policy Transfer in the European Union: An Institutionalist Perspective. *British Journal of Political Science* 35 (1): 103–126.

Chalk, Nigel, and Richard Hemming. 2000. Assessing Fiscal Sustainability in Theory and Practice. In *International Monetary Fund Working Paper WP/00/81*. Washington: International Monetary Fund.

Cox, Richard H., and Daniel Béland. 2013. Valence, Policy Ideas, and the Rise of Sustainability. *Governance* 26 (2): 307–328.

Cukier, Judith. 1997. Cost-Benefit Analysis of Telelearning: Developing a Methodology Framework. *Distance Education* 18 (1): 1357–1152.

Danielson, Caroline. 2007. Social Experiments and Public Policy. In *Handbook of Public Policy Analysis: Theory, Politics and Methods*, ed. Frank Fisher, Gerald J. Miller, and Mara Sidney, 381–392. Boca Raton: CRC Press/Taylor & Francis.

Dixon, John A., and Louise A. Fallon. 1989. The Concept of Sustainability: Origins, Extensions, and Usefulness for Policy. *Society and Natural Resources* 2 (1): 73–84.

Dolowitz, David P., and David Marsh. 2000. Learning from Abroad: The Role of Policy Transfer in Contemporary Policy-Making. *Governance* 13 (1): 5–53.
Donders, Karen, Caroline Pauwels, and Jan Loisen. 2014. *The Palgrave Handbook of European Media Policy*. London: Palgrave Macmillan.
Dovers, Stephen R. 1996. Sustainability: Demands on Policy. *Journal of Public Policy* 16 (3): 303–318.
Druckman, James, Donald P. Green, James H. Kuklinski, and Arthur Lupia, eds. 2011. *Cambridge Handbook of Experimental Political Science*. Cambridge: Cambridge University Press.
Eliassen, Kjell A., Marit Sjovaag Nfa, and Marit Sjovaag, eds. 1999. *European Telecommunications Liberalisation*. London: Routledge.
Ettelt, S., N. Mays, and P. Allen. 2015. Policy Experiments: Investigating Effectiveness or Confirming Direction? *Evaluation* 21 (3): 292–307.
Feintuck, Mike, and Mike Varney. 2006. *Media Regulation, Public Interest and the Law*. 2nd ed. Edinburgh: Edinburgh University Press.
Finkelstein, Neal D., ed. 2000. *Transparency in Public Policy: Great Britain and the United States*. Berlin: Springer.
Fonow, Mary Margaret, and Judith A. Cook. 2005. Feminist Methodology: New Applications in the Academy and Public Policy. *Signs: Journal of Women in Culture and Society* 30 (4): 2211–2236.
Fox, Justin. 2007. Government Transparency and Policymaking. *Public Choice* 131 (1–2): 23–44.
Freedman, Des. 2008. *The Politics of Media Policy*. Cambridge: Polity Press.
Gale, Trevor. 2001. Critical Policy Sociology: Historiography, Archaeology and Genealogy as Methods of Policy Analysis. *Journal of Education Policy* 16 (5): 379–393.
Gardner, Annette, and Claire Brindis. 2017. *Advocacy and Policy Change Evaluation: Theory and Practice*. Stanford: Stanford University Press.
Garnham, Nicholas. 2005. From Cultural to Creative Industries. *International Journal of Cultural Policy* 11 (1): 15–29.
Gillett, Sharon E., and Ingo Vogelsang, eds. 1999. *Competition, Regulation and Convergence: Current Trends in Telecommunication Policy Research*. Mahwah: Lawrence Erlbaum.
Gillwald, Alison. 2005. Good Intentions, Poor Outcomes: Telecommunications Reform in South Africa. *Telecommunications Policy* 29 (7): 469–491.
Goldsmith, Jack, and Tim Wu. 2008. *Who Controls the Internet? Illusions of a Borderless World*. Oxford: Oxford University Press.
Hacker, Jacob S. 2004. Privatizing Risk Without Privatizing the Welfare State: The Hidden Politics of Social Policy Retrenchment in the United States. *American Political Science Review* 98 (02): 243–260.
Hacker, Jacob S., Paul Pierson, and Kathleen Thelen. 2015. Drift and Conversion: Hidden Faces of Institutional Change. In *Advances in Comparative-Historical Analysis*, ed. James Mahoney and Kathleen Thelen, 180–210. Cambridge: Cambridge University Press.
Hajer, Maartin. 2002. Discourse Analysis and the Study of Policy Making. *European Political Science* 2 (1): 61–65.
Hawksworth, Mary. 1994. Policy Studies Within a Feminist Frame. *Policy Sciences* 27 (1–2): 97–118.

Herzog, Christian, and Christopher Ali. 2015. Elite Interviewing in Media and Communications Policy Research. *International Journal of Media and Cultural Politics* 11 (1): 37–54.

Herzog, Christian, and Hanno Beck. 2016. Experimental Media Policy. *International Journal of Digital Television* 7 (3): 315–330.

Horwitz, Robert B. 1991. *The Irony of Regulatory Reform: The Deregulation of American Telecommunications*. Oxford: Oxford University Press.

———. 2001. *Communication and Democratic Reform in South Africa*. Cambridge: Cambridge University Press.

Humphreys, Peter. 1996. *Mass Media and Media Policy in Western Europe*. Manchester: Manchester University Press.

Iosifidis, Petros. 2011. *Global Media and Communication Policy: An International Perspective*. London: Palgrave Macmillan.

Jaeger, Paul T. 2006. Telecommunications Policy and Individuals with Disabilities: Issues of Accessibility and Social Inclusion in the Policy and Research Agenda. *Telecommunications Policy* 30 (1): 112–124.

John, Richard R. 2010. *Network Nation: Inventing American Telecommunications*. Cambridge: Cambridge University Press.

———. 2015. Projecting Power Oversees: U.S. Postal Policy and International Standards Setting at the 1863 Paris Postal Conference. *Journal of Policy History* 27 (3): 416–438.

Johns Hopkins Center for Civil Society Studies. 2003. *Policy Tools and Government Performance: Report on a Conference Co-Sponsored by the U.S. General Accounting Office, the U.S. Office of Management and Budget, and the Johns Hopkins University*. Baltimore: The Johns Hopkins Center for Civil Society Studies.

Jome, Hiram L. 1925. Public Policy Toward Radio Broadcasting. *The Journal of Land & Public Utility Economics* 1 (2): 198–214.

Just, Natascha, and Manuel Puppis, eds. 2012. *Trends in Communication Policy Research: New Theories, Methods and Subjects*. Bristol: Intellect.

Kielbowicz, Richard B. 1989. *News in the Mail: The Press, Post Office, and Public Information, 1700–1860s*. Greenwood: Praeger.

———. 1990. Postal Subsidies for the Press and the Business of Mass Culture, 1880–1920. *Business History Review* 64 (3): 451–488.

———. 2005–2006. Preserving Universal Postal Service as a Communication Safety Net: A Policy History and Proposal. *Seton Hall Legislative Journal* 30: 383.

Kim, Sung-Kil, and Junseok Oh. 2018. Information Science Techniques for Investigating Research Areas: A Case Study in Telecommunications Policy. *The Journal of Supercomputing* 74 (12): 6691–6718.

Kim, Han-joo, Sang-kyu Byun, and Myeong-cheol Park. 2004. Mobile Handset Subsidy Policy in Korea: Historical Analysis and Evaluation. *Telecommunications Policy* 28 (1): 23–42.

Krieg, Jessica. 2004. There's no Business Like Show Business: Child Entertainers and the Law. *University of Pennsylvania Journal of Labor and Employment Law* 6 (2): 429–449.

Larouche, Pierre. 2000. *Competition Law and Regulation in European Telecommunications*. Oxford: Hart Publishing.

Lee, Karen. 2017. ACMA Varies Compliance and Monitoring Arrangements for the Telecommunications Consumer Protections Code. *Australian Journal of Competition and Consumer Law* 25 (1): 62–64.

Leeuw, Frans L. 2003. Reconstructing Program Theories: Methods Available and Problems to be Solved. *American Journal of Evaluation* 24 (1): 5–20.

Leff, Nathaniel H. 1984. Externalities, Information Costs, and Social Benefit-Cost Analysis for Economic Development: An Example from Telecommunications. *Economic Development and Social Change* 32 (2): 255–276.

Levitt, S.D., and J.A. List. 2009. Field Experiments in Economics: The Past, the Present, and the Future. *European Economic Review* 53 (1): 1–18.

Liu, Chun, and Krishna Jayakar. 2012. The Evolution of Telecommunications Policymaking: Comparative Analysis of China and India. *Telecommunications Policy* 36 (1): 13–28.

Livingstone, Sonia. 2011. Regulating the Internet in the Interests of Children: Emerging European and International Approaches. In *The Handbook of Global Media and Communication Policy*, ed. Robin Mansell and Marc Raboy, 505–524. Oxford: Wiley-Blackwell.

Lunt, Peter, and Sonia Livingstone. 2011. *Media Regulation: Governance and the Interests of Citizens and Consumers.* London: Sage.

Majchrzak, Ann, and M. Lynne Markus. 2013. *Methods for Policy Research: Taking Socially Responsible Action.* 2nd ed. London: Sage.

Mansell, Robin, and Marc Raboy, eds. 2014. *The Handbook of Global Media and Communication Policy.* Oxford: Wiley-Blackwell.

Manyozo, Linje. 2012. *Media, Communication and Development: Three Approaches.* London: Sage.

Martin, Steve, and Ian Sanderson. 1999. Evaluating Public Policy Experiments: Measuring Outcomes, Monitoring Processes or Managing Pilots? *Evaluation* 5 (3): 245–258.

Mathew, Bobjoseph, and Thomas Cottier, eds. 2003. *Telecom Regulatory Framework and Effect on Competition: The WTO Agreements on Telecommunications.* New York: Peter Lang.

May, Peter J. 1992. Policy Learning and Failure *Journal of Public Policy* 12 (4): 331–354.

May, Christopher. 2000. *A Global Political Economy of Intellectual Property Rights.* London: Routledge.

———. 2006. *World Intellectual Property Organization (WIPO): Resurgence and Development Agenda.* London: Routledge.

Mayer, Vicki. 2018. Media Policy and Governance. *Feminist Media Histories* 4 (2): 113–116.

Mazur, Amy G. 2002. *Theorizing Feminist Policy.* Oxford: Oxford University Press.

McChesney, Robert W. 1993 *Telecommunications, Mass Media, and Democracy: The Battle for the Control of U.S. Broadcasting, 1928–1935.* New York: Oxford University Press.

McConnell, Allan. 2010. Policy Success, Policy Failure and Grey Areas In-Between. *Journal of Public Policy* 30 (3): 345–362.

McCubbins, Mathew D., Roger G. Noll, and Barry R. Weingast. 1987. Administrative Procedures as Instruments of Political Control. *Journal of Law, Economics, and Organization* 3 (2): 243–277.

McPhail, Beverly A. 2003. Feminist Policy Analysis Framework. *The Social Policy Journal* 2 (2–3): 39–61.

Morton, Rebecca, and Kenneth Williams. 2010. *Experimental Political Science and the Study of Causality: From Nature to the Lab.* Cambridge: Cambridge University Press.

Murschetz, Paul Clemens, and Roland Teichmann. 2018. *Handbook of State Aid for Film: Finance, Industries and Regulation.* Berlin: Springer.

Napoli, Philip M. 2001. *Foundations of Communication Policy: Principles and Process in the Regulation of Electronic Media*. New York: Hampton Press.
Nielsen, Rasmus Kleis. 2014. 'Frozen' Media Subsidies During a Time of Media Change: A Comparative Analysis of Media Policy Drift in Six Western Democracies. *Global Media and Communication* 10 (2): 121–138.
Noske-Turner, Jessica. 2017. *Rethinking Media Development Through Evaluation: Beyond Freedom*. London: Palgrave Macmillan.
Nuechterlein, Jonathan E., and Philip J. Weiser. 2013. *Digital Crossroads: Telecommunications Law and Policy in the Internet Age*. Cambridge, MA: MIT Press.
Ots, Mart. 2009. Efficient Servants of Pluralism or Marginalized Media Policy Tools? *Journal of Communication Inquiry* 33 (4): 376–392.
Padovani, Claudia, and Elena Pavan. 2011. Actors and Interactions in Global Communication Governance: The Heuristic Potential of a Network Approach. In *The Handbook of Global Media and Communication Policy*, ed. Robin Mansell and Marc Raboy, 543–581. Oxford: Wiley-Blackwell.
Pandit, Sushmita. 2019. Public Policy and the Digital Deadline: The Implementation of the Digital Addressable System (DAS) in West Bengal. *Journal of Digital Media and Policy* 10 (2): 217–228.
Picard, Robert G. 1986. State Press Aid During the Era of Economic Readjustment: A Case Study of Scandinavian Nations. *European Studies Journal* 3: 1–8.
———. 2017. Monitoring Media Sustainability: Economic and Business Revisions to Development Indicators. In *What Is Sustainable Journalism? Integrating the Environmental, Social, and Economic Challenges of Journalism*, ed. Peter Berglez, Ulrika Olausson, and Mart Ots. New York: Peter Lang.
Picard, Robert G., and Mikko Grönlund. 2003. Development and Effects of Finnish Press Subsidies. *Journalism Studies* 4 (1): 105–119.
Pickard, Victor. 2014. *America's Battle for Media Democracy: The Triumph of Corporate Libertarianism and the Future of Media Reform*. Cambridge: Cambridge University Press.
Polishuk, Paul. 1976. Telecommunications Policymaking and Institutions of the U.S. Government. *Telecommunications Policy* 1 (1): 52–67.
Poort, Joost, and Barbara Baarsma. 2016. Measuring the Welfare Effects of Public Television. *Journal of Media Economics* 29 (1): 31–48.
Prado, Marianna Mota. 2013. Bureaucratic Resistance to Regulatory Reforms: Contrasting Experiences in Electricity and Telecommunications in Brazil. In *The Rise of the Regulatory State in the South: Infrastructure and Development in Emerging Economies*, ed. Navroz K. Dubash and Bronwen Morgan, 75–97. Oxford: Oxford University Press.
Price, Monroe. 2002. *Media and Sovereignty: The Global Information Revolution and Its Challenge to State Power*. Boston: MIT Press.
Radaelli, Claudio M. 2000. Policy Transfer in the European Union: Institutional Isomorphism as a Source of Legitimacy. *Governance* 13 (1): 25–43.
———. 2009. Measuring Policy Learning: Regulatory Impact Assessment in Europe. *Journal of European Public Policy* 16 (8): 1145–1164.
Rennie, Ellie. 2013. Unintended Consequences: Satellite Policy and Indigenous Television Media. *Media Information Australia* 149 (1): 92–103.
Rodrigo, Delia, Lorenzo Allio, and Pedro Andres-Amo. 2009. *Multi-Level Regulatory Governance: Policies, Institutions and Tools for Regulatory Quality and Policy Coherence*. OECD Working Papers on Public Governance, No. 13. Paris: OECD Publishing.

Rowland, Williard D. 1986. American Telecommunications Policy Research: Its Contradictory Origins and Influences. *Media, Culture & Society* 8 (2): 159–182.
Sanderson, Ian. 2002. Evaluation, Policy Learning and Evidence-Based Policy Making. *Public Administration* 80 (1): 1–22.
Sarikakis, Katharine, ed. 2007. *Media and Cultural Policy in the European Union*. Amsterdam: Rodopi.
Schneider, Volker, Godefroy Dang-Nguyen, and Raymond Werle. 1994. Corporate Actor Networks in European Policy-Making: Harmonizing Telecommunications Policy. *Journal of Common Market Studies* 32 (4): 473.
Schneir, Juan R., and Yupeng Xiong. 2016. A Cost Study of Fixed Broadband Access Networks for Rural Areas. *Telecommunications Policy* 40 (8): 755–773.
Schulz, Wolfgang, Peggy Valcke, and Kristina Irion, eds. 2013. *The Independence of the Media and its Regulatory Agencies*. Bristol: Intellect.
Scull, Tracy Marie, and Janis Beth Kupersmidt. 2011. An Evaluation of a Media Literacy Program Training Workshop for Late Elementary School Teachers. *Journal of Media Literacy Education* 2 (3): 199–208.
Simpson, Seamus, Manuel Puppis, and Hilde van den Bulck, eds. 2016. *European Media Policy for the Twenty First Century: Assessing the Past, Setting Agendas for the Future*. London: Routledge.
Stone, Diane. 1999. Learning Lessons and Transferring Policy across Time, Space and Disciplines. *Politics* 19 (1): 51–59.
Streeter, Thomas. 1996. *Selling the Air: A Critique of the Policy of Commercial Broadcasting in the United States*. Chicago: University of Chicago Press.
———. 2009. The Cable Fable Revisited: Discourse, Policy, and the Making of Cable Television. *Critical Studies in Mass Communication* 4 (2): 174–200.
———. 2013. Policy, Politics, and Discourse. *Communication, Culture & Critique* 6 (4): 488–501.
Sutherland, Ewan. 2016. The Case Study in Telecommunications Policy Research. *Info* 18 (1): 16–30.
Talvi, Ernesto, and Carlos Végh. 1998. Fiscal Policy Sustainability: A Basic Framework. In *Inter-American Development Bank, Working Paper 107*. Washington, DC: Inter-American Development Bank.
Taylor, Matthew, and Jake Thorold. 2017. Is Policy Failure Inevitable. *Royal Society of Arts Blog*. https://www.thersa.org/discover/publications-and-articles/matthew-taylor-blog/2017/03/is-policy-failure-inevitable?id=newsletter/fellowship/100417. Accessed 3 Dec 2018.
Terzis, Georgios, ed. 2008. *European Media Governance. The Brussels Dimension*. Bristol: Intellect.
Valcke, Peggy. 2006. The Future of Must-Carry: From Must-Carry to a Concept of Universal Service in the Info-Communications Sector. *Media Law and Policy* 15: 247–265.
van den Bulck, Hilde. 2012. Towards a Media Policy Process Analysis Model and Its Methodological Implications. In *Trends in Communication Policy Research: New Theories, Methods and Subjects*, ed. Natascha Just and Manuel Puppis. Bristol: Intellect.
van den Bulck, Manuel Puppis Hilde, Karen Donders, and Leo van Audenhove, eds. 2019. *The Palgrave Handbook of Methods for Media Policy Research*. London: Palgrave Macmillan.

van Dijk, Teun A. 1993. Principles of Critical Discourse Analysis. *Discourse & Society* 4 (2): 249–283.
van Kranenburg, Hans, ed. 2017. *Innovation Policies in the European News Media Industry: A Comparative Study*. Berlin: Springer.
Vanclay, Frank, Ana M. Esteves, Ilse Aucamp, and Daniel M. Franks. 2015. *Social Impact Assessment: Guidance for Assessing and Managing Social Impact of Projects*. Fargo: International Association for Impact Assessment.
Vedung, Evert. 2000. *Public Policy and Program Evaluation*. London: Routledge.
Walden, Ian. 2018. *Telecommunications Law and Regulation*. 5th ed. Oxford: Oxford University Press.
Ward, David. 2004. *The European Union Democratic Deficit and the Public Sphere: An Evaluation of EU Media Policy*. Amsterdam: IOS Press.
Wasko, Janet. 1999. The Political Economy of Film. In *A Companion to Film Theory*, ed. Toby Miller and Robert Stam, 221–233. Oxford: Blackwell Publishing.
———. 2005. Critiquing Hollywood: The Political Economy of Motion Pictures. In *A Concise Handbook of Movie Industry Economics*, ed. Charles C. Moul, 5–31. Cambridge: Cambridge University Press.
Weiss, Carol H. 1997. *Evaluation: Methods for Studying Programs and Policies*. 2nd ed. Upper Saddle River: Prentice Hall.
Weiss, Carol Hirschon. 1999. The Interface Between Evaluation and Public Policy. *Evaluation* 5 (4): 468–486.
Wetherell, Margaret, Stephanie Taylor, and Simeon J. Yates. 2001. *Discourse as Data: A Guide for Analysis*. London: Sage.
Winseck, Dwayne. 2002. The WTO, Emerging Policy Regimes and the Political Economy of Transnational Communications. In *Global Media Policy in the New Millennium*, ed. Marc Raboy, 19–38. Luton: University of Luton Press.
Wodak, Ruth, and Michael Meyer. 2009. *Methods for Critical Discourse Analysis*. London: Sage.
Wollmann, Helmut. 2006. Policy Evaluation and Evaluation Research. In *Handbook of Public Policy Analysis: Theory, Politics, and Methods*, ed. Frank Fischer and Gerald J. Miller, 393–404. Boca Raton: CRC Press/Taylor & Francis.

Suggested Readings

van den Bulck, Hilde, Manuel Puppis, Karen Donders, and Leo van Audenhove, eds. 2019. *The Palgrave Handbook of Methods for Media Policy Research*. London: Palgrave Macmillan.
Vedung, Evert. 2000. *Public Policy and Program Evaluation*. London: Routledge.
Weiss, Carol H. 1997. *Evaluation: Methods for Studying Programs and Policies*, 2nd. Prentice Hall.
Wollmann, H. 2006. Policy Evaluation and Evaluation Research. In *Handbook of Public Policy Analysis: Theory, Politics, and Methods*, ed. Frank Fischer, and Gerald J. Miller, 393–404. Boca Raton: CRC Press/Taylor & Francis.

CHAPTER 10

Policy Advocacy

Policy advocacy is engaging in the social decision-making processes on behalf of a cause, course of action or policy proposal. It involves arguing the case for the chosen point of view publicly and within political, economic, cultural and social institutions. Advocacy involves activities in multiple forums where ideas are raised, discussed and debated. It requires the expectation that other points of view will be presented, preparation to present the best arguments in policy debates and determination on how to counter the arguments of others.

Although advocacy by businesses and industries with economic interests in policy has existed informally and formally for several centuries, most non-business advocacy emerged in the second half of the twentieth century as social movements and not-for-profit entities in the areas of social policy, medicine, ecology and the environment developed. Advocacy emerged to bring attention to overlooked or emerging issues, to give voice to alternative voices and to respond to increasingly organized and coordinated advocacy by business interests.

Initial advocacy organizations in media and communications tended to focus on free expression and protection of journalists. These included the organizations Freedom House, PEN, Article 19, Reporters sans frontiers/Reporters without Borders, Committee to Protect Journalists and later the Electronic Frontier Foundation. In most countries, advocacy for other types of media and communications policies by non-industry actors has been limited and infrequent, typically by temporary citizens groups or scholars. Only a few well-organized and better funded advocacy groups such as Voice of the Listener in the U.K. and Alliance for Children's Television and Free Press in the U.S. have sustained larger-scale activities over time. A variety of smaller organizations concerned with issues such as community media, children and media, violence in media content and media literacy tend to scale up activities when their interests are addressed in policy processes (Shade 2011).

Fewer organized telecommunications advocacy groups exist focused on citizen interests, but a number have emerged to promote consumer interests,

R. G. Picard, *Media and Communications Policy Making*, Palgrave Global Media Policy and Business,
https://doi.org/10.1007/978-3-030-35173-1_10

usually as an activity of consumer advocacy groups, exemplified by the Consumer Guidance Society of India and the Africa Network of Consumer Associations of Information and Communication Technologies. Some advocacy groups focus on issues such as digital governance and rural telecommunications development.

Advocacy groups tend to rise and fall with the appearance of new issues and technologies. The largest growth of media and communications activism occurred in the mid-1960s and 1970s in response to broadcast policy changes and the appearance of cable TV. In the 1980s, information issues and advocacy of computer-related issues emerged, producing a new wave of activist groups surrounding digital issues in the 1990s (Mueller 2004). The most consistent advocacy tends to be produced by scholars and telecommunications policy research centers at universities.

This chapter explores the roles and concepts of advocacy, the structures and practices those who undertake it, how it can be considered and researched and ethical issues faced by those involved in advocacy.

Society, Markets and Policy

The broader interests of society are not represented in markets and market activity, which are subject primarily to economic forces involving producers, suppliers and consumers. Consequently, social concerns must be represented through policy-making activities or the weight of public opinion brought to bear on companies to behave responsibly as part of a larger public sphere.

These activities are typically undertaken through civil society organizations, recognizing that policy doesn't belong only to policy makers. *Civil society* is a conception that accounts for the activities of persons, groups and organizations influencing society, such as voluntary, nongovernmental organizations and social and reform movements that participate in policy-making processes (Alexander 1998; Edwards 2011).

The concept of civil society is debated, and there is significant debate over whether the notion of the market should be included in models of civil society. One stream of thought draws upon the traditions of Hegel and Marx and argues that civil society is a distinct sphere of activity next to the market and the state. A second perspective emanates from the work of Gramsci and Habermas, which portrays civil society as distinct from the market and state, but not separate and constantly relating to market and state but with autonomy.

Whatever conceptualization is accepted, civil society can only be represented if its views are represented through participation in public debate and policy processes. Advocacy has been shown as a way for civil society to engage the state in India, for example (Kumar 2012). Successful communications advocacy can occur within and outside formal policy structures, and civil society groups have achieved some preferred digital policies using both mechanisms at the international level (Hintz 2012). A study of civil society groups found they are being integrated into internet governance policy activities, but many doubt their effectiveness compared to diplomatic stakeholders and established institutions (Cammaerts 2011).

Advocacy and representation at times challenge state institutions and can produce regulatory backlash, especially in authoritarian states (Bolleyer 2019). Even many democratic states place significant constraints on the amount and forms of advocacy permitted under charities laws.

Most advocacy groups operate domestically because regional and global advocacy requires far greater organization, resources and creation of collaborative networks and coalitions. At times, however, broader non-domestic advocacy is used to pursue results through intergovernmental organizations and private governance when domestic policy results have been elusive.

Advocacy Networks and Coalitions

Advocacy networks and coalitions are designed to strengthen policy making by increasing the capacity of participants and the information brought into policy processes. They connect smaller organizations and help to give them a larger context and create the perception of greater support and apparent structure.

Networks and coalitions involve individuals and advocacy groups with varying focuses, perspectives and activities that share some common overriding objectives and are willing to work together as a unified force for change. Networks are informal groups of policy actors that work together to address issues and improve capabilities of members of such networks. These could be activist groups in cities across a country or around the world. The primary characteristic is that they are not guided by a central organization but embrace various groups with similar interests. Network research provides means for examining such networks, the complex relations and power in governance of global communications, and better understanding of policy spaces in which governance activities take place (Padovani and Pavan 2011).

In recent years, not-for-profit organizations with differing focuses of interest have formed associations to improve their knowledge and operations, and these have worked to increase the capacity of their members to engage in public policy activity (Balassiano and Chandler 2010). Advocacy coalitions involve multiple parties, often stakeholders, working to address common issues. These tend to create stability in activities and sustainability for change that takes longer periods of time to achieve.

To be an effective participant or observer, it is important to understand policy subsystems of coalitions of public and private partners that incorporate participants with varying goals but are working to achieve consensus (Sabatier and Weible 2007). Research on coalitions often uses the *Advocacy Coalition Framework* that conceptualizes policy competition among policy coalitions (Sabatier and Jenkins-Smith 1993; Sabatier and Weible 2007). Although policy advocacy involves multiple actors and complex relations among them, coalitions can be formed when shared beliefs and general agreement on a solution exist (John 2003).

Communication among network and coalition is crucial to their cohesiveness. A study of use of the internet among civil society groups and activists attempting to influence internet governance revealed its importance for intramovement networking and access to policy processes, but argued technologically based communications cannot replace all face-to-face interactions (Cammaerts 2011).

One or more coalitions may emerge to address an issue. A study of coalitions in debates over new public broadcasting management in the Flemish region of Belgium, for example, identified two major coalitions working privately and publicly to influence decisions—one supporting economic and commercial interests and the other public interests (van den Bulck and Donders 2014). A review of media policy involving children's issues found that children's advocacy groups, often working together although holding differing focuses, produced both public and private regulatory outcomes (Jordan 2008).

Varying priorities, organizational goals and practices can reduce the willingness to cooperate. Such differences created divisions among advocacy groups during the U.S. Federal Communications Commission's Open Internet proceedings (Löblich 2016). A study of advocacy coalitions addressing European Union broadcasting policy found a great deal of complexity in relations among the coalition stakeholders and argued that coalitions and relations among their participants at the European level would differ at the domestic level (van den Bulck and Donders 2014).

Limited knowledge about conditions that induce the media and the state to respond to media reform efforts makes it difficult to pursue success through reform coalitions, a factor shown to be important in case studies of Latin American civic coalitions (Waisbord 2010).

There are concerns whether studying policy networks links and connections between actors is effective (Dowding 1995), but advances in social network analysis improve the ability to study ad hoc coalitions and negotiations among participants (Varone et al. 2017). Informal collaboration and digital networking are creating decentralized, transborder advocacy groups, often driven by highly proficient technical activists that spur traditional multi-stakeholder policy activities (Milan and Hintz 2013).

Networks and coalitions can exist in many policy systems, but some research has shown that linkages to institutional actors enhance the effectiveness of such advocacy in authoritarian countries (Li et al. 2017). However, it may sometimes be necessary to sidestep undemocratic institutions to work for change from below or within (Sakr 2006) and to create new forums and venues for discussion of issues and alternatives in policy systems that are less willing to integrate advocacy groups (Lam and Chan 2017). Some groups, such as Russian nonprofit organizations, have tended to employ advocacy tactics that primarily focus on organizational sustainability and on obtaining help for individuals, rather than pursuing systemic change (Ljubownikow and Crotty 2016).

Whether influence on policy is sought or systemic changes are pursued influence the way in which advocacy groups, networks and coalitions operate, how and the extent to which they expect change to occur and the time frame for change.

Advocacy Activities

Advocacy, its roles and its purposes cannot be fully comprehended and contextualized without understanding the basic activities and practices that it involves.

Advocacy combines the range of communication activities involved in public relations with the practices of social movements and other political actors pursuing change. It involves educating the public and policy makers, persuading them that the issues are salient and that the perspectives advocated are valuable and negotiating with other parties to achieve the best possible outcome (Hoefer 2015). The most effective advocacy is part of an ongoing activity, and not merely an occasional advocacy action (Mosley 2013).

Strategically, advocacy needs to work to enhance participation in policy making, raise issues and positions to prominence, influence policy makers, promote reform of existing conditions or policy and ensure effective implementation and change (Gen and Wright 2013). It attempts to link its activities to the policy process (Hoefer 2015). To do so, advocacy efforts need to be well organized and use a range of organizational and communication techniques to ensure that views representing public interests are present in decision-making as equally as are those of private interests (Hessenius 2007). Activism requires building capacity and gaining attention, but also building trust with policy makers as well (Yanacopulos 2015).

Developing strategy, priorities and plans for advocacy is crucial. Advocacy groups, nonprofit organizations and others need to establish a mission statement and policy principles that will guide these activities, create an organization within which activities will take place, develop internal processes for deciding policy positions, decide who will be involved in the decision-making and advocacy activities, establish timelines and designate who can speak for the group (Fig. 10.1).

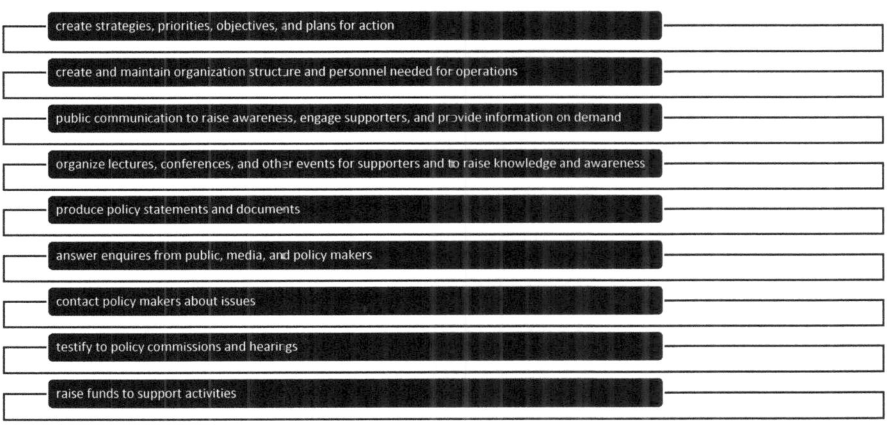

Fig. 10.1 Typical activities of advocacy groups

A critical early activity is building a case to attract supporters and bringing attention to it. An initial step for advocacy groups is constructing a carefully crafted, succinct description about the issue and what advocates are trying to do about it. This is normally no more than one paragraph and is written in language understandable to the average person. This short statement is usually supplemented by a one-page fact sheet that quickly lays out the issues, context and solutions being sought. Groups also produce policy statements promoting or responding to policy developments, and fuller policy analyses will need to be produced. The construction of these key messages and narratives is used to build support and provide information to supporters, the public and policy makers. They help develop issue recognition and acknowledgment of the needs for action.

Effective advocacy groups and NGOs work to understand the policy environment and other stakeholders, develop strategic and operational plans and seek engagement opportunities. Understanding the interests and values of stakeholders and other advocacy groups makes it possible to identify potential allies and develop alliances. Engaging supporters and the public through communications activities and events is a central activity. Activist groups use media, websites, social media, meetings, events and rallies to engage supporters and potential supporters and then to mobilize that support for more advocacy.

Learning activities are often organized to help build awareness, knowledge, support and engagement. Workshops, seminars, conferences and teach-ins all promote learning about issues and potential responses, as well as political learning and knowledge about policy making.

A variety of other public activities are used if they are appropriate for the type of advocacy organization and its reputation. Fundraising walks, tournaments, events, celebrations and demonstrations can build engagement, promote awareness and raise money needed for operations.

Communication activities are central to the policy process for building awareness, issue recognition and pushing issues onto the public and policy agendas. Attracting media coverage that helps build awareness of the issues among the public and policy makers is a primary activity of advocacy groups. This usually entails being readily accessible to reporters seeking information and responses to developments, writing opinion pieces and making appearances on public affairs radio and television.

Formalized groups that employ routine advocacy tactics and mobilize large numbers of people often try to align their messages with media concerns for local growth and well-being. Those that do so effectively tend to gain more attention from news media (Andrews and Caren 2010). Media reform organizations, however, may experience difficulties in obtaining coverage because mainstream media are motivated to deny coverage (Napoli 2009; Gibson 2010). Some advocacy groups are reticent to jeopardize coverage needed for other activities by promoting policies opposed by major media firms (Hackett and Anderson 2011).

Media operated by interest groups and digital media are creating a secondary space and public sphere in which nondominant views can more easily be conveyed and discussed (Downey and Fenton 2016). Digital and social media are effective for advocacy and organizational goals and are increasingly relied upon by NGOs and other advocacy groups (Hackett and Anderson 2011; Obar et al. 2012; Guo and Saxton 2014). They also help empower and amplify voices of marginalized publics (Ciszek 2013).

Ethical Issues for Advocacy Groups

Advocacy groups need to be perceived as trustworthy to gain the respect of policy makers and citizens, so that their activities are persuasive and effective. Ethical characteristics of respected advocacy groups include:

- Exhibiting integrity by acting in an honest and principled matter
- Developing a reputation for veracity by speaking truthfully and avoiding deception and evasion
- Providing objective policy analysis that does not mischaracterize research and facts to mislead policy makers
- Being transparent about interests represented and sources of funding
- Grounding positions and activities in social interests and not merely narrow private interests

Ethics in advocacy thus involves adherence of values of respect for others truthfulness, equity, and justice. These require ethical practices in persuasion and persuasive techniques employed (Edgett 2002) and care in choice of issues represented and those who pay for the advocacy (Nelson 1994).

Raising issues and preferred policy approaches in presentations at public meetings is a traditional tactic, as is producing written submissions to public consultations and legislative and administrative agencies that may also result in invitations to testify at hearings. Advocates make the case for their preferred options for addressing an issue and use these activities to develop common understandings of the issues among stakeholders and others concerned that might produce avenues for negotiation or consensus.

All these advocacy activities require having staff and supporters with strong communication, persuasion and policy skills because such presentations require professionalism and need to be constructed and presented in styles traditional for the body involved—statements, briefs, affidavits or draft legislation. Established advocacy groups and coalitions sometimes utilize celebrities to gain notice as one of the spokespersons in public and in public hearings because their fame and endorsement focuses attention on issues and often produces additional media coverage.

As the scope of activities rise, funding becomes a significant issue for advocacy organizations because participation in legislative, administrative and judicial proceedings can be very expensive. Obtaining contributions, grants and other revenue requires regular activity and may require that the group seek legal recognition, protection and benefits as an organization or charity.

Making direct contacts with policy makers to discuss the issues with them, influence their thinking and persuade them to support particularly policy measures are critical tactics of advocates. Lobbying generally begins with contacts with policy makers' staff, who need to understand issues and various approaches taken. This is often done through mail, introducing the advocacy group and its issues, and then followed up with phone calls and visits. Board members of nonprofit organizations are often active, well known in their communities and have connection to policy makers. These advantages can be used when trying to get the organizations' policy messages directly to policy makers and their staffs and trying to develop their support.

When policy making is underway, advocacy groups often meet with policy makers and their staffs or publicly respond to draft legislation, suggesting alternatives or revisions. Media reform groups have been criticized for being primarily reactive toward policy developments underway rather than working effectivity to help fashion policy beforehand (Napoli 2007).

Direct contacts with officials are sometime governed by laws and regulations about which advocates need to be aware (Libby 2012). These rules most often apply only to lobbyists paid for their efforts in directly contacting lawmakers, but sometimes apply to leaders of ministries and administrative agencies. Groups and individuals engaging in advocacy need to be aware of the regulations in the country(ies) in which they conduct advocacy.

To be effective in influencing policy, advocacy groups must have a high level of subject matter knowledge and expertise, develop evidence necessary to support their positions and be willing to engage with policy makers and other stakeholders. When dealing with issues affecting minorities and marginalized groups, a significant question is whether the advocacy group speaks on their behalf or provides means to them to speak for themselves or to others speaking on their behalf matters (DeSantis 2010).

The central issues of representation are whether the group can legitimately speak on behalf of those affected by the policy issue and whether advocacy could be perceived as paternalism and interference with self-determination. It is usually more effective for such groups to speak for themselves and be part of the advocacy group, drawing on the additional knowledge, evidence, expertise and support provided by the advocacy organization to be successful if the advocacy is on behalf of a small minority. Increasing activism and policy demands by persons of Latin American origin in the United States seeking more inclusion in media policy making have been possible because they represent a larger ethnic group that has well-established advocacy organizations (Smith and Abreu 2019).

Why Advocacy Activities Fail

Advocacy activities can fail to gain backing or to achieve their objectives for multiple reasons. Policy advocates must carefully consider and reconsider their strategies and plans over time to respond to or avoid inadequate accomplishments and failure.

Major causes of disappointment often result from insufficient organization and inability to develop public support. This may result from not attracting or utilizing supporters well, not garnering attention to the issue needed to generate policy interest, not making an effective case for preferred policy, suffering resource limitations that interfere with activities needed, insufficient networking and participation in coalitions and other factors internal to the operations of the advocacy group.

Disappointing outcomes often result from poor advocacy strategy and implementation, engaging in too much oppositional advocacy rather than in promoting realistic alternatives, insufficient focus on criteria of success and whether it will occur incrementally or all at once and lack of realism about the time required for policy to develop and change.

Other failures are caused by mistrust of the political or policy system, reluctance to work with other stakeholders and unwillingness to compromise. Failure can also result because of the issue leading to advocacy being so large it requires systemic changes or numerous complex public and private choices. Issues such as poverty reduction, environmental sustainability or climate change require multiple, complex and coordinated policies and are likely to produce advocacy failures unless they are addressed through advocacy of multiple discrete individual policies—such as pre-school education, reduction of plastic waste or reduction in use of fossil fuels—that individually contribute to solving the broader issue. Achieving large-scale change requires clear objectives, time and sustained effort.

An appraisal of efforts to gain inclusion of gender issues in global communications policy debates and outcomes, for example, found significant limitations in placing it on the policy agenda because of resistance of policy makers to expand the focus of existing or planned policies and because some feminists have been slow to organize and engage in effective advocacy in the domain of media and communications policy advocacy (Gallagher 2011).

Media and Communication Reform Advocacy as a Social Movement

Social movements are a form of large group action to promote or resist change that can develop when large-scale consciousness of injustice or need for action emerges, organizational structures and strength develop and political opportunities to challenge existing conditions appear (McAdam et al. 1996; Tarrow 2011). They tend to emerge when normal political processes are not responsive or are oppositional.

As social movements arise, their abilities to grow become dependent on their ability to organize and mobilize people (della Porta and Diani 2018). Social movements tend to begin as informal groupings of individuals who enter alliances because of coalescing identity (Tarrow 2011), and these tend to promote organization within the movement, sometimes through formally organized leadership by coordinating groups. Social movements can grow out of advocacy groups and vice versa.

There have been some efforts to cast media and communications reform advocacy as a social movement, particularly that surrounding media democratization efforts (Hackett and Adam 1999), but that advocacy has yet to engage significant number of citizens in most countries or globally. The lack of common frames of reference among advocacy groups, poor collaboration between groups and inability to create a large constituency have kept media and communications policy advocacy from growing into a social movement yet (Napoli 2007, 2008).

It has been suggested that creating an effective media reform movement will require communication of different issues to varying constituencies, engaging a variety of NGOs and casting change in positive rather than oppositional frames (Hackett and Anderson 2011).

Challenges of Scholars as Advocates

Discussions of ethics of scholars engaged in advocacy have taken place in fields ranging from history (Tobey 1986) to biomedicine (Dresser 2001), and from education (Zaretsky 2004) to law (Fallon Jr. 2012). These discussions focus on issues related to the ethics of practices in which scholars engage as advocates, the extent to which their research and scholarship becomes advocacy and their responsibilities when engaging in advocacy. Concerns about advocacy and lobbying practices have been addressed in public relations as business ethics matters (Fitzpatrick and Bronste 2006; Berg 2012), but the activities of scholars have rarely been addressed in media and communications policy circles.

The fundamental questions that scholars engaging in advocacy must answer are whether they are speaking as citizens or scholars and how their participation is presented to and perceived by others. Academics, scholarly researchers at other institutions and independent scholars have the rights of all citizens to engage in advocacy. However, once they place scholarly degrees following their name in advocacy activities, or list institutional affiliations, they accept the mantle of responsibilities involving scholarly ethics, norms and practices. These are sometimes specified in codes of conduct and codes of ethics promulgated by leading associations in various disciplines, by educational and research institutions and in employment contracts to ensure that activities do not harm the reputations of disciplines and academia.

Because society has invested in the education and development of scholars, there is an obligation for scholars to share knowledge and insights, not just in the classroom and scholarly journals, but also in debates and forums wrestling with decisions affecting society. The very term professor denotes professing what one knows and believes to be true. Participation in policy process is thus aligned with the work of scholars.

There are multiple ways that scholarly communications advocacy contributes to policy debates, but there are tensions between scholars addressing immediate policy issues and activists seeking longer term systemic change (Napoli and Aslama 2011). Scholar advocates have played important roles in European media policy making both through policy analyses and direct advocacy activities (van den Bulck and Donders 2014).

When taking part as scholars, however, individuals have a responsibility to provide fact-based advocacy that uses their expertise to provide technical information, facts and options, and that separates facts from opinion and policy prescription. They should not mislead the public and policy makers or not misrepresent the body of literature or specific research.

Forecasting presents special professional ethics issues because forecasts are based on assumptions that need to be transparent and explained. Forecasts are sometimes highly subjective or skewed to the benefit of those commissioning them but are subsequently presented as valid and reliable and following the principles and methods of science (Wachs 1990).

Scholars can also risk their reputations if they engage in too much advocacy and too little scholarship, so they need to ensure that they balance their activities and be transparent about the roles they are playing.

The bulk of advocacy undertaken by media and telecommunications scholars focuses on media- and digital content-related issues, primarily because there are more scholars in media than telecommunications. In some countries, such as Canada, there is limited governmental support for academic policy advocacy, but it has been argued that it is necessary to assert public interest values (Shepherd et al. 2014). Other countries welcome scholarly intervention because of the expertise and broader perspectives it brings to policy discussions.

Final Words

Policy advocacy is a central component of social decision-making because advocates often have expertise and differing perspectives from those of policy makers and stakeholders. Ensuring those are represented in the decision-making processes is necessary if the best choices are to be made. Despite the importance of advocacy, there is very little literature on advocacy group effectiveness, and, when it exists, inordinate attention is given to large, well-established advocacy groups (Andrews and Edwards 2004).

It has been argued that media and communications graduates are often unprepared to take part in advocacy efforts and need more than law and regulatory coursework. Some assert that more advocacy and lobbying strategy, skills and ethics should be taught in universities (Griffin and Thurber 2015) and that media policy studies and student internships or apprenticeships with advocacy groups are needed (Lentz 2014). At the very least, law and policy coursework should not merely teach existing policy approaches but also include more about processes involved and should increase skills in producing policy analyses and evaluations and policy advocacy mission statements, visions and fact sheets.

Advocacy and engagement are particularly important in pursuing stronger public interest components in media and communication policy, factors addressed in a review of Canadian telecommunications and digital policy (Moll and Shade 2011). Media and communications advocacy are not without its critics, particularly for embracing the traditional elitist theories of media and democracy and not embracing more participatory view of democratic participation (Gibson 2010).

Advocacy is an important part of the public sphere in which policy issues are discussed and policy decisions considered. Without such advocacy, the range of ideas and perceptions of policy options would be diminished.

Chapter Summary

- Policy advocacy involves public support for an issue or cause and presenting the chosen point of view about it.
- Advocacy groups appear with the emergence of new issues, and many are short-lived.
- Markets and market activity do not represent broader social interests and needs, requiring advocacy in political and policy processes.
- Advocacy networks and coalitions can help raise awareness of issues and develop policy capabilities.
- Organizational and communication abilities are needed for effective policy advocacy.
- Scholars engaged in advocacy need to behave ethically and ensure that their activities do not harm their individual reputations or those of their disciplines.

Points for Discussion

1. Why are strategy and planning important activities for advocacy groups?
2. What kinds of activities or events might conflict with the objectives of some types of advocacy organizations?
3. What ethical breaches might occur in advocating for a policy in a public forum?
4. How should an organization respond to the failure of its advocacy activities?

Bibliography

Alexander, Jeffery C. 1998. *The Civil Sphere*. Oxford: Oxford University Press.

Andrews, Kenneth T., and Neal Caren. 2010. Making the News: Movement Organizations, Media Attention, and the Public Agenda. *American Sociological Review* 75 (6): 841–866.

Andrews, Kenneth T., and Bob Edwards 2004. Advocacy Organizations in the U.S. Political Process. *Annual Review of Sociology* 30: 479–506.

Balassiano, Katia, and Susan M. Chandler. 2010. The Emerging Role of Nonprofit Associations in Advocacy and Public Policy: Trends, Issues, and Prospects. *Nonprofit and Volunteer Sector Quarterly* 39 (5): 946–955.

Berg, Kati Tusinski. 2012. The Ethics of Lobbying: Testing an Ethical Framework for Advocacy in Public Relations. *Journal of Mass Media Ethics* 27 (2): 97–114.

Bolleyer, Nicole. 2019. *The State and Civil Society: Regulating Interest Groups, Parties, and Public Benefit Organizations in Contemporary Democracies*. Oxford: Oxford University Press.

Cammaerts, Bart. 2011. Power Dynamics in Multi-Stakeholder Policy Processes and Intra-civil Society Networking. In *The Handbook of Global Media and Communication Policy*, ed. Robin Mansell and Marc Raboy, 131–147. Oxford: Wiley-Blackwell.

Ciszek, Erica. 2013. Advocacy and Amplification: Nonprofit Outreach and Empowerment Through Participatory Media. *The Public Relations Journal* 7 (2): 187–213.

della Porta, Donatella, and Mario Diani, eds. 2018. *The Oxford Handbook of Social Movements*. Oxford: Oxford University Press.

DeSantis, Gloria. 2010. Voices from the Margins: Policy Advocacy and Marginalized Communities. *Canadian Journal of Nonprofit and Social Economy Research* 1 (1): 23–45.

Dowding, Keith. 1995. Model or Metaphor? A Critical Review of the Policy Network Approach. *Political Studies* 43 (1): 136–158.

Downey, John, and Natalie Fenton. 2016. New Media, Counter Publicity and the Public Sphere. *New Media & Society* 5 (2): 185–202.

Dresser, Rebecca. 2001. *When Science Offers Salvation: Patient Advocacy and Research Ethics*. Oxford: Oxford University Press.

Edgett, Ruth. 2002. Toward an Ethical Framework for Advocacy in Public Relations. *Journal of Public Relations Research* 14 (1): 1–26.

Edwards, Michael, ed. 2011. *The Oxford Handbook of Civil Society*. Oxford: Oxford University Press.

Fallon, Richard H., Jr. 2012. Scholars' Briefs and the Vocation of a Law Professor. *Journal of Legal Analysis* 4 (1): 223–269.

Fitzpatrick, Kathy, and Carolyn Bronste, eds. 2006. *Ethics in Public Relations: Responsible Advocacy*. Thousand Oaks: Sage.

Gallagher, Margaret. 2011. Gender and Communication Policy: Struggling for Space. In *The Handbook of Global Media and Communication Policy*, ed. Robin Mansell and Marc Raboy, 451–466. Oxford: Wiley-Blackwell.

Gen, Sheldon, and Amy Conley Wright. 2013. Policy Advocacy Organizations: A Framework Linking Theory and Practice. *Journal of Policy Practice* 12 (3): 163–193.

Gibson, Timothy A. 2010. The Limits of Media Advocacy. *Communication, Culture and Critique* 3 (1): 44–65.

Griffin, Patrick, and James A. Thurber. 2015. Teaching Public Policy Advocacy by Combining Academic Knowledge and Professional Wisdom. *Interest Groups & Advocacy* 4 (1): 40–51.
Guo, Chao, and Gregory D. Saxton. 2014. Tweeting Social Change: How Social Media Are Changing Nonprofit Advocacy. *Nonprofit and Voluntary Sector Quarterly* 43 (1): 57–79.
Hackett, Robert, and Megan Adam. 1999. Is Media Democratization a Social Movement? *Peace Review* 11 (1): 125–131.
Hackett, Robert, and Steve Anderson. 2011. Democratizing Communication Policy in Canada: A Social Movement Perspective. *Canadian Journal of Communication* 36 (1): 161–168.
Hessenius, Barry. 2007. *Hardball Lobbying for Nonprofits: Real Advocacy for Nonprofits in the New Century*. London: Palgrave Macmillan.
Hintz, Arne. 2012. Challenging the Digital Gatekeepers: International Policy Initiatives for Free Expression. *Journal of Information Policy* 2: 128–150.
Hoefer, Richard. 2015. *Advocacy Practice for Social Justice*. 3rd ed. Oxford: Oxford University Press.
John, Peter. 2003. Is There Life After Policy Streams, Advocacy Coalitions, and Punctuations: Using Evolutionary Theory to Explain Policy Change? *Policy Studies Journal* 31 (4): 481–498.
Jordan, Amy B. 2008. Children's Media Policy. *The Future of Children* 18 (1): 235–253.
Kumar, V.Anil. 2012. Speaking Truth to Power? Civil Society and Policy Advocacy in India. *Journal of Asian Public Policy* 5 (1): 41–47.
Lam, Wai Fung, and Kwan Nok Chan. 2017. Policy Advocacy in Transitioning Regimes: Comparative Lessons from the Case of Harbour Protection in Hong Kong. *Journal of Comparative Policy Analysis: Research and Practice* 19 (1): 54–71.
Lentz, Becky. 2014. The Media Policy Tower of Babble: A Case for "Policy Literacy Pedagogy". *Critical Studies in Media Communication* 31 (2): 134–140.
Li, Hui, Carlos Wing Hung Lo, and Shui Yan Tang. 2017. Nonprofit Policy Advocacy Under Authoritarianism. *Public Administration Review* 77 (1): 103–117.
Libby, Pat. 2012. *The Lobbying Strategy Handbook: 10 Steps to Advancing Any Cause Effectively*. Thousand Oaks: Sage Publications.
Ljubownikow, Serge, and Jo Crotty. 2016. Nonprofit Influence on Public Policy: Exploring Nonprofit Advocacy in Russia. *Nonprofit and Voluntary Sector Quarterly* 45 (2): 314–332.
Löblich, Maria. 2016. Dissent and Political Participation: The Many Faces of Communication Policy Advocacy and Activism. *Communication, Culture, & Critique* 9 (3): 395–416.
McAdam, Doug, John D. McCarthy, and Mayer N. Zald, eds. 1996. *Comparative Perspectives on Social Movements: Political Opportunities, Mobilizing Structures, and Cultural Framings*. Cambridge: Cambridge University Press.
Milan, Stefania, and Arne Hintz. 2013. Networked Collective Action and the Institutionalized Policy Debate: Bringing Cyberactivism to the Policy Arena? *Policy & Internet* 5 (1): 7–26.
Moll, Marita, and Leslie Regan Shade, eds. 2011. *The Internet Tree: The State of Telecom Policy in Canada 3.0*. Ottawa: Canadian Centre for Policy Alternatives.
Mosley, Jennifer. 2013. Recognizing New Opportunities: Reconceptualizing Policy Advocacy in Everyday Organizational Practice. *Social Work* 58 (3): 231–239.

Mueller, Milton. 2004. Reinventing Media Activism: Public Interest Advocacy in the Making of U.S. Communication-Information Policy, 1960–2002. *The Information Society* 20 (3): 169–187.

Napoli, Philip M. 2007. Public Interest Media Activism and Advocacy as a Social Movement: A Review of the Literature. McGannon Center Working Paper Series, No. 21. Available at: https://fordham.bepress.com/mcgannon_working_papers/21/. Accessed 5 June 2019.

———. 2008. Bridging Cultural Policy and Media Policy. *The Journal of Arts Management, Law, and Society* 37 (4): 311–330.

———. 2009. Public Interest Media Advocacy and Activism as a Social Movement. *Annals of the International Communication Association* 33 (1): 385–429.

Napoli, Philip, and Minna Aslama, eds. 2011. *Communications Research in Action: Scholar-Activist Collaborations for a Democratic Public Sphere*. New York: Fordham University.

Nelson, Richard A. 1994. Issue Communication and Advocacy: Contemporary Ethical Challenges. *Public Relations Review* 20 (3): 225–231.

Obar, Jonathan A., Paul Zube, and Clifford Lampe. 2012. Advocacy 2.0: An Analysis of How Advocacy Groups in the United States Perceive and Use Social Media as Tools for Facilitating Civic Engagement and Collective Action. *Journal of Information Policy* 2: 1–25.

Padovani, Claudia, and Elena Pavan. 2011. Actors and Interactions in Global Communication Governance: The Heuristic Potential of a Network Approach. In *The Handbook of Global Media and Communication Policy*, ed. Robin Mansell and Marc Raboy, 543–581. Oxford: Wiley-Blackwell.

Sabatier, Paul A., and Hank C. Jenkins-Smith. 1993. *Policy Change and Learning: An Advocacy Coalition Approach*. Boulder: Westview Press.

Sabatier, Paul A., and Christopher M. Weible. 2007. The Advocacy Coalition Framework: Innovations and Clarifications. In *Theories of the Policy Process*, ed. Paul A. Sabatier, 2nd ed., 189–220. Boulder: Westview Press.

Sakr, Naomi. 2006. Foreign Support for Media Freedom Advocacy in the Arab Mediterranean: Globalization from Above or Below? *Mediterranean Politics* 11 (1): 1–20.

Shade, Leslie Regan. 2011. Media Reform in the United States and Canada: Activism and Advocacy for Media Policies in the Public Interest. In *The Handbook of Global Media and Communication Policy*, ed. Robin Mansell and Marc Raboy, 147–165. Oxford: Wiley Blackwell.

Shepherd, Tamara, Gregory Taylor, and Catherine Middleton. 2014. A Tale of Two Regulators: Telecom Policy Participation in Canada. *Journal of Information Policy* 4: 1–22.

Smith, Jason A., and Randy Abreu. 2019. OU or an IOU? Latina/OS and the Racialization of Media Policy. *Ethnic and Racial Studies* 42 (4): 607–625.

Tarrow, Sidney G. 2011. *Power in Movement: Social Movements and Contentious Politics*. 3rd ed. Cambridge: Cambridge University Press.

Tobey, Ronald C. 1986. The Public Historian as Advocate: Is Special Attention to Professional Ethics Necessary? *The Public Historian* 8 (1): 21–30.

van den Bulck, Hilde, and Karen Donders. 2014. Of Discourses, Stakeholders and Advocacy Coalitions in Media Policy: Tracing Negotiations Towards the New Management Contract of Flemish Public Broadcaster VRT. *European Journal of Communication* 29 (1): 83–99.

Varone, Frédéric, Karin Ingold, Charlotte Jourdain, and Volker Schneider. 2017. Studying Policy Advocacy Through Social Network Analysis. *European Political Science* 16 (3): 322–336.
Wachs, Martin. 1990. Ethics and Advocacy in Forecasting for Public Policy. *Business & Professional Ethics Journal* 9 (1/2): 141–157.
Waisbord, Silvio. 2010. The Pragmatic Politics of Media Reform: Media Movements and Coalition-Building in Latin America. *Global Media and Communication* 6 (2): 133–153.
Yanacopulos, Helen. 2015. *International NGO Engagement, Advocacy, Activism: The Faces and Spaces of Change*. London: Palgrave Macmillan.
Zaretsky, Lindy. 2004. Advocacy and Administration: From Conflict to Collaboration. *Journal of Educational Administration* 42 (2): 270–286.

Suggested Readings

Gen, Sheldon, and Amy Conley Wright. 2013. Policy Advocacy Organizations: A Framework Linking Theory and Practice. *Journal of Policy Practice* 12(3): 163–193.
Hessenius, Barry. 2007. *Hardball Lobbying for Nonprofits: Real Advocacy for Nonprofits in the New Century*. London: Palgrave Macmillan.
Libby, Pat. 2012. *The Lobbying Strategy Handbook: 10 Steps to Advancing Any Cause Effectively*. Thousand Oaks: Sage Publications.

CHAPTER 11

Looking Forward

This volume explored the context and methods of policy and policy making by focusing on the stimuli, systems, institutions, influences and choices that produce or impede policy and strengthen or weaken its application. It described best practices for policy processes, participation in policy making and conducting research about policy and policy making. It made the case that good policy research does more than merely describe or critique existing policy, law and intervention, criticize the absence of policy or argue for systemic change.

The book provided essential definitions, terms, concepts and frameworks for understanding and investigating policy making. It revealed the importance of exploring institutions, procedures and participants, and the importance of addressing differences among the environments, locales and processes in which policy emerges. It explored why and how policy issues arise, choices are contested and decisions taken. It emphasized the importance of analysis, evaluation and examination of policy and the methods frequently used in those activities.

This volume has revealed how policy studies focus on institutions, processes and actors in policy making, the principles and major concepts of policy studies, how those elements can be explored and applied in studies of specific policy and how policies and policy making can be compared across countries. Policy studies theories, concepts and research approaches provide additional avenues for researchers and scholars to apply in media and communications scholarship. Policy studies concepts can strengthen research that until now has primarily relied on other explanatory approaches and tended not to rely on, test or develop theory. Employing policy studies ideas in conjunction with the varied types of traditional media and communications research will make those studies contextually and theoretically stronger and expand the audience for the research by attracting scholars from a wider variety of disciplines.

R. G. Picard, *Media and Communications Policy Making*, Palgrave Global Media Policy and Business,
https://doi.org/10.1007/978-3-030-35173-1_11

Policy studies concepts open possibilities for exploring how political systems affect choices of policy tools and the effectiveness of various interventions in media and communications. They facilitate investigations of how top-down or bottom-up policy making affects choices of policy and the ability to influence processes. They provide perspectives within which to examine differences in policy and policy outcomes between converged or separated media and communications administrative agencies.

The approaches of policy studies allow consideration of differences among policy analyses produced by stakeholders and the capacity of differing stakeholders to engage in advocacy and their effects on policy outcomes. Policy studies provide means for exploring the effectiveness and challenges of coalitions and networks and whether and the extent to which advocacy by non-business groups produces policy changes that may or may not be in the interest of citizens and consumers.

Policy studies approaches make it possible to investigate whether privacy, consumer protection or media policy regimes are better suited for addressing data algorithms or whether direct legislation or administrative agency regulations and rules better serve democratic needs.

Policy studies conceptualizations can alter perceptions of telecommunications policy, which has conventionally focused on issues of system availability, capacity and reliability, with firms creating and operating the infrastructures. Researchers can consider the institutions of policy making to determine whether converged communications administrative agencies that have emerged in recent years are capable and competent to oversee the wider array of issues created by their expansion into network management, cloud services network security, and new personal, home and business applications being facilitated by the shift to 5G technology. These developments raise complex and central public questions because national economies, commerce and essential services such as energy, transportation, water and sewer systems, health care and education are becoming dependent on this telecommunications infrastructure and the implications of that dependence. Policy studies approaches will help researchers investigate what new types of policy, policy regimes and agencies will be appropriate in the coming years. The approaches can be used to inquire whether current disconnected policies across multiple policy regimes will be adequate to address issues of consumer privacy and the security of financial, health and other records and information held in services offered by telecommunications firms.

Multiple issues involving the internet policy remain open and in need of policy making. Most governance has focused on operability concerns, but significant questions of who, how and at what level the internet should be governed remain open. Policy makers in countries around the world are increasingly stepping in to address issues of cybersecurity, harassment, violent and sexual content, misinformation and disinformation, digital inequalities and human rights to communicate and access communication. In most countries, the fundamental policy question of whether the internet is an essential service that should be governed as a public utility or is a private product has not been directly asked and answered. How to address network effects and winner-take-all approaches by firms remains salient because competition law has difficulty defining the relevant market for digital systems and platform operations, and most media and communications agencies lack legal competency.

Questions raised by information and communications technologies decision-making and machine learning are rising with increased reliance on artificial intelligence systems. Even fundamental policies of how liability will be established regarding injury and deaths to humans and damage to property resulting from these technological advances remain open. The uses and effects of algorithms in determining what information and content are easily available to users remain debated, and multiple policy questions related to user manipulation and lack of control are still unanswered.

Overall, there is a need to employ better research methods and to engage in more comparative research to explore effectiveness of policy tools used in media and communications and compare policy among states, including those with differing political, economic and social systems. More research is needed to explore how specific policies have moved through policy processes, identifying the most important influences exercised on them, documenting where and how those occur, suggesting means for rectifying deficiencies and determining means for addressing inequities in those processes in future policy making.

More stakeholder research recognizing multiple points of view and identifying the forums and mechanism used to gain dominant support for some needs to be undertaken. Research about mechanisms that can be used to better recognize, represent and promote citizen and consumer concerns in policy processes should be undertaken. Issues of freedom of expression and democratic participation need to be raised in more policy regimes than those directly associated with media and communications. Means for improving public and civil society participation and representation at all governance levels need to be sought, especially those at regional and global levels, where most participation and representation is governmental and commercial.

Communication is central to the functioning of humans and society. The means of communications are not merely machines and technological infrastructures and systems, but fundamental systems for interaction and transaction. They facilitate conveyance of ideas, opinions, information, social values, experiences and entertainment. They carry and create culture and norms of society. They help to define and create our individual, professional, community and national identities. They support social cohesiveness and democratic activities.

Communications systems, platforms and media are highly influenced by technological, social, economic and political forces, however. Because communication is necessary for the functioning and well-being of society, policy needs to address elements that deny or skew the benefits of the operations of those systems, platforms and media. Contemporary communications are altering relationships, cultures, economies and governance worldwide. Individuals, institutions and society are struggling to comprehend and adjust to the new environment and to social and political fractures resulting from that transformation. Pursuing better public policies toward media and communications is crucial to the future of individuals and society.

Glossary

A

Administrative agency An executive or independent government agency charged with overseeing policy and implementing its laws. Agencies make rules and regulations required for the policy to be applied, based on their authorizing laws. Agencies may be placed within governmental ministries or departments or located externally and given some degree of autonomy. See Executive agency and Independent agency.

Authority The right to act or command through formally delegated power. Authority provides the mandate and power to make and enforce decisions through mechanisms established by the state and government.

B

Bilateral Refers to relations, agreements or treaties involving two sovereign states or recognized political entities that address issues of interest or with specific provisions that many not be of interest to multiple states. Contrast with Multilateral.

C

Communications policy Governance focused on systems, infrastructures and networks that facilitate communications and content distribution. Policy may be designed to create and improve these technologies and provision or to oversee their operations.

Competency A legislature's or administrative agency's right to address specific topics and make laws and interventions regarding it. Competency is granted through authorizing laws that establish and guide its operations.

R. G. Picard, *Media and Communications Policy Making*, Palgrave Global Media Policy and Business,
https://doi.org/10.1007/978-3-030-35173-1

Competition policy A policy domain focused on ensuring that markets operate effectively through decisions promoting competition and restricting activities that harm competitors or consumers and reduce competition and rivalry in markets. Most competition policy is enforced through antitrust/anticartel agencies or ministries, but promotion of competition can also be pursued through actions by other ministries and administrative agencies, including those involved in media and communications policy.

Consultation A formal information and discussion activity as part of deliberations about the need for policy making, options available or a specific policy proposal. Consultations may be open to submissions from anyone or limited to participation by specific stakeholders.

Consumer tools Intervention means designed to assist consumers in decision-making. These typically involve disclosure requirements concerning ingredients, services, terms and pricing. Tools may also provide protection to consumers against unfair and harmful actions by suppliers of goods and services.

Cultural policy The policy domain focused on promoting and protecting heritage and expressions of culture. It is usually a domestic policy activity but can involve regional and global governance. Cultural policy is made separately from media and communications policy but may influence those policies, particularly in areas affecting film and broadcasting. Most cultural policy is under the purview of ministries of culture, but some is often placed in the sphere of activities of administrative agencies for media and communications.

D

Disincentive A policy disadvantage or penalty that is implemented with the intent of discouraging some behavior through negative financial or administrative consequences. Disincentives do not mandate that the behavior ceases, but continuation comes at a cost that often produces compliance.

E

Economic(s) Knowledge and actions related to production, consumption, transactions, allocation of resources, decision-making and transfer of wealth. Economic laws, theories and concerns influence policy making and choices. Many analyses and policy examinations use economic methods to investigate potential outcomes of policy options.

Economic interest A national interest in achieving and maintaining economic growth, development, stability and the financial well-being of citizens and enterprises as a whole. At an individual or enterprise level, economic interest refers to private financial benefits obtained through ownership and other economic activities.

Evidence-based policy making The use of quantitative and qualitative evidence to help guide decision-making. It is based on seeking reliable evidence produced through rigorous and objective research, rather than relying on anecdotes and perceptions of what is occurring and how policy choices will affect the situation or problem considered.

Executive The branch of government made up of ministries and administrative agencies that implement laws and conduct the functions of government. Structures and forms of executive branches vary depending on the political system and governance needs.

Executive agency An administrative agency of government under the control of the executive branch. Administrative agencies may be established within ministries or departments or as stand-alone executive bodies. Contrast with Independent agency.

F

Facilitation tools Tools that create a beneficial operating environment for industries by providing structure, standards and processes that make it possible to operate an industry, stabilize an industry or coordinate policy across jurisdictions for simpler operation. The purposes of these interventions are to assist the industry, improve its development and support its sustainability.

Fiscal advantages Intervention that provides advantages to firms through reduced fees or rates or preferred treatment for services or collections by government agencies or controlled entities. These tools are used when policy makers wish to assist firms for economic development or other public purposes.

Framing Asserting policy arguments in a way that influences perceptions of them by stimulating psychological responses predisposed in individual's memory and information processing methods. Framing is designed to allow simpler messaging in political and policy communication.

Framework Principles, theories, bodies of knowledge and general objectives formed as a conceptual context with which to approach policy making regarding a particular topic. Use of established frameworks reduces the need to fully explain mechanisms being used in policy development.

G

General aid State support that can be used in any way by the recipient. This state aid, usually a subsidy, is given without specification of how it must be used. Contrast to Specific aid.

Governance Policy making and control activities of states, intergovernmental organizations, nongovernmental organizations and private actors. The term developed to include governance actions and influences outside state activities. Use of the term is debated because of limited agreed-upon uses and definitions.

H

Harmonization Coordinating policies, laws and regulations to bring them into agreement, clarify boundaries between them or simplify relationships between them. This may occur within a state by harmonizing policy across levels of government or various policy domains. It may also occur among states under international or regional governance activities.

Head of government The individual responsible for day-to-day operations of government and political activities, such as a prime minister or chancellor. See also Head of state.

Head of state The highest representative of a sovereign state, such as a monarch, emperor or president. Depending upon the structure of the state, the head of state may or may not also be the head of government.

Hierarchy Classification of persons or things in terms of importance, power and authority. In a hierarchy, those below the leader or top of the list are subordinate and have less agency to act or import.

I

Incentive A policy advantage or reward provided as an inducement to promote desired voluntary behavior to obtain beneficial financial or other consequences in exchange for specified actions. Incentives include tax reductions, subsidies and preferential treatment in licensing. Tools using this mechanism are designed to encourage and motivate firms and individuals to act in ways that support public purposes.

Independent agency An administrative agency that has authority separate from that of the executive, so that it can act independently of direct control. This structure is designed to provide some autonomy and ability to withstand political pressures. Contrast to Executive agency.

Industrial policy A policy domain in which strategic intervention is designed to produce growth and competitiveness in sectors of the economy. It can include use of both protective and supportive mechanisms and tools.

Information policy Governance of activities involved in the flow, processing, storage and use of data, information and related content. This is an increasingly important and disputed area of policy because of issues involving privacy, data protection, algorithms, and misinformation and disinformation.

Infrastructure Fundamental installations and facilities necessary for operations of network systems such as canals, roads, electricity and telecommunications. In media and communications policy infrastructure tends to most involve fixed and mobile communications systems, microwave and satellite systems, broadband networks and other distribution systems.

Innovation policy Policy domain focused on promoting and facilitating innovation through public and private activities. It is typically concerned with obtaining economic and social benefits for a country or province by encouraging and supporting scientific and technical research and innovation, planning and its application.

Institution(s) Established organizations, structures, processes, rules and practices through which collective activities take place and influence policy development, progress and outcomes Institutions are established and maintained by authority, practice or social norms.

Intergovernmental organization An official organization made up of member states created to address common issues through treaties and other regulations. Intergovernmental organizations are voluntary organizations focused on specific issues that operate according to a founding treaty. They may operate at the international or regional levels of governance.

International organization A voluntary nongovernmental body created to facilitate and govern multinational activities that does not carry the force of international law but exists by acceptance of states and other stakeholders because of common interests. These often are focused more on industry issues than general public issues. Lack of parallel governmental action can place them in de facto control of policy affecting the public worldwide.

Internet An interconnected network of telecommunications and computers facilitating communication, commerce, and the monitoring and control of mechanical and electronic systems. There are multiple private internets used primarily by governments and companies, in addition to the publicly available global internet and some public internets limited to national operation.

Internet governance Policies and practices put in place to facilitate internet operations and guide activities of telecommunications firms, service providers, platforms and users. Most internet governance has been private governance by international organizations, but there is an increasing demand for governance by an intergovernmental organization.

Intervention Describes activities in which the government intercedes in the market to proscribe and prescribe activities by private firms, provides incentives or disincentives for particular actions or engages in public provision.

J

Judiciary The court authorities, structures and personnel of a country that interpret and apply law and regulation to issues and actions being adjudicated. The independence and authority of the judiciary vary widely among nations.

L

Law Statutes, regulations, rules and practices established by legislative and executive action or judicial decisions within an existing governance system. These establish a system of procedures and rules that regulate actions of firms, individuals and government entities, address criminal and civil matters, and can provide penalties or remedies.

Legislative body A body of citizen representatives that enacts and approves policy, makes laws and conducts governmental business within the authority given by the national political system in which it is located. The degree of autonomy and scope of action vary widely in different governmental structures.

Legitimacy Acceptance of authority and power exercised through a governance system as being rightful and appropriate. The continuation of all governments and rulers is dependent on their legitimacy being accepted by those governed.

License Governmental permission to own, operate or use regulated resources or take part in regulated activities. Licenses are provided by an authority allowing the activity to take place under regulations governing the issuance of licenses. They may be used to organize and facilitate the industry, to regulate the structure of industry ownership or to control those allowed to participate in the industry.

Loan Lending money with repayment and interest payments specified over time or providing other resources for use with the expectation that money or resources will be returned. Loans may be made by private, public or quasi-public entities.

Loan guarantees A contractual obligation guaranteeing loan repayment. Used by governments to assist firms to obtain loans or obtain lower interest rates when doing so is deemed to support a public purpose. Loans guaranteed by governments will be repaid by government if the entity is unable to do so.

M

Mandates A grant of authority to carry out a task or official orders for individuals or firms to carry out an action or to refrain from action. An administrative agency may thus be given a mandate from the government to oversee the internet and those who use it. That agency in turn may mandate that internet firms do not allow anonymous use of the internet, platforms or services and that all internet users must be identifiable.

Mandated aid State support that administrative agencies are required to provide if parties meet specified requirements. Mandated aid removes the discretion of regulators to provide or withhold the support. Contrast to Selective aid.

Market failure A phenomenon that occurs when market participants and market forces are unable to create efficient production, distribution and consumption of a good or service. When market failures are identified, state intervention may occur to address systemic weaknesses through a variety of policy mechanisms and tools if doing so is deemed to serve a public purpose.

Media capture A condition in which private media in a country are controlled by a regime or regime allies through voluntary acquiesce in exchange for privileges or wealth.

Media policy Governance activities related to enterprises that produce and distribute content, including structure, operations and content provided. Media policy is often concerned about the effects of content, types of content provided or neglected, ownership of media enterprises and systems, and the ability of diverse groups to participate and be self-represented in media activities.

Multilateral Involves relations, agreements and treaties involving many states or parties. Multilateral activities and governance tend to concentrate on issues with broad common interests because of widely differing concerns and political systems among participating states. A good deal of multilateral activity takes place in intergovernmental organizations. Contrast to Bilateral.

N

Nation A community sharing common language history, identity and culture, and its geographical location may or may not be within the boundaries of a single country. The Mohawk nation, for example, extends across the eastern Canadian-U.S. border.

Nation state A country based on a predominant nation, with its territory and national boundaries aligned. Fewer pure nation states exist at present in the world because of historical mergers of nations and territories and patterns of large-scale migration.

National interest(s) Goals and ambitions for a nation's economy, culture, well-being and relations with other countries. National interests differ from national security, but interests involving availability of crucial resources may become security issues as well.

National security Protection of the security, safety and well-being of the state, its citizens, economy, and institutions from foreign or domestic attack, interference or disruption.

Norms Expectations of how individuals, organizations and enterprises should behave. These are based on what is customary and standard social behavior. Norms can involve social roles, relationships and customs. Breaching norms can produce censure, shaming and shunning, and sometimes civil or criminal action.

O

Operational intervention tools Intervention that affects firms' operational choices and behavior by requiring some activities and constraining others. This form of intervention requires firms to recognize and comply with mandates from governmental actors within the scope provided by their authority.

Ownership regulation Governmental action that determines who may own firms, what firms can participate in an industry and the size and market impact of the firms. Ownership may be controlled for competition rationales, to support ownership diversity and pluralism or to maintain control of media and communications.

P

Policy Governance rationales, principles, frameworks and objectives that guide decision-making and intervention in response to issues, challenges and problems affecting society. Policy that is agreed is placed into law, used to create administrative structures and operations, and to implements its mechanisms and tools.

Policy agenda Policy demands and issues that have arisen in significance to the point that policy makers are aware of them and considering taking action on them over other issues not on the agenda and perceived to be less important. In states where public opinion plays important roles in governance, public pressures for action help put issues on the policy agenda. See Public agenda.

Policy analysis A process of considering and researching issues, identifying policy options and their viability that is undertaken to support policy decision-making. Analysis is designed to provide a comprehensive briefing that assists policy makers making choices.

Policy capture Condition in which private actors effectively control policy making and administrative agencies to produce beneficial outcomes for themselves. This capture may occur because of deliberate or unintentional factors.

Policy evaluation A process of reviewing the efficiency and outcomes of policy that has been in place with the purpose of determining whether it should be continued, revised or discontinued. Evaluations are based on criteria that determine the extent to which policy is producing desired results, unintended consequences, and is cost-effective.

Policy maker Actors in policy making that influence policy development and make policy decisions. These may be governmental actors or a range of stakeholders with interest in the issues or developments being considered.

Policy making The process by which purposive decisions are made within a governance system. It involves how policy is designed, taken up by policy-making institutions, influences exercised upon its development, its approval and its implementation.

Policy mechanism The general approach and institutionalized means applied when addressing a policy issue. Mechanisms involve beliefs that certain actions will produce outcomes. The choice of mechanism can determine the effectiveness of the policy in addressing issues and the tools selected.

Policy narrative Rhetorical explanations of issues within a concise framework for comprehension, analysis and action. Narratives are designed to be persuasive and align with preferred beliefs. Policy makers are often confronted with conflicting narratives from stakeholders and other political actors.

Policy principles Statements of foundational values and norms that are used to guide policy consideration and decisions. These fundamental tenets provide reference points for reflection when objectives, mechanisms and tools are considered.

Policy process Linear or cyclical conceptualizations of why and how policy emerges, is developed and considered and is implemented and reconsidered. The process is comprised of policy stages in which activities take place.

Policy stages Activities described as steps in a process by which awareness of the need for policy emerges and policy is subsequently developed and implemented. Used to allow easier conceptualization of policy making and the activities involved in it.

Policy tool Intervention instruments used to facilitate the working of policy mechanisms by inducing or influencing functions or interactions of the mechanism employed.

Policy trajectory The direction of policy development over time and its influence on subsequent policy development relevant to similar or adjacent topics by creating an example and expectations.

Political philosophy Political philosophies are built on concepts of power, authority, justice, liberty, equality, rights and property and their roles in social decision-making. These philosophies are normative positions that affect conceptualizations of states, governance, the right to rule and the responsibilities of states and rulers.

Polity A community based on common interests and identity that has organized structures for governance and decision-making. These are often the citizenry of states, provinces or municipalities and users of services of water and electrical associations, but they can also be associations, unions and other organizations.

Politics The processes and activities of deliberation and decision-making within a polity. It involves actions by political actors and parties through the institutions and mechanisms of governance.

Power Authority and capability to produce a purposeful outcome through command or influence. The exercise of power may or may not involve coercion and may be just or unjust.

Privacy The state of being free from attention and observation. Privacy preserves personal dignity and provides the ability to seclude oneself, to separate oneself from intrusion and to withhold personal matters and activities from public view.

Private regulation Policies, rules, regulations and processes created by private entities to govern activities of networks, systems and enterprises, to establish technical and operating standards or to respond to complaints from the public.

Public agenda Issues and developments that the public believe are significant and deserving of policy attention. It is essentially a prioritization of public concerns that can influence the policy agenda of policy makers.

Public opinion The views, desires and wants of members of the public. This can be expressed in political views and policy preferences and collective opinion measured by survey research.

Public provision Provision of public services through state-owned firms, quasi-governmental enterprises or public institutions. This mechanism is typically used to respond to developing markets, market failure or limitations on the provision of desirable public goods.

Public sphere The space in which public participation in deliberation and decision-making takes place. This space may be expansive or narrow, depending upon governance and political systems. An active, extensive public sphere is more likely to produce more ideas, concerns and discussion to be used in policy making.

Q

Quota A share of something that must be provided or receipt of which is fixed by governance. Content quotas, for example, typically fix a percentage of broadcast or print media content that must be devoted to specific types of content. Paper quotas may specify the amount of paper that can be used by newspapers or magazines in cases where production or import of paper is controlled.

R

Regulation A form of governance intervention by which behavior is proscribed or prescribed. Such intervention may prohibit charging rural customers more for telephone services than urban customers or require firms to invest at least 5 percent of their annual turnover in system maintenance.

Regulatory exemption Intervention in which firms or industries are exempted from compliance with regulations generally applicable to all firms. This provides advantages in comparison to other firms, allows actions that might not otherwise be permitted and can reduce operating costs.

Religion A form of cultural practice involving belief, rituals, morality and norms of behavior and explanations of the place of humans in the universe.

S

Selective aid State support that administrative agencies may choose to provide to parties that meet specified requirements. This provides the authority for administrative personnel to choose among applications from qualified applicants in providing support for audiovisual productions or to determine some are not worthy or qualified for assistance.

Social policy Involves public choices related to provision of social services, such as education, health care, pensions, child welfare and income loss. This policy domain focuses on issues involved in the well-being of society.

Sovereignty The right of states to self-govern without interference recognized by other states. The right is sometimes claimed by nations and territories in asserting independence.

Specific aid State support that can only be used by recipients for specified purposes. A specific subsidy given to support hiring of new journalists, for example, should not be diverted to acquire new technology.

Stakeholder(s) Individuals, groups, enterprises and others who are affected by objectives, policy choices and actions. They have an interest in the processes, arguments and decisions made in policy making and should be provided an opportunity to participate.

Standards, operating Rules set by public and private bodies that govern firms' behavior by specifying operating standards they should achieve. This may involve requirements that broadcasters devote a specified portion of their broadcast time to news and public affairs or that internet service providers and search firms provide search filters that reduce unwanted contact with materials of a violent or sexual nature.

Standards, technical Rules set by public and private bodies to ensure functionality of technologies, interconnectivity and reduction of costs for producers and consumers. These standards involve specification of equipment, materials, processes and their qualities.

State An organized community with a political structure and sovereign government, usually recognized as an independent country. The state and its governance system are empowered to operate on behalf of the country and its population.

State capture Condition in which state institutions, processes and policies are captive to private interests, often through corrupt practices. This condition is most often evident in transitional states.

Structural intervention tools Policy tools that create and control the structure and organization of an industry, its participants and its markets. Tools include licensing, ownership control and more.

Subsidy(ies) Intervention by which public funds are transferred to private entities to pursue a public purpose or expenditures made by the state to help reduce operating costs for firms. Subsidies take multiple forms and can be described by their purposes and administration. See General and Specific aid and Mandated and Selective aid.

Subsidy tools Policy instruments used to determine how much and how public funds will be transferred to private entities in the pursuit of public purposes.

Surveillance Observing and monitoring activities and behavior of individuals or groups through human or technical means for the purpose of influencing their actions, social control or investigation. Surveillance has traditionally been undertaken by the state, but major technology firms are now deeply involved in surveillance of their customers.

T

Tax A compulsory charge levied by a government to finance its budget or disincentive production or consumption. Taxes may be levied in many ways, including taxation of individual income, property, sales, businesses, goods and services traded among nations, and value added.

Tax credit Relief from paying a tax that is offered to incentivize specified activity or support certain conditions. Credits can cover part of the entire tax and are subtracted from taxes owed to the state.

Telecommunications policy Governance of telephony and broadcasting related activities, including elements related to infrastructures, operations and services. Because of technological change and convergence, this governance is increasingly subsumed under communications and media policies.

Trade barriers Restrictions on imports or exports created by governments, typically for an economic or security purpose. These may be taxes on imports or product requirements that limit the willingness of firms to engage in trade with a country.

Treaty An agreement made between two or more nations governing how particular issues will be jointly addressed or how they will behave toward each other. Treaties carry obligations enforceable under international law.

Treaty denunciation The exiting of a treaty by a former signatory, thus withdrawing it from its obligations. Processes for doing so are ensconced in international law and treaties themselves. Denunciation may occur for many reasons including new governments disagreeing with the obligations, belief that the treaty is ineffective or recognition that conditions that prompted the treaty have been altered.

Treaty ratification Agreement of a state to be bound by multinational or bilateral treaty provisions. The processes for ratification vary among states, but all provide for explicit decision to abide by the obligations of the treaty.

V

Values Ideals held by individuals and cultures about what is desirable or undesirable, good or bad, moral or immoral and acceptable or unacceptable. Values influence standards, principles, priorities, choices and behavior. Commonly held values inform policy-making principles and decisions.

Bibliography

Abrahamson, Bram Dov. 2001. Media Policy After Regulation. *International Journal of Cultural Studies* 4 (3): 301–326.

Acharya, Amitav, and Alastair Iain Johnston, eds. 2007. *Crafting Cooperation: Regional International Institutions in Comparative Perspective*. Cambridge: Cambridge University Press.

Ahearne, Jeremy, ed. 2002. *French Cultural Policy Debates: A Reader*. London: Routledge.

Alexander, Jeffery C. 1998. *The Civil Sphere*. Oxford: Oxford University Press.

Ali, Christopher. 2012. Media at the Margins: Policy and Practice in American, Canadian, and British Community Television. *International Journal of Communication* 6: 1119–1138. Available at: https://ijoc.org/index.php/ijoc/article/view/1316/750. Accessed 15 Oct 2019.

———. 2017. *Media Localism: The Policies of Place*. Urbana: University of Illinois.

Allison, Audrey L. 2014. *The ITU and Managing Satellite Orbital and Spectrum Resources in the 21st Century*. Berlin: Springer.

Althaus, Catherine, Peter Bridgman, and Glyn Davis. 2013. *The Australian Policy Handbook*. 5th ed. Crows Nest: Allen & Unwin.

Amos, Owen. 2009. 'Kitemark' Could Distinguish Journalism from 'Web Noise.' *PressGazette*, January 1. Available at: https://pressgazette.co.uk/kitemark-could-distinguish-journalism-from-web-noise/. Accessed 19 June 2019.

Ampuja, Marko. 2012. Globalization Theory, Media-Centrism and Neoliberalism: A Critique of Recent Intellectual Trends. *Critical Sociology* 38 (2): 281–301.

Amy, Douglas J. 1984. Toward a Post-Positivist Policy Analysis. *Policy Studies Journal* 13 (1): 207–211.

an Hulst, Merlijn, and Dvora Yanow. 2016. From Policy "Frames" to "Framing": Theorizing a More Dynamic, Political Approach. *The American Review of Public Administration* 46 (1): 92–112.

Anderson, Charles W. 1979. The Place of Principles in Policy Analysis. *The American Political Science Review* 73 (3): 711–723.

R. G. Picard, *Media and Communications Policy Making*, Palgrave Global Media Policy and Business,
https://doi.org/10.1007/978-3-030-35173-1

Andrews, Kenneth T., and Neal Caren. 2010. Making the News: Movement Organizations, Media Attention, and the Public Agenda. *American Sociological Review* 75 (6): 841–866.

Andrews, Kenneth T., and Bob Edwards. 2004. Advocacy Organizations in the U.S. Political Process. *Annual Review of Sociology* 30: 479–506.

Appadurai, Arjun. 1996. *Modernity at Large: Cultural Dimensions of Globalization*. Minneapolis: University of Minnesota Press.

Arnull, Anthony, and D. Wincott. 2003. *Accountability and Legitimacy in the European Union*. Oxford: Oxford University Press.

Atkins, William. 2002. *The Politics of Southeast Asia's New Media*. London: Routledge.

Aufderheide, Pat. 2006. The 1996 Telecommunications Act: Ten Years Later. *Federal Communications Law Journal* 58 (3): 407–413.

Aust, Anthony. 2014. *Modern Treaty Law and Practice*. 3rd ed. Cambridge: Cambridge University Press.

Australia, Department of Communications and the Arts. n.d. Telecommunications Self-Regulation. Available at: https://www.communications.gov.au/policy/policy-listing/telecommunications-self-regulation. Accessed 1 Apr 2019.

Austria. 2011. Media Transparency Act, Official Gazette 125/2011.

Ba, Alice D., Cheng-Chwee Kuik, and Sueo Sudo, eds. 2017. *Institutionalizing East Asia: Mapping and Reconfiguring Regional Cooperation*. London: Routledge.

Baasanjav, Undrah. 2016. The Public Interest and Mongolian Digital Television Transition. *International Journal of Digital Television* 7 (1): 7–22.

Bagdikian, Ben H. 1983. *The Media Monopoly*. Boston: Beacon Press.

Baker, C. Edwin. 2001. *Media, Markets and Democracy*. Cambridge: Cambridge University Press.

———. 2006. *Media Concentration and Democracy: Why Ownership Matters*. New York: Cambridge University Press.

Baker & McKenzie. 2012. *Guide to Media and Content Regulation in Asia Pacific*. Sydney: Baker & McKenzie.

Balassiano, Katia, and Susan M. Chandler. 2010. The Emerging Role of Nonprofit Associations in Advocacy and Public Policy: Trends, Issues, and Prospects. *Nonprofit and Volunteer Sector Quarterly* 39 (5): 946–955.

Baldwin, Robert, Martin Cave, and Martin Lodge. 2013. *Understanding Regulation: Theory, Strategy, and Practice*. 2nd ed. Oxford: Oxford University Press.

Ball, Stephen J. 1993. What Is Policy? Texts, Trajectories and Toolboxes. *Discourse: Studies in the Cultural Politics of Education* 13 (2): 10–17.

Bandyopadhyay, Sumana, and André Torre. 2017. *Regional Cooperation in South Asia: Socio-economic, Spatial, Ecological and Institutional Aspects*. Berlin: Springer.

Bardach, Eugene. 2005. *A Practical Guide for Policy Analysis*. 2nd ed. Washington, DC: Congressional Quarterly Press.

Barrow, Clyde W. 1993. *Critical Theories of the State: Marxist, Neo-Marxist, and Post-Marxist*. Madison: University of Wisconsin Press.

Bartle, Ian. 2005. *Globalisation and EU Policy-Making: The Neo-Liberal Transformation of Telecommunications and Electricity*. Manchester: Manchester University Press.

Barwise, Patrick, and Robert G. Picard. 2014. What If There Were No BBC Television? The Net Impact on UK Viewers. RISJ Report. Oxford: Reuters Institute, University of Oxford.

Bauer, Johannes M. 2010a. Learning from Each Other: Promises and Pitfalls of Benchmarking in Communications Policy. *Info* 12 (6): 8–20.

———. 2010b. Regulation, Public Policy, and Investment in Communications Infrastructure. *Telecommunications Policy* 34 (1-2): 65–79.

———. 2014. Platforms, Systems, Competition, and Innovation: Reassessing the Foundations of Communications Policy. *Telecommunications Policy* 38 (8-9): 662–673.

Becker, Henk A. 2001. Social Impact Assessment. *European Journal of Operational Research* 128 (2): 311–321.

Beder, S. 2001. Research Note – Neoliberal Think Tanks and Free Market Environmentalism, Environmental Politics. *Environmental Politics* 10 (2): 128–133.

Bemelmans-Videc, Marie-Louise, Ray C. Rist, and Evert Vedung, eds. 1998. *Carrots, Sticks & Sermons: Policy Instruments and Their Evaluation*. New Brunswick: Transaction Publishers.

Benington, John, and Mark Moore, eds. 2011. *Public Value: Theory and Practice*. Basingstoke: Palgrave Macmillan.

Benjamin, Stuart M., and James B. Speta. 2015. *Telecommunications Law and Policy*. 4th ed. Durham: Carolina Academic Press.

Benkler, Yochai, Hal Roberts, Robert Faris, Alicia Solow-Niederman, and Bruce Etling. 2015. Social Mobilization and the Networked Public Sphere: Mapping the SOPA-PIPA Debate. *Political Communication* 32 (4): 594–624.

Bennetts, Marc. 2019. Russia Passes Law to Jail People for 15 Days for 'Disrespecting' Government. *The Guardian*, March 6. Accessible at: https://www.theguardian.com/world/2019/mar/06/russian-parliament-outlaws-online-disrespect. Accessed 8 Mar 2019.

Berg, Elliot J. 1993. *Rethinking Technical Cooperation: Reforms for Capacity Building in Africa*. New York: United Nations Development Program.

Berg, Kati Tusinski. 2012. The Ethics of Lobbying: Testing an Ethical Framework for Advocacy in Public Relations. *Journal of Mass Media Ethics* 27 (2): 97–114.

Berger, Lee. 2001. Proposed Legal Structure for the Silksat Satellite Consortium: A Regional Intergovernmental Organization to Improve Telecommunications Infrastructure in Central Asia and the Trans-Caucasus Region. *Law and Policy in International Business* 3: 99–143.

Bernabei, Stefano. 2018. Italy Buys into Telecom Italia to Shield Strategic Interests. *Reuters*. Available at: https://www.reuters.com/article/us-telecom-italia-vivendi-cdp/italy-buys-into-telecom-italia-to-shield-strategic-interests-idUSKCN1HC0GJ. Accessed 12 Jan 2019.

Besley, Timothy, and Andrea Prat. 2006. Handcuffs for the Grabbing Hand? Media Capture and Government Accountability. *American Economic Review* 96 (3): 720–736.

Bickham, David S., and Ronald G. Slaby. 2012. Effects of a Media Literacy Program in the US on Children's Critical Evaluation of Unhealthy Media Messages About Violence, Smoking, and Food. *Journal of Children and Media* 6 (2): 255–271.

Biersteker, Thomas J., and Cynthia Weber, eds. 1996. *State Sovereignty as a Social Construct*. Cambridge: Cambridge University Press.

Birkland, Thomas A. 1998. Focusing Events, Mobilization, and Agenda Setting. *Journal of Public Policy* 18 (1): 53–74.

———. 2007. Agenda Setting in Public Policy. In *Handbook of Public Policy Analysis*, ed. Frank Fischer, Gerald J. Miller, and Mara S. Sidney, 63–78. Boca Raton: CRC Press.

———. 2015. *An Introduction to the Policy Process: Theories, Concepts, and Models of Public Policy Making*. 4th ed. Armonk: M.E. Sharpe.

Blackman, Colin R. 1998. Convergence Between Telecommunications and Other Media: How Should Regulation Adapt? *Telecommunications Policy* 22 (3): 163–170.

Blakely, Robert J. 1979. *To Serve the Public Interest: Educational Broadcasting in the United States.* Syracuse: Syracuse University Press.

Boardman, Anthony E., David H. Greenberg, Aidan R. Vining, and David L. Weimer. 2017. *Cost-Benefit Analysis: Concepts and Practice.* 4th ed. Cambridge: Cambridge University Press.

Bogenschneider, Karen, and Thomas J. Corbett. 2010. *Evidence-Based Policy Making: Insights from Policy-Minded Researchers and Research-Minded Policy Makers.* London: Routledge.

Bolleyer, Nicole. 2019. *The State and Civil Society: Regulating Interest Groups, Parties, and Public Benefit Organizations in Contemporary Democracies.* Oxford: Oxford University Press.

Bouwen, Pieter. 2002. Corporate Lobbying in the European Union: The Logic of Access. *Journal of European Public Policy* 9 (3): 365–390.

Bowman, Ann, and Richard C. Kearney. 2016. *State and Local Government.* 10th ed. Boston: Cengage Learning.

Boydstun, Amber E. 2013. *Making the News: Politics, the Media, and Agenda Setting.* Chicago: University of Chicago Press.

Braman, Sandra. 2004. Where Has Media Policy Gone? Defining the Field in the Twenty-First Century. *Communication Law and Policy* 9 (2): 153–182.

———, ed. 2006. *The Emergent Global Information Policy Regime.* London: Palgrave Macmillan.

Braun, Dietmar, and Fabrizio Gilardi. 2006. Taking 'Galton's Problem' Seriously: Towards a Theory of Policy Diffusion. *Journal of Theoretical Politics* 18 (3): 298–322.

Brousseau, Eric, Meryem Marzouki, and Cécile Méadel, eds. 2012. *Governance, Regulation and Powers on the Internet.* Cambridge: Cambridge University Press.

Brown, Allan. 2009. Economics, Public Service Broadcasting, and Social Values. *Journal of Media Economics* 9 (1): 3–15.

Bruce, Steve. 2003. *Politics and Religion.* Cambridge: Polity Press.

Brundenius, Claes, and Ricardo Torres Pérez, eds. 2014. *No More Free Lunch: Reflections on the Cuban Economic Reform Process and Challenges for Transformation.* Berlin: Springer.

Bulmer, Simon, and Stephen Padgett. 2004. Policy Transfer in the European Union: An Institutionalist Perspective. *British Journal of Political Science* 35 (1): 103–126.

Burstein, Paul. 2003. The Impact of Public Opinion on Public Policy: A Review and an Agenda. *Political Research Quarterly* 56 (1): 29–40.

Busterna, John C., and Robert G. Picard. 1993. *Joint Operating Agreements: The Newspaper Preservation Act and Its Application.* Norwood: Ablex Publishing.

Calabrese, Andrew, and Marco Briziarelli. 2011. Media imperialism: Bilateral Trade Agreements as Instruments of Media Governance. In *Handbook of Global Media and Communication Policy*, ed. Robin Mansell and Marc Raboy, 383–394. Oxford: Wiley-Blackwell.

Cammaerts, Bart. 2011. Power Dynamics in Multi-Stakeholder Policy Processes and Intra-Civil Society Networking. In *The Handbook of Global Media and Communication Policy*, ed. Robin Mansell and Marc Raboy, 131–147. Oxford: Wiley-Blackwell.

Cammaerts, Bart, and Nico Carpentier, eds. 2007. *Reclaiming the Media: Communication Rights and Democratic Media Roles.* Bristol: Intellect.

Campbell, Harry F., and Richard P.C. Brown. 2015. *Cost-Benefit Analysis*. 2nd ed. London: Routledge.

Campos, Nauro F., and Francesco Giovannoni. 2007. Lobbying, Corruption and Political Influence. *Public Choice* 131 (1–2): 1–21.

Canada, Canadian Revenue Agency. 2018. Advertising. https://www.canada.ca/en/revenue-agency/services/tax/businesses/topics/sole-proprietorships-partnerships/report-business-income-expenses/completing-form-t2125/line-8521-advertising.html. Accessed 26 Dec 2018.

Canada, Ministère de la Culture et des Communications. 2018. Secteurs de Intervention. https://www.mcc.gouv.qc.ca/index.php?id=9. Accessed 21 Jan 2018.

Canadian Infrastructure Bank. n.d.. Available at: https://cib-bic.ca/en/lobby. Accessed 6 May 2019.

Canedo, Daniele, and Carmina Crusafon. 2014. The European Audiovisual Policy Goes Abroad: The Case of Inter-Regional Cooperation with Mercosur. In *The Palgrave Handbook of European Media Policy*, ed. Karen Donders, Caroline Pauwels, and Jan Loisen, 526–541. London: Palgrave Macmillan.

Cardona, Jeannie. 2002. Cultural Statistics in Europe: Updates and Trends. UNESCO International Symposium on Cultural Statistics, Montréal, 21–23 October.

Carpenter, Daniel, and David A. Moss, eds. 2013. *Preventing Regulatory Capture*. Cambridge: Cambridge University Press.

Cartwright, Nancy, and Jeremy Hardie. 2012. *Evidence-Based Policy: A Practical Guide to Doing It Better*. Oxford: Oxford University Press.

Castells, Manuel. 2000. *The Information Age: Economy Society and Culture, 3 Vols*. Oxford: Blackwell.

———. 2008. The New Public Sphere: Global Civil Society, Communication Networks, and Global Governance. *Annals of the American Academy of Political and Social Science* 616 (1): 78–93.

Cave, Martin, and Peter Crowther. 1996. Determining the Level of Regulation in EU Telecommunications. A Preliminary Assessment. *Telecommunications Policy* 20 (10): 725–738.

Cave, Martin, and William Webb. 2016. *Spectrum Management: Using the Airwaves for Maximum Social and Economic Benefit*. Cambridge: Cambridge University Press.

Cecot, Caroline, and Scott Wallsten. 2009. South Asia Telecommunications Development and the Role of Regional Cooperation. In *The Service Revolution in South Asia*, ed. Ejaz Ghani, 296–306. Washington, DC: The International Bank for Reconstruction and Development/World Bank.

Centre for Media Pluralism and Media Freedom. 2016. *Assessing the Risk for Media Pluralism in EU and Beyond: Application of the Media Pluralism Monitor Tool (MPM2016) in 30 European Countries*. Florence: European University Centre. http://cmpf.eui.eu/News/All/1601MPM2016Grant.aspx. Accessed 09 Dec 2018.

Chalk, Nigel, and Richard Hemming. 2000. Assessing Fiscal Sustainability in Theory and Practice. International Monetary Fund Working Paper WP/00/81. Washington: International Monetary Fund.

Cheema, G. Shabbir, Christopher A. McNall, and Vesselin Popovski, eds. 2011. *Cross-Border Governance in Asia: Regional Issues and Mechanisms*. Tokyo: United Nations University.

Chilton, Paul. 2004. *Analysing Political Discourse: Theory and Practice*. London: Routledge.

Chong, Dennis, and James N. Druckman. 2007. Framing Theory. *Annual Review of Political Science* 10: 103–126.

Choudrie, Jyoti, and Catherine Middleton. 2013. *Management of Broadband Technology and Innovation: Policy, Deployment and Use.* London: Routledge.

Christians, Clifford G., Theodore L. Glasser, Denis McQuail, Kaarle Nordenstreng, and Robert A. White. 2009. *Normative Theories of the Media.* Urbana/Chicago: University of Illinois Press.

Ciszek, Erica. 2013. Advocacy and Amplification: Nonprofit Outreach and Empowerment Through Participatory Media. *The Public Relations Journal* 7 (2): 187–213.

Clarke, Thomas, and Christos Pitelis, eds. 1995. *The Political Economy of Privatization.* London: Routledge.

Cobb, John B., Jr. 2002. *Postmodernism and Public Policy: Reframing Religion, Culture, Education, Sexuality, Class, Race, Politics, and the Economy.* Albany: State University of New York Press.

Cochetti, Roger. 2015. *Mobile Satellite Communications Handbook.* 2nd ed. Hoboken: John Wiley & Sons.

Codding, George A., Jr. 1964. *The Universal Postal Union: Coordinator of the International Mails.* New York: New York University Press.

Codding, George A., Jr., and Anthony M. Rutkowski. 1982. *The International Telecommunication Union in a Changing World.* Boston: Artech House.

Coleman, Stephen, and Peter M. Shane, eds. 2012. *Connecting Democracy: Online Consultation and the Flow of Political Communication.* Cambridge, MA: MIT Press.

Collins, Richard, ed. 1995. *Converging Media? Converging Regulation?* London: Institute of Public Policy Research.

Commission for Communications Regulation and Ofcom, Band IV/V Bilateral Co-ordination Agreement Between the Administrations of Ireland and the United Kingdom of Great Britain and Northern Ireland, June 2012. http://static.ofcom.org.uk/static/broadcasting/Web_Ireland_United%20Kingdom%20800MHz%20DTT%20Clearance%20Agreement_06July12.pdf. Accessed 11 Nov 2018.

Communications Alliance. n.d. http://www.commsalliance.com.au/. Accessed 1 Apr 2019.

Council of Europe. 1989. European Convention on Transfrontier Television. Available at: https://heinonline.org/HOL/LandingPage?handle=hein.journals/intlm28&div=113&id=&pag e=. Accessed 13 Apr 2019.

Cowie, Campbell, and Christopher T. Marsden. 1998. Convergence, Competition and Regulation. *International Journal of Communications Law and Policy* 1 (1): 1–32.

Cox, Richard H., and Daniel Béland. 2013. Valence, Policy Ideas, and the Rise of Sustainability. *Governance* 26 (2): 307–328.

Crandall, Robert W., and Kenneth Flamm. 1989. *Changing the Rules: Technological Change, Competition, and Regulation in Communications.* Washington, DC: Brookings Institution Press.

Crawford, James. 2012. *Brownlie's Principles of Public International Law.* 8th ed. Oxford: Oxford University Press.

Cremer, Helmuth, Farid Gasmi, Andre Grimaud, and Jean Jacques Laffont. 2001. Universal Service: An Economic Perspective. *Annals of Public and Cooperative Economics* 72 (1): 5–43.

Crew, Michael A., and Paul R. Kleindorfer. 2000. Liberalization and the Universal Service Obligation in Postal Service. In *Current Directions in Postal Reform*, ed. Michael A. Crew and Paul R. Kleindorfer, 3–28. Boston: Springer.

Crusafon, Carmina. 2015. The European Audiovisual Space: How European Media Policy Has Set the Pace of Its Development. In *European Cinema and Television*, ed. Bondebjerg Ib, Eva Norrup Redvall, and Andres Higson, 81–101. London: Palgrave Macmillan.

Cukier, Judith. 1997. Cost-Benefit Analysis of Telelearning: Developing a Methodology Framework. *Distance Education* 18 (1): 1357–1152.

Curran, James. 2010. The Future of Journalism. *Journalism Studies* 11 (4): 464–476.

———. 2011. *Media and Democracy*. London: Taylor and Francis.

Curry, Bill, and Tamsin McMahon. 2019. Social-Media Giants Pledge Joint Action on Extremism at Summit with Trudeau, Other World Leaders. *The Globe and Mail*, May 15. Available at: https://www.theglobeandmail.com/politics/article-social-media-giants-pledge-joint-action-on-online-hate-at-summit-with/. Accessed 23 June 2019.

Daalmeijer, Joop. 2004. Public Service Broadcasting in The Netherlands. *Trends in Communication* 12 (1): 33–45.

Dahlgren, Peter, ed. 2009. *Media and Political Engagement: Citizens, Communication, and Democracy*. Cambridge: Cambridge University Press.

Danielson, Caroline. 2007. Social Experiments and Public Policy. In *Handbook of Public Policy Analysis: Theory, Politics and Methods*, ed. Frank Fisher, Gerald J. Miller, and Mara Sidney, 381–392. Boca Raton: CRC Press/Taylor and Francis.

Dawes, Sharon S. 2010. Stewardship and Usefulness: Policy Principles for Information-Based Transparency. *Government Information Quarterly* 27 (4): 377–383.

della Porta, Donatella, and Mario Diani, eds. 2018. *The Oxford Handbook of Social Movements*. Oxford: Oxford University Press.

DeSantis, Gloria. 2010. Voices from the Margins: Policy Advocacy and Marginalized Communities. *Canadian Journal of Nonprofit and Social Economy Research* 1 (1): 23–45.

Dinh, Hinh T. 2013. *Light Manufacturing in Vietnam: Creating Jobs and Prosperity in a Middle-Income Economy*. Washington, DC: International Bank for Reconstruction and Development/The World Bank.

Dixon, John A., and Louise A. Fallon. 1989. The Concept of Sustainability: Origins, Extensions, and Usefulness for Policy. *Society and Natural Resources* 2 (1): 73–84.

Djelic, Marie-Laure, and Kerstin Sahlin-Andersson, eds. 2006. *Transnational Governance: Institutional Dynamics of Regulation*. Cambridge: Cambridge University Press.

Dolowitz, David P., and David Marsh. 2000. Learning from Abroad: The Role of Policy Transfer in Contemporary Policy-Making. *Governance* 13 (1): 5–53.

Donders, Karen. 2012. *Public Service Media and Policy in Europe*. London: Palgrave Macmillan.

Donders, Karen, Caroline Pauwels, and Jan Loisen. 2014. *The Palgrave Handbook of European Media Policy*. London: Palgrave Macmillan.

Dovers, Stephen R. 1996. Sustainability: Demands on Policy. *Journal of Public Policy* 16 (3): 303–318.

Dowding, Keith. 1995. Model or Metaphor? A Critical Review of the Policy Network Approach. *Political Studies* 43 (1): 136–158.

Downey, John, and Natalie Fenton. 2016. New Media, Counter Publicity and the Public Sphere. *New Media & Society* 5 (2): 185–202.

Doyle, Gillian. 2002. *Media Ownership: The Economics and Politics of Convergence and Concentration in the UK and European Media*. London: Sage.

Dresser, Rebecca. 2001. *When Science Offers Salvation: Patient Advocacy and Research Ethics*. Oxford: Oxford University Press.

Druckman, James, Donald P. Green, James H. Kuklinski, and Arthur Lupia, eds. 2011. *Cambridge Handbook of Experimental Political Science*. Cambridge: Cambridge University Press.

Duffy, Matt. 2013. *Media Laws and Regulation of the GCC Countries*. Doha: Doha Center for Media Freedom.

Dymond, Andrew. 1987. Reducing the Number of Missing Links: Regional Cooperation and Telecommunications Development in Southern Africa. *Telecommunications Policy* 11 (2): 121–134.

Easton, David. 1965. *A Framework for Political Analysis*. New York: Prentice Hall.

Edgett, Ruth. 2002. Toward an Ethical Framework for Advocacy in Public Relations. *Journal of Public Relations Research* 14 (1): 1–26.

Edwards, Michael, ed. 2011. *The Oxford Handbook of Civil Society*. Oxford: Oxford University Press.

Edwards, Geoff, and Leonard Waverman. 2006. The Effects of Public Ownership and Regulatory Independence on Regulatory Outcomes: A Study of Interconnect Rates in EU Telecommunications. *Journal of Regulatory Economics* 29 (1): 23–67.

Elazar, Daniel J. 1997. Contrasting Unitary and Federal Systems. *International Political Science Review* 18 (3): 37–251.

Eliassen, Kjell A., Marit Sjovaag Nfa, and Marit Sjovaag, eds. 1999. *European Telecommunications Liberalisation*. London: Routledge.

Elman, Miriam Fendius. 1995. The Foreign Policies of Small States: Challenging Neorealism in its Own Backyard. *British Journal of Political Science* 25 (2): 171–217.

El-Nawawy, Mohammed, and Adel Iskandar. 2008. *Al-Jazeera: The Story of the Network That Is Rattling Governments*. New York: Basic Books.

Enikolopov, Ruben, and Maria Petrova. 2016. Media Capture: Empirical Evidence. In *Handbook of Media Economics*, ed. Simon P. Anderson, Joel Waldfogel, and David Strömberg, 687–700. Amsterdam: North Holland.

Eriksen, Thomas H. 2014. *Globalization: The Key Concepts*. 2nd ed. New York: Bloomsbury Academic.

Ettelt, S., N. Mays, and P. Allen. 2015. Policy Experiments: Investigating Effectiveness or Confirming Direction? *Evaluation* 21 (3): 292–307.

European Commission. 2001. Executive Summary: Identification and Evaluation of Financial Flows Within the European Cinema Industry by Comparison with the American Model. Study for the European Commission, Directorate General for Education and Culture, Unit C1. Brussels: European Commission.

Eurostat. 2001. *Special Feature on Publishing and Printing*. Brussels: Eurostat Structural Business Statistics Unit.

Fairclough, Isabela, and Norman Fairclough. 2012. *Political Discourse Analysis: A Method for Advanced Students*. London: Routledge.

Fallon, Richard H., Jr. 2012. Scholars' Briefs and the Vocation of a Law Professor. *Journal of Legal Analysis* 4 (1): 223–269.

Fan, Peilei, and Chihiro Watanabe. 2006. Promoting Industrial Development Through Technology Policy: Lessons from Japan and China. *Technology in Society* 28 (3): 303–320.

Farrington, David P., and Maria M. Ttofi. 2009. Reducing School Bullying: Evidence-Based Implications for Policy. *Crime and Justice* 38 (1): 281–345.

Faulhaber, Gerald R., Hal J. Singer, and Augustus H. Urschel. 2017. The Curious Absence of Economic Analysis at the Federal Communications Commission: An

Agency in Search of a Mission. *International Journal of Communication* 11: 1214–1233.

Fawn, Rick. 2013. *International Organizations and Internal Conditionality: Making Norms Matter*. London: Palgrave Macmillan.

Feintuck, Mike, and Mike Varney. 2006. *Media Regulation, Public Interest and the Law*. 2nd ed. Edinburgh: Edinburgh University Press.

Felipe, Jesus. 2016. *Development and Modern Industrial Policy in Practice: Issues and Country Experiences*. Cheltenham: Edward Elgar Publishing.

Ferguson, Charles H. 2004. *The Broadband Problem: Anatomy of a Market Failure and Policy Dilemma*. Washington, DC: Brookings Institution Press.

Ferrero, Mario, and Ronald Wintrobe, eds. 2009. *The Political Economy of Theocracy*. New York: Palgrave Macmillan.

Fine, Ben, Alfredo Saad-Filho, and Marco Boffo. 2013. *The Elgar Companion to Marxist Economics*. Cheltenham: Edward Elgar Publishers.

Finkelstein, Neal D., ed. 2000. *Transparency in Public Policy: Great Britain and the United States*. Berlin: Springer.

Fitzpatrick, Kathy, and Carolyn Bronstein, eds. 2006. *Ethics in Public Relations: Responsible Advocacy*. Thousand Oaks: Sage.

Flew, Terry. 2011. *The Creative Industries: Culture and Policy*. London: Sage.

Flew, Terry, Petros Iosifidis, and Jeanette Steemers, eds. 2016. *Global Media and National Policies: The Return of the State*. London: Palgrave Macmillan.

Fonnaini, Robert. 1990. *The Myth of Scientific Public Policy*. New Brunswick: Transaction.

Fonow, Mary Margaret, and Judith A. Cook. 2005. Feminist Methodology: New Applications in the Academy and Public Policy. *Signs: Journal of Women in Culture and Society* 30 (4): 2211–2236.

Fowler, Mark S., and Daniel L. Brenner. 1981. Marketplace Approach to Broadcast Regulation. *Texas Law Review* 60: 207.

Fox, Justin. 2007. Government Transparency and Policymaking. *Public Choice* 131 (1–2): 23–44.

Fransman, Martin. 2002. Mapping the Evolving Telecoms Industry: The Uses and Shortcomings of the Layer Model. *Telecommunications Policy* 26 (9): 473–483.

Frederking, Brian, and Paul F. Diehl, eds. 2015. *The Politics of Global Governance: International Organizations in an Interdependent World*. 5th ed. Boulder: Lynne Rienner Publishers.

Freedman, Robert. 1990. *The Marxist System: Economic, Political, and Social Perspectives*. Washington, DC: CQ Press.

Freedman, Des. 2006. Dynamics of Power in Contemporary Media Policy-Making. *Media, Culture and Society* 28 (6): 907–923.

———. 2008. *The Politics of Media Policy*. Cambridge: Polity Press.

———. 2010. Media Policy Silences: The Hidden Face of Communications Decision Making. *The International Journal of Press/Politics* 15 (3): 344–361.

———. 2015. Media Policy Fetishism. *Critical Studies in Media Communication* 32 (2): 96–111.

Frieden, Rob. 2003. Adjusting the Horizontal and Vertical in Telecommunications Regulation: A Comparison of the Traditional and a New Layered Approach. *Federal Communications Law Review* 55 (2): 208–250.

Friedlander, Amy. 1995. *Natural Monopoly and Universal Service: Telephones and Telegraphs in the U.S. Communications Infrastructure, 1837–1940*. Reston: Corp. for National Research Initiatives.
Gale, Trevor. 2001. Critical Policy Sociology: Historiography, Archaeology and Genealogy as Methods of Policy Analysis. *Journal of Education Policy* 16 (5): 379–393.
Gallagher, Margaret. 2011. Gender and Communication Policy: Struggling for Space. In *The Handbook of Global Media and Communication Policy*, ed. Robin Mansell and Marc Raboy, 451–466. Oxford: Wiley-Blackwell.
Galperin, Herman. 1999. Cultural Industries Policy in Regional Trade Agreements: The Cases of NAFTA, the European Union and MERCOSUR. *Media, Culture and Society* 21 (5): 627–648.
Garcia-Murillo, Martha, and Ian MacInnes. 2003. The Impact of Technological Convergence on the Regulation of ICT Industries. *International Journal on Media Management* 5 (1): 57–67.
Gardner, Annette, and Claire Brindis. 2017. *Advocacy and Policy Change Evaluation: Theory and Practice*. Stanford: Stanford University Press.
Garnham, Nicholas. 2005. From Cultural to Creative Industries. *International Journal of Cultural Policy* 11 (1): 15–29.
Gen, Sheldon, and Amy Conley Wright. 2013. Policy Advocacy Organizations: A Framework Linking Theory and Practice. *Journal of Policy Practice* 12 (3): 163–193.
Geradín, Damien, and David Luff, eds. 2004. *The WTO and Global Convergence in Telecommunications and Audio-Visual Services*. Cambridge: Cambridge University Press.
Gerrand, Peter. 2011. Unacceptable Quality of Service: Why Industry Self Regulation Is Not Working. *Telecommunication Journal of Australia* 61 (4): 541–543.
Gershgorn, Dave. 2018. The EU Is Giving Netflix and Amazon Two Years to Make 30% of Their Catalogs European. *Quartz*. https://qz.com/1508022/netflix-and-amazon-have-two-years-to-make-30-of-their-catalogs-european/. Accessed 19 Dec 2018.
Gershon, Richard A. 1993. International Deregulation and the Rise of Transnational Media Corporations. *Journal of Media Economics* 6 (2): 3–22.
Gibbons, Thomas. 2015. Active Pluralism: Dialogue and Engagement as Basic Media Policy Principles. *International Journal of Communication* 9: 1382–1399.
Gibson, Timothy A. 2010. The Limits of Media Advocacy. *Communication, Culture and Critique* 3 (1): 44–65.
Gilardi, Fabrizio, and Martino Maggetti. 2011. The Independence of Regulatory Authorities. In *Handbook on the Politics of Regulation*, ed. David Levi-Faur, 201–214. Cheltenham: Edward Elgar.
Gillett, Sharon E., and Ingo Vogelsang, eds. 1999. *Competition, Regulation and Convergence: Current Trends in Telecommunication Policy Research*. Mahwah: Lawrence Erlbaum.
Gillwald, Alison. 2005. Good Intentions, Poor Outcomes: Telecommunications Reform in South Africa. *Telecommunications Policy* 29 (7): 469–491.
Ginosar, Avshalom. 2013. Media Governance: A Conceptual Framework or Merely a Buzz Word? *Communication Theory* 23: 356–374.
Ginsberg, Roy. 2010. *Demystifying the European Union: The Enduring Logic of Regional Integration*. Plymouth: Rowman & Littlefield.
Glenn, Carol M. 2017. *Controlling Cyberspace: The Politics of Internet Governance and Regulation*. Santa Barbara: Praeger.
Goldsmith, Jack, and Tim Wu. 2008. *Who Controls the Internet? Illusions of a Borderless World*. Oxford: Oxford University Press.

Graz, Jean-Christophe, and Andreas Nölke, eds. 2008. *Transnational Private Governance and Its Limits*. London: Routledge.

Green-Pedersen, Christoffer, and Stefaan Walgrave, eds. 2014. *Agenda Setting, Policies, and Political Systems: A Comparative Approach*. Chicago: University of Chicago Press.

Greenstein, Shane. 2015. *How the Internet Became Commercial: Innovation, Privatization, and the Birth of a New Network*. Princeton: Princeton University Press.

Greenstein, Shane, and Victor Stango, eds. 2007. *Standards and Public Policy*. Cambridge: Cambridge University Press.

Greenwood, Justin. 2017. *Interest Representation in the European Union*. 4th ed. London: Palgrave.

Gregory, Paul R., and Robert C. Stuart. 2004. *Comparing Economic Systems in the Twenty-First Century*. 7th ed. Mason: South-Western/Cengage Learning.

Griffin, Patrick, and James A. Thurber. 2015. Teaching Public Policy Advocacy by Combining Academic Knowledge and Professional Wisdom. *Interest Groups & Advocacy* 4 (1): 40–51.

Gross, Peter. 2008. Back to the (Uncertain) Future. Politics, Business and the Media in Romania. *Global Media Journal* 1 (4): 51–68.

Guo, Chao, and Gregory D. Saxton. 2014. Tweeting Social Change: How Social Media Are Changing Nonprofit Advocacy. *Nonprofit and Voluntary Sector Quarterly* 43 (1): 57–79.

Hacker, Jacob S. 2004. Privatizing Risk Without Privatizing the Welfare State: The Hidden Politics of Social Policy Retrenchment in the United States. *American Political Science Review* 98 (02): 243–260.

Hacker, Jacob S., Paul Pierson, and Kathleen Thelen. 2015. Drift and Conversion: Hidden Faces of Institutional Change. In *Advances in Comparative-Historical Analysis*, ed. James Mahoney and Kathleen Thelen, 180–210. Cambridge: Cambridge University Press.

Hackett, Robert, and Megan Adam. 1999. Is Media Democratization a Social Movement? *Peace Review* 11 (1): 125–131.

Hackett, Robert, and Steve Anderson. 2011. Democratizing Communication Policy in Canada: A Social Movement Perspective. *Canadian Journal of Communication* 36 (1): 161–168.

Hague, Rod, Martin Harrop, and John McCormick. 2016. *Comparative Government and Politics: An Introduction*. 10th ed. London: Palgrave Macmillan.

Haines, Anjana. 2016. European Commission Unveils VAT Rules for E-commerce Businesses. *International Tax Review*. http://www.internationaltaxreview.com/Article/3647310/European-Commission-unveils-VAT-rules-for-e-commerce-businesses.html. Accessed 31 Dec 2018.

Hajer, Maartin 2002. Discourse Analysis and the Study of Policy Making. *European Political Science* 2 (1): 61–65.

Hale, Thomas, and David Held, eds. 2011. *The Handbook of Transnational Governance: Institutions and Innovations*. Cambridge: Polity.

Hale, Kathleen, and Ramona McNeal. 2011. Technology, Politics, and E-Commerce: Internet Sales Tax and Interstate Cooperation. *Government Information Quarterly* 28 (2): 262–270.

Hall, Peter A. 1989. *The Political Power of Economic Ideas: Keynesianism Across Nations*. Princeton: Princeton University Press.

Hall, Rodney B., and Thomas J. Biersteker, eds. 2002. *The Emergence of Private Authority in Global Governance*. Cambridge: Cambridge University Press.

Hanretty, Chris, and Christel Koop. 2012. Measuring the Formal Independence of Regulatory Agencies. *Journal of European Public Policy* 19 (2): 198–216.

———. 2013. Shall the Law Set Them Free? The Formal and Actual Independence of Regulatory Agencies. *Regulation & Governance* 7 (2): 195–214.

Hansberger, Anders. 2001. What Is the Policy Problem? Methodological Challenges in Policy Evaluation. *Evaluation* 7 (1): 45–62.

Harders, Cilja, and Matteo Lengrenzi, eds. 2016. *Beyond Regionalism? Regional Cooperation, Regionalism and Regionalization in the Middle East*. London: Routledge.

Harlow, Carol. 2002. *Accountability in the European Union*. Oxford: Oxford University Press.

Harrington, Alexandria. 2018. *International Organizations and the Law*. London: Routledge.

Hart, H.L.A., Leslie Green, Joseph Raz, and Penelope Bulloch. 2012. *The Concept of Law*. 3rd ed. Oxford: Oxford University Press.

Harvey, David. 2003. *The New Imperialism*. Oxford: Oxford University Press.

———. 2007. *A Brief History of Neoliberalism*. Oxford: Oxford University Press.

Haufler, Virginia. 2013. *A Public Role for the Private Sector: Industry Self-Regulation in a Global Economy*. New York: Carnegie Endowment for World Peace.

Hawdon, James. 1996. *Emerging Organizational Forms: The Proliferation of Regional Intergovernmental Organizations in the Modern World-System*. New York: Praeger.

Hawksworth, Mary. 1994. Policy Studies Within a Feminist Frame. *Policy Sciences* 27 (1–2): 97–118.

Hawton, Keith, and Kathryn Williams. 2005. Media Influences on Suicidal Behaviour: Evidence and Prevention. In *Prevention and Treatment of Suicidal Behaviour: From Science to Practice*, ed. Keith Hawton. Oxford: Oxford University Press.

Hayes, Michael T. 2001. *The Limits of Policy Change: Incrementalism, Worldview, and the Rule of Law*. Washington, DC: Georgetown University Press.

Hayton, Bill. 2011. *Vietnam: Rising Dragon*. New Haven: Yale University Press.

Hazlett, Thomas W. 1998. Assigning Property Rights to Radio Spectrum Users: Why Did FCC License Auctions Take 67 Years? *Journal of Law and Economics* 41 (2): 529–576.

Hellman, Joel, and Daniel Kaufmann. 2001. Confronting the Problem of State Capture in Transition Economies. *IMF Finance and Development* 38(3). Available at: http://www.imf.org/external/pubs/ft/fandd/2001/09/hellman.htm. Accessed 2 July 2019.

Hellman, Joel S., Geraint Jones, Daniel Kaufmann, and Mark Schankerman. 2000. *Measuring Governance, Corruption, and State Capture: How Firms and Bureaucrats Shape the Business Environment in Transition Economies*. Washington, DC: The International Bank for Reconstruction and Development/World Bank.

Hellman, Joel S., Geraint Jones, and Daniel Kaufmann. 2003. Seize the State, Size the Day: State Capture and Influence in Transition Economies. *Journal of Comparative Economics* 31 (4): 751–773.

Herzog, Christian, and Christopher Ali. 2015. Elite Interviewing in Media and Communications Policy Research. *International Journal of Media and Cultural Politics* 11 (1): 37–54.

Herzog, Christian, and Hanno Beck. 2016. Experimental Media Policy. *International Journal of Digital Television* 7 (3): 315–330.

Hesmondhalgh, David. 2005. Media and Cultural Policy as Public Policy: The Case of the British Labour Government. *International Journal of Cultural Policy* 11 (1): 95–109.

Hessenius, Barry. 2007. *Hardball Lobbying for Nonprofits: Real Advocacy for Nonprofits in the New Century*. London: Palgrave Macmillan.

Hill, Richard. 2014. *The New International Telecommunication Regulations and the Internet: A Commentary and Legislative History*. Berlin: Springer.

Hills, Jill. 1994. Dependency Theory and Its Relevance Today: International Institutions in Telecommunications and Structural Power. *Review of International Studies* 20 (2): 169–186.

Hills, Jill, and Maria Michalis. 1997. Technological Convergence: Regulatory Competition. The British Case of Digital Television. *Policy Studies* 18 (3–4): 219–237.

Hintz, Arne. 2012. Challenging the Digital Gatekeepers: International Policy Initiatives for Free Expression. *Journal of Information Policy* 2: 128–150.

Hoefer, Richard. 2015. *Advocacy Practice for Social Justice*. 3rd ed. Oxford: Oxford University Press.

Hoekman, Bernard M., and Petros C. Mavroidis. 2015. *World Trade Organization (WTO): Law, Economics, and Politics*. 2nd ed. London: Routledge.

Hofbauer, Jane A. 2016. *Sovereignty in the Exercise of the Right to Self-Determination*. Leiden: Martinus Nijhoff.

Holland, Jeremy. 2007. *Tools for Institutional, Political, and Social Analysis of Policy Reform: A Sourcebook for Development Practitioners*. Washington, DC: The International Bank for Reconstruction and Development/The World Bank.

Hollis, Duncan B. 2014. *The Oxford Guide to Treaties*. Oxford: Oxford University Press.

Holsti, K.J. 2004. *Taming the Sovereigns: Institutional Change in International Politics*. Cambridge: Cambridge University Press.

Holt, Jennifer. 2011. *Empires of Entertainment: Media Industries and the Politics of Deregulation, 1980–1996*. Rutgers: Rutgers University Press.

Hood, Christopher C., and Helen Z. Margetts. 2007. *The Tools of Government in the Digital Age*. 2nd ed. Houndmills: Palgrave Macmillan.

Horwitz, Robert B. 1991. *The Irony of Regulatory Reform: The Deregulation of American Telecommunications*. Oxford: Oxford University Press.

———. 2001. *Communication and Democratic Reform in South Africa*. Cambridge: Cambridge University Press.

Howlett, Michael, and M. Ramesh. 2003. *Studying Public Policy: Policy Cycles and Policy Subsystems*. Oxford: Oxford University Press.

Hoyle, Rick H., ed. 2014. *Handbook of Structural Equation Modeling*. New York: Guilford Press.

Hudson, Heather E. 1991. Telecommunications in Africa: The Role of the ITU. *Telecommunications Policy* 15 (4): 343–350.

———. 2006. *From Rural Village to Global Village: Telecommunications for Development in the Information Age*. New York: Routledge.

Humphreys, Peter. 1996. *Mass Media and Media Policy in Western Europe*. Manchester: Manchester University Press.

———. 2009. The Politics of Media Policy: How Political? *Cultural Trends* 18 (3): 263–272.

Hunter McMahon, Stephanie. 2018. *Principles of Tax Policy*. St. Paul: West Academic Publishing.

Hurd, Ian. 2017. *International Organizations: Politics, Law, Practice*. 3rd ed. Cambridge: Cambridge University Press.
International Telecommunication Union. n.d. *International Telecommunications Regulations*. https://www.itu.int/en/wcit-12/Pages/itrs.aspx. Accessed 11 Nov 2018.
Iosifidis, Petros. 1997. Pluralism and Media Concentration Policy in the European Union. *Javnost/The Public* 4 (1): 85–104.
———. 2002. Digital Convergence: Challenges for European Regulation. *Javnost/The Public* 9 (3): 27–47.
———, ed. 2010. *Reinventing Public Service Communication: European Broadcasters and Beyond*. London: Palgrave Macmillan.
———. 2011. *Global Media and Communication Policy: An International Perspective*. London: Palgrave Macmillan.
Jaeger, Paul T. 2006. Telecommunications Policy and Individuals with Disabilities: Issues of Accessibility and Social Inclusion in the Policy and Research Agenda. *Telecommunications Policy* 30 (1): 112–124.
Jann, Werner, and Kai Wegrich. 2006. Theories of the Policy Cycle. In *Handbook of Public Policy Analysis: Theory, Politics, and Methods*, ed. Frank Fischer, Gerald J. Miller, and Mara S. Sydney, 43–62. New York: Routledge.
Jenkins, William I. 1978. *Policy Analysis: A Political and Organizational Perspective*. London: Martin Robertson & Co.
Jensen, Nathan. 2019. *Incentives to Pander: How Politicians Use Corporate Welfare for Political Gain*. Cambridge: Cambridge University Press.
Jin, Dal Young. 2011. *Hands On Hands Off: The Korean State and the Market Liberalization of the Communication Industry*. Cresskill: Hampton Press.
Jin, Dal Yong. 2017. *Smartland Korea: Mobile Communication, Culture, and Society*. Ann Arbor: University of Michigan Press.
John, Peter. 2003. Is There Life After Policy Streams, Advocacy Coalitions, and Punctuations: Using Evolutionary Theory to Explain Policy Change? *Policy Studies Journal* 31 (4): 481–498.
John, Richard R. 2010. *Network Nation: Inventing American Telecommunications*. Cambridge: Cambridge University Press.
———. 2015. Projecting Power Oversees: U.S. Postal Policy and International Standards Setting at the 1863 Paris Postal Conference. *Journal of Policy History* 27 (3): 416–438.
John, Peter. 2017. *Field Experiments in Political Science and Public Policy: Practical Lessons in Design and Delivery*. London: Routledge.
Johns Hopkins Center for Civil Society Studies. 2003. *Policy Tools and Government Performance: Report on a Conference Co-Sponsored by the U.S. General Accounting Office, the U.S. Office of Management and Budget, and The Johns Hopkins University*. Baltimore: The Johns Hopkins Center for Civil Society Studies.
Jome, Hiram L. 1925. Public Policy Toward Radio Broadcasting. *The Journal of Land & Public Utility Economics* 1 (2): 198–214.
Jordan, Amy B. 2008. Children's Media Policy. *The Future of Children* 18 (1): 235–253.
Junisbai, Barbara. 2011. Oligarchs and Ownership: The Role of Financial-Industrial Groups. Controlling Kazakhstan's 'Independent' Media. In *After the Czars and Commissars: The Press in Post-Soviet Authoritarian Central Asia*, ed. Eric Freedman and Richard Shafer, 35–58. East Lansing: Michigan State University Press.

Just, Natascha, and Manuel Puppis, eds. 2012. *Trends in Communication Policy Research: New Theories, Methods and Subjects*. Bristol: Intellect.

Juwayeyi, Murendehle M. 2017. The Malawi Communications Regulatory Authority: Issues of De Jure and De Facto Independence. *Communication Law and Policy* 22 (2): 213–253.

Karns, Margaret P., Karen A. Mingst, and Kendall W. Stiles. 2015. *International Organizations: The Politics and Processes of Global Governance*. 3rd ed. Boulder: Lynne Rienner Publishers.

Karppinen, Kari, and Hallvard Moe. 2013. A Critique of 'Media Governance'. In *Communication and Media Policy in the Era of the Internet*, ed. Maria Löblich and Senta Pfaff-Rüdiger, 69–80. Baden-Baden: Nomos.

Kelly, James T. 2012. *Framing Democracy: A Behavioral Approach to Democratic Theory*. Princeton: Princeton University Press.

Keohane, Robert O. 1969. Lilliputians' Dilemmas: Small States in International Politics. *International Organization* 23 (2): 291–310.

Khetri, Nir. 2005. Information and Communication Technologies, Strategic Asymmetry and National Security. *Journal of International Management* 11 (4): 5M3–580.

Kielbowicz, Richard B. 1989. *News in the Mail: The Press, Post Office, and Public Information, 1700–1860s*. Greenwood: Praeger.

———. 1990. Postal Subsidies for the Press and the Business of Mass Culture, 1880–1920. *The Business History Review* 64 (3): 451–488.

———. 2005–2006. Preserving Universal Postal Service as a Communication Safety Net: A Policy History and Proposal. *Seton Hall Legislative Journal* 30: 383

Kim, Kyungmo, and George A. Barnett. 2000. The Structure of the International Telecommunications Regime in Transition: A Network Analysis of International Organizations. *International Interactions* 26 (1): 91–127.

Kim, Yongsoo, and Tim Kelly. 2010. *Building Broadband: Strategies and Policies for the Developing World*. Washington, DC: The International Bank for Reconstruction and Development/World Bank.

Kim, Sung-Kil, and Junseok Oh. 2018. Information Science Techniques for Investigating Research Areas: A Case Study in Telecommunications Policy. *The Journal of Supercomputing* 74 (12): 6691–6718.

Kim, Han-joo, Sang-kyu Byun, and Myeong-cheol Park. 2004. Mobile Handset Subsidy Policy in Korea: Historical Analysis and Evaluation. *Telecommunications Policy* 28 (1): 23–42.

Kingdon, John W. 2003. *Agendas, Alternatives, and Public Policies*. 2nd ed. New York: Longman.

Klein, Hans. 2002. ICANN and Internet Governance: Leveraging Technical Coordination to Realize Global Public Policy. *The Information Society: An International Journal* 18 (3): 193–207.

Kleinwächter, Wolfgang. 2000. ICANN Between Technical Mandate and Political Challenges. *Telecommunications Policy* 24 (6-7): 553–563.

Klemm, Alexander. 2009. *Causes, Benefits, and Risks of Business Tax Incentives*. Working Paper WP/09/21. Washington, DC: International Monetary Fund.

Klüver, Heike. 2013. *Lobbying in the European Union: Interest Groups, Lobbying Coalitions, and Policy Change*. Oxford: Oxford University Press.

Koch-Baumgarten, Sigrid, and Katrin Voltmer, eds. 2010. *Public Policy and the Mass Media: The Interplay of Mass Communication and Political Decision Making*. London: Routledge.

Kraft, Michael, and Scott Furlong. 2017. *Public Policy: Politics, Analysis, and Alternatives*. 6th ed. Washington, DC: CQ Press.

Kraidy, Marwan M. 2002. Arab Satellite Television Between Regionalization and Globalization. *Global Media Journal* 1 (1). Available at: http://repository.upenn.edu/asc_papers/186. Accessed 13 Apr 2019.

Kreijen, Gerald, ed. 2002. *State, Sovereignty, and International Governance*. Oxford: Oxford University Press.

Krieg, Jessica. 2004. There's No Business Like Show Business: Child Entertainers and the Law. *University of Pennsylvania Journal of Labor and Employment Law* 6 (2): 429–449.

Kroeber, Arthur R. 2016. *China's Economy: What Everyone Needs to Know*. Oxford: Oxford University Press.

Ku, Cheng-Yuan, Yi-Wen Chang, and David C. Yen. 2009. National Information Security Policy and its Implementation: A Case Study in Taiwan. *Telecommunications Policy* 33 (7): 371–384.

Kuhn, Max, and Kjell Johnson. 2013. *Applied Predictive Modeling*. Berlin: Springer.

Kumar, V.Anil. 2012. Speaking Truth to Power? Civil Society and Policy Advocacy in India. *Journal of Asian Public Policy* 5 (1): 41–47.

Kwakwa, Edward. 2006. Institutional and Procedural Reform at the World Intellectual Property Organization. *International Organizations Law Review* 3 (1): 143–152.

Lam, Wai Fung, and Kwan Nok Chan. 2017. Policy Advocacy in Transitioning Regimes: Comparative Lessons from the Case of Harbour Protection in Hong Kong. *Journal of Comparative Policy Analysis: Research and Practice* 19 (1): 54–71.

Larouche, Pierre. 2000. *Competition Law and Regulation in European Telecommunications*. Oxford: Hart Publishing.

Larson, James F. 1995. *The Telecommunications Revolution in Korea*. Oxford: Oxford University Press.

Latzer, Michael. 2007. Regulatory Choice in Communications Governance. *European Journal of Communication* 22 (3): 399–405.

Lee, Karen. 2017. ACMA Varies Compliance and Monitoring Arrangements for the Telecommunications Consumer Protections Code. *Australian Journal of Competition and Consumer Law* 25 (1): 62–64.

Leeuw, Frans L. 2003. Reconstructing Program Theories: Methods Available and Problems to be Solved. *American Journal of Evaluation* 24 (1): 5–20.

Leff, Nathaniel H. 1984. Externalities, Information Costs, and Social Benefit-Cost Analysis for Economic Development: An Example from Telecommunications. *Economic Development and Social Change* 32 (2): 255–276.

Leitner, Johannes, and Hannes Meissner, eds. 2016. *State Capture, Political Risks and International Business: Cases from Black Sea Region Countries*. London: Routledge.

Lemieux, Frederic. 2018. *Intelligence and State Surveillance in Modern Societies: An International Perspective*. Bingley: Emerald Publishing.

Lentz, Becky. 2014. The Media Policy Tower of Babble: A Case for 'Policy Literacy Pedagogy'. *Critical Studies in Media Communication* 31 (2): 134–140.

Leonard, Dick, and Robert Taylor. 2016. *The Routledge Guide to the European Union*. London: Routledge.

Levine, Michael E., and Jennifer L. Forrence. 1990. Regulatory Capture, Public Interest, and the Public Agenda: Toward a Synthesis. *Journal of Law, Economics, and Organization* 331: 167–198.

Levitt, S.D., and J.A. List. 2009. Field Experiments in Economics: The Past, the Present, and the Future. *European Economic Review* 53 (1): 1–18.

Levy, Brian, and Pablo T. Spiller, eds. 1996. *Regulations, Institutions, and Commitment: Comparative Studies of Telecommunications*. Cambridge: Cambridge University Press.

Lewis, Ted G. 2006. *Critical Infrastructure Protection in Homeland Security: Defending a Networked Nation*. New York: John Wiley & Sons.

Li, Wei, and Lixin Colin Xu. 2004. The Impact of Privatization and Competition in the Telecommunications Sector Around the World. *The Journal of Law and Economics* 47 (2): 395–430.

Li, Hui, Carlos Wing-Hung Lo, and Shui-Yan Tang. 2017. Nonprofit Policy Advocacy Under Authoritarianism. *Public Administration Review* 77 (1): 103–117.

Libby, Pat. 2012. *The Lobbying Strategy Handbook: 10 Steps to Advancing Any Cause Effectively*. Thousand Oaks: Sage Publications.

Lijphart, Arend. 2012. *Patterns of Democracy: Government Forms and Performance in Thirty-Six Countries*. 2nd ed. New Haven: Yale University Press.

Lin, Peng, Xiaojun Feng, and Qian Zhang. 2014. *Auction Design for the Wireless Spectrum Market*. Berlin: Springer.

Linder, Marc. 1990. From Street Urchins to Little Merchants: The Juridical Transvaluation of Child Newspaper Carriers. *Temple Law Review* 63: 829–864.

Linstone, Harold A., and Murray Turoff, eds. 1975. *Delphi Method: Techniques and Applications*. Boston: Addison-Wesley Educational Publishers.

Linz, Juan J. 2000. *Totalitarian and Authoritarian Regimes*. Boulder: Lynne Rienner Publishers.

Liu, Chun, and Krishna Jayakar. 2012. The Evolution of Telecommunications Policymaking: Comparative Analysis of China and India. *Telecommunications Policy* 36 (1): 13–28.

Livingstone, Sonia. 2011. Regulating the Internet in the Interests of Children: Emerging European and International Approaches. In *The Handbook of Global Media and Communication Policy*, ed. Robin Mansell and Marc Raboy, 505–524. Oxford: Wiley-Blackwell.

Ljubownikow, Serge, and Jo Crotty. 2016. Nonprofit Influence on Public Policy: Exploring Nonprofit Advocacy in Russia. *Nonprofit and Voluntary Sector Quarterly* 45 (2): 314–332.

Löblich, Maria. 2016. Dissent and Political Participation: The Many Faces of Communication Policy Advocacy and Activism. *Communication, Culture, & Critique* 9 (3): 395–416.

Lowe, Gregory F., and Christian E. Berg. 2013. The Funding of Public Service Media: A Matter of Value and Values. *International Journal on Media Management* 15 (2): 77–97.

Lowe, Gregory F., and Christian Nissen. 2011. *Small Among Giants: Television Broadcasting in Smaller Countries*. Göteborg: NORDICOM.

Lugo-Ocando, Jairo. 2008. *The Media in Latin America*. Maidenhead: Open University Press/McGraw-Hill.

Lukes, Steven. 1986. *Power*. New York: New York University Press.

Lunt, Peter, and Sonia Livingstone. 2011. *Media Regulation: Governance and the Interests of Citizens and Consumers*. London: Sage.

Lyall, Francis. 2016. *International Communications: The International Telecommunication Union and the Universal Postal Union*. London: Routledge.

Lyons, Gene M., and Michael Mastanduno, eds. 1995. *Beyond Westphalia?: National Sovereignty and International Intervention*. Baltimore: Johns Hopkins University Press.

Magee, John F. 1964. Decision Trees for Decision Making. *Harvard Business Review* 42 (4): 126–138.

Magnette, Paul. 2003. European Governance and Civic Participation: Beyond Elitist Citizenship? *Political Studies* 51 (1): 144–160.

Majchrzak, Ann, and M. Lynne Markus. 2013. *Methods for Policy Research: Taking Socially Responsible Action*. 2nd ed. London: Sage.

Mansell, Robin, and Marc Raboy, eds. 2014. *The Handbook of Global Media and Communication Policy*. Oxford: Wiley-Blackwell.

Manyozo, Linje. 2012. *Media, Communication and Development: Three Approaches*. London: Sage.

Marston, Greg, and Rob Watts. 2003. Tampering with the Evidence: A Critical Appraisal of Evidence-Based Policy Making. *The Drawing Board: An Australian Review of Public Affairs* 3 (3): 143–163.

Martin, Steve, and Ian Sanderson. 1999. Evaluating Public Policy Experiments: Measuring Outcomes, Monitoring Processes or Managing Pilots? *Evaluation* 5 (3): 245–258.

Mathew, Bobjoseph, and Thomas Cottier, eds. 2003. *Telecom Regulatory Framework and Effect on Competition: The WTO Agreements on Telecommunications*. New York: Peter Lang.

Matthews, Duncan. 2003. *Globalizing Intellectual Property Rights: The TRIPS Agreement*. London: Taylor & Francis.

May, Peter J. 1992. Policy Learning and Failure. *Journal of Public Policy* 12 (4): 331–354.

May, Christopher. 2000. *A Global Political Economy of Intellectual Property Rights*. London: Routledge.

———. 2006. *World Intellectual Property Organization (WIPO): Resurgence and Development Agenda*. London: Routledge.

———. 2009. *The Global Political Economy of Intellectual Property Rights: The New Enclosures*. 2nd ed. London: Taylor & Francis.

May, Peter J., Joshua Sapotichne, and Samuel Workman. 2006. Policy Coherence and Policy Domains. *Policy Studies Journal* 34 (3): 381–403.

Mayer, Vicki. 2018. Media Policy and Governance. *Feminist Media Histories* 4 (2): 113–116.

Mazar (Madjar), Haim. 2016. Radio Spectrum Management: Policies. In *Regulations and Techniques*. Chichester: Wiley.

Mazur, Amy G. 2002. *Theorizing Feminist Policy*. Oxford: Oxford University Press.

McAdam, Doug, John D. McCarthy, and Mayer N. Zald, eds. 1996. *Comparative Perspectives on Social Movements: Political Opportunities, Mobilizing Structures, and Cultural Framings*. Cambridge: Cambridge University Press.

McCallum, Zoe. 2019. Journalism vs Churnalism: The Push for "Quality Marks" in Online News. *Inforrm's Blog*, February 26. Available at: https://inforrm.org/2019/02/26/journalism-vs-churnalism-the-push-for-quality-marks-in-online-news-zoe-mccallum/. Accessed 19 June 2019.

McChesney, Robert W. 1993. *Telecommunications, Mass Media, and Democracy: The Battle for the Control of U.S. Broadcasting, 1928–1935*. New York: Oxford University Press.

———. 1999. *Rich Media, Poor Democracy: Communication Politics in Dubious Times.* Champaign: University of Illinois Press.

———. 2004. *The Problem of the Media: U.S. Communication Politics in the Twenty-First Century.* New York: Monthly Review Press.

———. 2012. Farewell to Journalism: Time for a Rethinking. *Journalism Practice* 6 (5–6): 614–626.

McChesney, Robert W., and Victor Pickard. 2011. *Will the Last Reporters Please Turn Out the Lights: The Collapse of Journalism and What Can Be Done About It.* New York: The New Press.

McCombs, Max. 2004. *Setting the Agenda: The Mass Media and Public Opinion.* Malden: Blackwell Publishing.

McCombs, Maxwell E., and Donald L. Shaw. 1972. The Agenda-Setting Function of Mass Media. *Public Opinion Quarterly* 36 (2): 176–187.

———. 1993. The Evolution of Agenda-Setting Research: Twenty-Five Years in the Marketplace of Ideas. *Journal of Communication* 43 (2): 58–67.

McConnell, Allan. 2010. Policy Success, Policy Failure and Grey Areas In-Between. *Journal of Public Policy* 30 (3): 345–362.

McCormick, Patricia K. 2005. The African Telecommunications Union: A Pan-African Approach to Telecommunications Reform. *Telecommunications Policy* 29 (7): 529–548.

McCormick, Patricia K., and Maury J. Mechanick. 2013. *The Transformation of Intergovernmental Satellite Organisations: Policy and Legal Perspectives.* Leiden: Martinus Nijhoff Publishers.

McCubbins, Mathew D., Roger G. Noll, and Barry R. Weingast. 1987. Administrative Procedures as Instruments of Political Control. *Journal of Law, Economics, and Organization* 3 (2): 243–277.

McGillivray, Fiona. 2004. *Privileging Industry: The Comparative Politics of Trade and Industrial Policy.* Princeton: Princeton University Press.

McLaughlin, Lisa, and Victor Pickard. 2005. What Is Bottom-Up About Internet Governance? *Global Media and Communication* 1 (3): 357–373.

McPhail, Beverly A. 2003. Feminist Policy Analysis Framework. *The Social Policy Journal* 2 (2–3): 39–61.

Menashri, David. 2001. *Post-Revolutionary Politics in Iran: Religion, Society and Power.* London: Routledge.

Mikler, John. 2018. *The Political Power of Global Corporations.* Cambridge: Polity.

Milan, Stefania, and Arne Hintz. 2013. Networked Collective Action and the Institutionalized Policy Debate: Bringing Cyberactivism to the Policy Arena? *Policy & Internet* 5 (1): 7–26.

Miles, Hugh. 2005. *Al Jazeera: The Inside Story of the Arab News Channel That Is Challenging the West.* New York: Grove Press.

Miller, Hugh T. 2002. *Postmodern Public Policy.* Albany: State University of New York Press.

Mindel, Joshua L., and Douglas C. Sicker. 2006. Leveraging the EU Regulatory Framework to Improve a Layered Model for U.S. Telecommunications Markets. *Telecommunications Policy* 30 (2): 136–148.

Moll, Marita, and Leslie Regan Shade, eds. 2011. *The Internet Tree: The State of Telecom Policy in Canada 3.0.* Ottawa: Canadian Centre for Policy Alternatives.

Montoya, Miguel Á., and Francesc Trillas. 2007. The Measurement of the Independence of Telecommunications Regulatory Agencies in Latin America and the Caribbean. *Utilities Policy* 15 (3): 182–190.
Moore, Mark. 1995. *Creating Public Value: Strategic Management in Government*. Cambridge, MA: Harvard University Press.
Morçöl, Göktuğ, and Nadezda P. Ivanova. 2010. Methods Taught in Public Policy Programs: Are Quantitative Methods Still Prevalent? *Journal of Public Affairs Education* 16 (2): 255–277.
Morris, Brigit Morris, and Máire Messenger Davies. 2018. Can Children's Privacy Rights Be Adequately Protected Through Press Regulation? What Press Regulation Can Learn from the Courts. *Journal of Media Law* 10 (1): 92–113.
Morton, Rebecca, and Kenneth Williams. 2010. *Experimental Political Science and the Study of Causality: From Nature to the Lab*. Cambridge: Cambridge University Press.
Mosley, Jennifer. 2013. Recognizing New Opportunities: Reconceptualizing Policy Advocacy in Everyday Organizational Practice. *Social Work* 58 (3): 231–239.
Moss, Scott. 2002. Policy Analysis from First Principles. *Proceedings of the National Academy of Sciences of the United States of America*, Vol. 99, No. 10, Supplement 3: Arthur M. Sackler Colloquium of the National Academy of Sciences. Sackler Colloquium on Adaptive Agents, Intelligence, and Emergent Human Organization: Capturing Complexity Through Agent-Based Modeling (May 14, 2002), 7267–7274.
Mossberger, Karen, and Harold Wolman. 2003. Policy Transfer as a Form of Prospective Policy Evaluation: Challenges and Recommendations. *Public Administration Review* 63 (4): 428–440.
Mueller, Milton. 2004. Reinventing Media Activism: Public Interest Advocacy in the Making of U.S. Communication-Information Policy, 1960–2002. *The Information Society* 20 (3): 169–187.
Mueller, Milton L., Brenden N. Kuerbis, and Christiane Pagé. 2007. Democratizing Global Communication? Global Civil Society and the Campaign for Communication Rights in the Information Society. *International Journal of Communication* 1 (1): 267–296.
Mukasa, Stanford G. 1992. Toward Pan-African Cooperation in Satellite Communication: An Analysis of the RASCOM Project. *Africa Media Review* 6 (2): 13–30.
Mulaik, Stanley A. 2009. *Linear Causal Modeling with Structural Equations*. Boca Raton: CRC Press.
Mureithi, Muriuki. 2002. Evolution of Telecommunications Policy Reforms in East Africa: Setting New Policy Strategies to Anchor Benefits of Policy Reforms. *The African Journal of Information and Communication* 3: 58–54.
Murschetz, Paul. 1998. State Support for the Daily Press in Europe: A Critical Appraisal: Austria, France, Norway and Sweden Compared. *European Journal of Communication* 13 (3): 291–313.
———, ed. 2013. *State Aid for Newspapers: Theories, Cases, Actions*. Berlin: Springer.
Murschetz, Paul Clemens, and Roland Teichmann. 2018. *Handbook of State Aid for Film: Finance, Industries and Regulation*. Berlin: Springer.
Musiani, Francesca, Derrick L. Cogburn, Laura DeNardis, and Nanette S. Levinson, eds. 2015. *The Turn to Infrastructure in Internet Governance*. London: Palgrave Macmillan.
Nagel, Stuart S. 2002. *Handbook of Public Policy Evaluation*. Thousand Oaks: Sage.
Nair, G. Madhavan. 2008. Role of Communications Satellites in National Development. *IETE Technical Review* 25 (1): 3–8.

Napoli, Philip M. 1999. The Unique Nature of Communications Regulation: Evidence and Implications for Communications Policy Analysis. *Journal of Broadcasting & Electronic Media* 43 (3): 565–581.

———. 2001. *Foundations of Communication Policy: Principles and Process in the Regulation of Electronic Media*. New York: Hampton Press.

———. 2007. Public Interest Media Activism and Advocacy as a Social Movement: A Review of the Literature. McGannon Center Working Paper Series, No. 21. Available at: https://fordham.bepress.com/mcgannon_working_papers/21/. Accessed 5 June 2019.

———. 2008. Bridging Cultural Policy and Media Policy. *The Journal of Arts Management, Law, and Society* 37 (4): 311–330.

———. 2009. Public Interest Media Advocacy and Activism as a Social Movement. *Annals of the International Communication Association* 33 (1): 385–429.

Napoli, Philip, and Minna Aslama, eds. 2011. *Communications Research in Action: Scholar-Activist Collaborations for a Democratic Public Sphere*. New York: Fordham University.

Natalicchi, Giorgio. 2001. *Wiring Europe. Reshaping the European Telecommunication Regime*. London: Rowman and Littlefield.

Naughton, Barry J. 2018. *The Chinese Economy: Adaptation and Growth*. 2nd ed. Cambridge, MA: MIT Press.

Nazzini, Renato. 2012. *The Foundations of European Union Competition Law: The Objectives and Principles of Article 102*. Oxford: Oxford University Press.

Negrine, Ralph, ed. 2013. *Satellite Broadcasting: The Politics and Implications of the New Media*, Reprint ed. London: Routledge.

Nelson, Richard A. 1994. Issue Communication and Advocacy: Contemporary Ethical Challenges. *Public Relations Review* 20 (3): 225–231.

Nielsen, Rasmus Kleis. 2014. 'Frozen' Media Subsidies During a Time of Media Change: A Comparative Analysis of Media Policy Drift in Six Western Democracies. *Global Media and Communication* 10 (2): 121–138.

Nielsen, Rasmus Kleis with Geert Linnebank. 2011. *Public Support for Media: A Six-Country Overview of Direct and Indirect Subsidies*. RISJ Report. Oxford: Reuters Institute for the Study of Journalism, University of Oxford.

Nigeria, Federal Ministry of Communication Technology. 2012. *Nigeria's National Broadband Plan 2013–2018*. https://www.researchictafrica.net/countries/nigeria/Nigeria_National_Broadband_Plan_2013-2018.pdf. Accessed 24 Dec 2018.

Nigeria, National Broadcasting Commission. n.d. Procedure of Obtaining a Broadcast License. Available at: http://www.nbc.gov.ng/pages/licensing. Accessed 30 Dec 2018.

Nissen, Christian S., ed. 2006. *Making a Difference: Public Service Broadcasting in the European Media Landscape*. Eastleigh: John Libbey Publishing.

Noam, Eli, ed. 1999. *Telecommunications in Africa*. New York: Oxford University Press.

Nordenstreng, Kaarle, and Herbert I. Schiller. 1993. *Beyond National Sovereignty: International Communications in the 1990s*. Greenwood: Praeger.

Noske-Turner, Jessica. 2017. *Rethinking Media Development Through Evaluation: Beyond Freedom*. London: Palgrave Macmillan.

Nuechterlein, Jonathan E., and Philip J. Weiser. 2013. *Digital Crossroads: Telecommunications Law and Policy in the Internet Age*. Cambridge, MA: MIT Press.

Ó Siochrú, Sean, Bruce Girard, and Amy Mahan. 2002. *Global Media Governance: A Beginner's Guide*. Lanham: Rowman and Littlefield.

O'Regan, Tom, and Ben Goldsmith. 2006. Making Cultural Policy: Meeting Cultural Objectives in a Digital Environment. *Television and New Media* 7 (1): 68–91.

Obar, Jonathan A., Paul Zube, and Clifford Lampe. 2012. Advocacy 2.0: An Analysis of How Advocacy Groups in the United States Perceive and Use Social Media as Tools for Facilitating Civic Engagement and Collective Action. *Journal of Information Policy* 2: 1–25.

OECD. 2017. *Preventing Policy Capture: Integrity in Public Decision Making*. Paris: Organization for Economic Co-operation and Development.

Olsen, Jonathan, and John McCormick. 2016. *The European Union: Politics and Policies*. 6th ed. Boulder: Westview Press.

Ots, Mart. 2009. Efficient Servants of Pluralism or Marginalized Media Policy Tools? *Journal of Communication Inquiry* 33 (4): 376–392.

Ots, Mart, Arne H. Krumsvik, Marko Ala-Fossi, and Pernilla Rendahl. 2016. The Shifting Role of Value-Added Tax (VAT) as a Media Policy Tool: A Three-Country Comparison of Political Justifications. *Javnost/The Public* 23 (2): 170–187.

Padovani, Claudia, and Elena Pavan. 2011. Actors and Interactions in Global Communication Governance: The Heuristic Potential of a Network Approach. In *The Handbook of Global Media and Communication Policy*, ed. Robin Mansell and Marc Raboy, 543–581. Oxford: Wiley-Blackwell.

Page, Benjamin I., and Robert Y. Shapiro. 1983. Effects of Public Opinion on Policy. *American Political Science Review* 77 (1): 175–190.

———. 1992. *The Rational Public: Fifty Years of Trends in Americans' Policy Preferences*. Chicago: University of Chicago Press.

Pandit, Sushmita. 2019. Public Policy and the Digital Deadline: The Implementation of the Digital Addressable System (DAS) in West Bengal. *Journal of Digital Media and Policy* 10 (2): 217–228.

Panke, Diana. 2012. Small States in Multilateral Negotiations. What Have We Learned? *Cambridge Review of International Affairs* 25 (3): 387–398.

Parisia, Francesco, Norbert Schulz, and Jonathan Klick. 2006. Two Dimensions of Regulatory Competition. *International Review of Law and Economics* 26 (1): 56–66.

Parker, David, and Colin Kirkpatrick. 2005. Privatisation in Developing Countries: A Review of the Evidence and the Policy Lessons. *Journal of Development Studies* 41 (4): 513–541.

Pauwels, Caroline, and Jan Loisen. 2003. The WTO and the Audiovisual Sector: Economic Free Trade or Cultural Horse Trading. *European Journal of Communication* 18 (3): 291–313.

Pawson, Ray. 2006. *Evidence Based Policy: A Realistic Approach*. London: Sage.

Peters, B. Guy, and Jon Pierre. 2016. *Comparative Governance: Rediscovering the Functional Dimension of Governing*. Cambridge: Cambridge University Press.

Petrova, Maria. 2008. Inequality and Media Capture. *Journal of Public Economics* 92 (1–2): 183–212.

Pew Research Center. 2017. Public Comments to the Federal Communications Commission About Net Neutrality Contain Many Inaccuracies and Duplicates. November 29. Available at: http://www.pewinternet.org/2017/11/29/public-comments-to-the-federal-communications-commission-about-net-neutrality-contain-many-inaccuracies-and-duplicates/. Accessed 6 Mar 2019.

Phalen, Sean. 2014. *Neoliberalism, Media and the Political*. London: Palgrave Macmillan.

Picard, Robert G. 1983. State Intervention in U.S. Press Economics. *Gazette* 30: 3–11.

———. 1985. Patterns of State Intervention in Western Press Economics. *Journalism Quarterly* 62 (1): 3–9.
———. 1986. State Press Aid During the Era of Economic Readjustment: A Case Study of Scandinavian Nations. *European Studies Journal* 3: 1–8.
———. 1995. Free Press and Government: The Ignored Relationships of U.S. Newspapers. In *Media Structure and the State: Concepts, Issues, Measures*, ed. Karl Erik Gustafsson, 133–148. Göteborg: Göteborg University, School of Economics and Commercial Law.
———. 2007a. The Challenges of Public Functions and Commercialized Media. In *The Politics of News: The News of Politics*, ed. Doris Graber, Denis McQuail, and Pippa Norris, 2nd ed., 211–229. Washington, DC: Congressional Quarterly Press.
———. 2007b. Natural Death, Euthanasia, and Suicide: The Demise of Joint Operating Agreements. *Journal of Media Business Studies* 4 (2): 41–54.
———. 2008. Subsidies for the Media. In *The International Encyclopedia of Communication*, ed. Wolfgang Donsbach, vol. 11, 4891–4895. Oxford: Wiley-Blackwell.
———. 2011. Economic Approaches to Media Policy. In *The Handbook of Global Media and Communication Policy*, ed. Robin Mansell and Marc Raboy, 355–375. Oxford: Wiley-Blackwell.
———. 2015. Business and Market Challenges and Their Effects on the Foundations and Trajectory of U.S. Broadcast Policy. *Journal of Media Business Studies* 8 (2): 45–62.
———. 2016. Isolated and Particularised: The State of Contemporary Media and Communications Policy Research. *Javnost/The Public* 23 (2): 135–152.
———. 2017a. The Sisyphean Pursuit of Media Pluralism: European Efforts to Establish Policy and Measurable Evidence. *Communication Law and Policy* 22 (3): 255–273.
———. 2017b. Monitoring Media Sustainability: Economic and Business Revisions to Development Indicators. In *What Is Sustainable Journalism? Integrating the Environmental, Social, and Economic Challenges of Journalism*, ed. Peter Berglez, Ulrika Olausson, and Mart Ots. New York: Peter Lang.
Picard, Robert G., and Mikko Grönlund. 2003. Development and Effects of Finnish Press Subsidies. *Journalism Studies* 4 (1): 105–119.
Picard, Robert G., and Victor S. Pickard. 2016. Essential Principles for Contemporary Media and Communications Policymaking. RISJ Report, April 2017. Oxford: Reuters Institute for the Study of Journalism, University of Oxford.
Picard, Robert G., and Timo E. Toivonen. 2004. Issues in Assessment of the Economic Impact of Copyright. *Review of Economic Research on Copyright Issues* 1 (1): 20–29.
Picard, Robert G., and Steven S. Wildman, eds. 2015. *Handbook of the Economics of the Media*. Cheltenham: Edward Elgar Publishing.
Picard, Robert G., Valerie Belair-Gagnon, and Sofia Ranchordás, ed. 2016a. The Impact of Charity and Tax Law and Regulation on Not-for-Profit News Organizations. Reuters Institute, University of Oxford, and Information Society Project, Yale Law School, Yale University.
Picard, Robert G., Charles Davis, Franco Papandrea, and Sora Park. 2016b. Platform Proliferation and Its Implications for Domestic Content Policies. *Telematics and Informatics* 33: 683–692.
Pickard, Victor. 2007. Neoliberal Visions and Revisions in Global Communications Policy from NWICO to WSIS. *Journal of Communication Inquiry* 31 (2): 118–139.

———. 2014a. *America's Battle for Media Democracy: The Triumph of Corporate Libertarianism and the Future of Media Reform*. Cambridge: Cambridge University Press.

———. 2014b. The Great Evasion: Confronting Market Failure in American Media Policy. *Critical Studies in Media Communication* 31 (2): 153–159.

Polishuk, Paul. 1976. Telecommunications Policymaking and Institutions of the U.S. Government. *Telecommunications Policy* 1 (1): 52–67.

Polońska, Eva, and Charlie Beckett, eds. 2019. *Public Service Broadcasting and Media Systems in Troubled European Democracies*. London: Palgrave Macmillan.

Poort, Joost, and Barbara Baarsma. 2016. Measuring the Welfare Effects of Public Television. *Journal of Media Economics* 29 (1): 31–48.

Prado, Marianna Mota. 2013. Bureaucratic Resistance to Regulatory Reforms: Contrasting Experiences in Electricity and Telecommunications in Brazil. In *The Rise of the Regulatory State in the South: Infrastructure and Development in Emerging Economies*, ed. Navroz K. Dubash and Bronwen Morgan, 75–97. Oxford: Oxford University Press.

Price, Monroe. 2002. *Media and Sovereignty: The Global Information Revolution and Its Challenge to State Power*. Boston: MIT Press.

Puppis, Manuel. 2007. Media Governance as a Horizontal Extension of Media Regulation: The Importance of Self- and Co-regulation. *Communications* 32 (3): 330–336.

———. 2008. National Media Regulation in the Era of Free Trade: The Role of Global Media Governance. *European Journal of Communication* 23 (4): 405–424.

———. 2009. Media Regulation in Small States. *International Communication Gazette* 71 (1–2): 7–17.

———. 2010. Media Governance: A New Concept for the Analysis of Media Policy and Regulation. *Communication, Culture & Critique* 3: 134–149.

Qiang, Christine Zhen-Wei, and Alexander Pitt. 2003. *Contribution of Information and Communication Technologies to Growth*. Washington, DC: The International Bank for Reconstruction and Development/World Bank.

Raats, Tim, Tom Evens, and Sanne Ruelens. 2016. Challenges for Sustaining Local Audio-Visual Ecosystems: Analysis of Financing and Production of Domestic TV Fiction in Small Media Markets. *Journal of Popular Television* 4 (1): 129–147.

Raboy, Marc, ed. 2002. *Global Media Policy in the New Millennium*. Luton: University of Luton Press.

Raboy, Marc, and Claudia Padovani. 2010. Mapping Global Media Policy: Concepts, Frameworks, Methods. *Communication, Culture & Critique* 3 (2): 150–169.

Radaelli, Claudio M. 2000. Policy Transfer in the European Union: Institutional Isomorphism as a Source of Legitimacy. *Governance* 13 (1): 25–43.

———. 2009. Measuring Policy Learning: Regulatory Impact Assessment in Europe. *Journal of European Public Policy* 16 (8): 1145–1164.

Randon, Perri A. 1994. Constraining Campaigning: The Legal Treatment of Non-Profit Policy Advocacy Across 24 Countries. *Voluntas: International Journal of Voluntary and Nonprofit Organizations* 5 (1): 27–58.

Reed, David P. 2006. Critiquing the Layered Regulatory Model. *Journal on Telecommunications and High Technology Law* 4 (2): 281–298.

Reinalda, Bob, ed. 2013. *Routledge Handbook of International Organization*. London: Routledge.

Rennie, Ellie. 2013. Unintended Consequences: Satellite Policy and Indigenous Television Media. *Media Information Australia* 149 (1): 92–103.

Richardson, Jeremy, ed. 1982 and 2012. *Policy Styles in Western Europe*. London: Allan & Unwin/Taylor & Francis.

Rockwell, R., and N. Janus. 2002. The Politics of Coercion: Advertising, Media and State Power in Central America. *Journalism* 3 (3): 331–353.

Rodrigo, Delia, Lorenzo Allio, and Pedro Andres-Amo. 2009. Multi-Level Regulatory Governance: Policies, Institutions and Tools for Regulatory Quality and Policy Coherence. OECD Working Papers on Public Governance, No. 13. Paris: OECD Publishing.

Roland, Gérard, and Joseph E. Stiglitz. 2008. *Privatization: Successes and Failures*. New York: Columbia University Press.

Rothman, Steven B., Utpal Vyas, and Yoichiro Sato, eds. 2017. *Regional Institutions, Geopolitics and Economics in the Asia-Pacific: Evolving Interests and Strategies*. London: Routledge.

Rothstein, Robert L. 1968. *Alliances and Small Powers*. New York: Columbia University Press.

Rowland, Willard D. 1986. American Telecommunications Policy Research: Its Contradictory Origins and Influences. *Media, Culture and Society* 8 (2): 159–182.

Ryan, Patrick S. 2005. European Spectrum Management Principles. *Journal of Computer and Information Law* 23: 277–324.

Sabatier, Paul A., and Hank C. Jenkins-Smith. 1993. *Policy Change and Learning: An Advocacy Coalition Approach*. Boulder: Westview Press.

Sabatier, Paul A., and Christopher M. Weible. 2007. The Advocacy Coalition Framework: Innovations and Clarifications. In *Theories of the Policy Process*, ed. Paul A. Sabatier, 2nd ed., 189–220. Boulder: Westview Press.

Sakr, Naomi. 2006. Foreign Support for Media Freedom Advocacy in the Arab Mediterranean: Globalization from Above or Below? *Mediterranean Politics* 11 (1): 1–20.

Salamon, Lester M. 2002. *The Tools of Government: A Guide to the New Governance*. Oxford: Oxford University Press.

Salanié, Bernard. 2000. *Microeconomics of Market Failure*. Cambridge, MA: MIT Press.

Sanderson, Ian. 2002. Evaluation, Policy Learning and Evidence-Based Policy Making. *Public Administration* 80 (1): 1–22.

Sarikakis, Katharine, ed. 2007. *Media and Cultural Policy in the European Union*. Amsterdam: Editions Rodopi.

Sarikakis, Katharine, and Sarah Ganter. 2014. Priorities in Global Media Policy Transfer: Audiovisual and Digital Policy Mutations in the EU, MERCOSUR and US Triangle. *European Journal of Communication* 29 (1): 17–33.

Sarooshi, Dan. 2005. *International Organizations and Their Exercise of Sovereign Powers*. Oxford: Oxford University Press.

Saudi Arabia, Communication and Information Technology Commission. http://www.citc.gov.sa/English/Pages/default.aspx. Accessed 7 May 2016.

Saudi Arabia, King Abdulaziz City for Science and Technology. http://www.kacst.edu.sa/eng/Pages/default.aspx. Accessed 7 May 2016.

Saudi Arabia, Ministry of Communication and Information Technology. http://www.mcit.gov.sa/En/Pages/default.aspx. Accessed 7 May 2016.

Saudi Arabia, Ministry of Culture and Communication. http://www.saudinf.com/main/c6e.htm. Accessed 7 May 2016.

Saunders, Robert J. 1983. *Telecommunications and Economic Development*. Baltimore: World Bank/Johns Hopkins University Press.

Scharpf, Fritz W. 2000. Institutions in Comparative Policy Research. *Comparative Policy Studies* 33 (6–7): 762–790.

Scheufele, Dietram A., and David Tewksbury. 2007. Framing, Agenda Setting, and Priming: The Evolution of Three News Media Effects Models. *Journal of Communication* 57 (1): 9–20.

Schiller, Herbert I. 1989. *Culture, Inc.: The Corporate Takeover of Public Expression*. New York: Oxford University Press.

Schiller, Dan. 2008. The Militarization of U.S. Communications. *Communication, Culture & Critique* 1 (1): 126–138.

Schneider, Volker. 2001. Institutional Reform in Telecommunications: The European Union in Transnational Policy Diffusion. In *Europeanization and Domestic Change*, ed. Maria Green Cowles, James Caporaso, and Thomas Rissee, 60–78. Ithaca: Cornell University Press.

Schneider, Anne, and Helen Ingram. 1990. Behavioral Assumptions of Policy Tools. *The Journal of Politics* 52 (2): 510–529.

Schneider, Volker, Godefroy Dang-Nguyen, and Raymond Werle. 1994. Corporate Actor Networks in European Policy-Making: Harmonizing Telecommunications Policy. *Journal of Common Market Studies* 32 (4): 473–498.

Schneir, Juan R., and Yupeng Xiong. 2016. A Cost Study of Fixed Broadband Access Networks for Rural Areas. *Telecommunications Policy* 40 (8): 755–773.

Schulz, Wolfgang, and Thorsten Held. 2004. *Regulated Self-Regulation as a Form of Modern Government: A Comparative Analysis with Case Studies from Media and Telecommunications Law*. Bloomington: Indiana University Press.

Schulz, Wolfgang, Peggy Valcke, and Kristina Irion, eds. 2013. *The Independence of the Media and Its Regulatory Agencies*. Bristol: Intellect Books.

Scull, Tracy Marie, and Janis Beth Kupersmidt. 2011. An Evaluation of a Media Literacy Program Training Workshop for Late Elementary School Teachers. *Journal of Media Literacy Education* 2 (3): 199–208.

Semati, Mehdi, ed. 2008. *Media, Culture and Society in Iran: Living with Globalization and the Islamic State*. London: Routledge.

Sengara, Ryan, Sal Humphreys, Jock Given, Marion McCutcheon, and Claire Milne. 2009. *Future Consumer: Emerging Consumer Issues in Telecommunications and Convergent Communications and Media*. Petersham: Australian Communications Consumer Action Network.

Shade, Leslie Regan. 2011. Media Reform in the United States and Canada: Activism and Advocacy for Media Policies in the Public Interest. In *The Handbook of Global Media and Communication Policy*, ed. Robin Mansell and Marc Raboy, 147–165. Oxford: Wiley Blackwell.

Shaheen, Irum. 2013. South Asian Association for Regional Cooperation (SAARC): Its Role, Hurdles and Prospects. *IOSR Journal of Humanities and Social Science* 15 (6): 1–9.

Shanahan, Elizabeth A., Mark K. McBeth, and Paul L. Hathaway. 2011. Narrative Policy Framework: The Influence of Media Policy Narratives on Public Opinion. *Politics & Policy* 39 (3): 373–400.

Sharkey, William W. 1982. *The Theory of Natural Monopoly*. Cambridge: Cambridge University Press.

Shaver, Mary Alice, and Soontae An, eds. 2014. *The Global Advertising Regulation Handbook*. London: Routledge.

Shaw, Malcolm M. 2017. *International Law*. 8th ed. Cambridge: Cambridge University Press.

Shepherd, Tamara, Gregory Taylor, and Catherine Middleton. 2014. A Tale of Two Regulators: Telecom Policy Participation in Canada. *Journal of Information Policy* 4: 1–22.

Shoup, Laurence H. 2015. *Think Tank: The Council on Foreign Relations and the Empire of Neoliberal Geopolitics, 1976–2014*. New York: Monthly Review Press.

Sicker, Douglas C., and Lisa Blumensaadt. 2006. Misunderstanding the Layered Model(s). *Journal on Telecommunications and High Technology Law* 4 (2): 299–320.

Simpson, Seamus, Manuel Puppis, and Hilde Van den Bulck, eds. 2016. *European Media Policy for the Twenty-First Century: Assessing the Past, Setting Agendas for the Future*. London: Routledge.

Slobogin, Christopher. 2007. *Privacy at Risk: The New Government Surveillance and the Fourth Amendment*. Chicago: University of Chicago Press.

Smith, Martin J. 2009. *Power and the State*. London: Palgrave Macmillan.

Smith, Rachael Craufurd. 2015. Determining Regulatory Competence for Audiovisual Media Services in the European Union. *Journal of Media Law* 3 (2): 263–285.

Smith, Jason A., and Randy Abreu. 2019. OU or an IOU? Latina/os and the Racialization of Media Policy. *Ethnic and Racial Studies* 42 (4): 607–625.

Smith, Kevin B., and Christopher W. Larimer. 2013. *The Public Policy Theory Primer*. Boulder: Westview Press.

Sonwalkar, P. 2001. Opposition to the Entry of Foreign Press in India, 1991–1995: The Hidden Agenda. *Modern Asian Studies* 35 (3): 743–763.

Soper, J. Christopher, and Joel S. Fetzer. 2018. *Religion and Nationalism in Global Perspective*. Cambridge: Cambridge University Press.

Steffak, Jens, Claudia Kissling, and Patricia Nanz, eds. 2007. *Emergent Patterns of Civil Society Participation in Global and European Governance*. Basingstoke: Palgrave Macmillan.

Stephenson, Phillip. 2008. *Telecommunications and Growth*. Saarbrücken: VDM Verlag.

Stevenson, Charles A. 2013. *America's Foreign Policy Toolkit: Key Institutions and Processes*. Los Angeles: CQ Press.

Stoker, Gerry, ed. 2016. *Evidence-Based Policy Making in the Social Sciences*. Cambridge: Polity Press.

Stone, Diane. 1999. Learning Lessons and Transferring Policy across Time, Space and Disciplines. *Politics* 19 (1): 51–59.

Streeter, Thomas. 1996. *Selling the Air: A Critique of the Policy of Commercial Broadcasting in the United States*. Chicago: University of Chicago Press.

———. 2009. The Cable Fable Revisited: Discourse, Policy, and the Making of Cable Television. *Critical Studies in Mass Communication* 4 (2): 174–200.

———. 2013. Policy, Politics, and Discourse. *Communication, Culture and Critique* 6 (4): 488–501.

Sutherland, Ewan. 2016. The Case Study in Telecommunications Policy Research. *Info* 18 (1): 16–30.

Svolik, Milan W. 2012. *The Politics of Authoritarian Rule*. Cambridge: Cambridge University Press.

Swain, John W., and Kathleen Dolan Swain. 2015. *Effective Writing in the Public Sector*. London: Routledge.

Sweet, Pat. 2019. Spain to Introduce Digital Services Tax. *Accountancy Daily*, January 22. Available at: https://www.accountancydaily.co/spain-introduce-digital-services-tax. Accessed 4 Mar 2019.

Sydney, Mara S. 2007. Policy Formulation: Design and Tools. In *Handbook of Public Policy Analysis*, ed. Frank Fischer, Gerald J. Miller, and Mara S. Sidney, 79–88. Boca Raton: CRC Press.

Talvi, Ernesto, and Carlos Végh. 1998. Fiscal Policy Sustainability: A Basic Framework. Inter-American Development Bank. Working Paper 107. Washington, DC: Inter-American Development Bank.

Tamkin, Emily. 2019. With Putin's Signature, 'Fake News' Bill Becomes Law. *Washington Post*, March 18. Available at: https://www.washingtonpost.com/world/2019/03/18/with-putins-signature-fake-news-bill-becomes-law/?utm_term=.3f5767d87d39. Accessed 28 Mar 2019.

Tarrow, Sidney G. 2011. *Power in Movement: Social Movements and Contentious Politics*. 3rd ed. Cambridge: Cambridge University Press.

Taylor, William B., Jr. 1977. *A Survey of Policy Tools Available to Local Governments to Influence Industrial Development*. Cambridge, MA: John F. Kennedy School of Government, Harvard University.

Taylor, Matthew, and Jake Thorold. 2017. "Is Policy Failure Inevitable" Royal Society of Arts Blog. https://www.thersa.org/discover/publications-and-articles/matthew-taylor-blog/2017/03/is-policy-failure-inevitable?id=newsletter/fellowship/100417. Accessed 12 Dec 2018.

Terzis, Georgios, ed. 2008. *European Media Governance. The Brussels Dimension*. Bristol: Intellect.

Thatcher, Mark. 2002. Delegation to Independent Regulatory Agencies: Pressures, Functions and Contextual Mediation. *West European Politics* 25 (1): 125–147.

Timberg, Craig, Drew Harwell, Hamza Shaban, Andrew Ba Tran, and Brian Fung. 2019. The New Zealand Shooting Shows How YouTube and Facebook Spread Hate and Violent Images—Yet Again. *New York Times*, March 15. Available at: https://www.washingtonpost.com/technology/2019/03/15/facebook-youtube-twitter-amplified-video-christchurch-mosque-shooting/?utm_term=.99416f057b97. Accessed 29 Mar 2019.

Tobey, Ronald C. 1986. The Public Historian as Advocate: Is Special Attention to Professional Ethics Necessary? *The Public Historian* 8 (1): 21–30.

Torero, Maximo, and Joachim von Braun, eds. 2006. *Information and Communication Technologies for Development and Poverty Reduction: The Potential of Telecommunications*. Baltimore: Johns Hopkins University Press.

Tracey, Michael. 1998. *Decline and Fall of Public Service Broadcasting*. New York: Oxford University Press.

Trappel, Josef. 1991. Born Losers or Flexible Adjustment? The Media Policy Dilemma of Small States. *European Journal of Communication* 6 (3): 355–371.

Trkman, Peter, Borka Jerman Blazic, and Tomaz Turka. 2008. Factors of Broadband Development and the Design of a Strategic Policy Framework. *Telecommunications Policy* 32 (2): 101–115.

Turner, Rachel S. 2008. *Neo-liberal Ideology: History, Concepts and Policies*. Edinburgh: Edinburgh University Press.

Turnpenny, John, Måns Nilsson, Duncan Russel, Andrew Jordan, Julia Hertin, and Björn Nykvist. 2008. Why Is Integrating Policy Assessment So Hard? A Comparative

Analysis of the Institutional Capacities and Constraints. *Journal of Environmental Planning and Management* 51 (6): 759–775.

United States, Agency for Global Media. 2018. https://www.bbg.gov/. Accessed 31 Dec 2018.

United States, Communications Act of 1934. Available at: https://transition.fcc.gov/Reports/1934new.pdf. Accessed 30 Dec 2018

United States, Telecommunications Act of 1996, Sec. 5. Available at: https://transition.fcc.gov/Reports/tcom1996.txt. Accessed 31 Dec 2018.

United States US Central Intelligence Agency and US Department of State. 2012. *Saudi Arabia: A Brief Comprehensive Study of Saudi Arabia, Country Studies.* Washington, DC: Zay's Place.

Valcke, Peggy. 2006. The Future of Must-Carry: From Must-Carry to a Concept of Universal Service in the Info-Communications Sector. *Media Law and Policy* 15: 247–265.

Valcke, Peggy, Robert Picard, Miklos Sükösd, Beata Klimkiewicz, Brankica Petkovic, and Cinzia dal Zotto. 2010. The European Media Pluralism Monitor: Bridging Law, Economics, and Media Studies as a First Step towards Risk-Based Regulation in Media Markets. *Journal of Media Law* 2 (1): 85–113.

Valcke, Peggy, Miklos Sukosd, and Robert G. Picard, eds. 2015. *Media Pluralism and Diversity: Concepts, Risks and Global Trends.* London: Palgrave Macmillan.

van Cuilenburg, Jan. 2003. Media Policy Paradigm Shifts: Toward New Communications Policy Paradigm. *European Journal of Communications* 18 (2): 181–207.

van den Bossche, Peter, and Werner Zdouc. 2013. *The Law and Policy of the World Trade Organization.* 3rd ed. Cambridge: Cambridge University Press.

van den Bulck, Hilde. 2012. Towards a Media Policy Process Analysis Model and Its Methodological Implications. In *Trends in Communication Policy Research: New Theories, Methods and Subjects*, ed. Natascha Just and Manuel Puppis. Intellect: Bristol.

van den Bulck, Hilde, and Karen Donders. 2014a. Analyzing European Media Policy: Stakeholders and Advocacy Coalition. In *The Palgrave Handbook of European Media Policy*, ed. Karen Donders, Caroline Pauwels, and Jan Loisen, 19–35. London: Palgrave Macmillan.

———. 2014b. Of Discourses, Stakeholders and Advocacy Coalitions in Media Policy: Tracing Negotiations towards the New Management Contract of Flemish Public Broadcaster VRT. *European Journal of Communication* 29 (1): 83–99.

van den Bulck, Hilde, Manuel Puppis, Karen Donders, and Leo van Audenhove, eds. 2019. *The Palgrave Handbook of Methods for Media Policy Research.* London: Palgrave Macmillan.

van Dijk, Teun A. 1993. Principles of Critical Discourse Analysis. *Discourse & Society* 4 (2): 249–283.

van Kranenburg, Hans, ed. 2017. *Innovation Policies in the European News Media Industry: A Comparative Study.* Berlin: Springer.

van Schewick, Barbara. 2015. Network Neutrality and Quality of Service: What a Nondiscrimination Rule Should Look Like. *Stanford Law Review* 67: 1–166.

Vanclay, Frank, Ana M. Esteves, Ilse Aucamp, and Daniel M. Franks. 2015. *Social Impact Assessment: Guidance for Assessing and Managing Social Impact of Projects.* Fargo: International Association for Impact Assessment.

Varone, Frédéric, Karin Ingold, Charlotte Jourdain, and Volker Schneider. 2017. Studying Policy Advocacy Through Social Network Analysis. *European Political Science* 16 (3): 322–336.

Vedung, Evert. 2000. *Public Policy and Program Evaluation*. London: Routledge.
Veselý, Arnošt. 2007. Problem Delimitation in Public Policy Analysis. *Central European Journal of Public Policy* 1 (1): 80–100.
Vital, David. 1967. *The Inequality of States: A Study of Small Power in International Relations*. Oxford: Oxford University Press.
Volgy, Thomas J., Zlatko Šabič, Petra Roter, and Andrea K. Gerlak. 2009. *Mapping the New World Order*. Chichester: Wiley-Blackwell.
Vonortas, Nicholas S., Phoebe C. Rouge, and Anwar Aridi, eds. 2015. *Innovation Policy: A Practical Introduction*. Berlin: Springer.
Wachs, Martin. 1990. Ethics and Advocacy in Forecasting for Public Policy. *Business & Professional Ethics Journal* 9 (1/2): 141–157.
Waisbord, Silvio. 2010. The Pragmatic Politics of Media Reform: Media Movements and Coalition-Building in Latin America. *Global Media and Communication* 6 (2): 133–153.
Walden, Ian. 2018. *Telecommunications Law and Regulation*. 5th ed. Oxford: Oxford University Press.
Walsh, Tim. 2000. Globalization, Posts, and the Universal Postal Union: A Functional Critique. In *Current Directions in Postal Reform*, ed. Michael A. Crew and Paul R. Kleindorfer, 483–506. Boston: Springer.
Ward, David. 2004. *The European Union Democratic Deficit and the Public Sphere: An Evaluation of EU Media Policy*. Amsterdam: IOS Press.
———. 2006. Can the Market Provide: Public Service Media, Market Failure and Public Goods. In *Making a Difference: Public Service Broadcasting in the European Media Landscape*, ed. Christian S. Nissen, 51–64. Eastleigh: John Libbey Publishing.
Wasko, Janet. 1999. The Political Economy of Film. In *A Companion to Film Theory*, ed. Toby Miller and Robert Stam, 221–233. Oxford: Blackwell Publishing.
———. 2005. Critiquing Hollywood: The Political Economy of Motion Pictures. In *A Concise Handbook of Movie Industry Economics*, ed. Charles C. Moul, 5–31. Cambridge: Cambridge University Press.
Watts, Ronald L. 1998. Federalism, Federal Political Systems, and Federations. *Annual Review of Political Science* 1 (1): 117–137.
Wavre, Veronique. 2018. *Policy Diffusion and Telecommunications Regulations*. London: Palgrave Macmillan.
Weaver, David H. 2007. Thoughts on Agenda Setting, Framing, and Priming. *Journal of Communication* 57 (1): 142–147.
Weber, Rolf H. 2009. *Shaping Internet Governance: Regulatory Challenges*. Berlin: Springer.
Webster, Amalie M. 2003. The Council of Europe's Convention on Cybercrime. *Berkeley Technology Law Journal* 18 (1): 425–446.
Weible, Christopher M., and Paul A. Sabatier, eds. 2018. *Theories of the Policy Process*. 4th ed. London: Routledge.
Weiss, Carol H. 1997. *Evaluation: Methods for Studying Programs and Policies*. 2nd ed. Upper Saddle River: Prentice Hall.
Weiss, Carol Hirschon. 1999. The Interface between Evaluation and Public Policy. *Evaluation* 5 (4): 468–486.
Westbrook, Tom, and Charlotte Greenfield. 2019. New Zealand Bans Military Type Semi-Automatic Weapons Used in Mosque Massacre. *Reuters*, March 21. Available at: https://www.reuters.com/article/us-newzealand-shootout-ardern-guncontrol-idUSKCN1R205Z. Accessed 29 Mar 2019.

Wetherell, Margaret, Stephanie Taylor, and Simeon J. Yates. 2001. *Discourse as Data: A Guide for Analysis*. London: Sage Publication.

Whitt, Richard. 2004. A Horizontal Leap Forward: Formulating a New Communications Public Policy Framework Based on the Network Layers Model. *Federal Communications Law Journal* 56 (3): 587–672.

Whittiker, Zach. 2019. California to Close Data Breach Notification Loopholes Under New Law. *Tech Crunch*, February 21. Available at: https://techcrunch.com/2019/02/21/california-data-breach-laws/. Accessed 1 July 2019.

Winseck, Dwayne. 2002. The WTO, Emerging Policy Regimes and the Political Economy of Transnational Communications. In *Global Media Policy in the New Millennium*, ed. Marc Raboy, 19–38. Luton: University of Luton Press.

Winseck, Dwayne, and Jefferson D. Pooley. 2017. A Reply to Faulhaber, Singer, and Urschel's Curious Tale of Economics and Common Carriage (Net Neutrality) at the FCC. *International Journal of Communication* 11 (2017): 2702–2733. https://ijoc.org/index.php/ijoc/article/view/7543/2077. Accessed 18 Oct 2019.

Wodak, Ruth, and Michael Meyer. 2009. *Methods for Critical Discourse Analysis*. London: Sage.

Wollmann, Helmut. 2006. Policy Evaluation and Evaluation Research. In *Handbook of Public Policy Analysis: Theory, Politics, and Methods*, ed. Frank Fischer and Gerald J. Miller, 393–404. Boca Raton: CRC Press/Taylor & Francis.

World Intellectual Property Organization. 2018. Zimbabwe Broadcasting Services Act 3/2001, 22/2001, 26/200, 6/2003. Available at: https://www.wipo.int/edocs/lexdocs/laws/en/zw/zw036en.pdf. Accessed 31 Dec 2018

———. 2019. WIPO Performances and Phonograms Treaty. Available at: https://www.wipo.int/treaties/en/ip/wppt/. Accessed 29 Mar 2019.

Wu, Irene. 2004. Canada, South Korea, Netherlands and Sweden: Regulatory Implications of the Convergence of Telecommunications, Broadcasting and Internet Services. *Telecommunications Policy* 28 (1): 79–96.

Yanacopulos, Helen. 2015. *International NGO Engagement, Advocacy, Activism: The Faces and Spaces of Change*. London: Palgrave Macmillan.

Young, Sally. 2007. Following the Money Trail: Government Advertising, the Missing Millions and the Unknown Effects. *Public Policy* 2 (2): 104–118.

Zahariadis, Nikolaos, ed. 2016. *Handbook of Public Policy Agenda Setting*. Cheltenham: Edward Elgar Publishing.

Zaretsky, Lindy. 2004. Advocacy and Administration: From Conflict to Collaboration. *Journal of Educational Administration* 42 (2): 270–286.

Zboralska, Emelia, and Charles Davis. 2017. Transnational Over-the-Top Media Distribution as a Business and Policy Disruptor: The Case of Netflix in Canada. *The Journal of Media Innovations* 4 (1): 4–25.

Zimbabwe Broadcasting Corporation. 2018. Available at: http://www.zbccorporate.co.zw/. Accessed 31 Dec 2018.

Zittrain, Jonathan. 2008. Privacy 2.0. *University of Chicago Legal Forum* 2008 (1): 65–119.

Zuckerberg, Mark. 2019. Mark Zuckerberg: The Internet Needs New Rules. Let's Start in These Four Areas. *Washington Post*, March 30. Available at: https://www.washingtonpost.com/opinions/mark-zuckerberg-the-internet-needs-new-rules-lets-start-in-these-four-areas/2019/03/29/9e6f0504-521a-11e9-a3f7-78b7525a8d5f_story.html?noredirect=on&utm_term=.391b2de524e1. Accessed 23 June 2019.

Index[1]

[1] Note: Page numbers followed by 'n' refer to notes.

R. G. Picard, *Media and Communications Policy Making*, Palgrave Global Media Policy and Business,
https://doi.org/10.1007/978-3-030-35173-1

GPSR Compliance
The European Union's (EU) General Product Safety Regulation (GPSR) is a set of rules that requires consumer products to be safe and our obligations to ensure this.

If you have any concerns about our products, you can contact us on

ProductSafety@springernature.com

In case Publisher is established outside the EU, the EU authorized representative is:

Springer Nature Customer Service Center GmbH
Europaplatz 3
69115 Heidelberg, Germany

www.ingramcontent.com/pod-product-compliance
Ingram Content Group UK Ltd.
Pitfield, Milton Keynes, MK11 3LW, UK
UKHW020202290926
15471UKWH00005B/1027

* 9 7 8 3 0 3 0 3 5 1 7 2 4 *